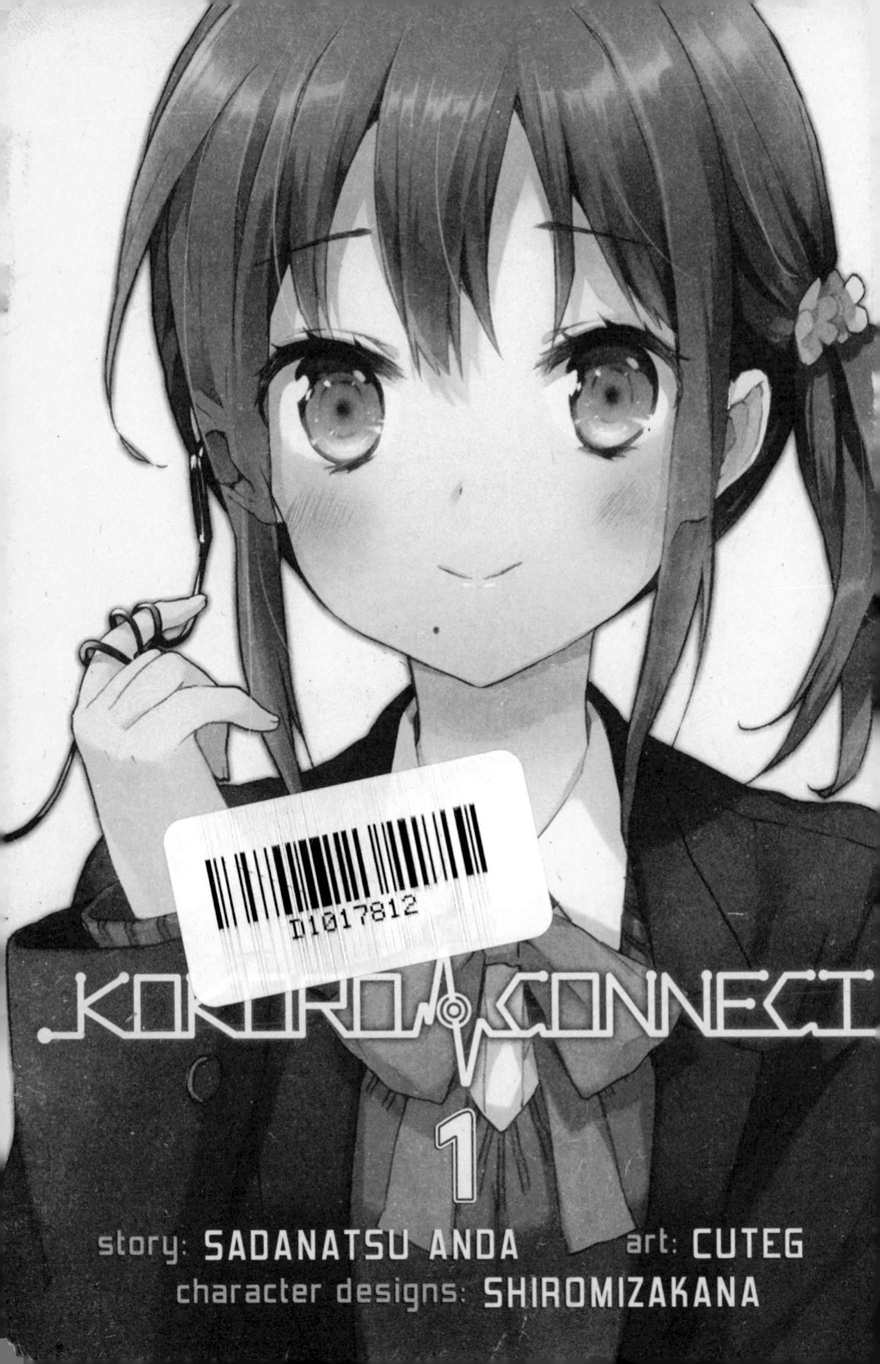
KOKORO CONNECT
1
story: SADANATSU ANDA
art: CUTEG
character designs: SHIROMIZAKANA
D1017812

SEVEN SEAS ENTERTAINMENT PRESENTS

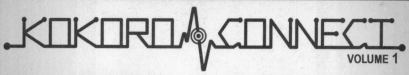

KOKORO CONNECT

VOLUME 1

Story: **SADANATSU ANDA** / Character Designs: **SHIROMIZAKANA** / Art: **CUTEG**

TRANSLATION
Nan Rymer

ADAPTATION
Shannon Fay

COPY EDITOR
Lee Otter

LETTERING AND LAYOUT
Mia Chiresa

COVER DESIGN
Nicky Lim

MANAGING EDITOR
Adam Arnold

PUBLISHER
Jason DeAngelis

First published in Japan in 2011 by KADOKAWA CORPORATION ENTERBRAIN. English translation rights arranged with KADOKAWA CORPORATION ENTERBRAIN through TOHAN CORPORATION, Tokyo.

ISBN: 978-1-626920-72-9

Printed in Canada

First Printing: August 2014

10 9 8 7 6 5 4 3 2 1

FOLLOW US ONLINE: ***www.gomanga.com***

READING DIRECTIONS

This book reads from ***right to left***, Japanese style. If this is your first time reading manga, you start reading from the top right panel on each page and take it from there. If you get lost, just follow the numbered diagram here. It may seem backwards at first, but you'll get the hang of it! Have fun!!

1
2
3
4
5
6
7
8
9

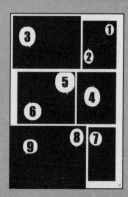

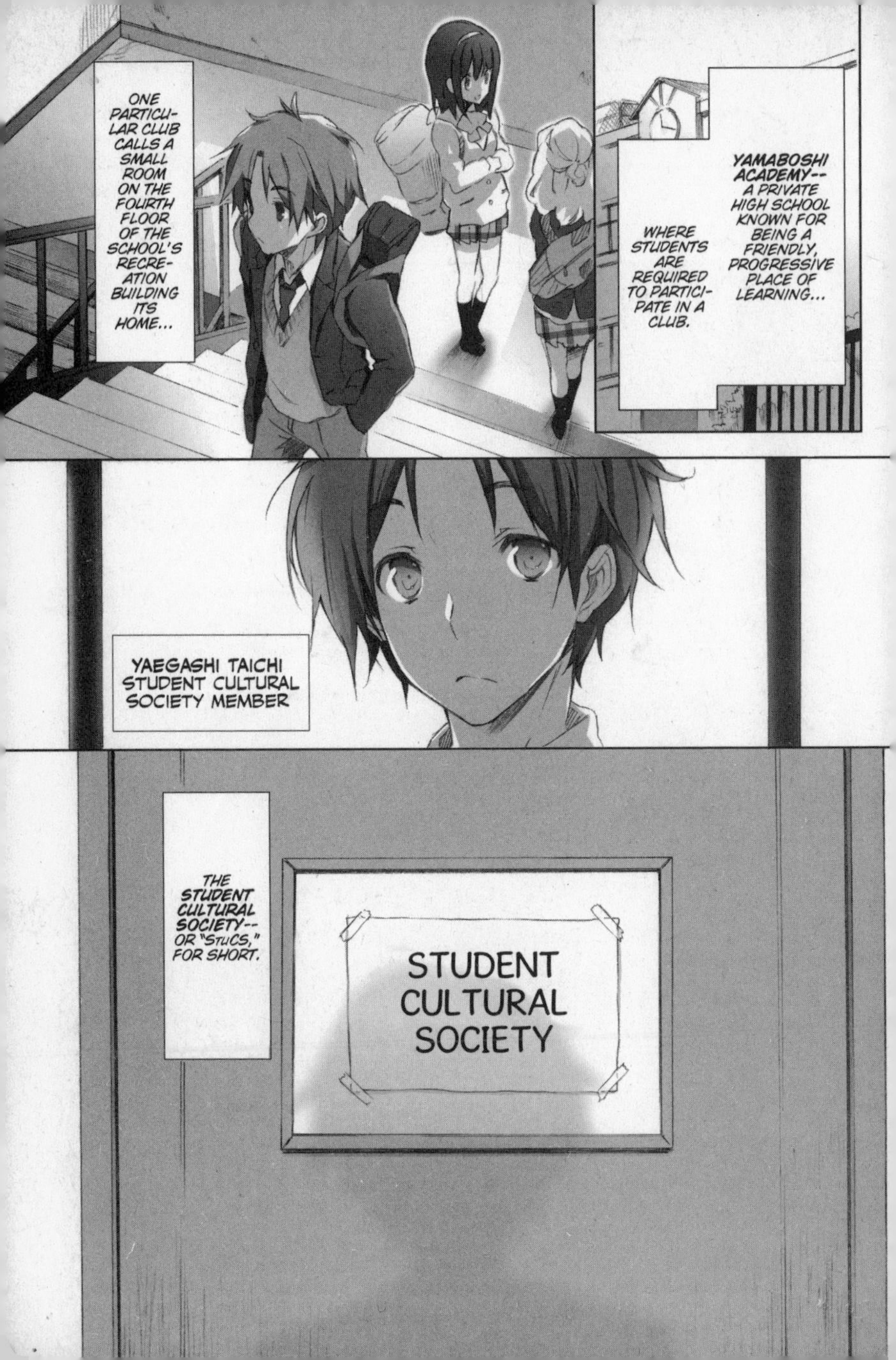
YAMABOSHI ACADEMY-- A PRIVATE HIGH SCHOOL KNOWN FOR BEING A FRIENDLY, PROGRESSIVE PLACE OF LEARNING...
WHERE STUDENTS ARE REQUIRED TO PARTICIPATE IN A CLUB.
ONE PARTICULAR CLUB CALLS A SMALL ROOM ON THE FOURTH FLOOR OF THE SCHOOL'S RECREATION BUILDING ITS HOME...
YAEGASHI TAICHI STUDENT CULTURAL SOCIETY MEMBER
THE STUDENT CULTURAL SOCIETY-- OR "StuCS," FOR SHORT.
STUDENT CULTURAL SOCIETY

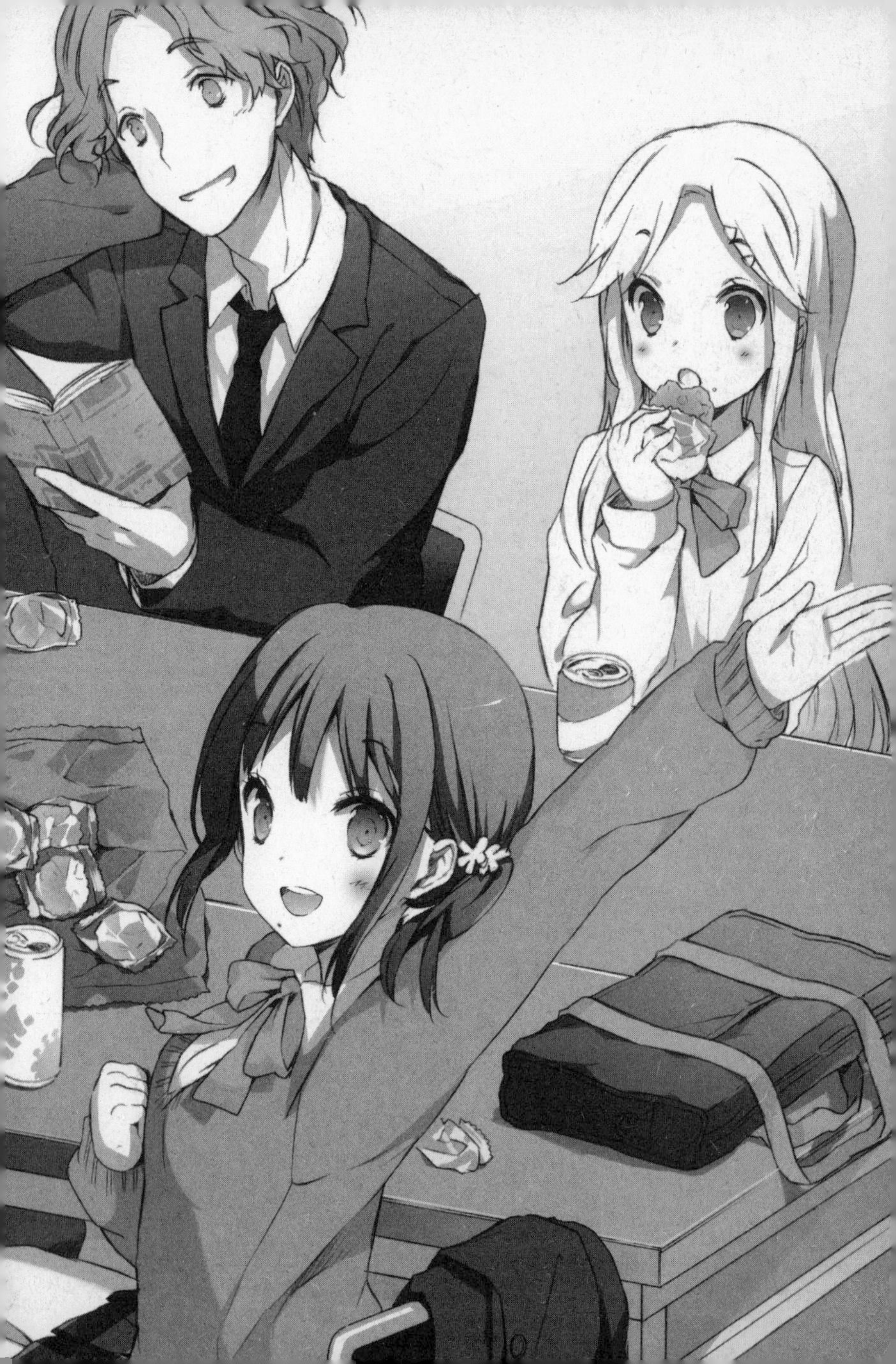

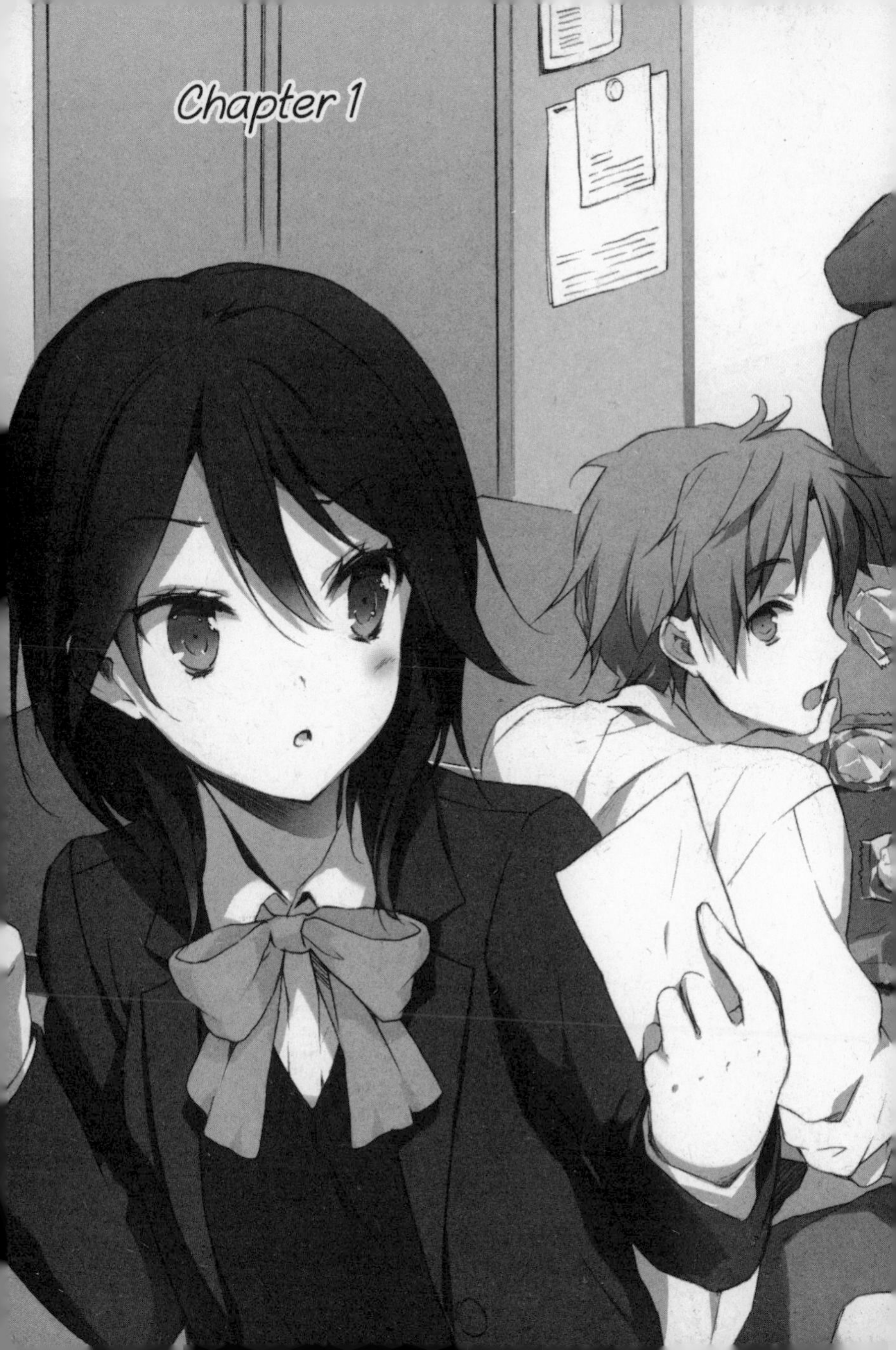
Chapter 1

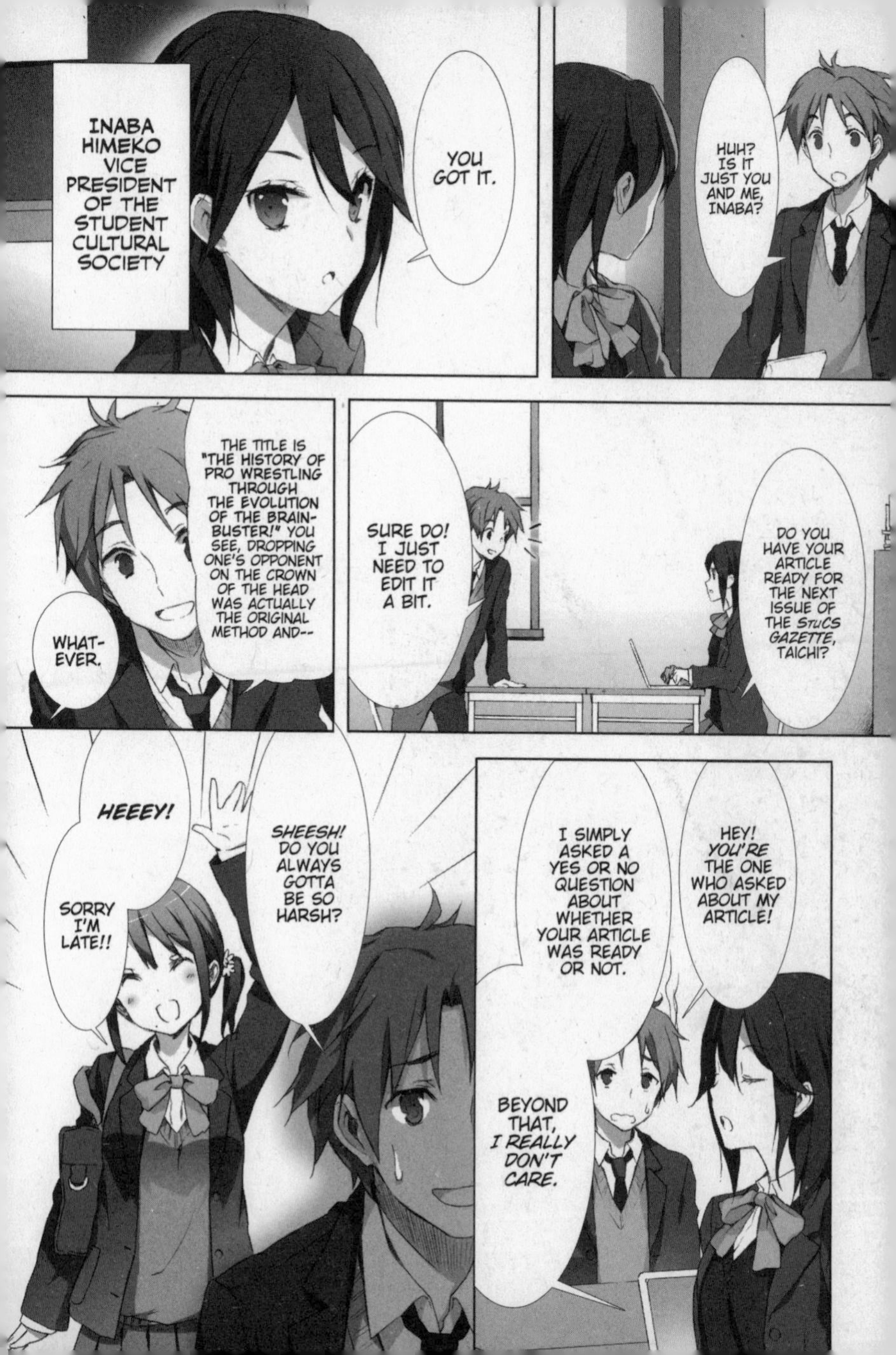
HUH? IS IT JUST YOU AND ME, INABA?
YOU GOT IT.
INABA HIMEKO VICE PRESIDENT OF THE STUDENT CULTURAL SOCIETY
DO YOU HAVE YOUR ARTICLE READY FOR THE NEXT ISSUE OF THE StuCS GAZETTE, TAICHI?
SURE DO! I JUST NEED TO EDIT IT A BIT.
THE TITLE IS "THE HISTORY OF PRO WRESTLING THROUGH THE EVOLUTION OF THE BRAIN-BUSTER!" YOU SEE, DROPPING ONE'S OPPONENT ON THE CROWN OF THE HEAD WAS ACTUALLY THE ORIGINAL METHOD AND--
WHAT-EVER.
HEY! YOU'RE THE ONE WHO ASKED ABOUT MY ARTICLE!
I SIMPLY ASKED A YES OR NO QUESTION ABOUT WHETHER YOUR ARTICLE WAS READY OR NOT.
BEYOND THAT, I REALLY DON'T CARE.
SHEESH! DO YOU ALWAYS GOTTA BE SO HARSH?
HEEEY!
SORRY I'M LATE!!

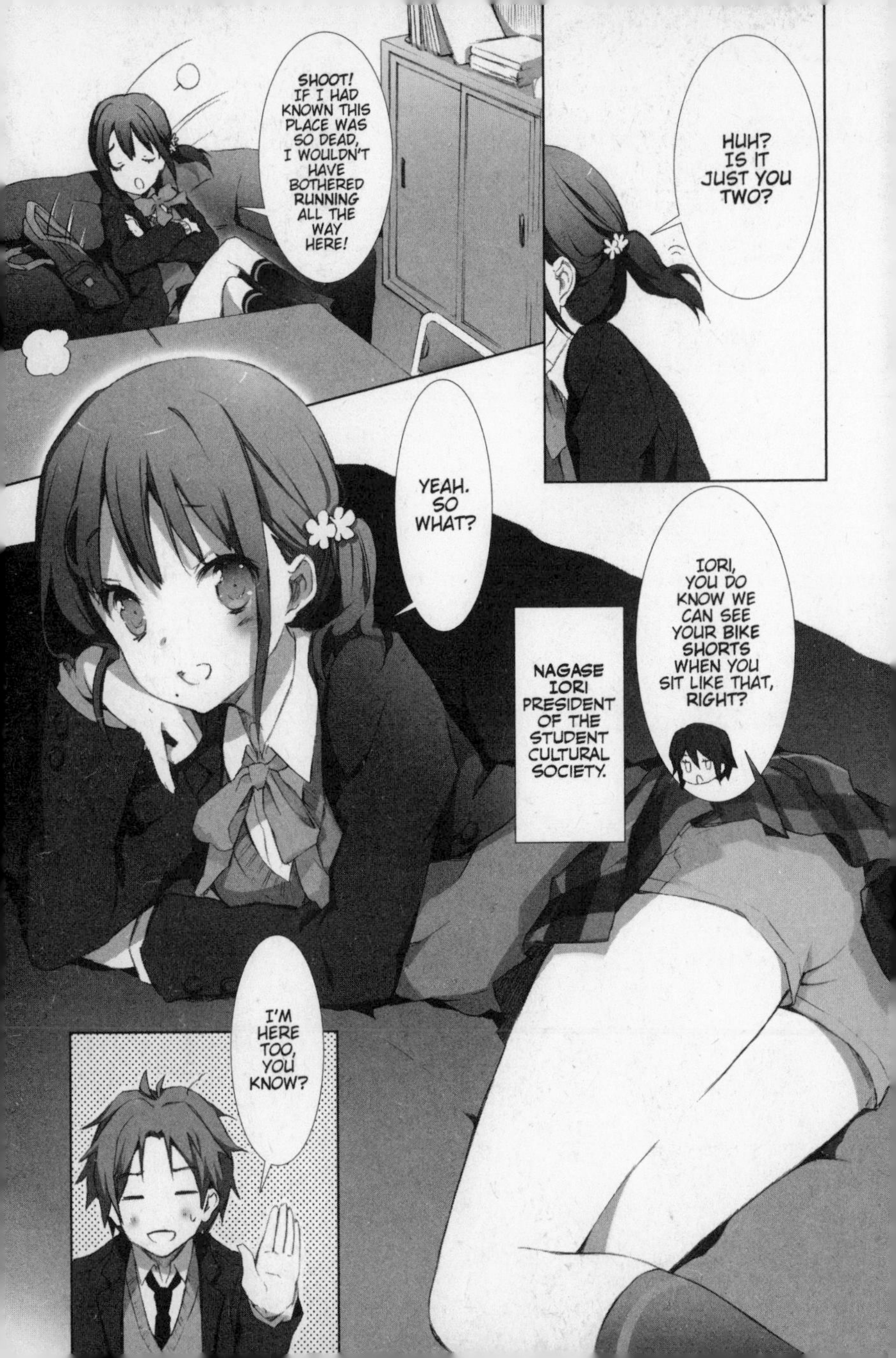
HUH? IS IT JUST YOU TWO?
SHOOT! IF I HAD KNOWN THIS PLACE WAS SO DEAD, I WOULDN'T HAVE BOTHERED RUNNING ALL THE WAY HERE!
IORI, YOU DO KNOW WE CAN SEE YOUR BIKE SHORTS WHEN YOU SIT LIKE THAT, RIGHT?
YEAH. SO WHAT?
NAGASE IORI PRESIDENT OF THE STUDENT CULTURAL SOCIETY.
I'M HERE TOO, YOU KNOW?

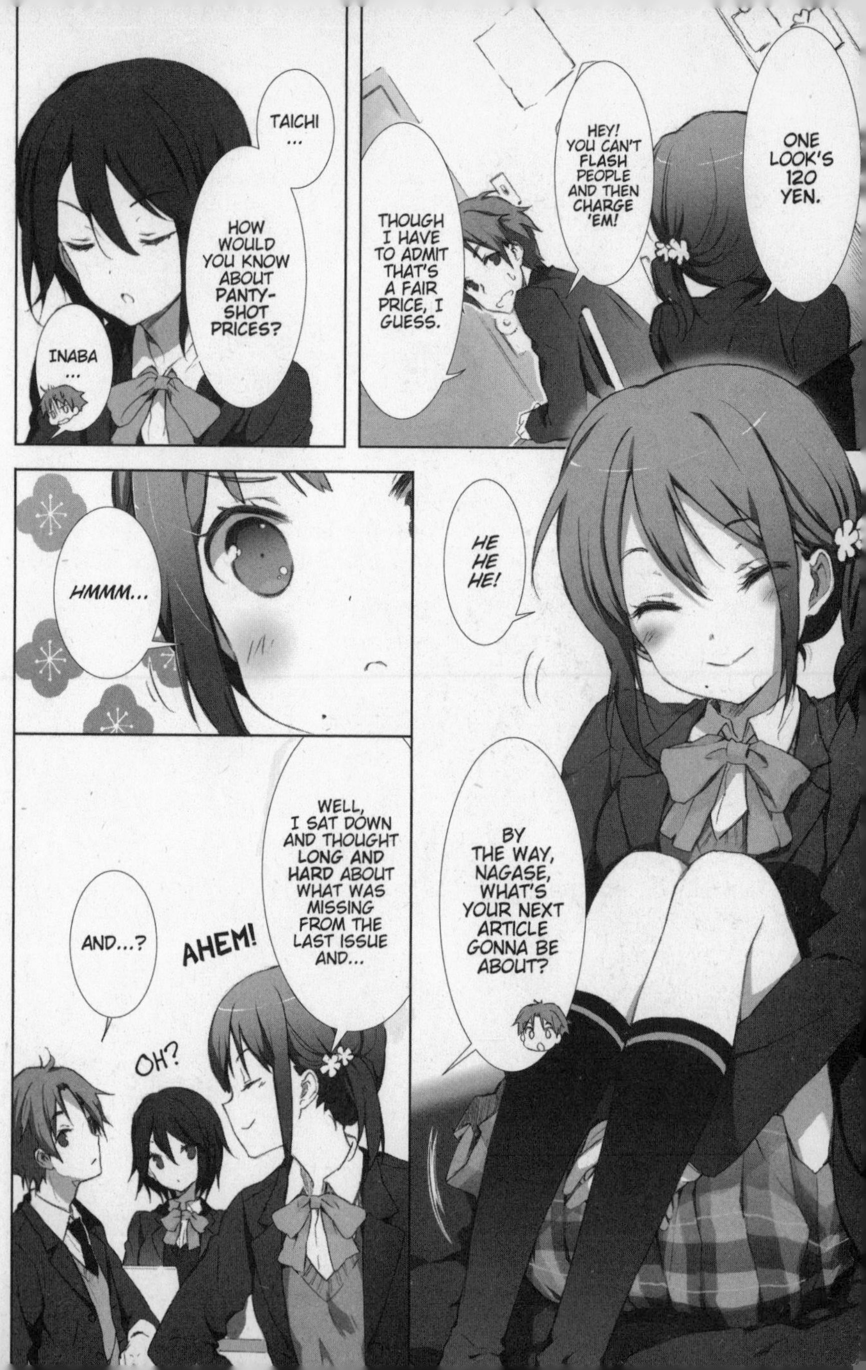
ONE LOOK'S 120 YEN.
HEY! YOU CAN'T FLASH PEOPLE AND THEN CHARGE 'EM!
THOUGH I HAVE TO ADMIT THAT'S A FAIR PRICE, I GUESS.
TAICHI ...
HOW WOULD YOU KNOW ABOUT PANTY-SHOT PRICES?
INABA ...
HE HE HE!
BY THE WAY, NAGASE, WHAT'S YOUR NEXT ARTICLE GONNA BE ABOUT?
HMMM...
WELL, I SAT DOWN AND THOUGHT LONG AND HARD ABOUT WHAT WAS MISSING FROM THE LAST ISSUE AND...
AHEM!
AND...?
OH?

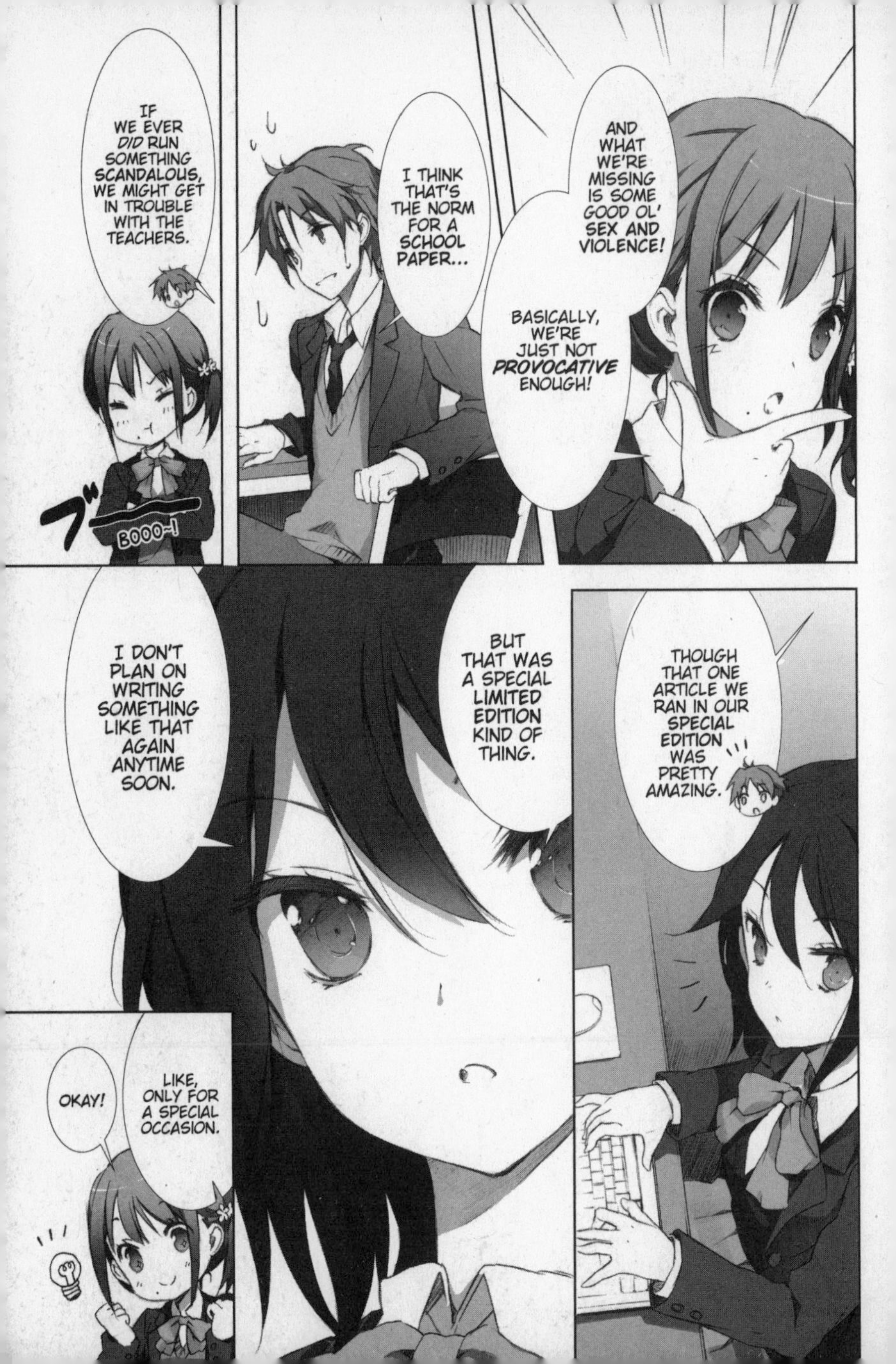
AND WHAT WE'RE MISSING IS SOME GOOD OL' SEX AND VIOLENCE!
BASICALLY, WE'RE JUST NOT *PROVOCATIVE* ENOUGH!
I THINK THAT'S THE NORM FOR A SCHOOL PAPER...
IF WE EVER *DID* RUN SOMETHING SCANDALOUS, WE MIGHT GET IN TROUBLE WITH THE TEACHERS.
BOOO~!
THOUGH THAT ONE ARTICLE WE RAN IN OUR SPECIAL EDITION WAS PRETTY AMAZING.
BUT THAT WAS A SPECIAL LIMITED EDITION KIND OF THING.
I DON'T PLAN ON WRITING SOMETHING LIKE THAT AGAIN ANYTIME SOON.
LIKE, ONLY FOR A SPECIAL OCCASION.
OKAY!

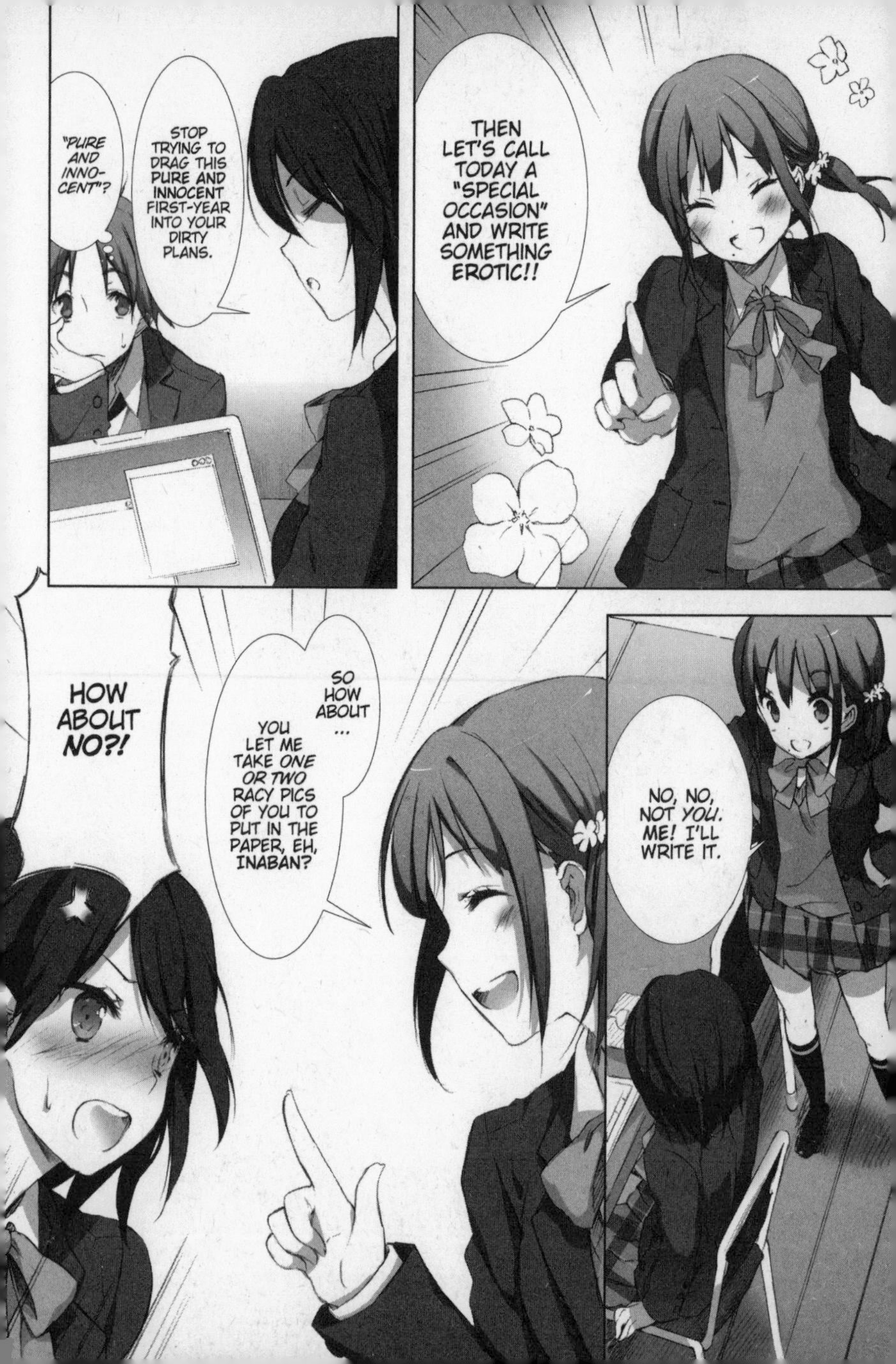
THEN LET'S CALL TODAY A "SPECIAL OCCASION" AND WRITE SOMETHING EROTIC!!
STOP TRYING TO DRAG THIS PURE AND INNOCENT FIRST-YEAR INTO YOUR DIRTY PLANS.
"PURE AND INNO-CENT"?
NO, NO, NOT *YOU*. ME! I'LL WRITE IT.
SO HOW ABOUT ... YOU LET ME TAKE *ONE OR TWO* RACY PICS OF YOU TO PUT IN THE PAPER, EH, INABAN?
HOW ABOUT *NO*?!

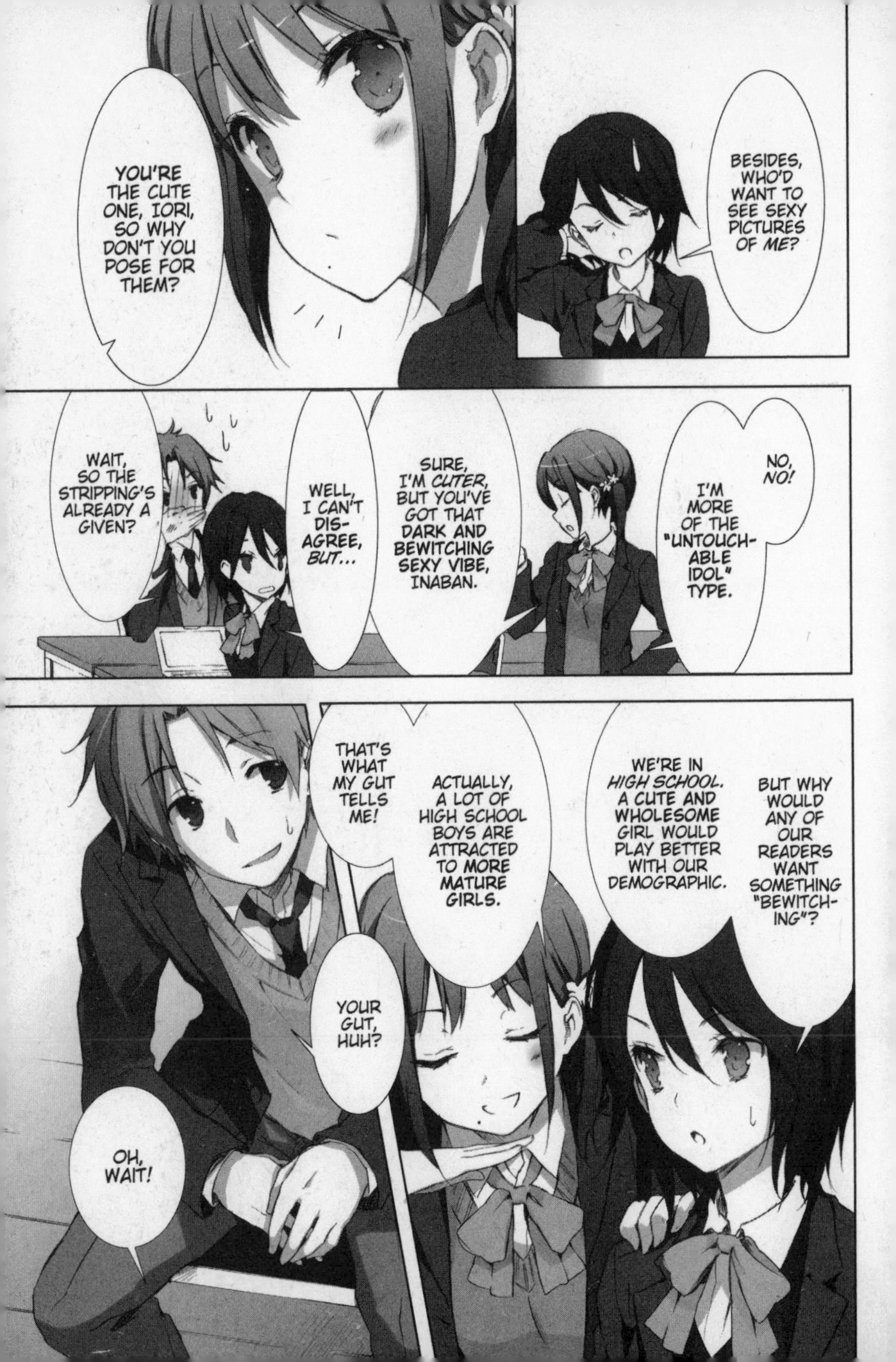
BESIDES, WHO'D WANT TO SEE SEXY PICTURES OF *ME*?
YOU'RE THE CUTE ONE, IORI, SO WHY DON'T YOU POSE FOR THEM?
NO, *NO!*
I'M MORE OF THE "UNTOUCHABLE IDOL" TYPE.
SURE, I'M *CUTER*, BUT YOU'VE GOT THAT DARK AND BEWITCHING SEXY VIBE, INABAN.
WELL, I CAN'T DISAGREE, *BUT*...
WAIT, SO THE STRIPPING'S ALREADY A GIVEN?
BUT WHY WOULD ANY OF OUR READERS WANT SOMETHING "BEWITCHING"?
WE'RE IN *HIGH SCHOOL*. A CUTE AND WHOLESOME GIRL WOULD PLAY BETTER WITH OUR DEMOGRAPHIC.
ACTUALLY, A LOT OF HIGH SCHOOL BOYS ARE ATTRACTED TO MORE MATURE GIRLS.
THAT'S WHAT MY GUT TELLS ME!
YOUR GUT, HUH?
OH, WAIT!

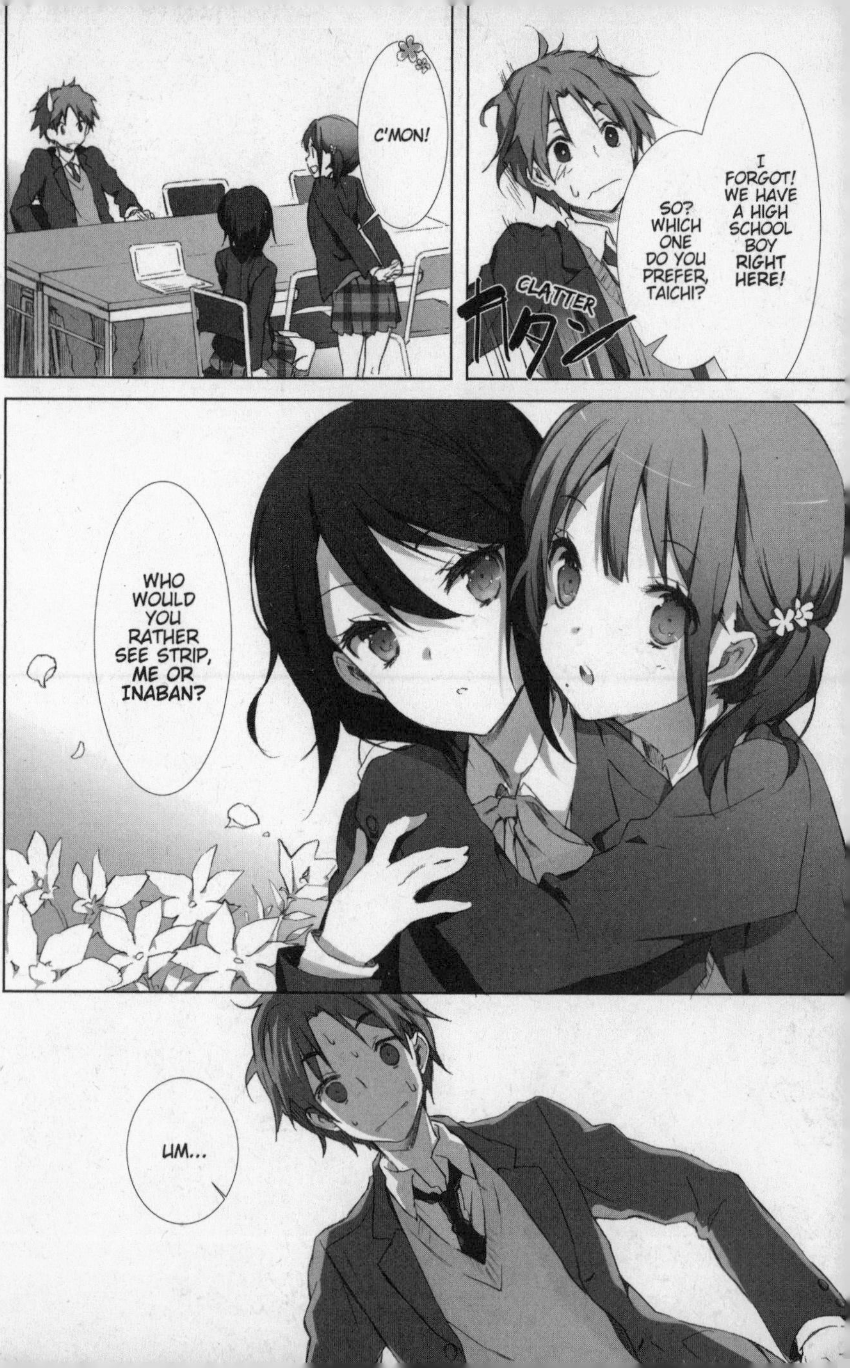
I FORGOT! WE HAVE A HIGH SCHOOL BOY RIGHT HERE!
SO? WHICH ONE DO YOU PREFER, TAICHI?
CLATTER
カタン
C'MON!
WHO WOULD YOU RATHER SEE STRIP, ME OR INABAN?
UM...

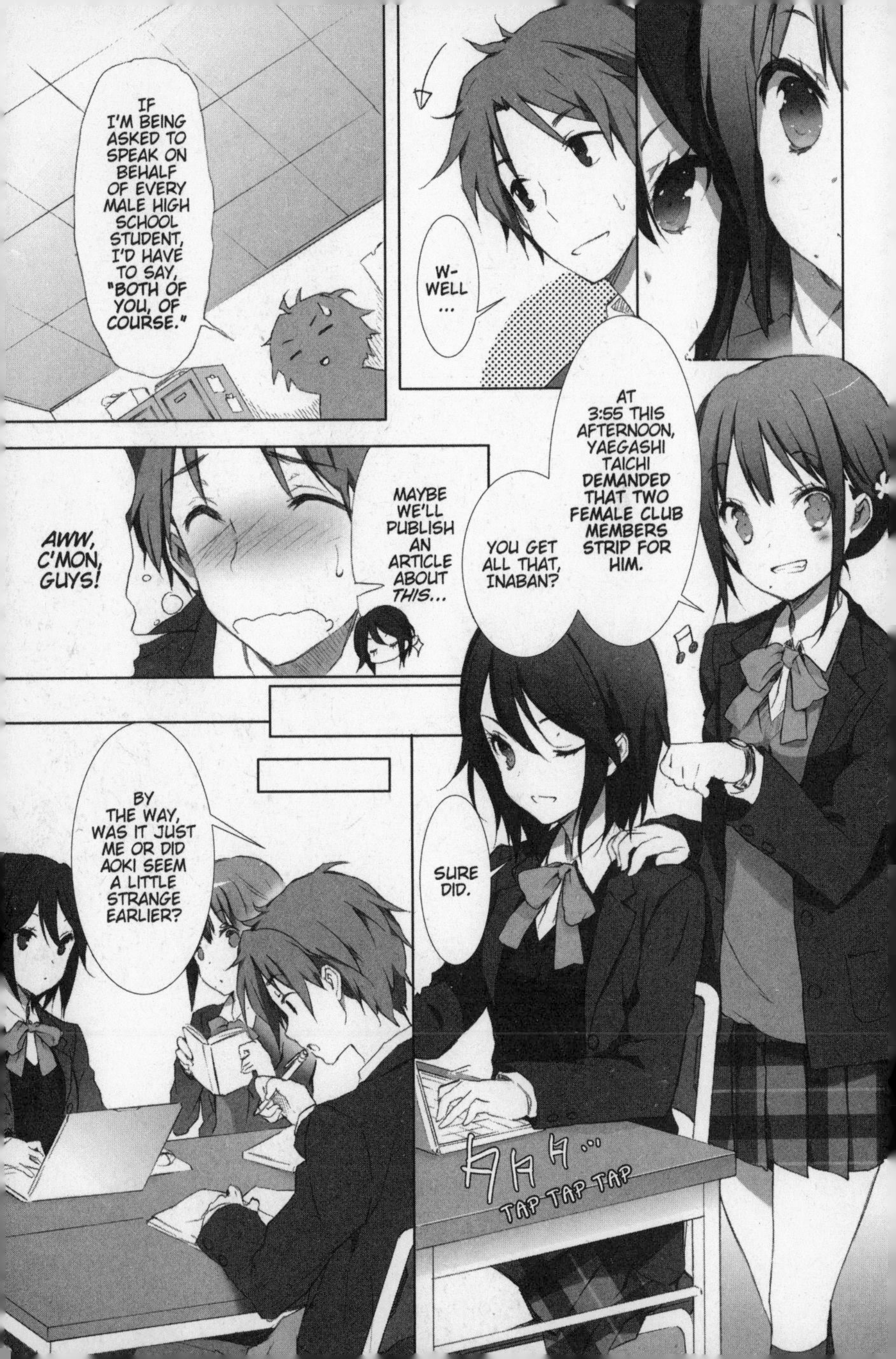
W-WELL...
IF I'M BEING ASKED TO SPEAK ON BEHALF OF EVERY MALE HIGH SCHOOL STUDENT, I'D HAVE TO SAY, "BOTH OF YOU, OF COURSE."
AT 3:55 THIS AFTERNOON, YAEGASHI TAICHI DEMANDED THAT TWO FEMALE CLUB MEMBERS STRIP FOR HIM.
YOU GET ALL THAT, INABAN?
SURE DID.
TAP TAP TAP
MAYBE WE'LL PUBLISH AN ARTICLE ABOUT *THIS*...
AWW, C'MON, GUYS!
BY THE WAY, WAS IT JUST ME OR DID AOKI SEEM A LITTLE STRANGE EARLIER?

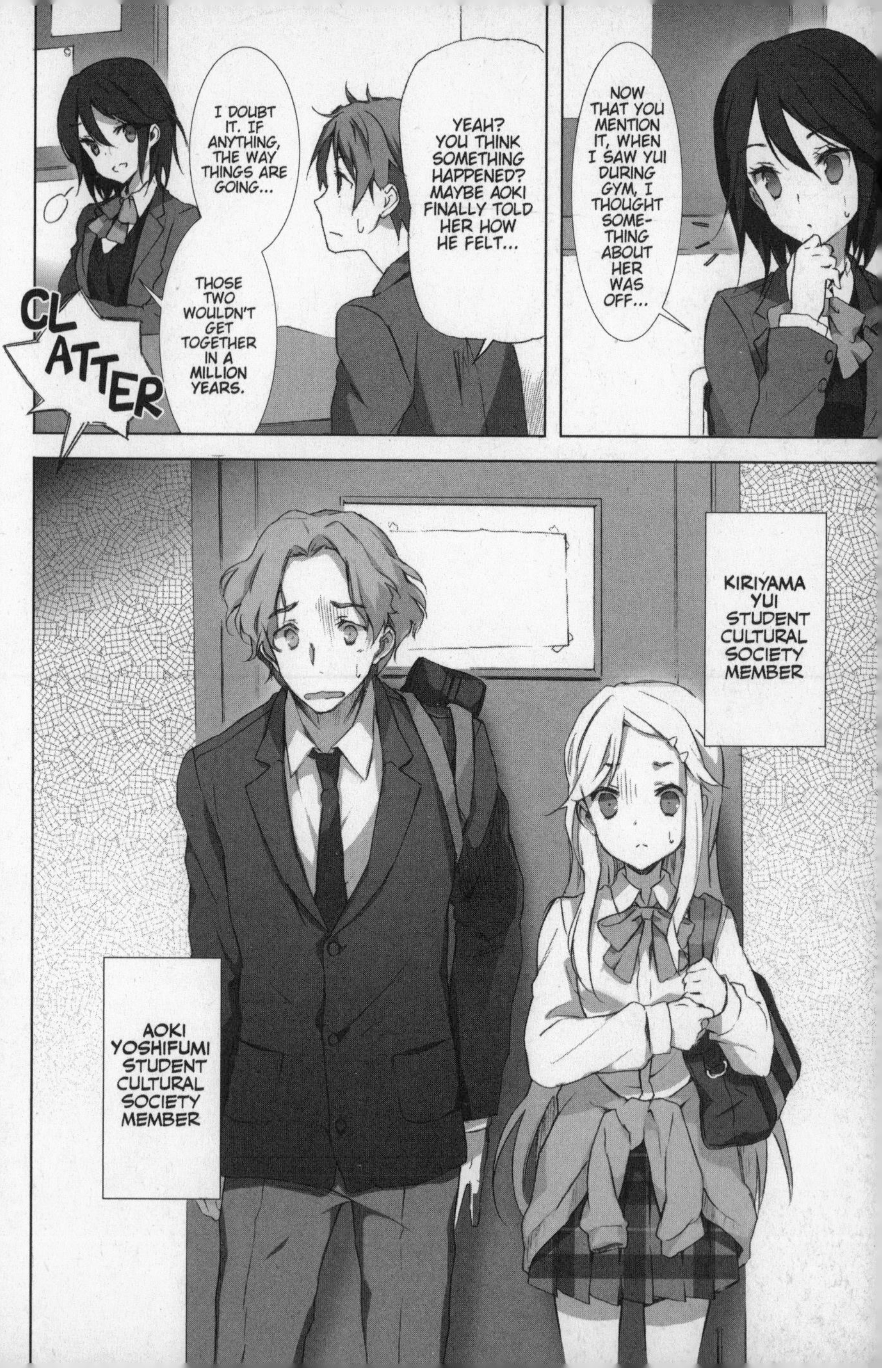
NOW THAT YOU MENTION IT, WHEN I SAW YUI DURING GYM, I THOUGHT SOME-THING ABOUT HER WAS OFF...
YEAH? YOU THINK SOMETHING HAPPENED? MAYBE AOKI FINALLY TOLD HER HOW HE FELT...
I DOUBT IT. IF ANYTHING, THE WAY THINGS ARE GOING...
THOSE TWO WOULDN'T GET TOGETHER IN A MILLION YEARS.
CLATTER
KIRIYAMA YUI STUDENT CULTURAL SOCIETY MEMBER
AOKI YOSHIFUMI STUDENT CULTURAL SOCIETY MEMBER

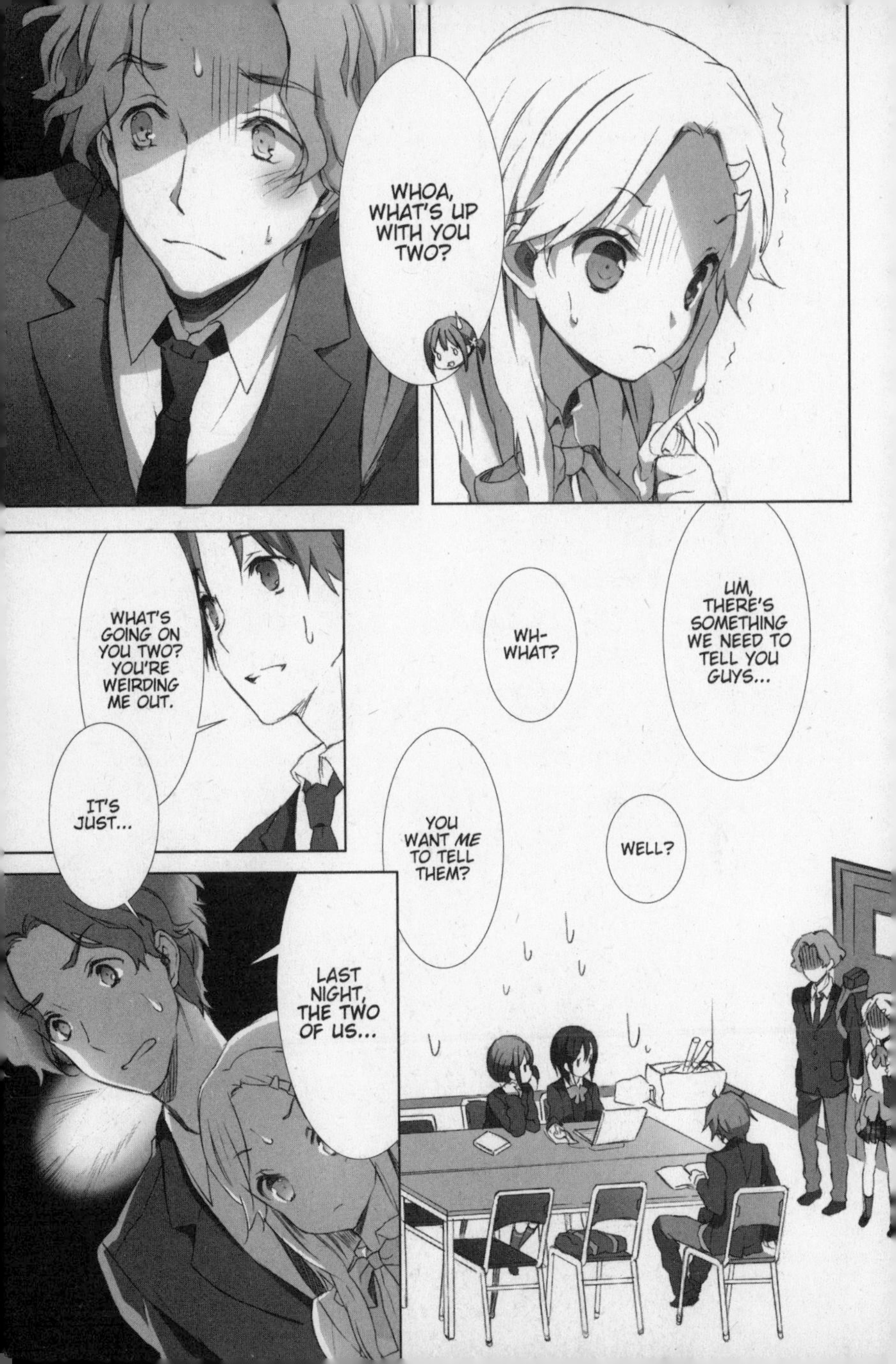
WHOA, WHAT'S UP WITH YOU TWO?
UM, THERE'S SOMETHING WE NEED TO TELL YOU GUYS...
WH-WHAT?
WELL?
YOU WANT *ME* TO TELL THEM?
WHAT'S GOING ON YOU TWO? YOU'RE WEIRDING ME OUT.
IT'S JUST...
LAST NIGHT, THE TWO OF US...

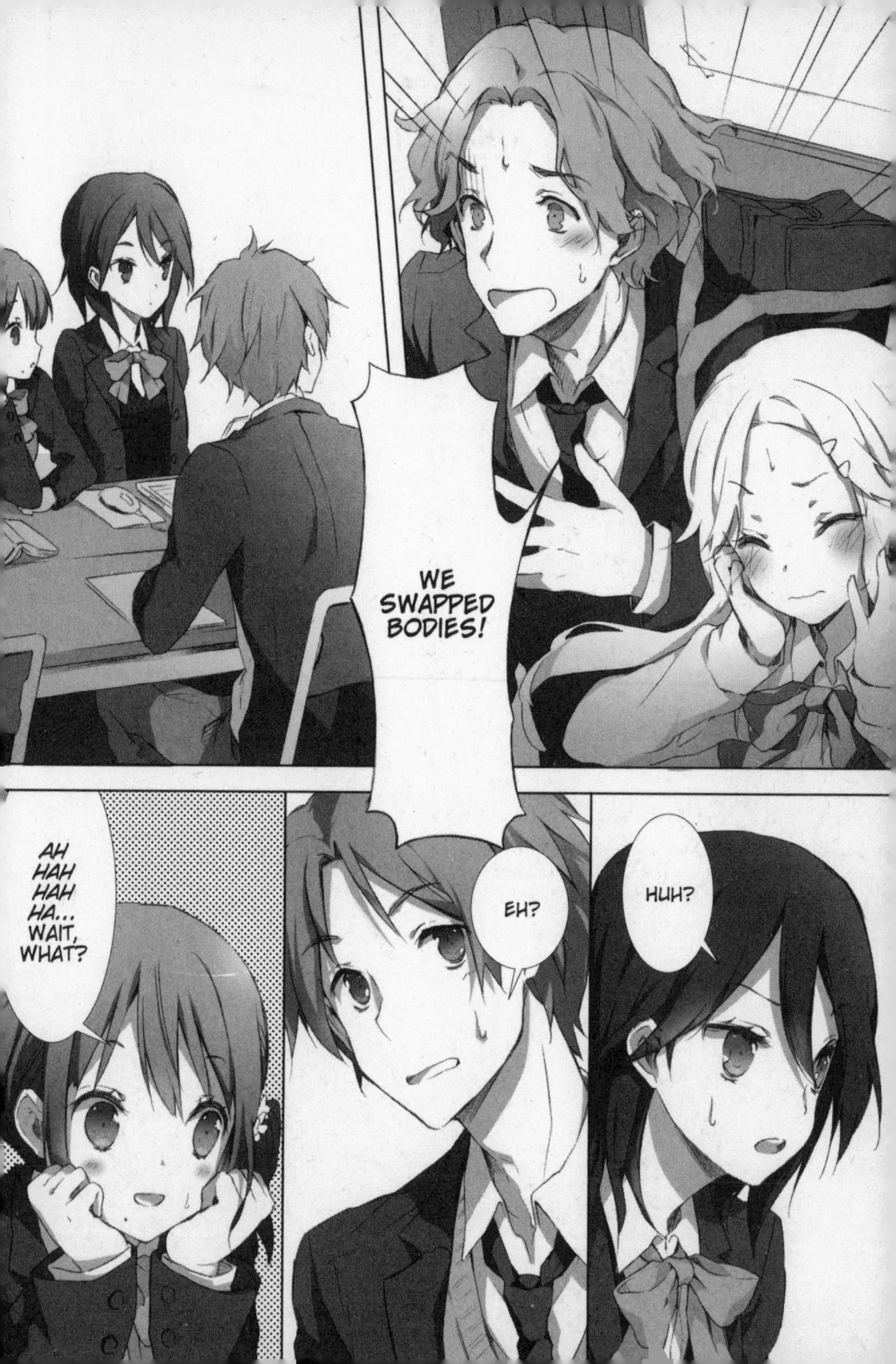
WE SWAPPED BODIES!
HUH?
EH?
AH HAH HAH HA... WAIT, WHAT?

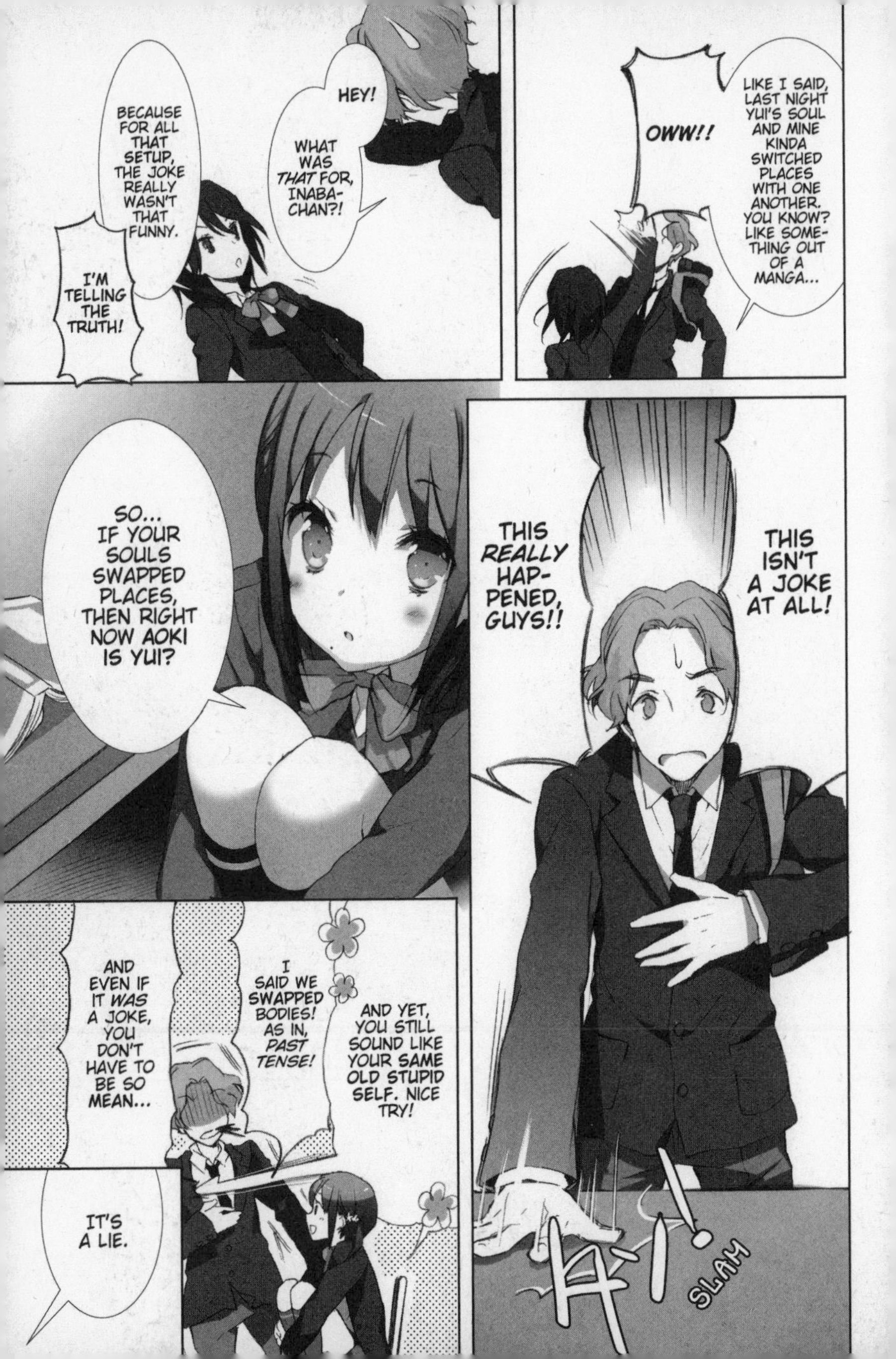
LIKE I SAID, LAST NIGHT YUI'S SOUL AND MINE KINDA SWITCHED PLACES WITH ONE ANOTHER. YOU KNOW? LIKE SOME-THING OUT OF A MANGA...
OWW!!
HEY!
WHAT WAS *THAT* FOR, INABA-CHAN?!
BECAUSE FOR ALL THAT SETUP, THE JOKE REALLY WASN'T THAT FUNNY.
I'M TELLING THE TRUTH!
THIS ISN'T A JOKE AT ALL!
THIS *REALLY* HAP-PENED, GUYS!!
SLAM
SO... IF YOUR SOULS SWAPPED PLACES, THEN RIGHT NOW AOKI IS YUI?
I SAID WE SWAPPED BODIES! AS IN, *PAST TENSE!*
AND YET, YOU STILL SOUND LIKE YOUR SAME OLD STUPID SELF. NICE TRY!
AND EVEN IF IT *WAS* A JOKE, YOU DON'T HAVE TO BE SO MEAN...
IT'S A LIE.

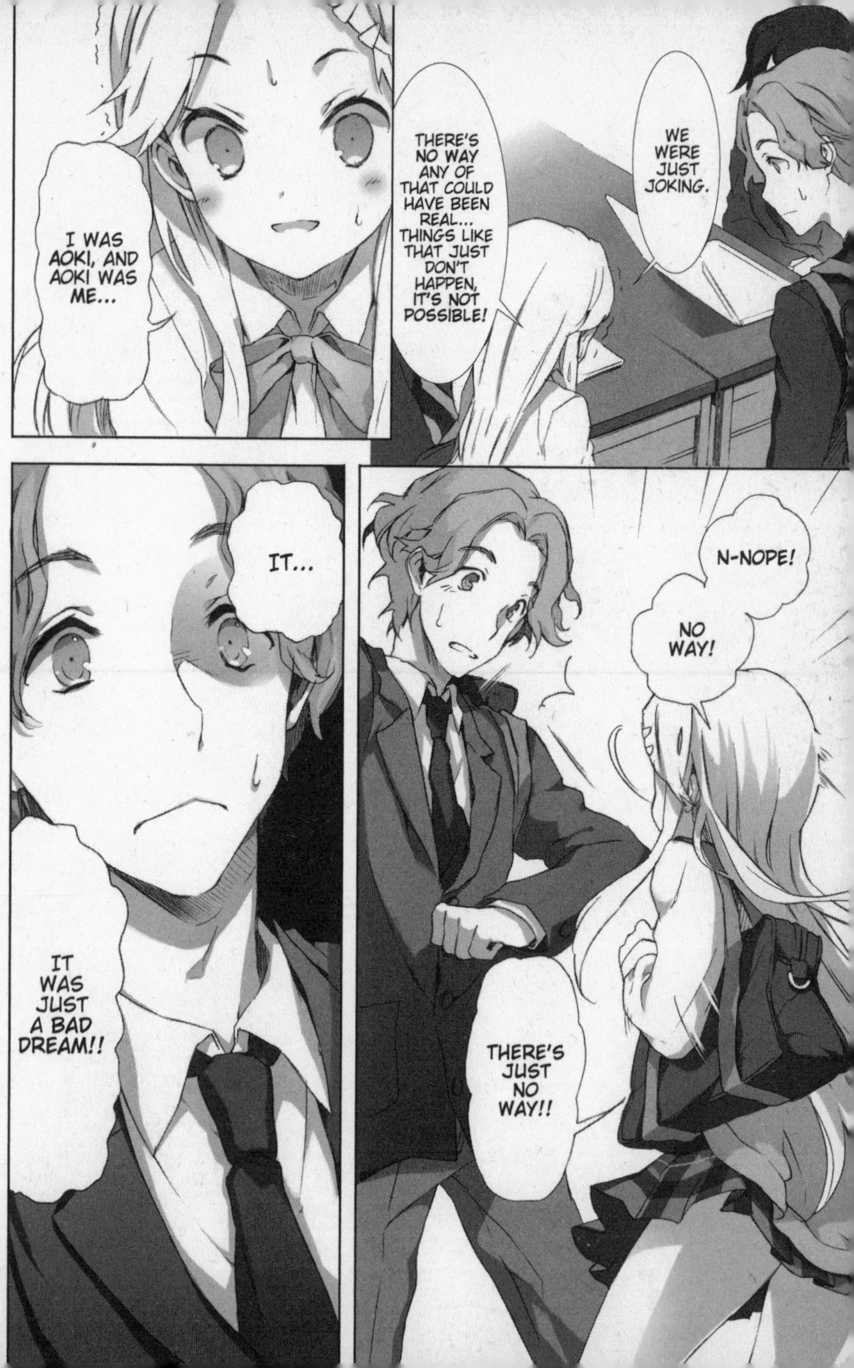
WE WERE JUST JOKING.
THERE'S NO WAY ANY OF THAT COULD HAVE BEEN REAL... THINGS LIKE THAT JUST DON'T HAPPEN, IT'S NOT POSSIBLE!
I WAS AOKI, AND AOKI WAS ME...
N-NOPE!
NO WAY!
THERE'S JUST NO WAY!!
IT...
IT WAS JUST A BAD DREAM!!

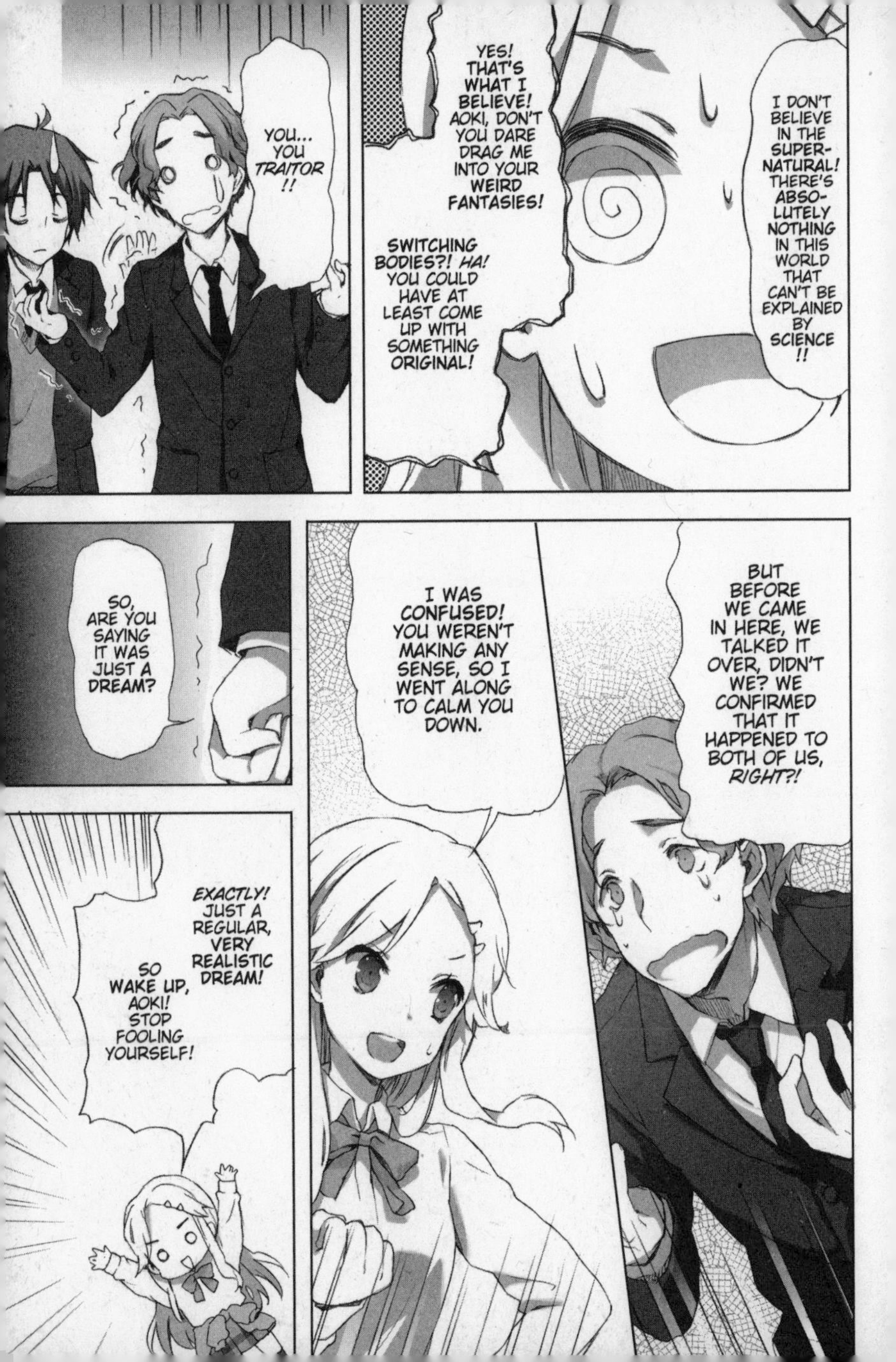

I DON'T BELIEVE IN THE SUPER-NATURAL! THERE'S ABSO-LUTELY NOTHING IN THIS WORLD THAT CAN'T BE EXPLAINED BY SCIENCE!!
YES! THAT'S WHAT I BELIEVE! AOKI, DON'T YOU DARE DRAG ME INTO YOUR WEIRD FANTASIES!
SWITCHING BODIES?! HA! YOU COULD HAVE AT LEAST COME UP WITH SOMETHING ORIGINAL!
YOU... YOU TRAITOR!!
BUT BEFORE WE CAME IN HERE, WE TALKED IT OVER, DIDN'T WE? WE CONFIRMED THAT IT HAPPENED TO BOTH OF US, RIGHT?!
I WAS CONFUSED! YOU WEREN'T MAKING ANY SENSE, SO I WENT ALONG TO CALM YOU DOWN.
SO, ARE YOU SAYING IT WAS JUST A DREAM?
EXACTLY! JUST A REGULAR, VERY REALISTIC DREAM!
SO WAKE UP, AOKI! STOP FOOLING YOURSELF!

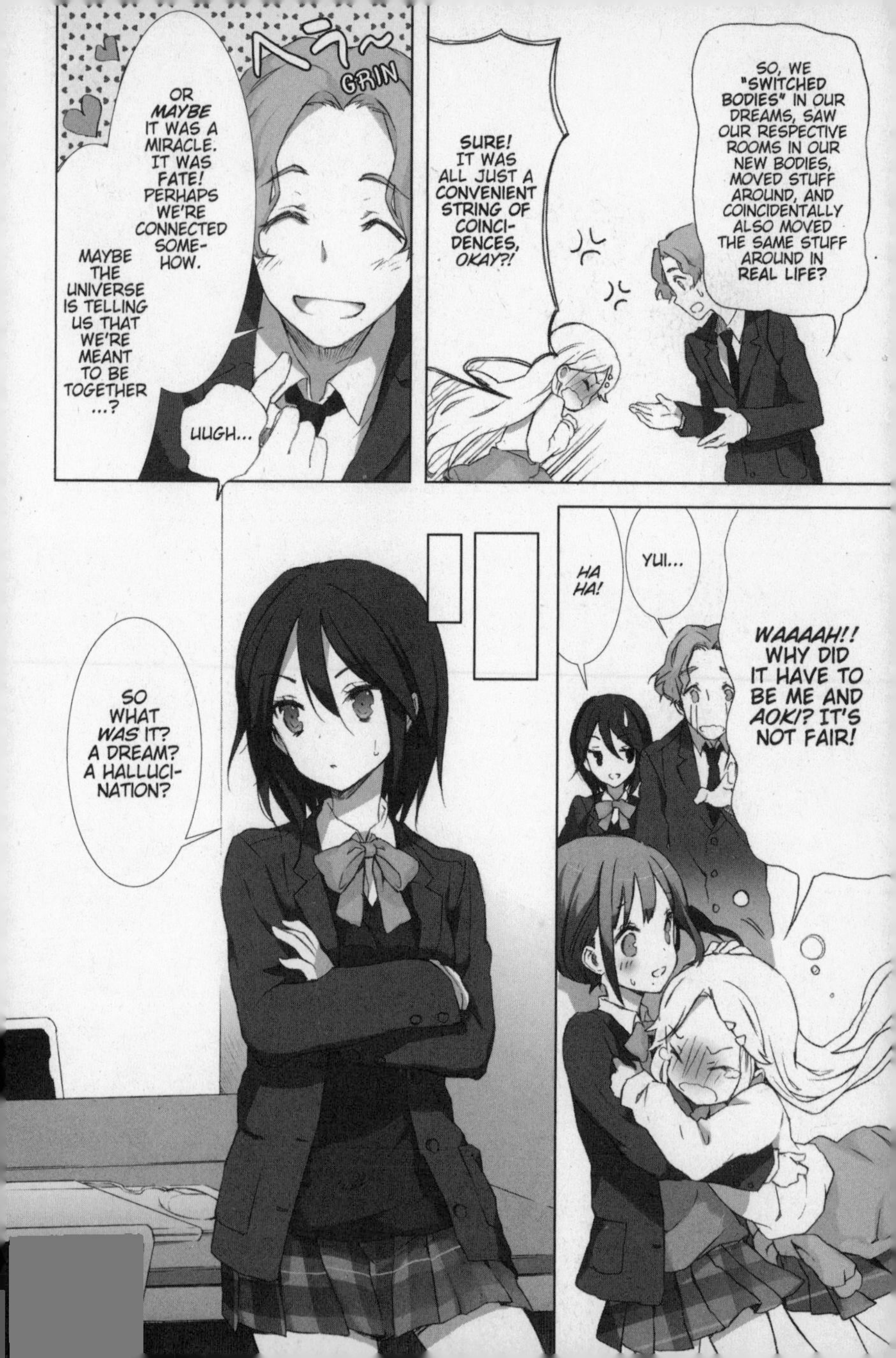
SO, WE "SWITCHED BODIES" IN OUR DREAMS, SAW OUR RESPECTIVE ROOMS IN OUR NEW BODIES, MOVED STUFF AROUND, AND COINCIDENTALLY ALSO MOVED THE SAME STUFF AROUND IN REAL LIFE?
SURE! IT WAS ALL JUST A CONVENIENT STRING OF COINCI-DENCES, *OKAY?!*
へえ～
GRIN
OR *MAYBE* IT WAS A MIRACLE. IT WAS FATE! PERHAPS WE'RE CONNECTED SOME-HOW.
MAYBE THE UNIVERSE IS TELLING US THAT WE'RE MEANT TO BE TOGETHER ...?
UUGH...
WAAAAH!! WHY DID IT HAVE TO BE ME AND *AOKI*? IT'S NOT FAIR!
YUI...
HA HA!
SO WHAT *WAS* IT? A DREAM? A HALLUCI-NATION?

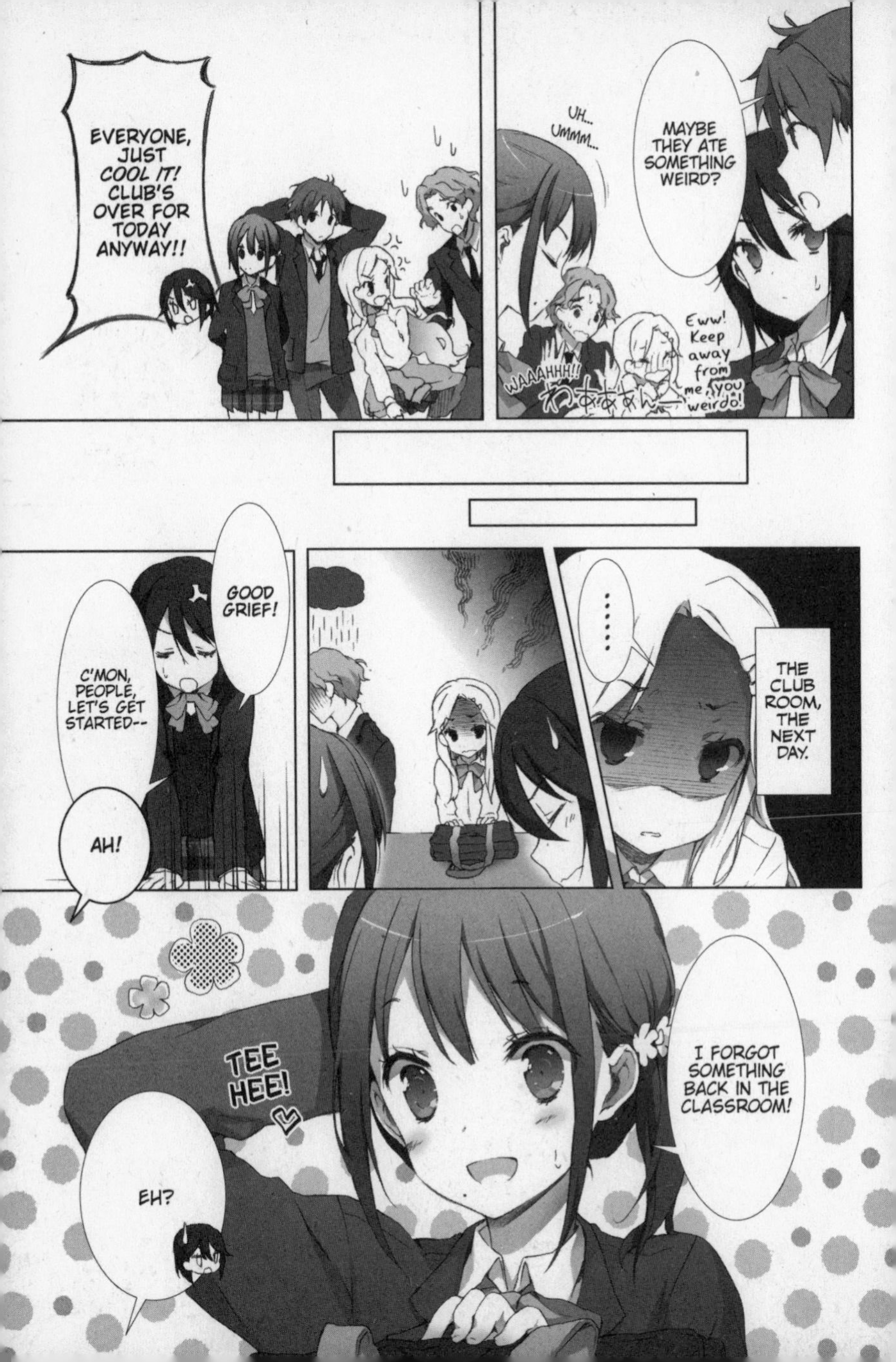
MAYBE THEY ATE SOMETHING WEIRD?
UH... UMMM...
Eww! Keep away from me, you weirdo!
WAAAHHH!!
EVERYONE, JUST COOL IT! CLUB'S OVER FOR TODAY ANYWAY!!
THE CLUB ROOM, THE NEXT DAY.
......
GOOD GRIEF!
C'MON, PEOPLE, LET'S GET STARTED--
AH!
I FORGOT SOMETHING BACK IN THE CLASSROOM!
TEE HEE!
EH?

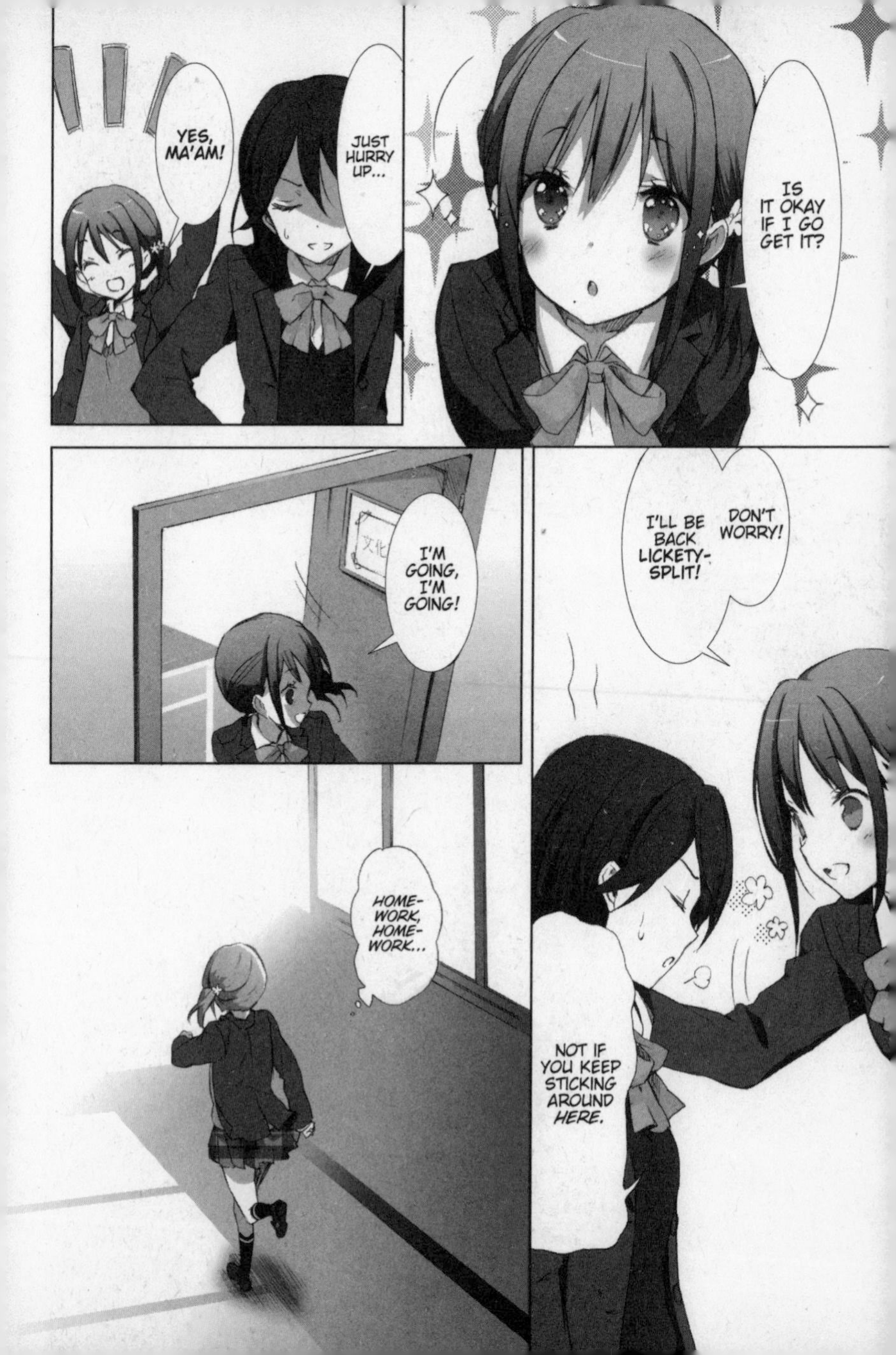
IS IT OKAY IF I GO GET IT?
JUST HURRY UP...
YES, MA'AM!
DON'T WORRY!
I'LL BE BACK LICKETY-SPLIT!
NOT IF YOU KEEP STICKING AROUND HERE.
I'M GOING, I'M GOING!
HOME-WORK, HOME-WORK...

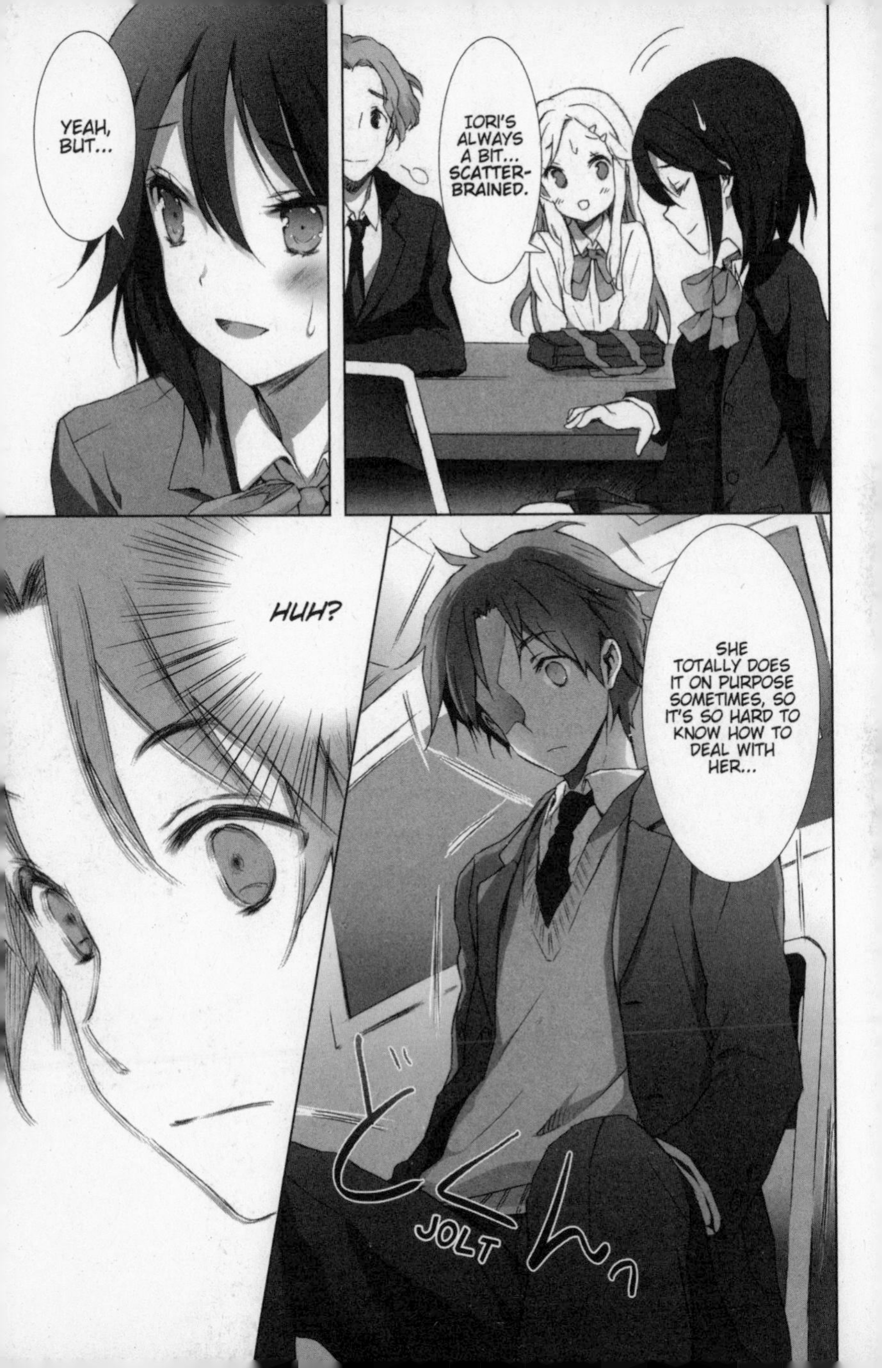
IORI'S ALWAYS A BIT... SCATTER-BRAINED.
YEAH, BUT...
SHE TOTALLY DOES IT ON PURPOSE SOMETIMES, SO IT'S SO HARD TO KNOW HOW TO DEAL WITH HER...
どくん
JOLT
HUH?

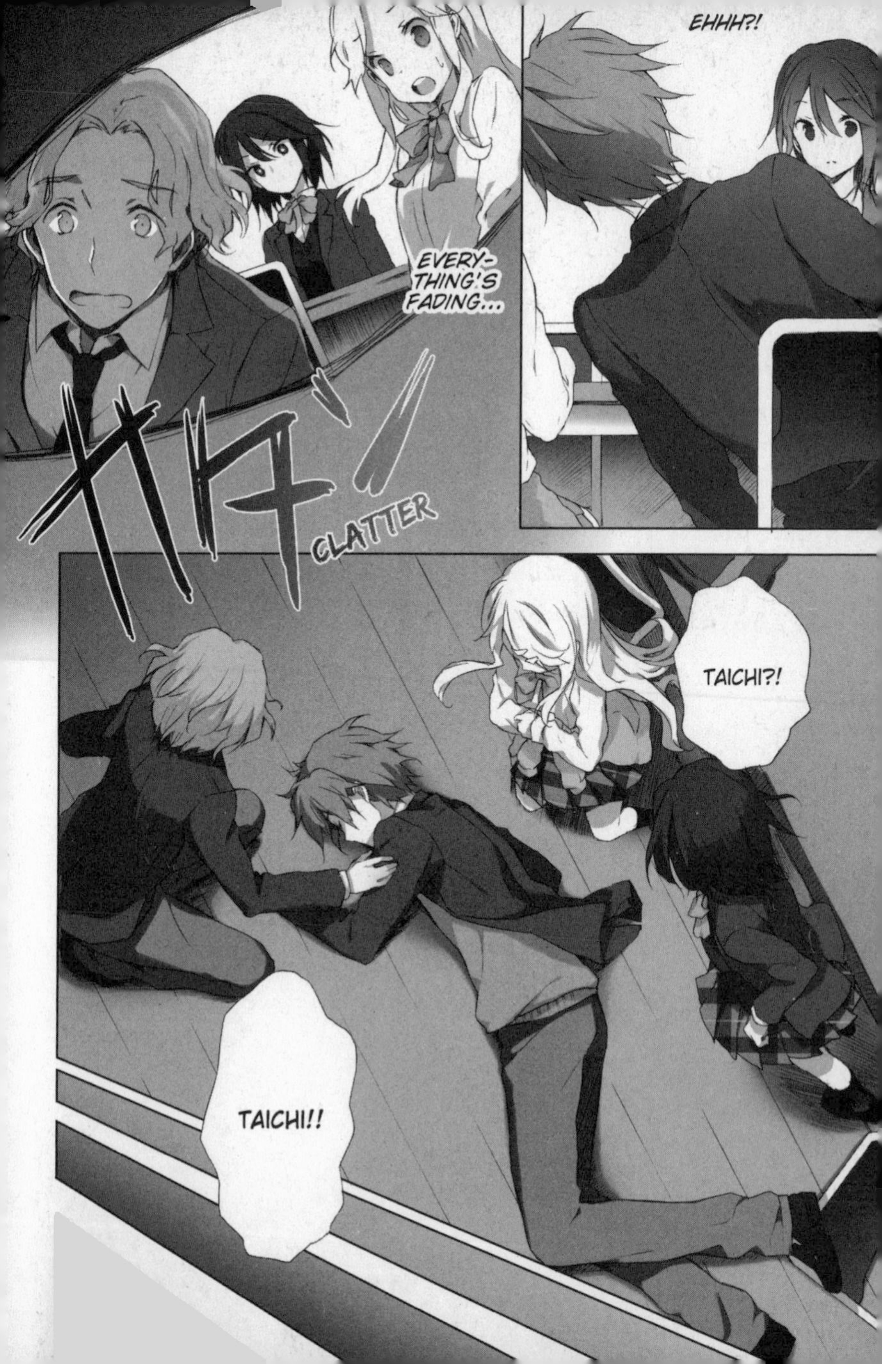
EHHH?!
EVERY-THING'S FADING...
CLATTER
TAICHI?!
TAICHI!!

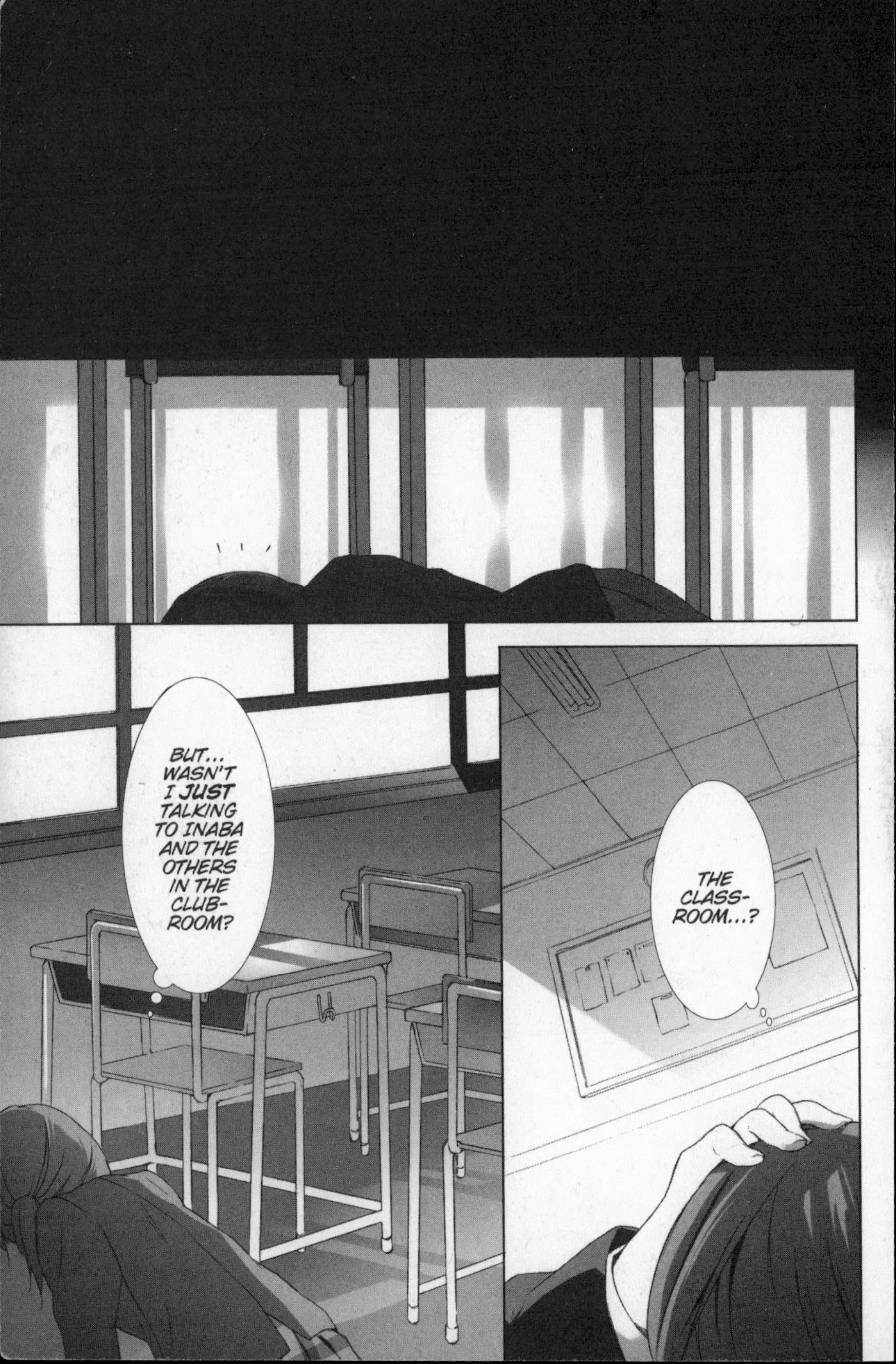
THE CLASS-ROOM...?
BUT... WASN'T I JUST TALKING TO INABA AND THE OTHERS IN THE CLUB-ROOM?

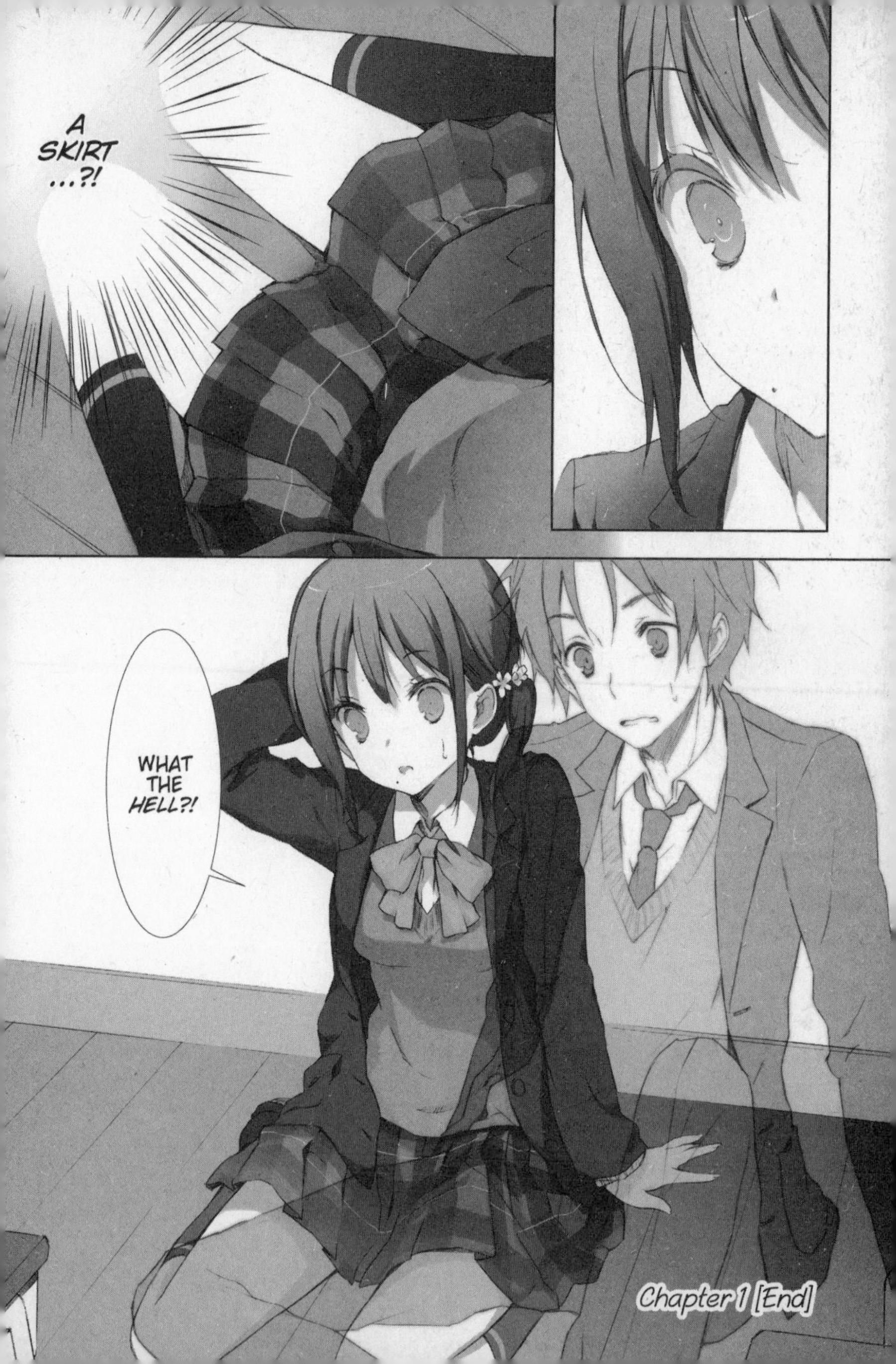
A SKIRT ...?!
WHAT THE HELL?!
Chapter 1 [End]

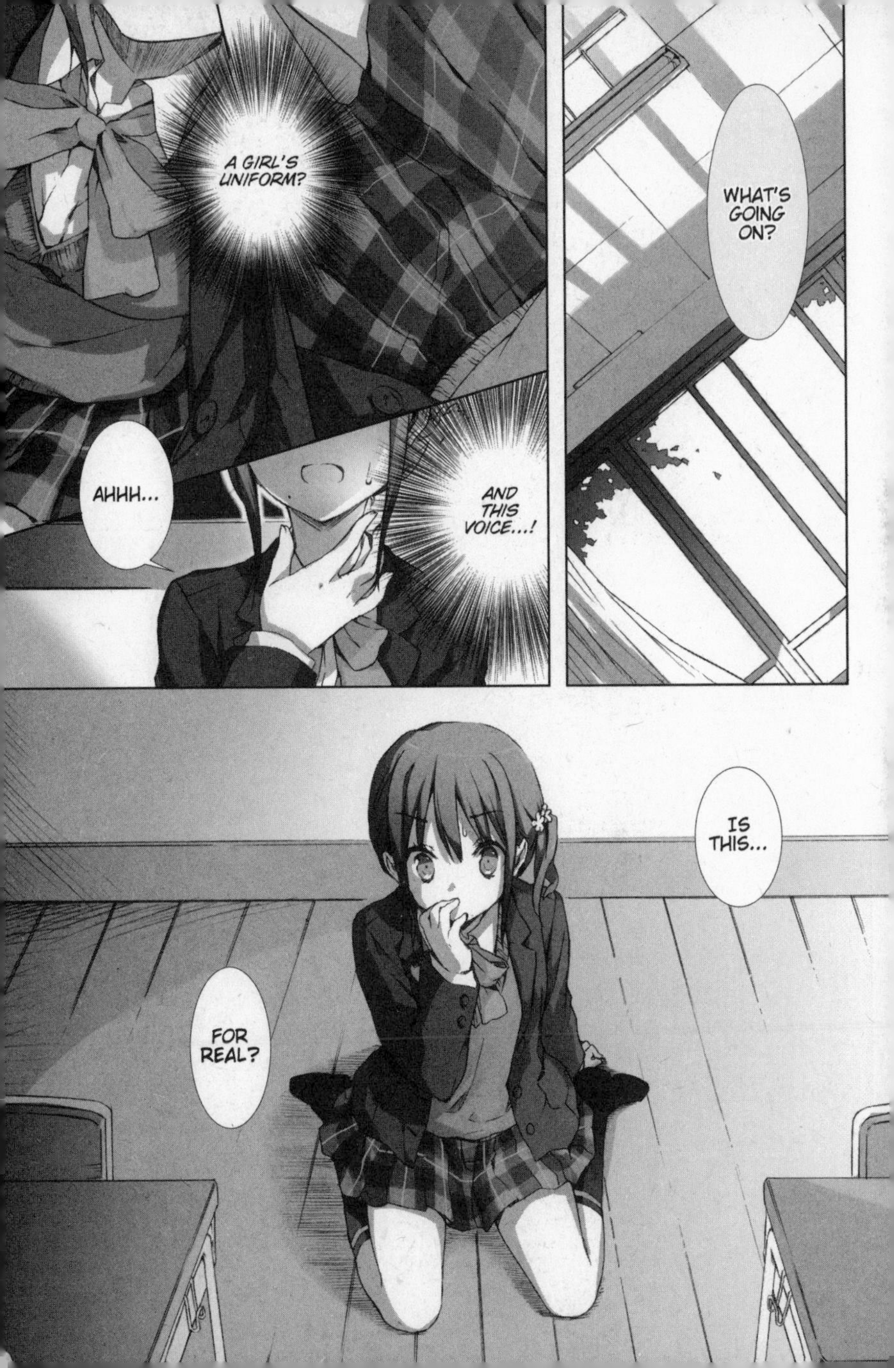
WHAT'S GOING ON?
A GIRL'S UNIFORM?
AND THIS VOICE...!
AHHH...
IS THIS...
FOR REAL?

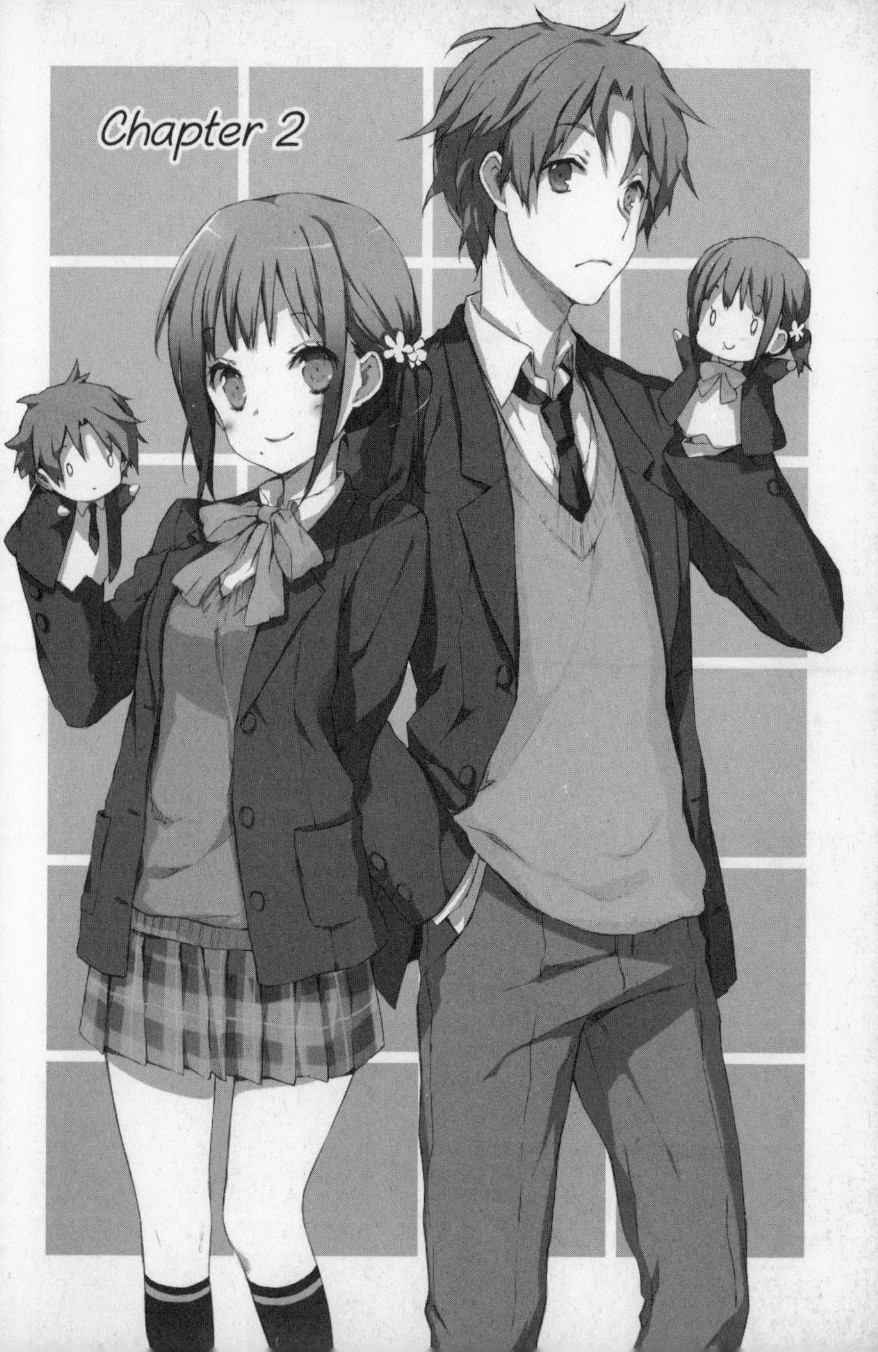
Chapter 2

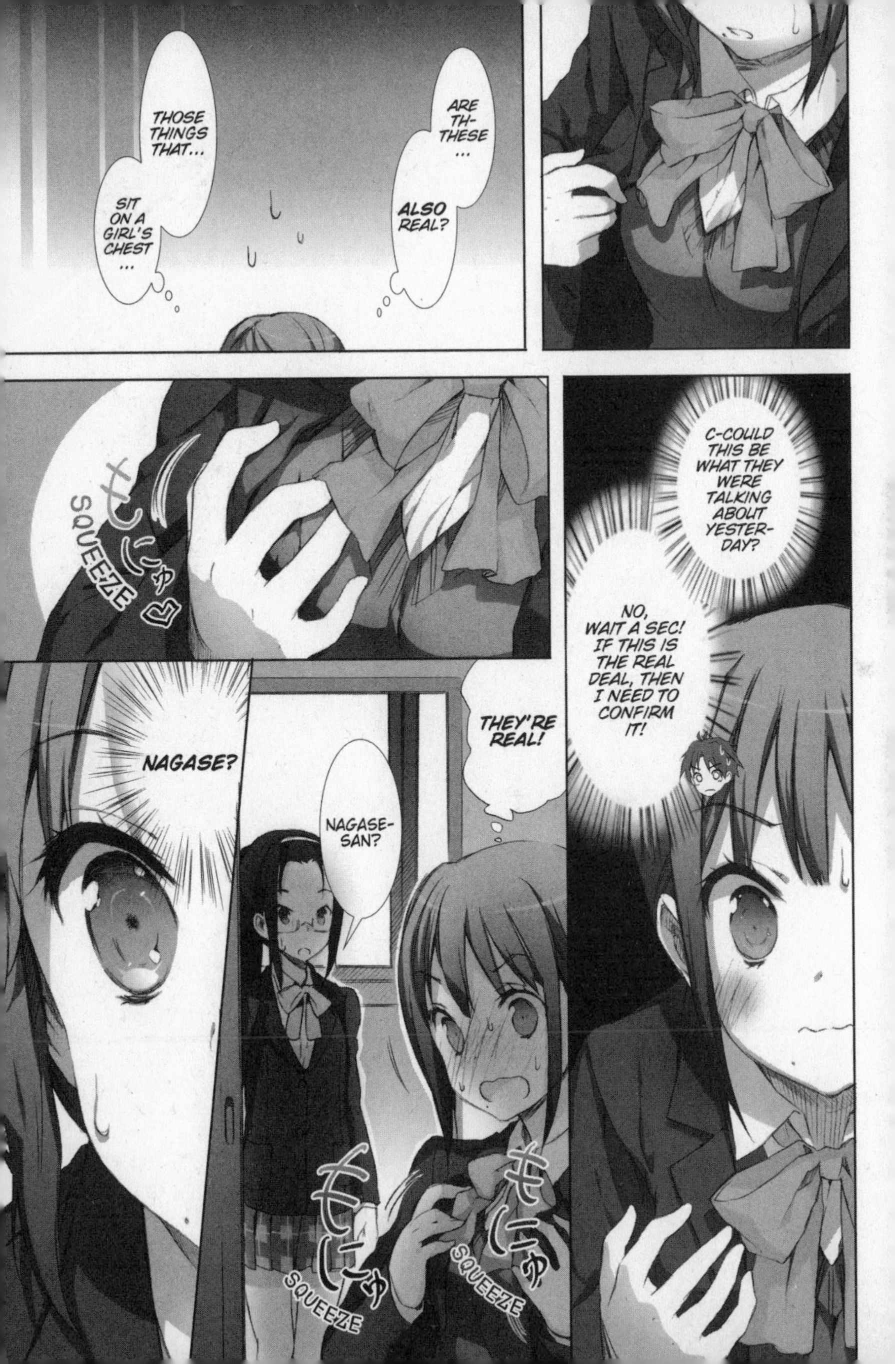
ARE TH-THESE... ALSO REAL?
THOSE THINGS THAT... SIT ON A GIRL'S CHEST...
C-COULD THIS BE WHAT THEY WERE TALKING ABOUT YESTERDAY?
NO, WAIT A SEC! IF THIS IS THE REAL DEAL, THEN I NEED TO CONFIRM IT!
もにゅ
SQUEEZE
THEY'RE REAL!
NAGASE-SAN?
もにゅ
SQUEEZE
もにゅ
SQUEEZE
NAGASE?

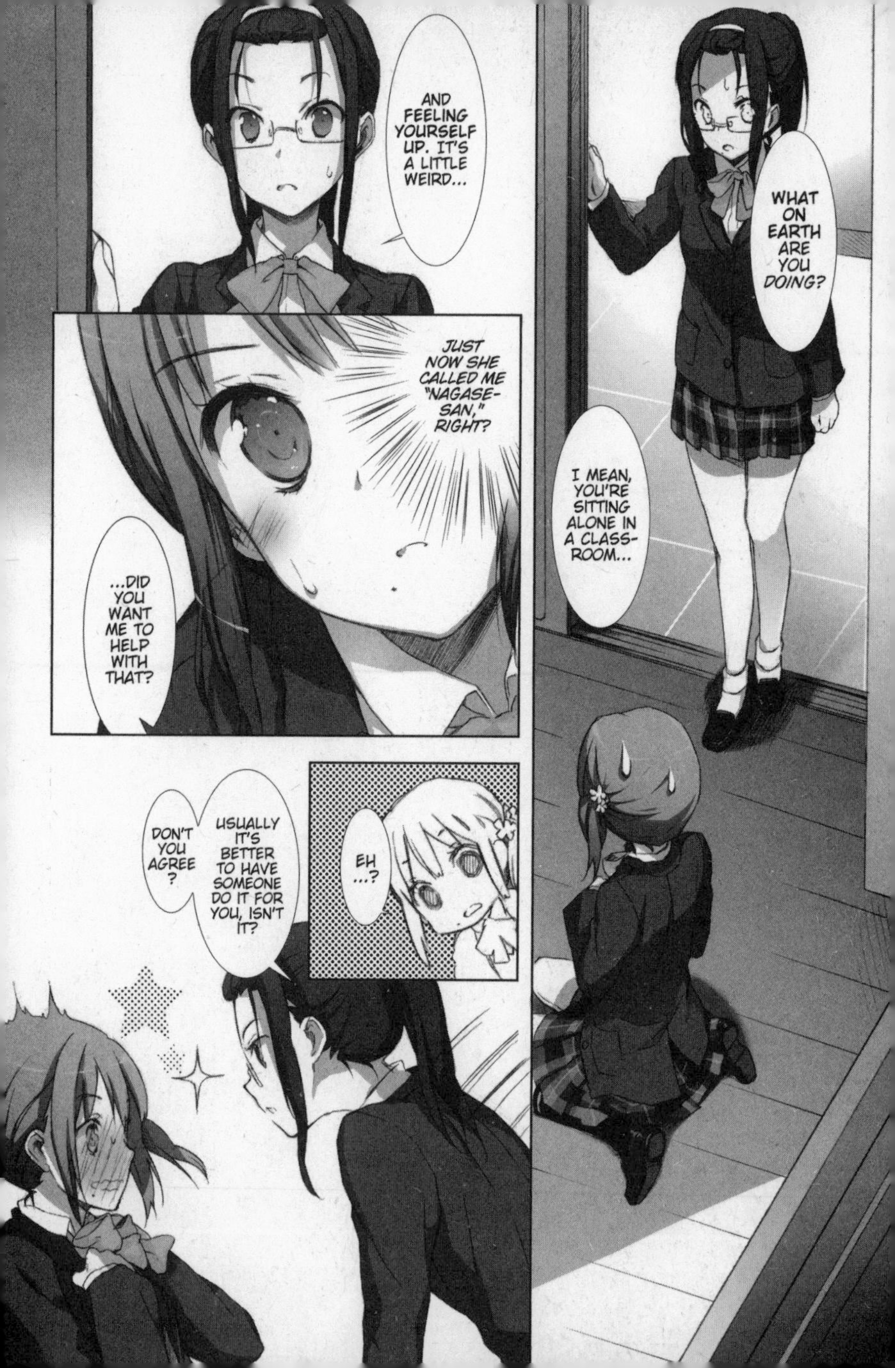

WHAT ON EARTH ARE YOU DOING?
I MEAN, YOU'RE SITTING ALONE IN A CLASS-ROOM...
AND FEELING YOURSELF UP. IT'S A LITTLE WEIRD...
JUST NOW SHE CALLED ME "NAGASE-SAN," RIGHT?
...DID YOU WANT ME TO HELP WITH THAT?
EH ...?
USUALLY IT'S BETTER TO HAVE SOMEONE DO IT FOR YOU, ISN'T IT?
DON'T YOU AGREE?

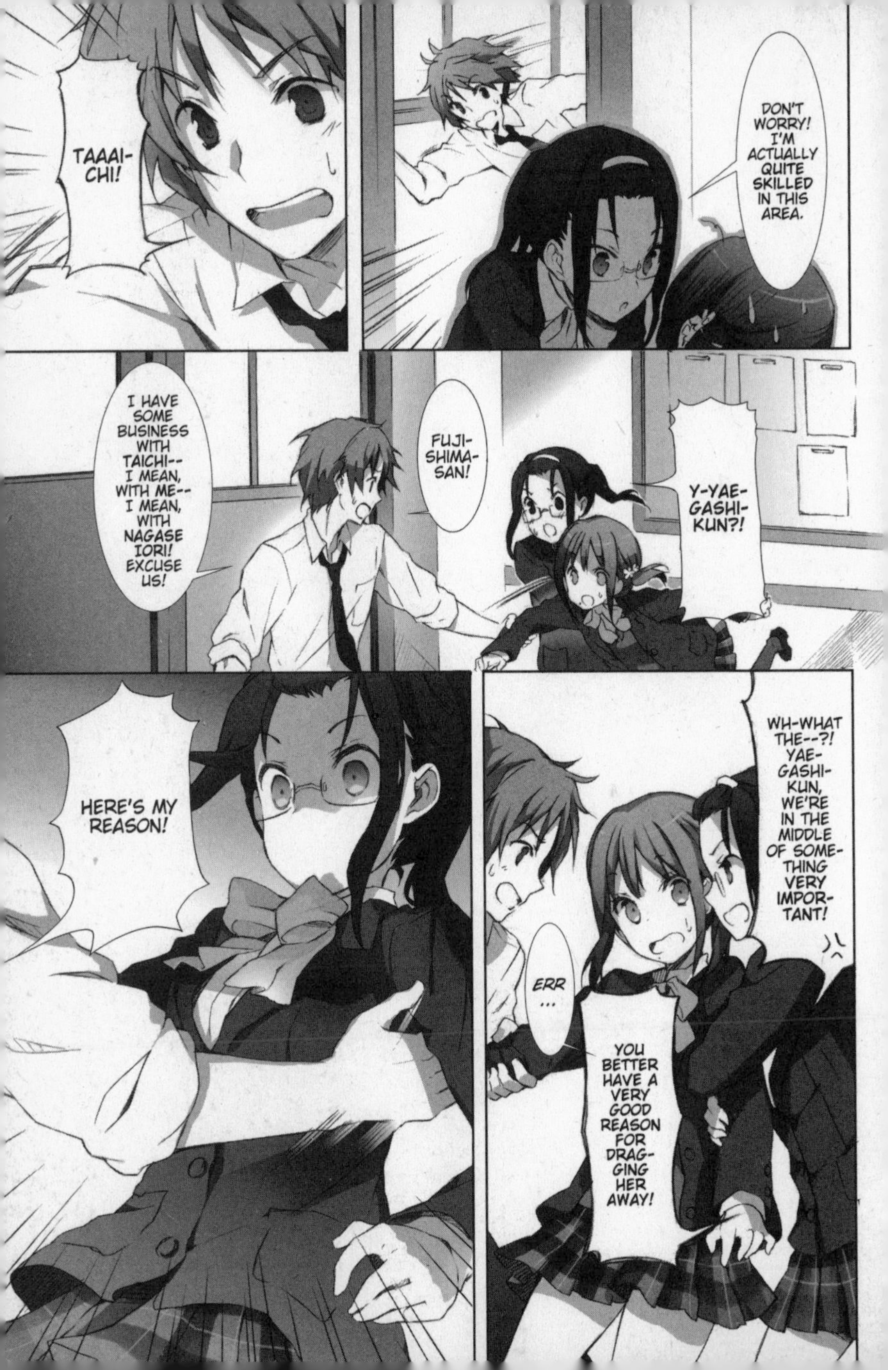
DON'T WORRY! I'M ACTUALLY QUITE SKILLED IN THIS AREA.
TAAAI-CHI!
Y-YAE-GASHI-KUN?!
FUJI-SHIMA-SAN!
I HAVE SOME BUSINESS WITH TAICHI-- I MEAN, WITH ME-- I MEAN, WITH NAGASE IORI! EXCUSE US!
WH-WHAT THE--?! YAE-GASHI-KUN, WE'RE IN THE MIDDLE OF SOME-THING VERY IMPOR-TANT!
ERR ...
YOU BETTER HAVE A VERY GOOD REASON FOR DRAG-GING HER AWAY!
HERE'S MY REASON!

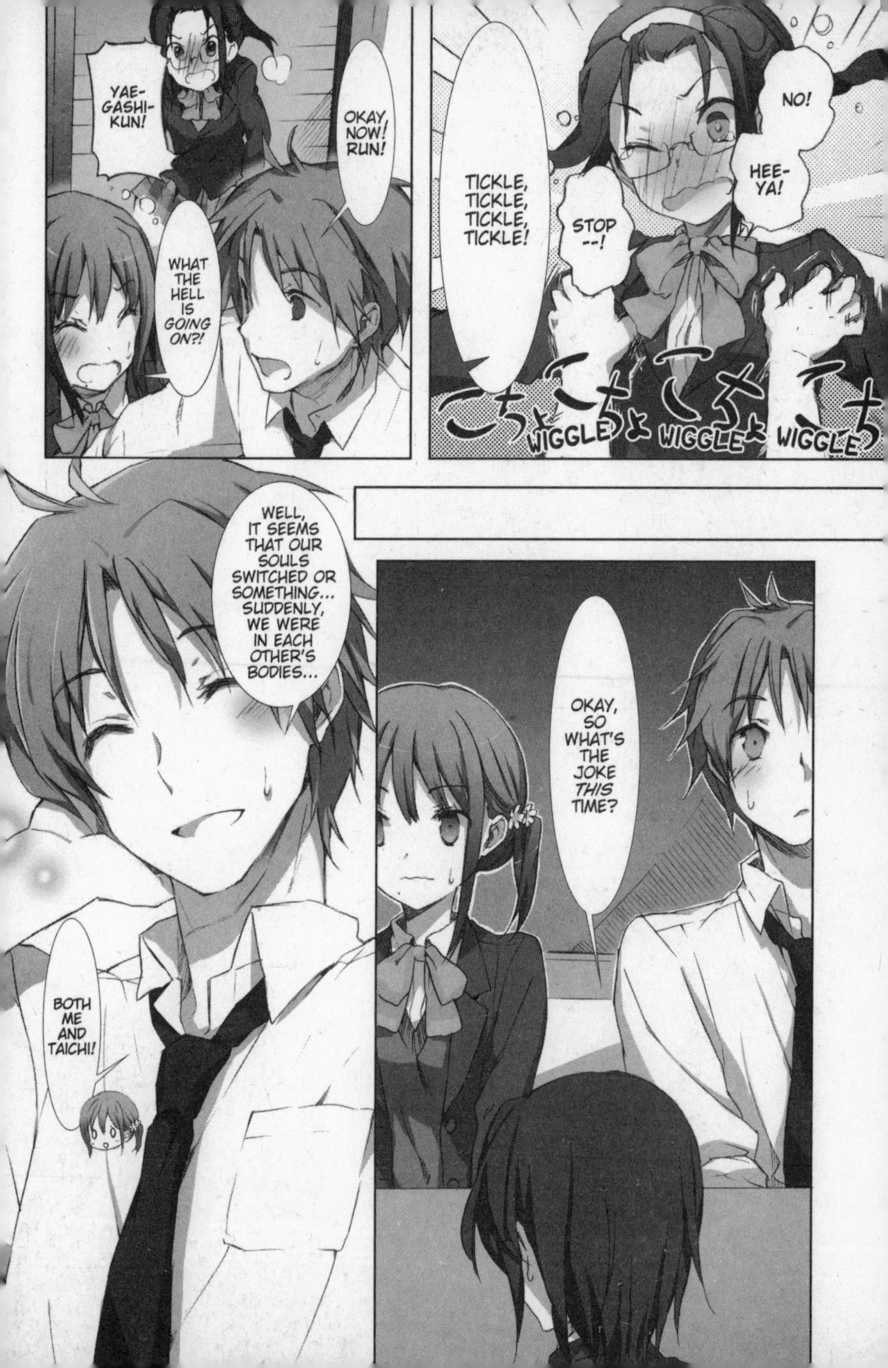
NO!
HEE-YA!
TICKLE, TICKLE, TICKLE, TICKLE!
STOP --!
こちょこちょこちょこち
WIGGLE WIGGLE WIGGLE
OKAY, NOW! RUN!
YAE-GASHI-KUN!
WHAT THE HELL IS *GOING* ON?!
OKAY, SO WHAT'S THE JOKE *THIS* TIME?
WELL, IT SEEMS THAT OUR SOULS SWITCHED OR SOMETHING... SUDDENLY, WE WERE IN EACH OTHER'S BODIES...
BOTH ME AND TAICHI!

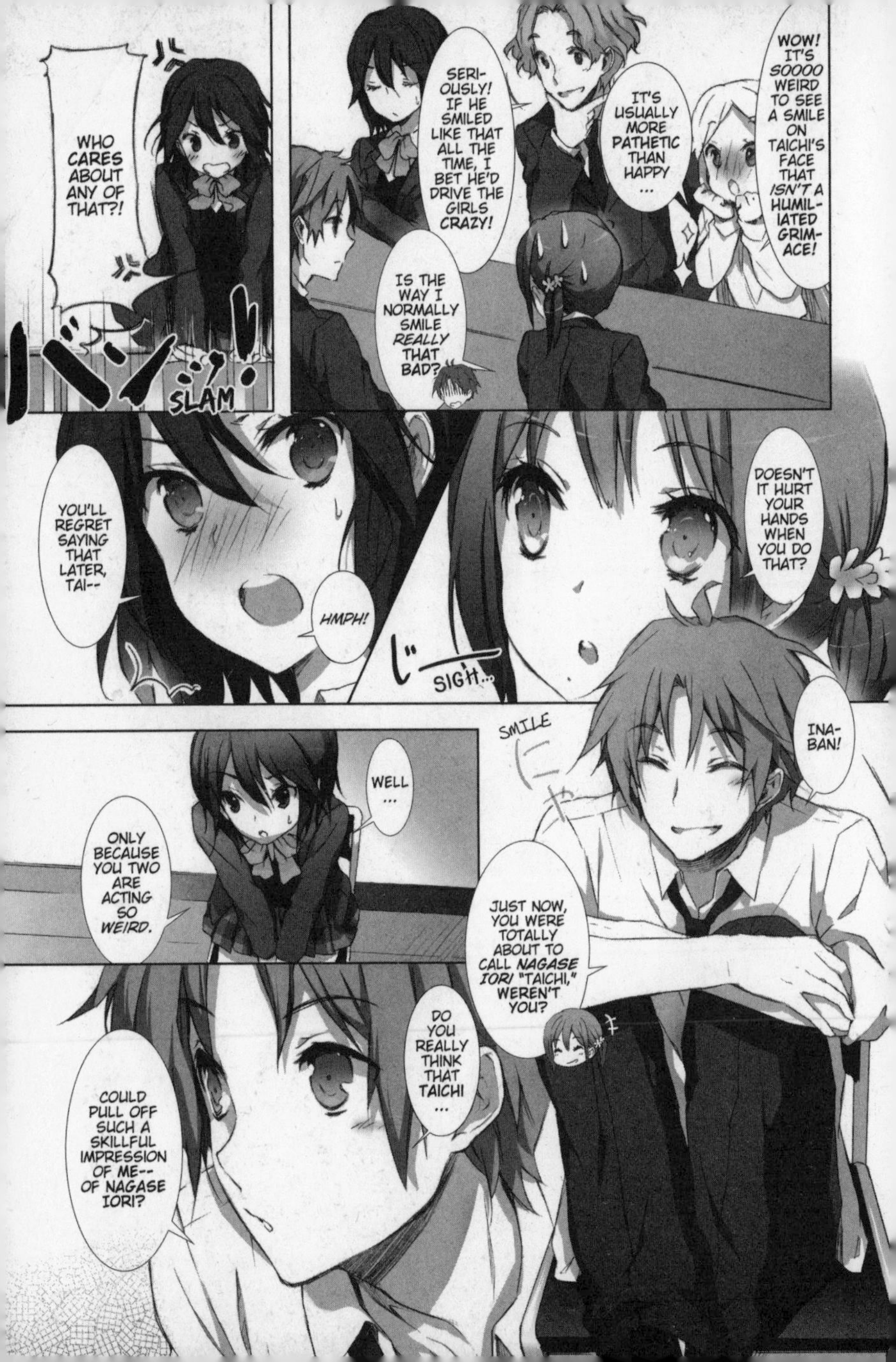
WOW! IT'S SOOOO WEIRD TO SEE A SMILE ON TAICHI'S FACE THAT ISN'T A HUMILIATED GRIMACE!
IT'S USUALLY MORE PATHETIC THAN HAPPY...
SERIOUSLY! IF HE SMILED LIKE THAT ALL THE TIME, I BET HE'D DRIVE THE GIRLS CRAZY!
IS THE WAY I NORMALLY SMILE REALLY THAT BAD?
WHO CARES ABOUT ANY OF THAT?!
SLAM
DOESN'T IT HURT YOUR HANDS WHEN YOU DO THAT?
SIGH...
YOU'LL REGRET SAYING THAT LATER, TAI--
HMPH!
INA-BAN!
SMILE
JUST NOW, YOU WERE TOTALLY ABOUT TO CALL NAGASE IORI "TAICHI," WEREN'T YOU?
WELL...
ONLY BECAUSE YOU TWO ARE ACTING SO WEIRD.
DO YOU REALLY THINK THAT TAICHI...
COULD PULL OFF SUCH A SKILLFUL IMPRESSION OF ME-- OF NAGASE IORI?

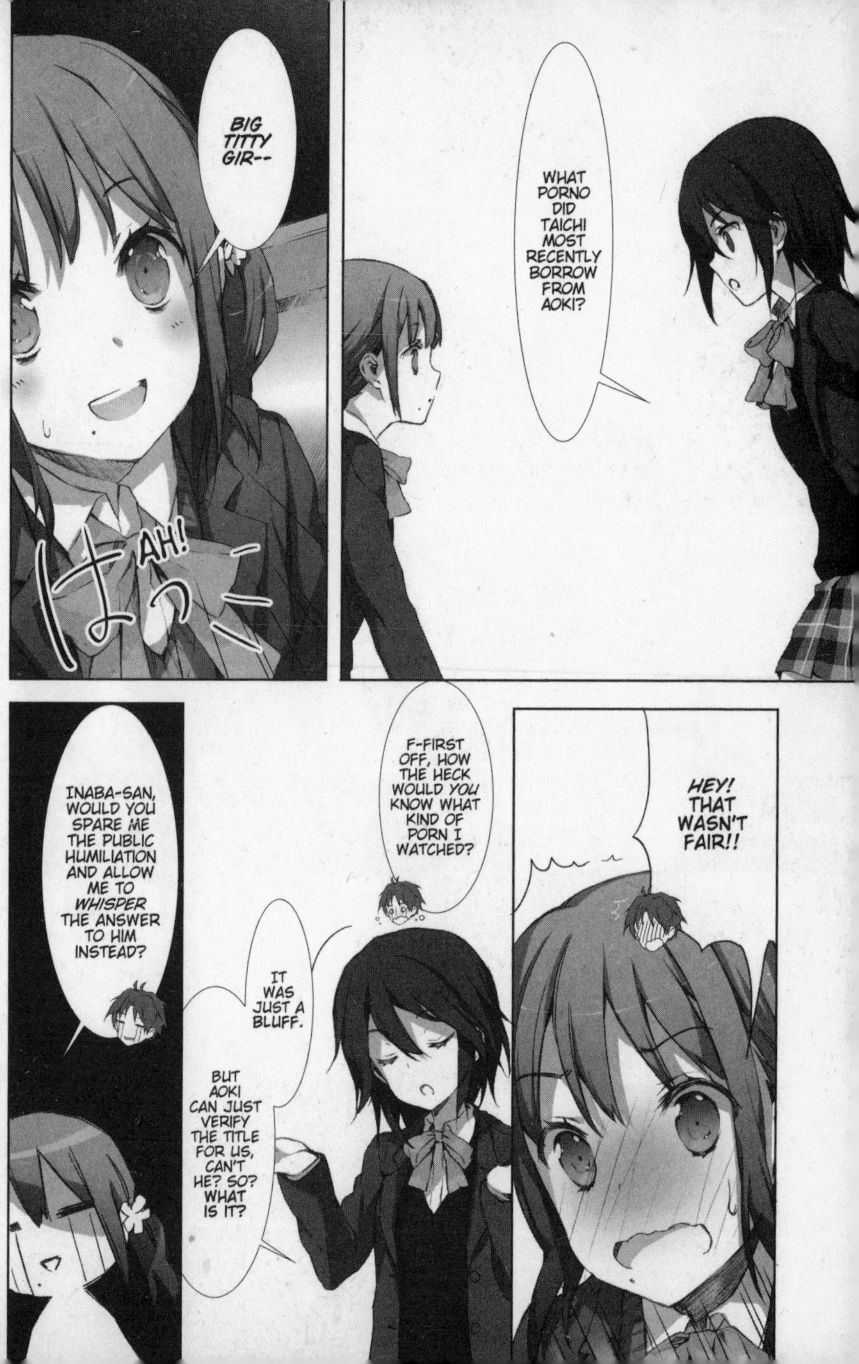
WHAT PORNO DID TAICHI MOST RECENTLY BORROW FROM AOKI?
BIG TITTY GIR--
AH!
はっ
HEY! THAT WASN'T FAIR!!
F-FIRST OFF, HOW THE HECK WOULD YOU KNOW WHAT KIND OF PORN I WATCHED?
IT WAS JUST A BLUFF.
BUT AOKI CAN JUST VERIFY THE TITLE FOR US, CAN'T HE? SO? WHAT IS IT?
INABA-SAN, WOULD YOU SPARE ME THE PUBLIC HUMILIATION AND ALLOW ME TO WHISPER THE ANSWER TO HIM INSTEAD?

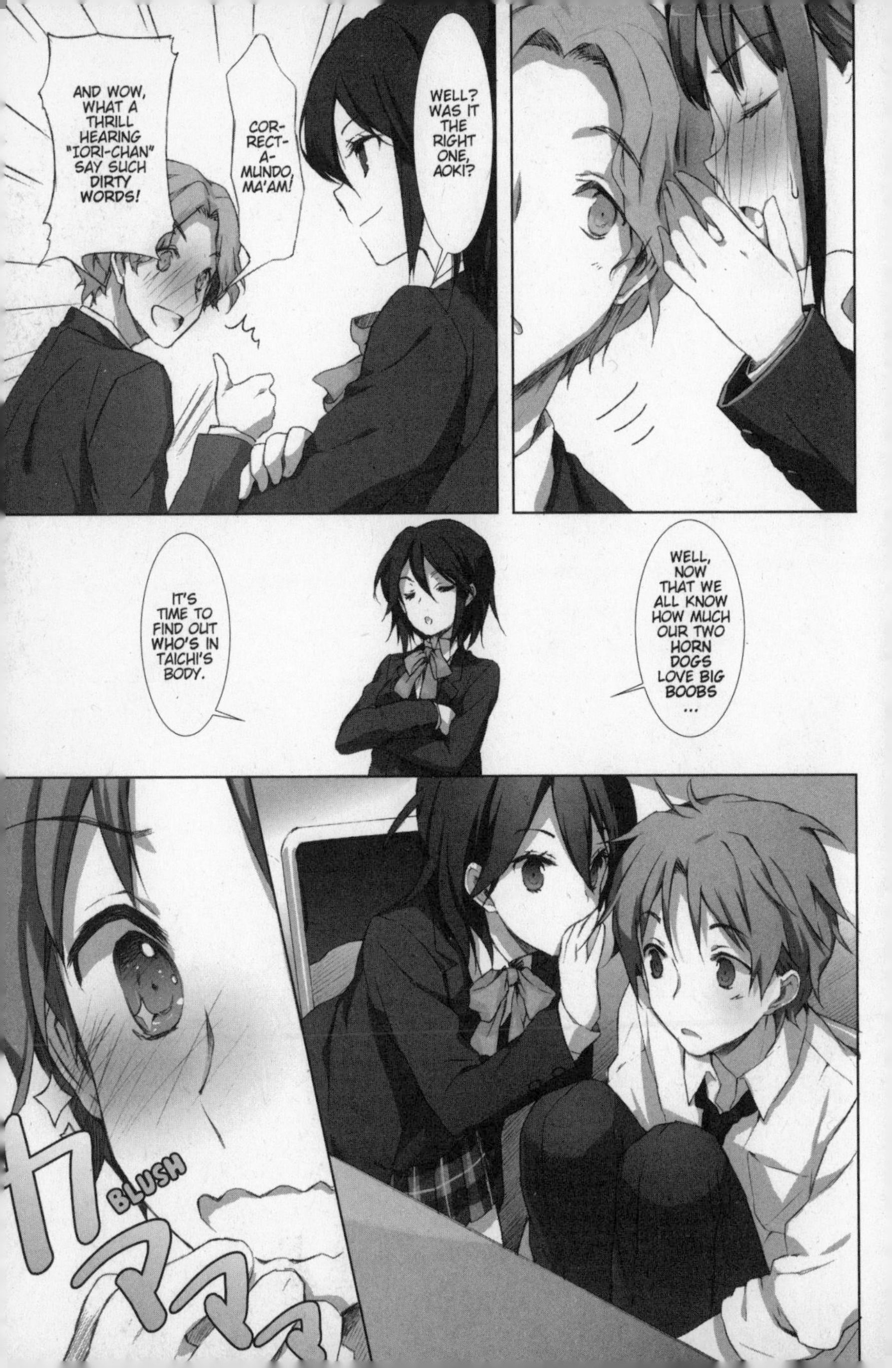
WELL? WAS IT THE RIGHT ONE, AOKI?
CORRECT-A-MUNDO, MA'AM!
AND WOW, WHAT A THRILL HEARING "IORI-CHAN" SAY SUCH DIRTY WORDS!
WELL, NOW THAT WE ALL KNOW HOW MUCH OUR TWO HORN DOGS LOVE BIG BOOBS...
IT'S TIME TO FIND OUT WHO'S IN TAICHI'S BODY.
BLUSH

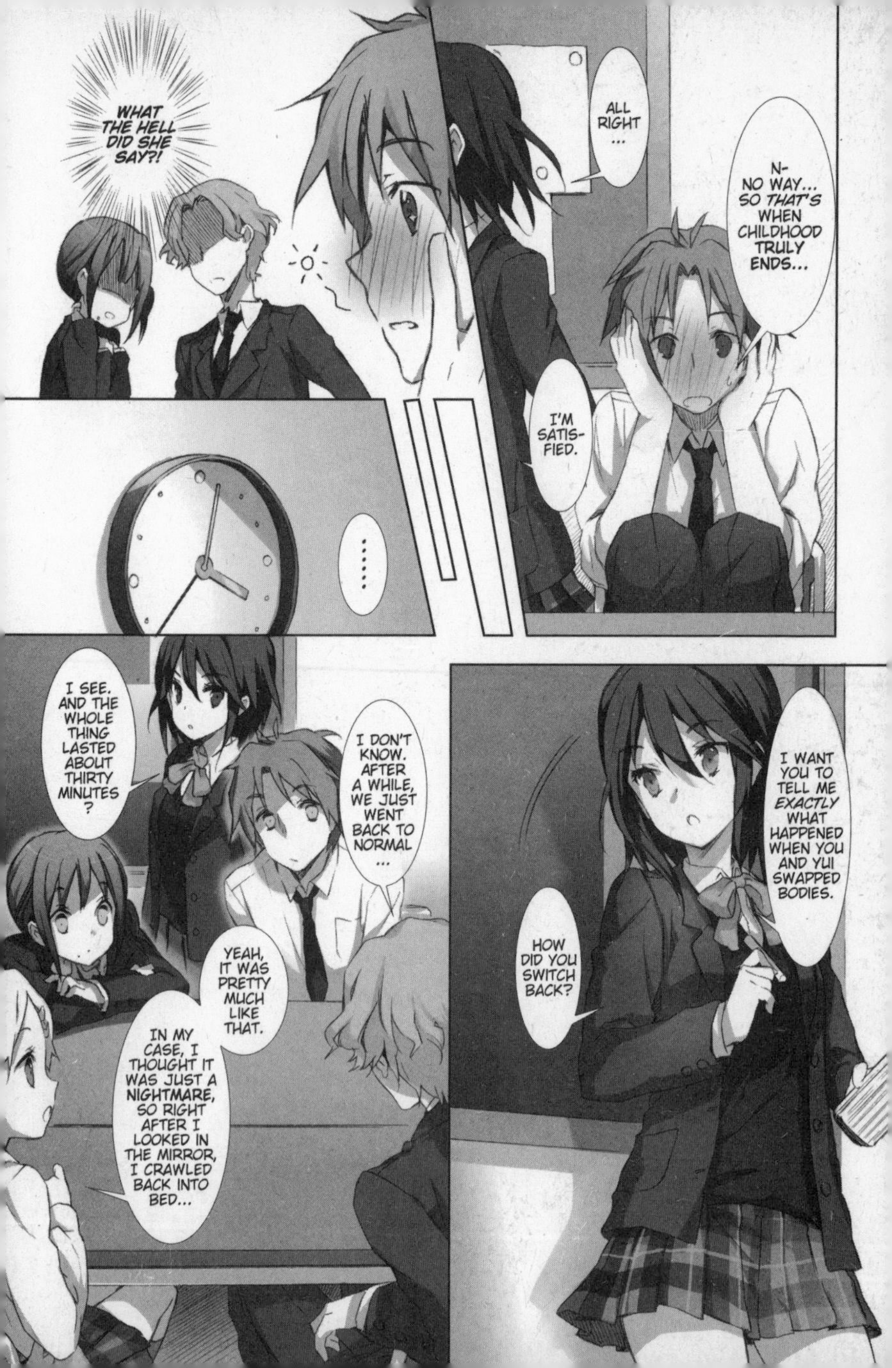
N- NO WAY... SO *THAT'S* WHEN CHILDHOOD TRULY ENDS...
ALL RIGHT...
I'M SATIS- FIED.
WHAT THE HELL DID SHE SAY?!
......
I WANT YOU TO TELL ME *EXACTLY* WHAT HAPPENED WHEN YOU AND YUI SWAPPED BODIES.
HOW DID YOU SWITCH BACK?
I DON'T KNOW. AFTER A WHILE, WE JUST WENT BACK TO NORMAL...
I SEE. AND THE WHOLE THING LASTED ABOUT THIRTY MINUTES?
YEAH, IT WAS PRETTY MUCH LIKE THAT.
IN MY CASE, I THOUGHT IT WAS JUST A NIGHTMARE, SO RIGHT AFTER I LOOKED IN THE MIRROR, I CRAWLED BACK INTO BED...

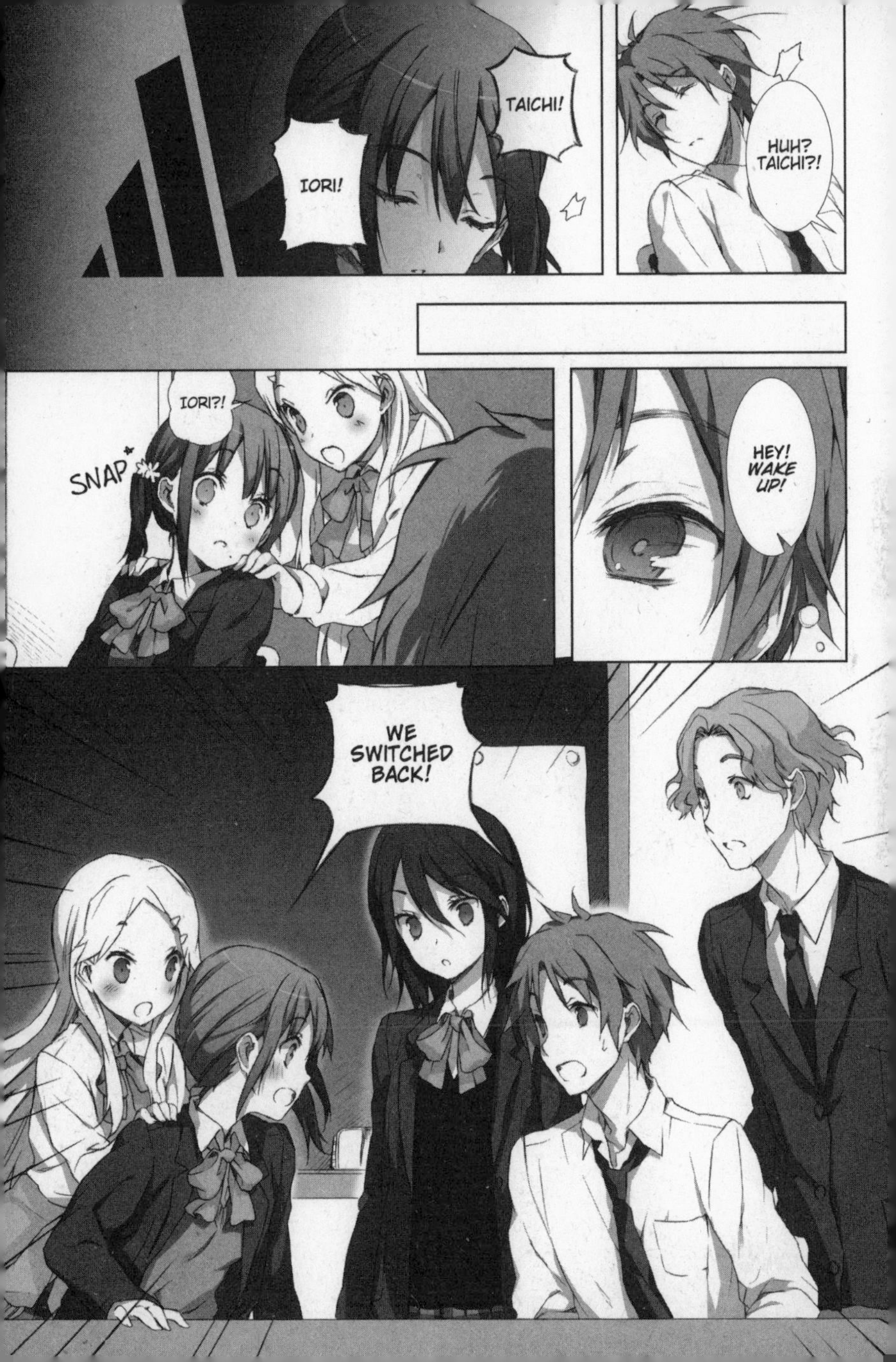
HUH? TAICHI?!
TAICHI!
IORI!
HEY! WAKE UP!
IORI?!
SNAP
WE SWITCHED BACK!

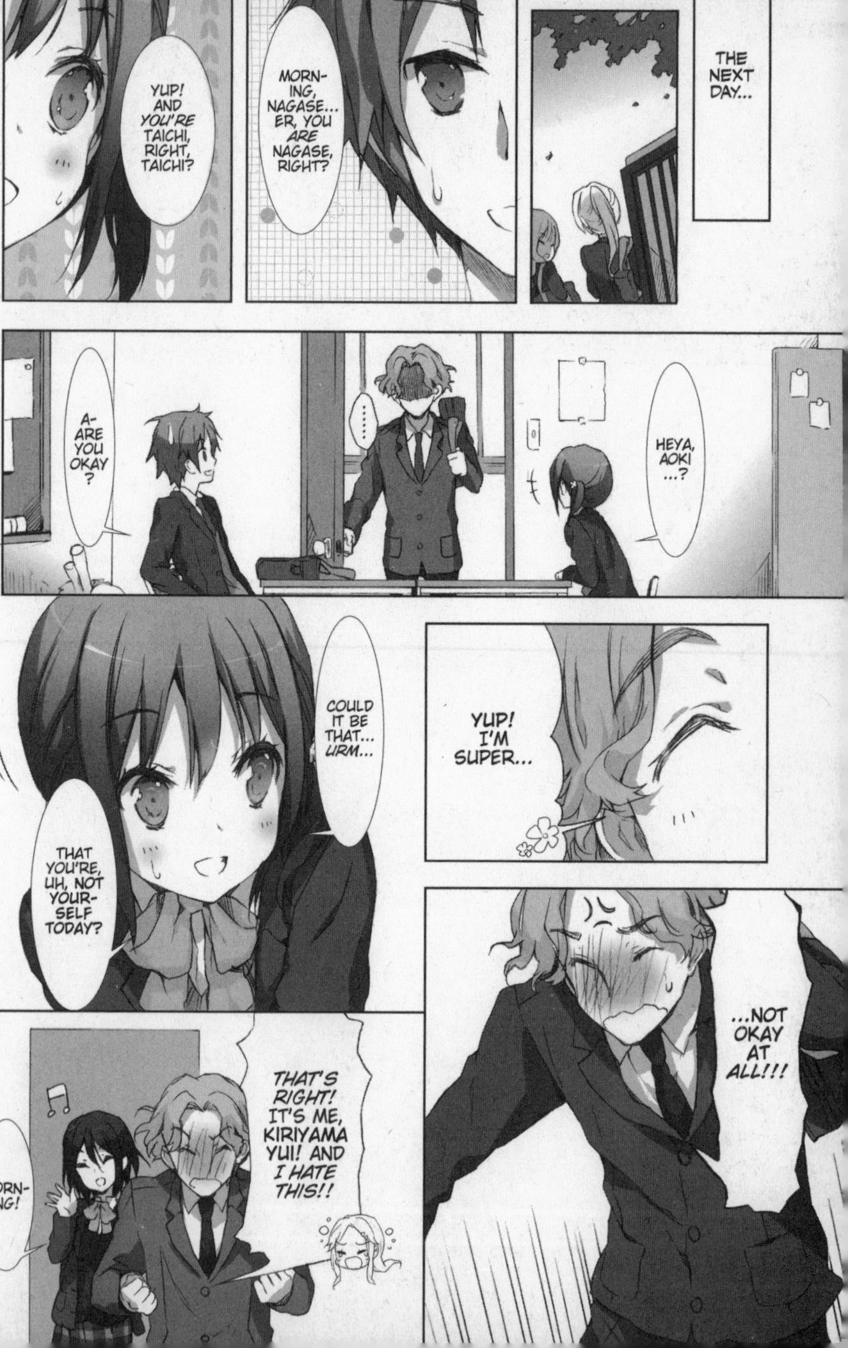
THE NEXT DAY...
MORNING, NAGASE... ER, YOU ARE NAGASE, RIGHT?
YUP! AND YOU'RE TAICHI, RIGHT, TAICHI?
HEYA, AOKI...?
......
A-ARE YOU OKAY?
YUP! I'M SUPER...
...NOT OKAY AT ALL!!!
COULD IT BE THAT... URM...
THAT YOU'RE, UH, NOT YOURSELF TODAY?
THAT'S RIGHT! IT'S ME, KIRIYAMA YUI! AND I HATE THIS!!
MORNING!

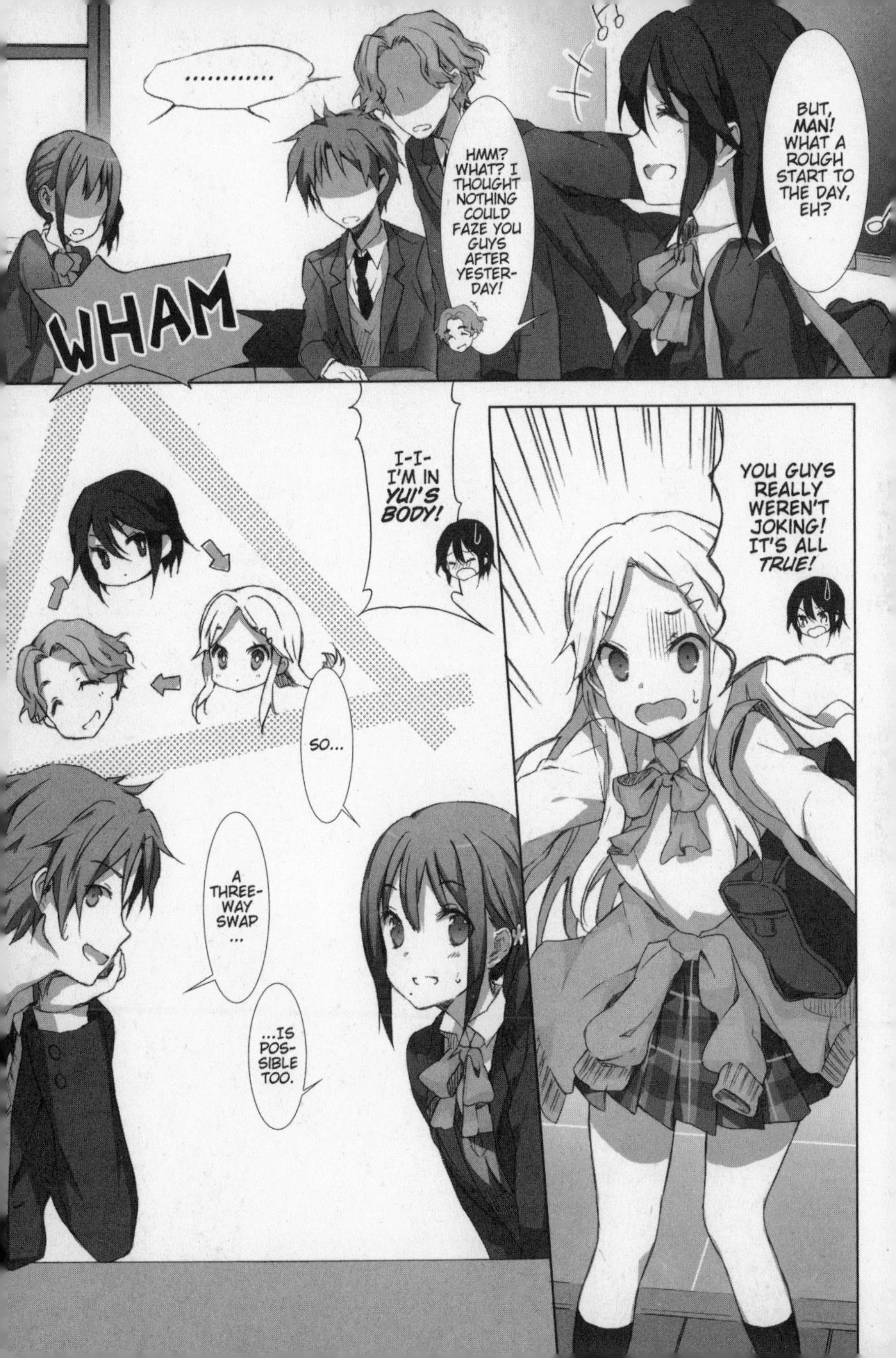
BUT, MAN! WHAT A ROUGH START TO THE DAY, EH?
HMM? WHAT? I THOUGHT NOTHING COULD FAZE YOU GUYS AFTER YESTER-DAY!
....
WHAM
YOU GUYS REALLY WEREN'T JOKING! IT'S ALL *TRUE!*
I-I-I'M IN *YUI'S BODY!*
SO...
A THREE-WAY SWAP...
...IS POSSIBLE TOO.

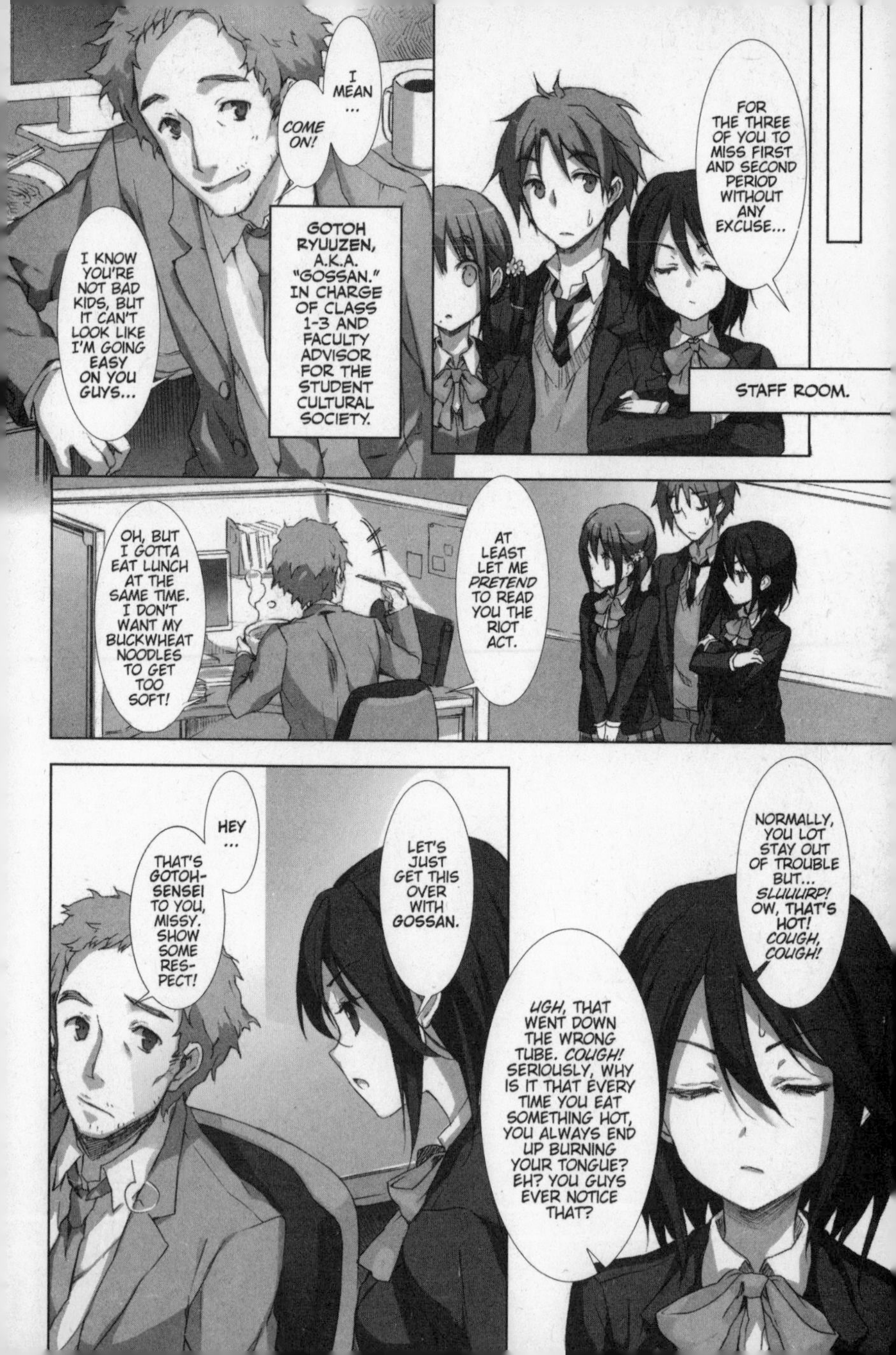
FOR THE THREE OF YOU TO MISS FIRST AND SECOND PERIOD WITHOUT ANY EXCUSE...
STAFF ROOM.
I MEAN ...
COME ON!
GOTOH RYUUZEN, A.K.A. "GOSSAN." IN CHARGE OF CLASS 1-3 AND FACULTY ADVISOR FOR THE STUDENT CULTURAL SOCIETY.
I KNOW YOU'RE NOT BAD KIDS, BUT IT CAN'T LOOK LIKE I'M GOING EASY ON YOU GUYS...
AT LEAST LET ME *PRETEND* TO READ YOU THE RIOT ACT.
OH, BUT I GOTTA EAT LUNCH AT THE SAME TIME. I DON'T WANT MY BUCKWHEAT NOODLES TO GET TOO SOFT!
NORMALLY, YOU LOT STAY OUT OF TROUBLE BUT... *SLUUURP!* OW, THAT'S HOT! *COUGH, COUGH!*
UGH, THAT WENT DOWN THE WRONG TUBE. *COUGH!* SERIOUSLY, WHY IS IT THAT EVERY TIME YOU EAT SOMETHING HOT, YOU ALWAYS END UP BURNING YOUR TONGUE? EH? YOU GUYS EVER NOTICE THAT?
LET'S JUST GET THIS OVER WITH GOSSAN.
HEY ...
THAT'S GOTOH-SENSEI TO YOU, MISSY. SHOW SOME RESPECT!

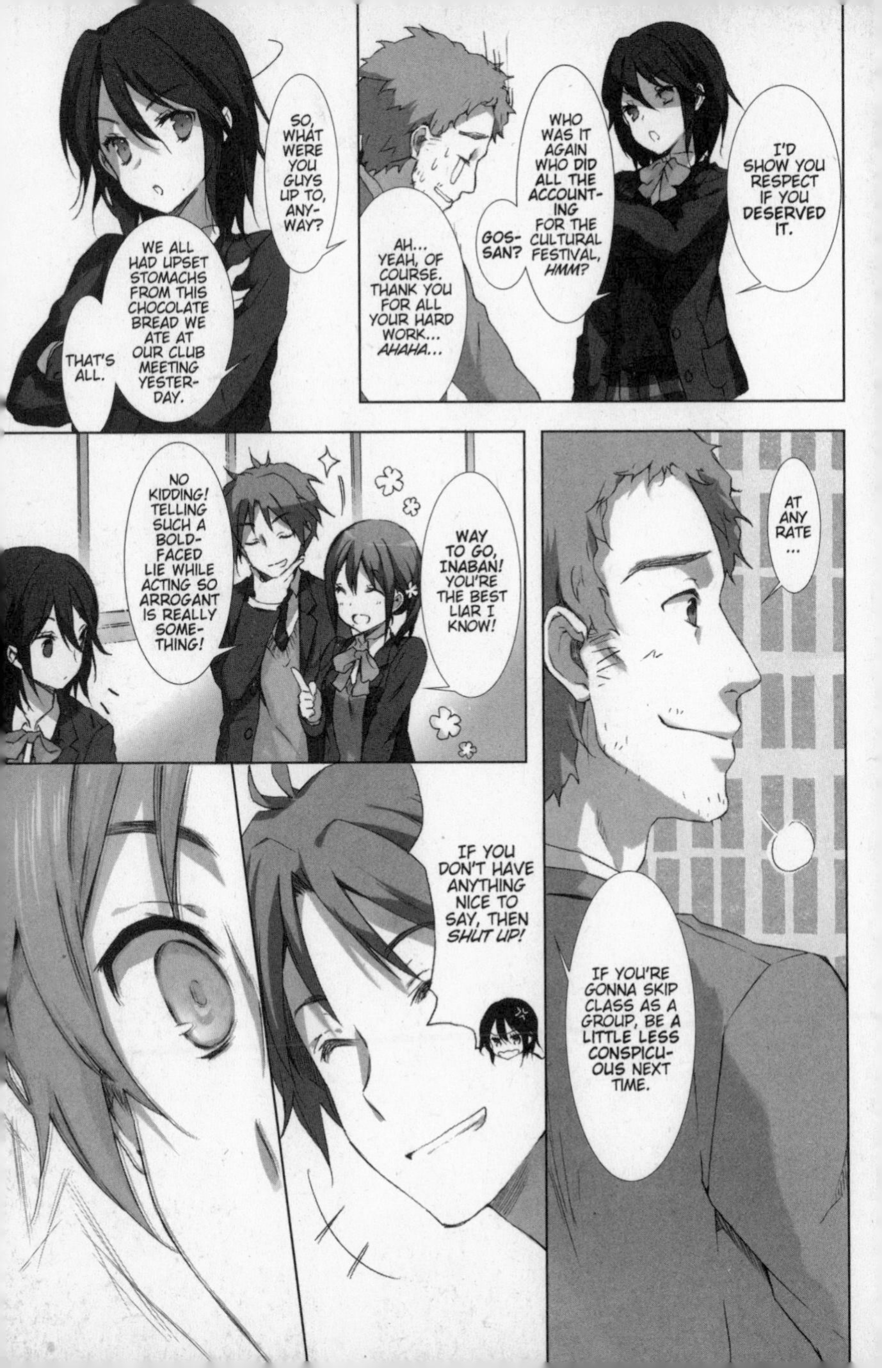
I'D SHOW YOU RESPECT IF YOU DESERVED IT.
WHO WAS IT AGAIN WHO DID ALL THE ACCOUNTING FOR THE CULTURAL FESTIVAL, *HMM?*
GOS-SAN?
AH... YEAH, OF COURSE. THANK YOU FOR ALL YOUR HARD WORK... *AHAHA...*
SO, WHAT WERE YOU GUYS UP TO, ANYWAY?
WE ALL HAD UPSET STOMACHS FROM THIS CHOCOLATE BREAD WE ATE AT OUR CLUB MEETING YESTERDAY.
THAT'S ALL.
AT ANY RATE...
IF YOU'RE GONNA SKIP CLASS AS A GROUP, BE A LITTLE LESS CONSPICUOUS NEXT TIME.
WAY TO GO, INABAN! YOU'RE THE BEST LIAR I KNOW!
NO KIDDING! TELLING SUCH A BOLD-FACED LIE WHILE ACTING SO ARROGANT IS REALLY SOMETHING!
IF YOU DON'T HAVE ANYTHING NICE TO SAY, THEN *SHUT UP!*

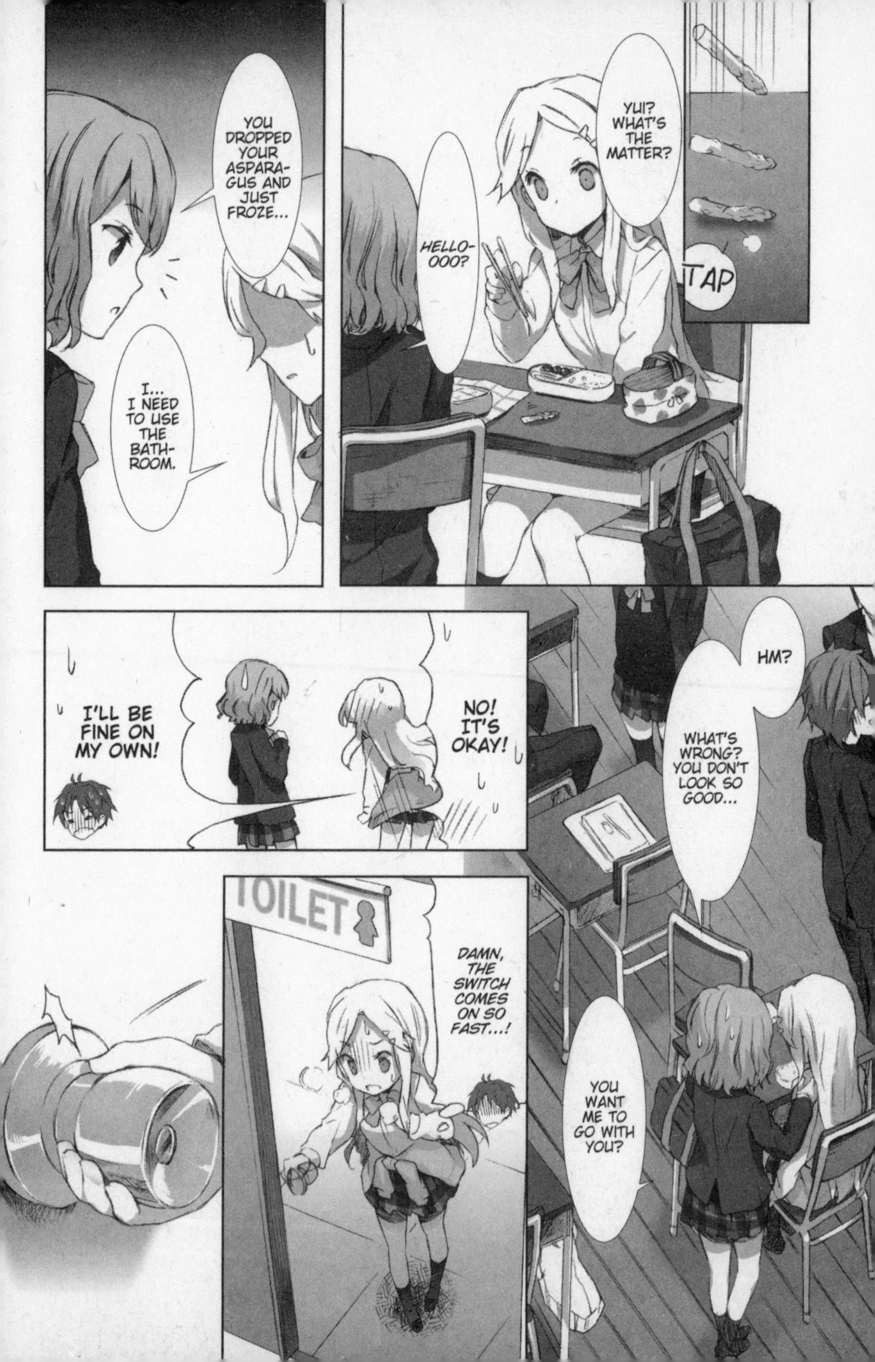
TAP
YUI? WHAT'S THE MATTER?
HELLO-OOO?
YOU DROPPED YOUR ASPARAGUS AND JUST FROZE...
I... I NEED TO USE THE BATHROOM.
HM?
WHAT'S WRONG? YOU DON'T LOOK SO GOOD...
YOU WANT ME TO GO WITH YOU?
NO! IT'S OKAY!
I'LL BE FINE ON MY OWN!
TOILET
DAMN, THE SWITCH COMES ON SO FAST...!

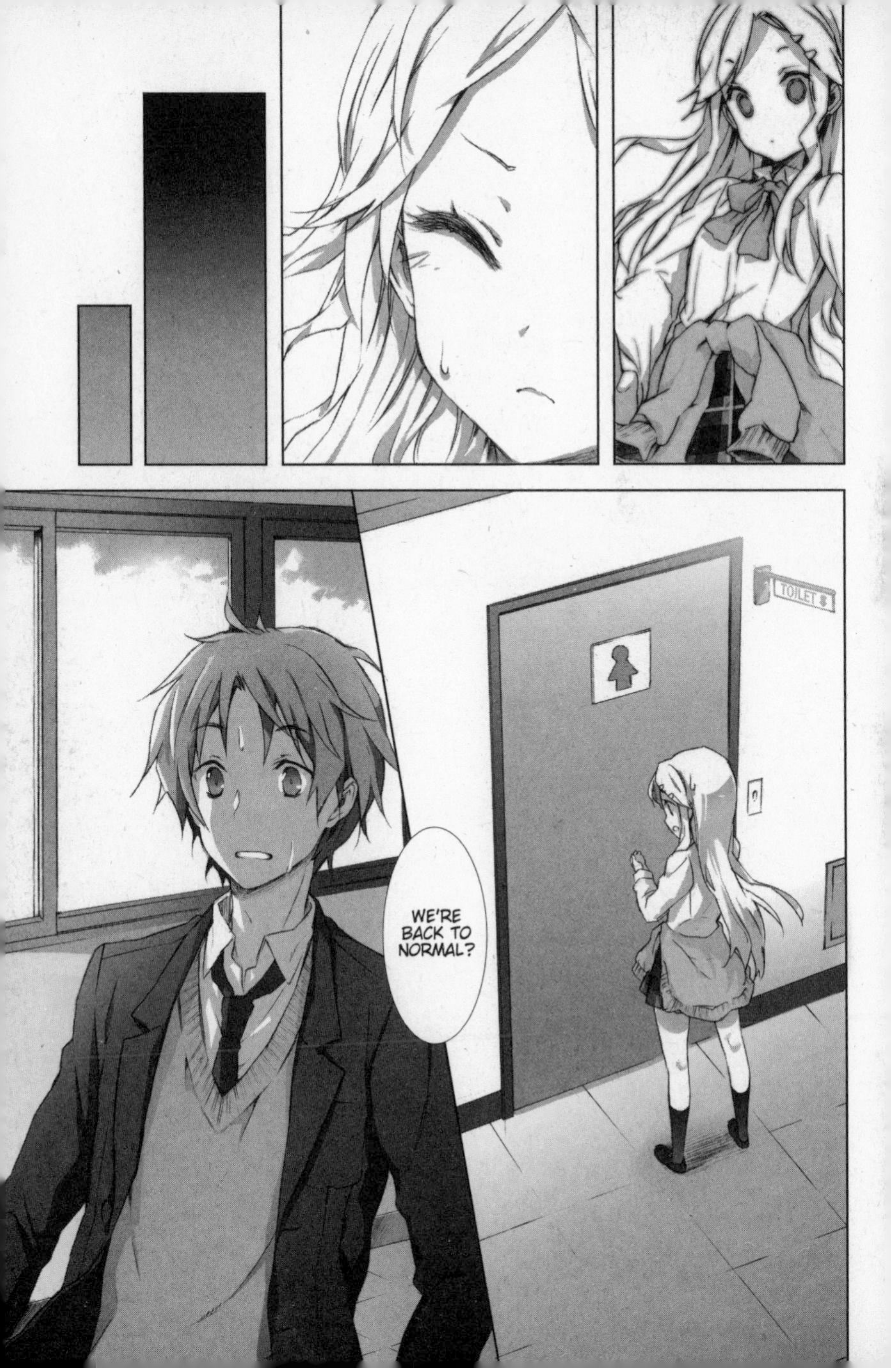
TOILET
WE'RE BACK TO NORMAL?

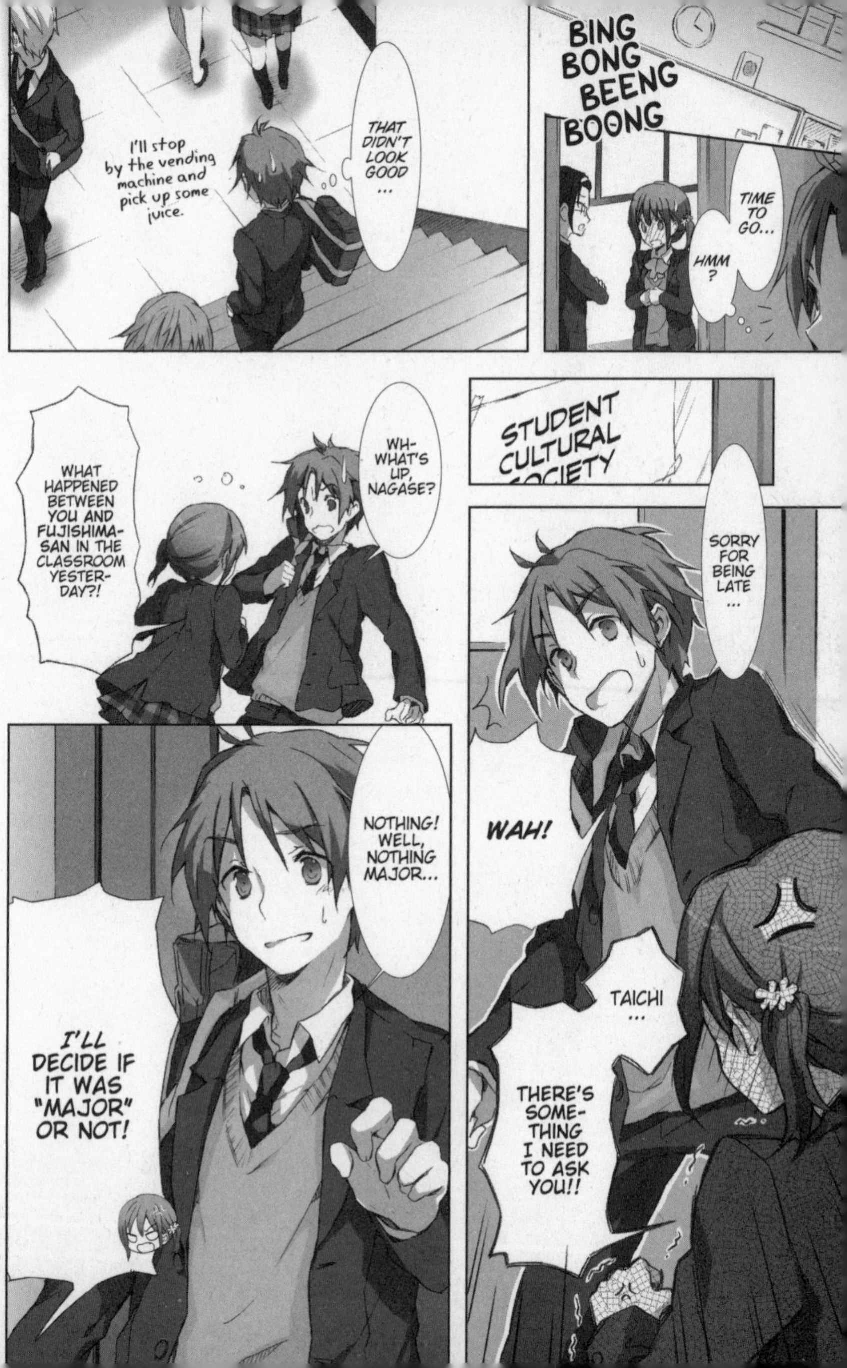
BING BONG BEENG BOONG
TIME TO GO...
HMM?
THAT DIDN'T LOOK GOOD...
I'll stop by the vending machine and pick up some juice.
STUDENT CULTURAL SOCIETY
SORRY FOR BEING LATE...
WAH!
TAICHI...
THERE'S SOMETHING I NEED TO ASK YOU!!
WH-WHAT'S UP, NAGASE?
WHAT HAPPENED BETWEEN YOU AND FUJISHIMA-SAN IN THE CLASSROOM YESTER-DAY?!
NOTHING! WELL, NOTHING MAJOR...
I'LL DECIDE IF IT WAS "MAJOR" OR NOT!

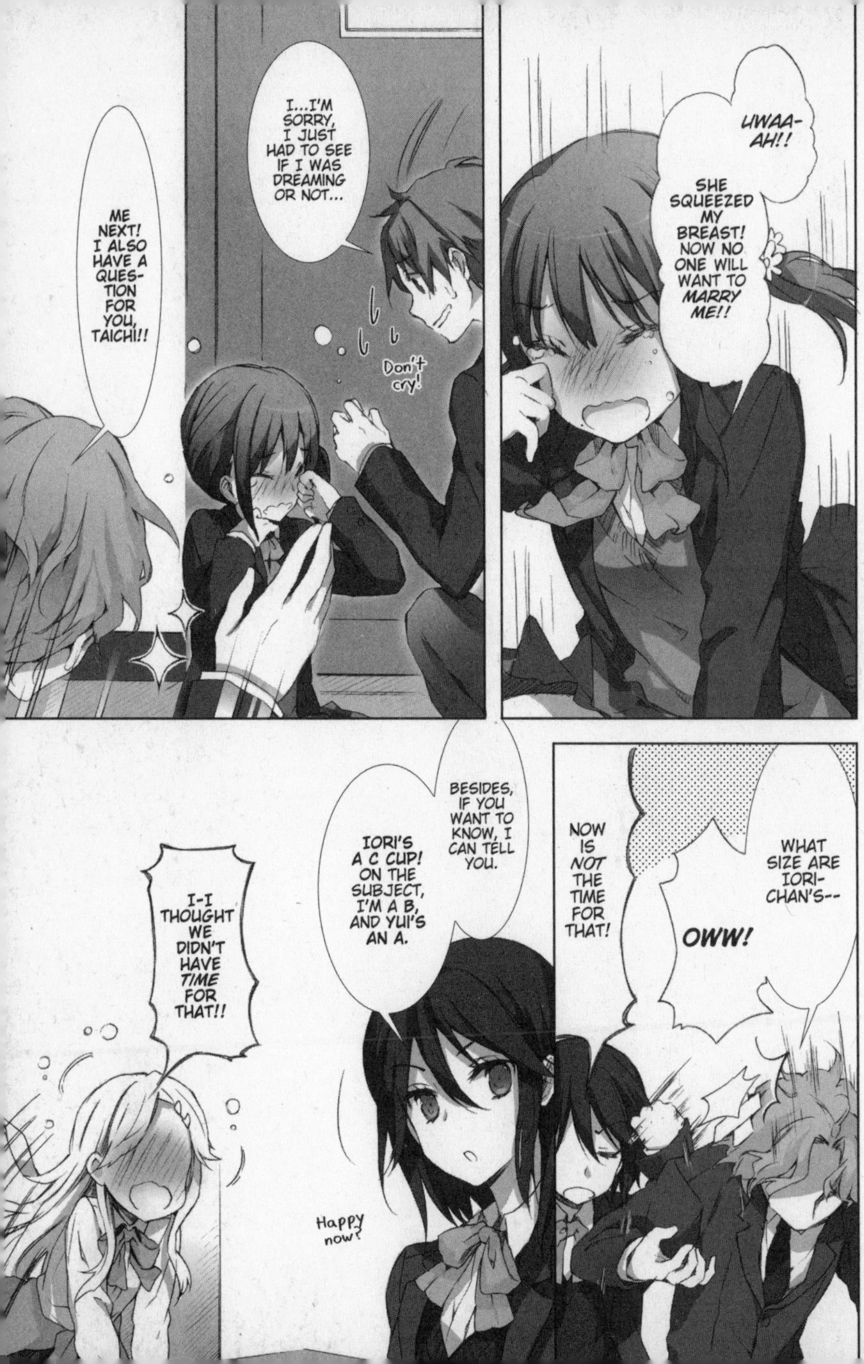
UWAA-AH!!
SHE SQUEEZED MY BREAST! NOW NO ONE WILL WANT TO *MARRY* ME!!
I...I'M SORRY, I JUST HAD TO SEE IF I WAS DREAMING OR NOT...
Don't cry!
ME NEXT! I ALSO HAVE A QUES-TION FOR YOU, TAICHI!!
WHAT SIZE ARE IORI-CHAN'S--
OWW!
NOW IS *NOT* THE TIME FOR THAT!
BESIDES, IF YOU WANT TO KNOW, I CAN TELL YOU.
IORI'S A C CUP! ON THE SUBJECT, I'M A B, AND YUI'S AN A.
Happy now?
I-I THOUGHT WE DIDN'T HAVE *TIME* FOR THAT!!

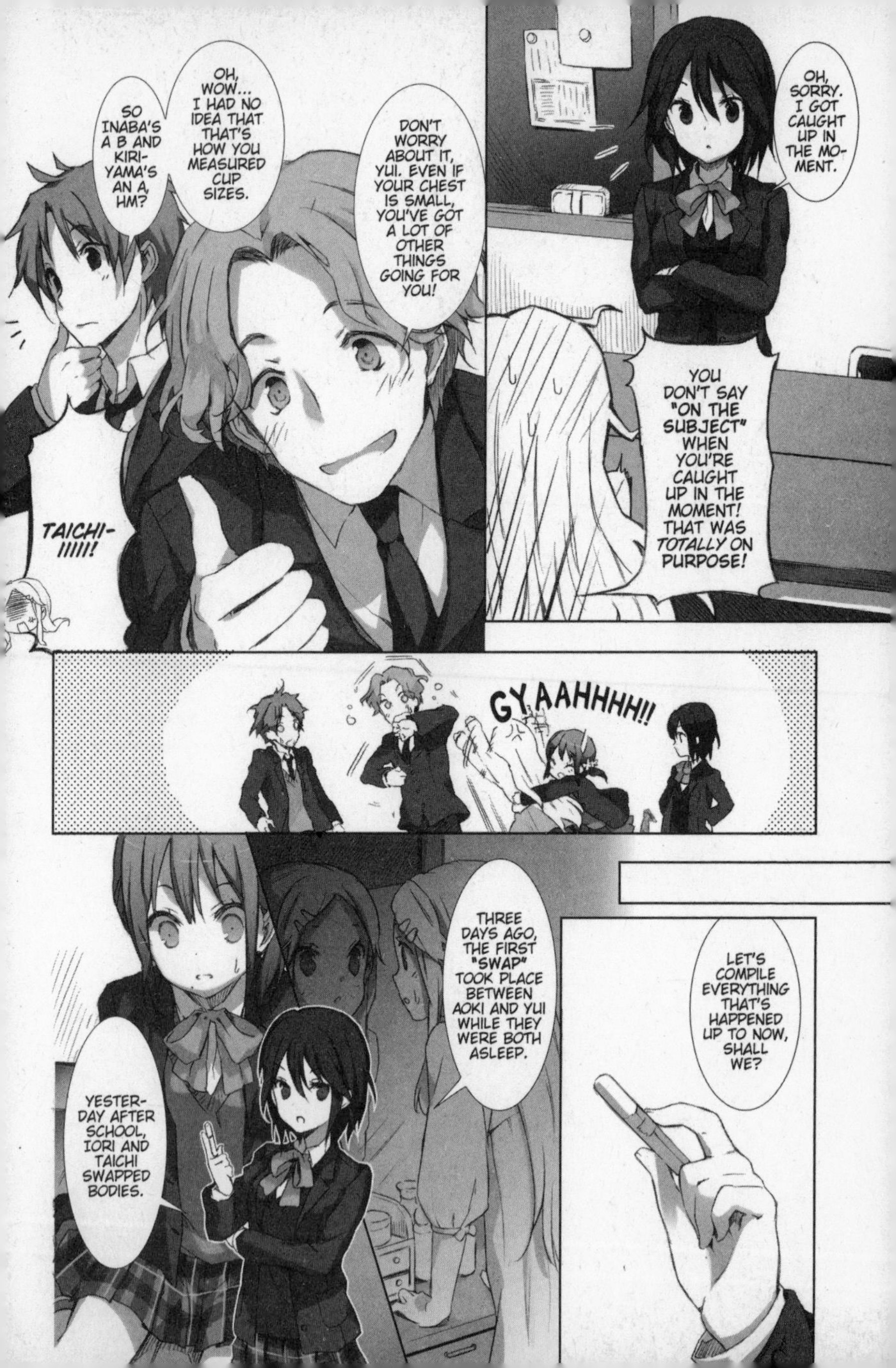
OH, SORRY. I GOT CAUGHT UP IN THE MOMENT.
YOU DON'T SAY "ON THE SUBJECT" WHEN YOU'RE CAUGHT UP IN THE MOMENT! THAT WAS *TOTALLY* ON PURPOSE!
DON'T WORRY ABOUT IT, YUI. EVEN IF YOUR CHEST IS SMALL, YOU'VE GOT A LOT OF OTHER THINGS GOING FOR YOU!
OH, WOW... I HAD NO IDEA THAT THAT'S HOW YOU MEASURED CUP SIZES.
SO INABA'S A B AND KIRIYAMA'S AN A, HM?
TAICHI-IIIIII!
GYAAHHHH!!
LET'S COMPILE EVERYTHING THAT'S HAPPENED UP TO NOW, SHALL WE?
THREE DAYS AGO, THE FIRST "SWAP" TOOK PLACE BETWEEN AOKI AND YUI WHILE THEY WERE BOTH ASLEEP.
YESTERDAY AFTER SCHOOL, IORI AND TAICHI SWAPPED BODIES.

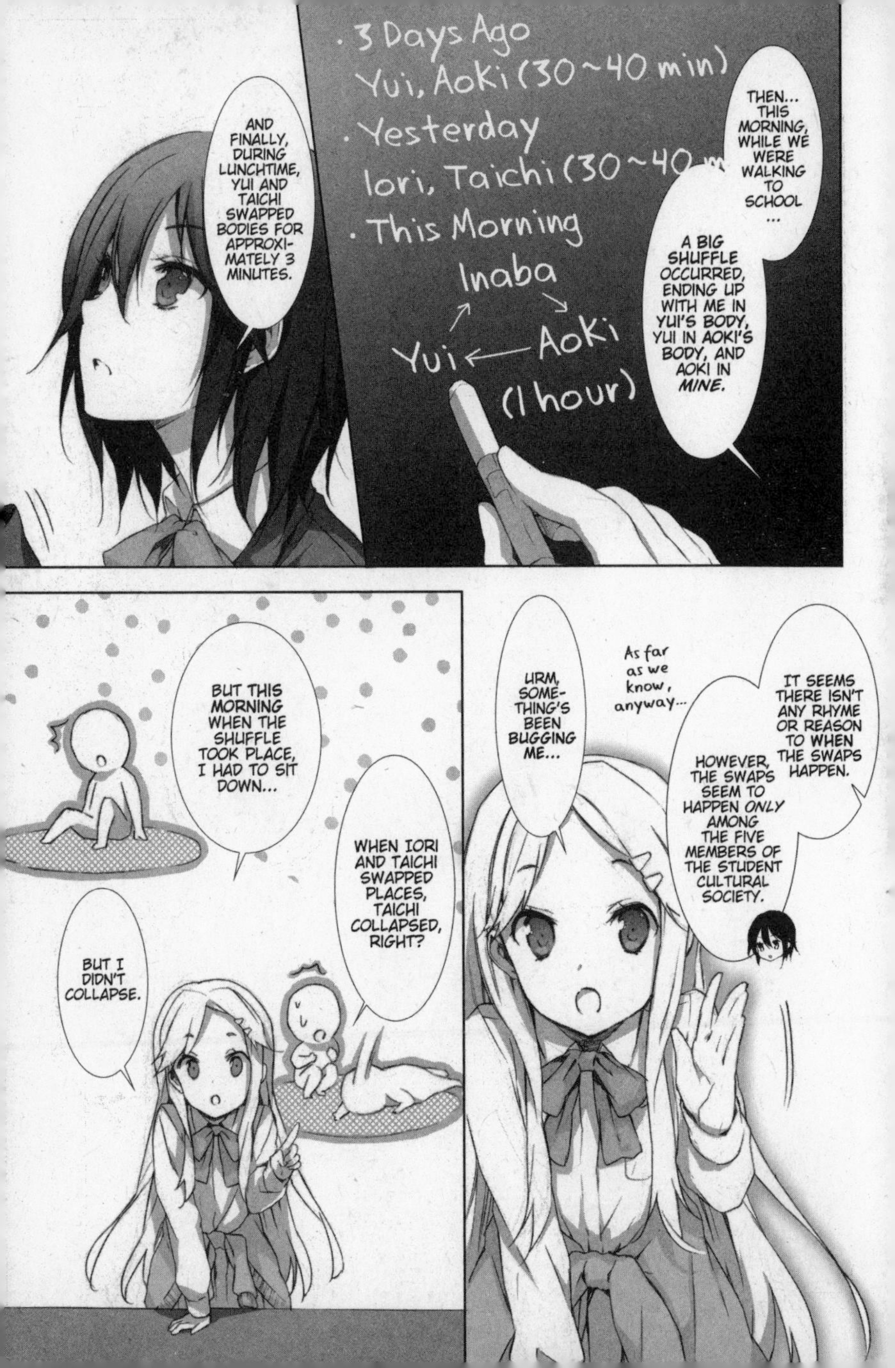

· 3 Days Ago
Yui, Aoki (30~40 min)
· Yesterday
Iori, Taichi (30~40 m
· This Morning
Inaba → Aoki → Yui → Inaba
(1 hour)
THEN... THIS MORNING, WHILE WE WERE WALKING TO SCHOOL...
A BIG SHUFFLE OCCURRED, ENDING UP WITH ME IN YUI'S BODY, YUI IN AOKI'S BODY, AND AOKI IN *MINE*.
AND FINALLY, DURING LUNCHTIME, YUI AND TAICHI SWAPPED BODIES FOR APPROXIMATELY 3 MINUTES.
IT SEEMS THERE ISN'T ANY RHYME OR REASON TO WHEN THE SWAPS HAPPEN.
HOWEVER, THE SWAPS SEEM TO HAPPEN *ONLY* AMONG THE FIVE MEMBERS OF THE STUDENT CULTURAL SOCIETY.
As far as we know, anyway...
URM, SOMETHING'S BEEN BUGGING ME...
WHEN IORI AND TAICHI SWAPPED PLACES, TAICHI COLLAPSED, RIGHT?
BUT THIS MORNING WHEN THE SHUFFLE TOOK PLACE, I HAD TO SIT DOWN...
BUT I DIDN'T COLLAPSE.

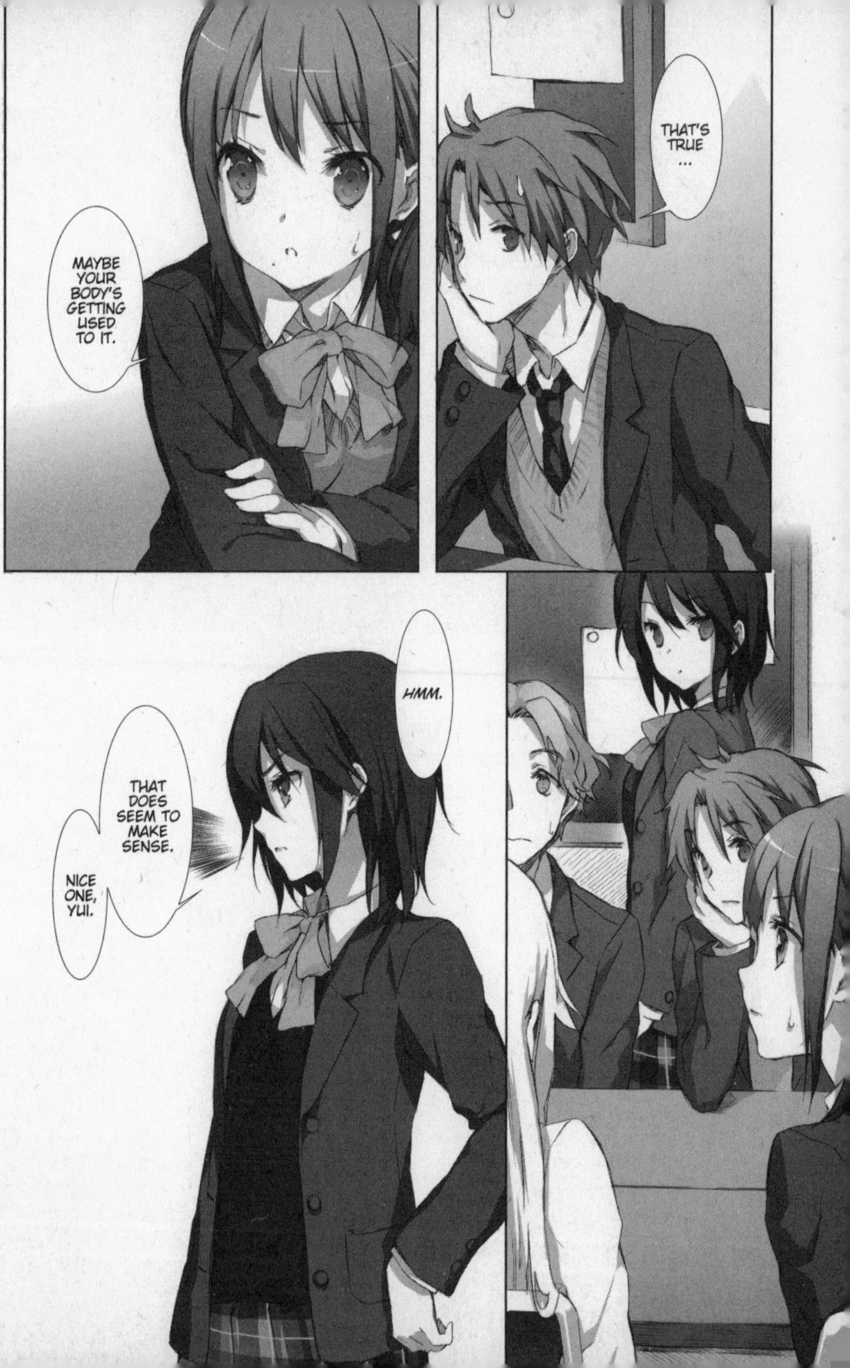
THAT'S TRUE ...
MAYBE YOUR BODY'S GETTING USED TO IT.
HMM.
THAT DOES SEEM TO MAKE SENSE.
NICE ONE, YUI.

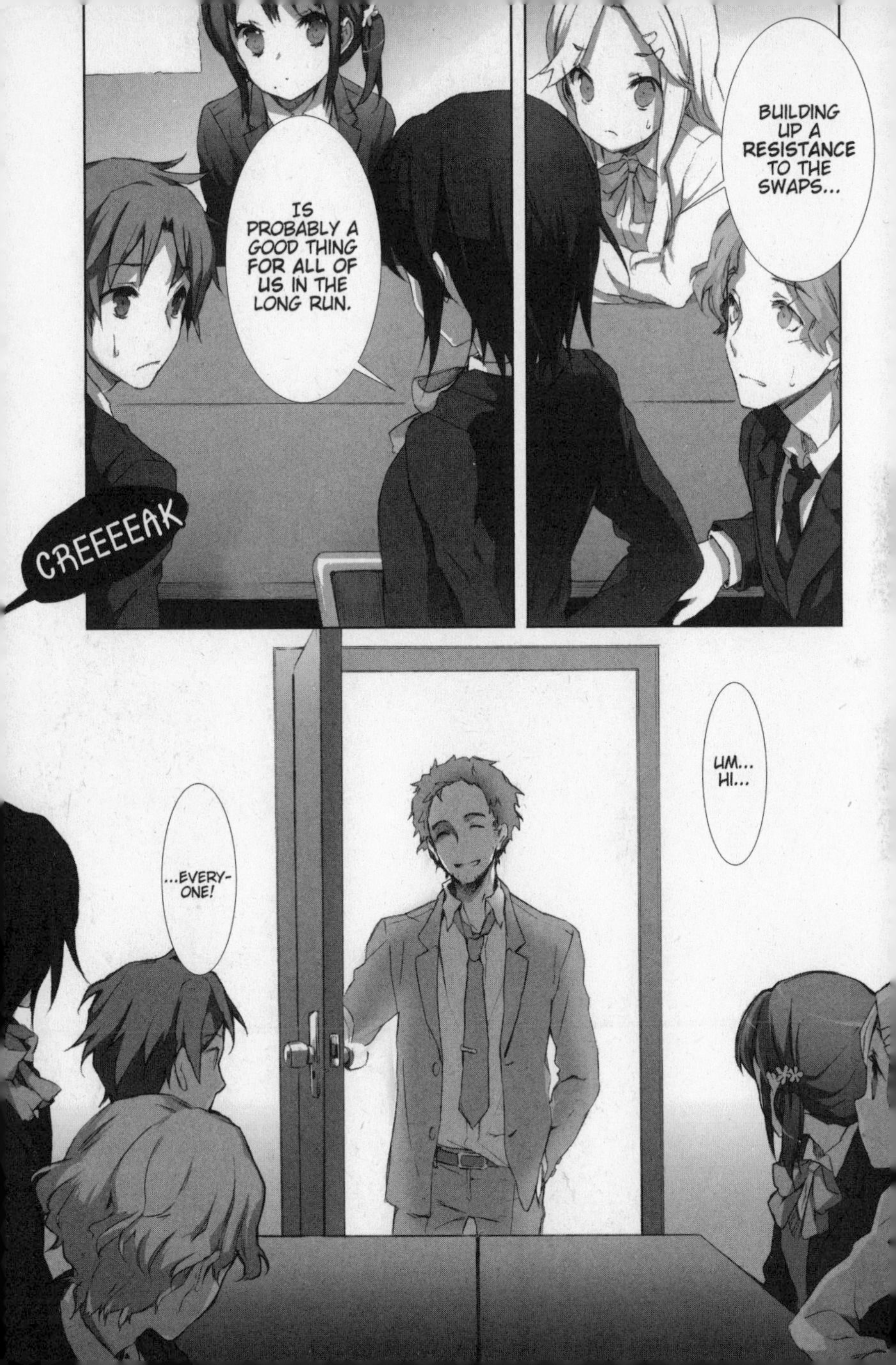
BUILDING UP A RESISTANCE TO THE SWAPS...
IS PROBABLY A GOOD THING FOR ALL OF US IN THE LONG RUN.
CREEEEEAK
UM... HI...
...EVERY-ONE!

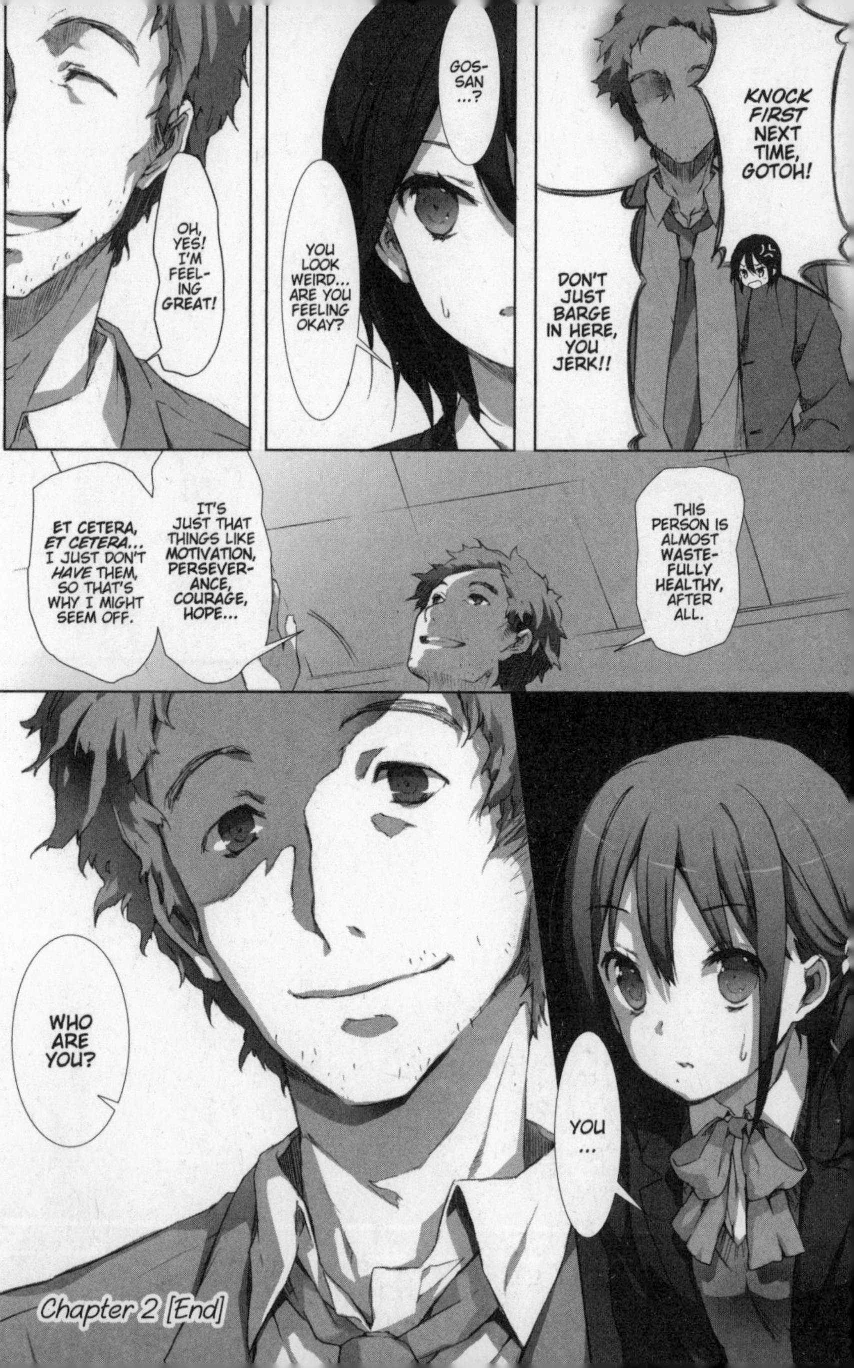
KNOCK FIRST NEXT TIME, GOTOH!
DON'T JUST BARGE IN HERE, YOU JERK!!
GOS-SAN ...?
YOU LOOK WEIRD... ARE YOU FEELING OKAY?
OH, YES! I'M FEEL-ING GREAT!
THIS PERSON IS ALMOST WASTE-FULLY HEALTHY, AFTER ALL.
IT'S JUST THAT THINGS LIKE MOTIVATION, PERSEVER-ANCE, COURAGE, HOPE...
ET CETERA, *ET CETERA*... I JUST DON'T *HAVE* THEM, SO THAT'S WHY I MIGHT SEEM OFF.
YOU ...
WHO ARE YOU?
Chapter 2 [End]

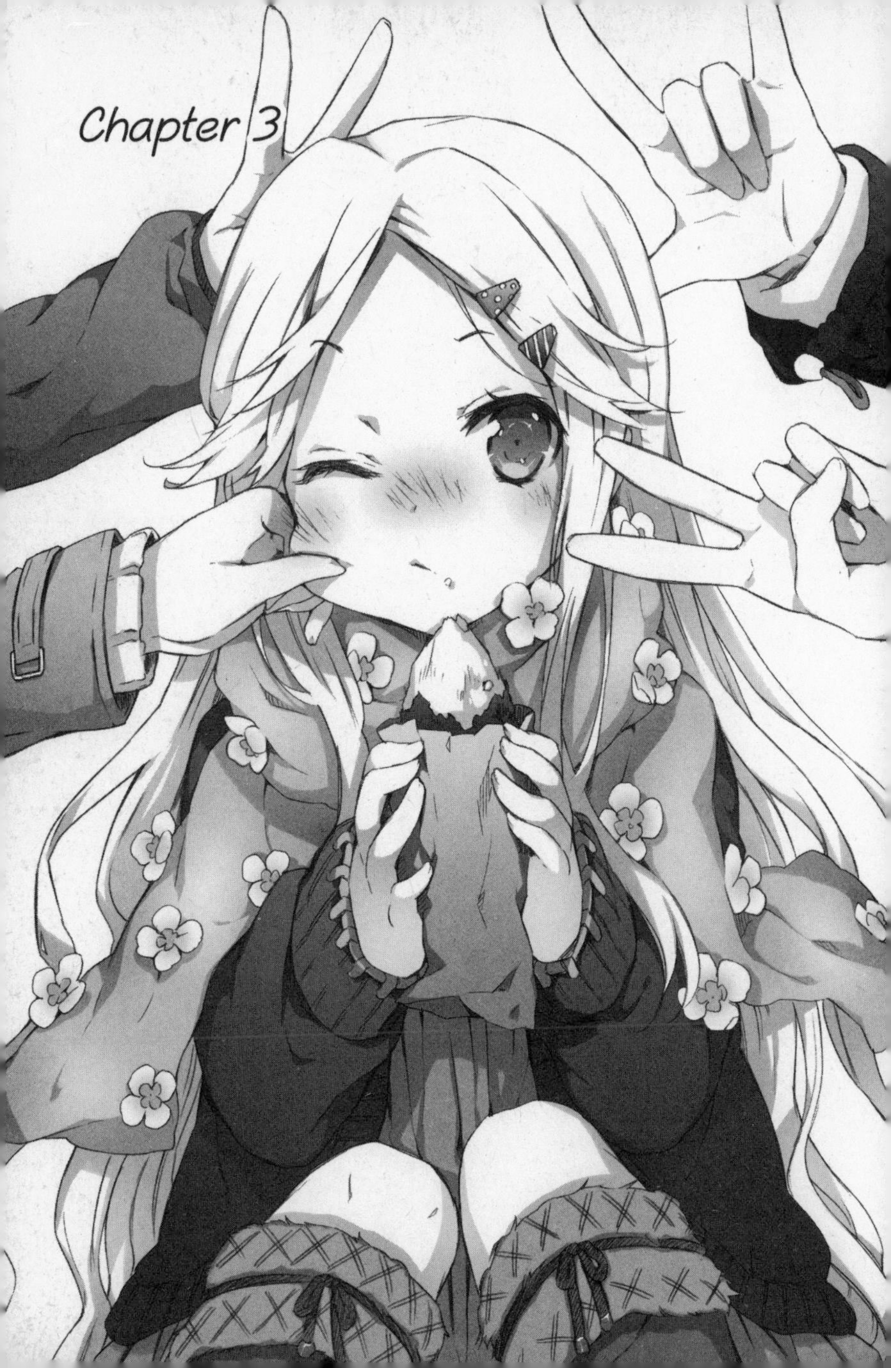
Chapter 3

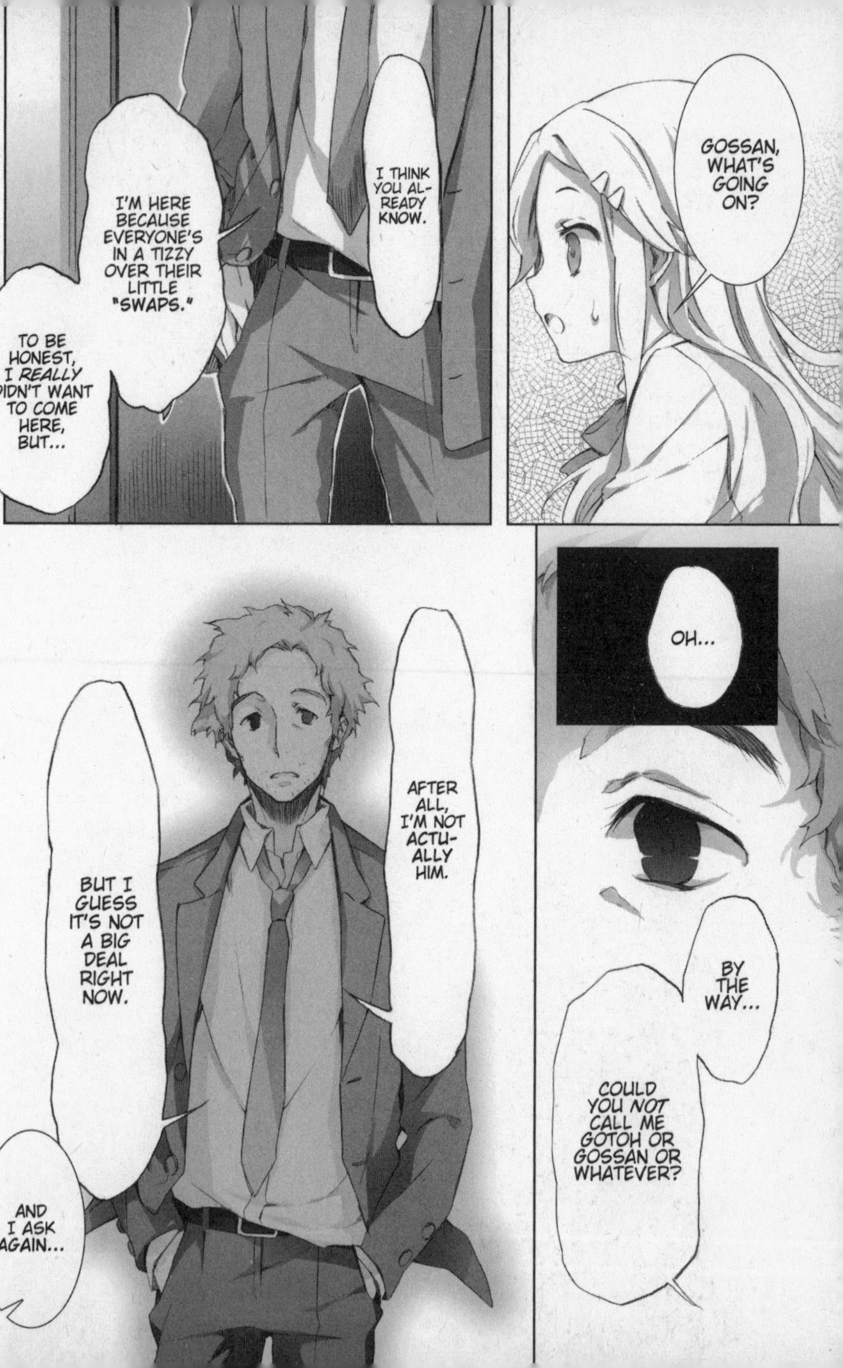
GOSSAN, WHAT'S GOING ON?
I THINK YOU AL-READY KNOW.
I'M HERE BECAUSE EVERYONE'S IN A TIZZY OVER THEIR LITTLE "SWAPS."
TO BE HONEST, I *REALLY* DIDN'T WANT TO COME HERE, BUT...
OH...
BY THE WAY...
COULD YOU *NOT* CALL ME GOTOH OR GOSSAN OR WHATEVER?
AFTER ALL, I'M NOT ACTU-ALLY HIM.
BUT I GUESS IT'S NOT A BIG DEAL RIGHT NOW.
AND I ASK AGAIN...

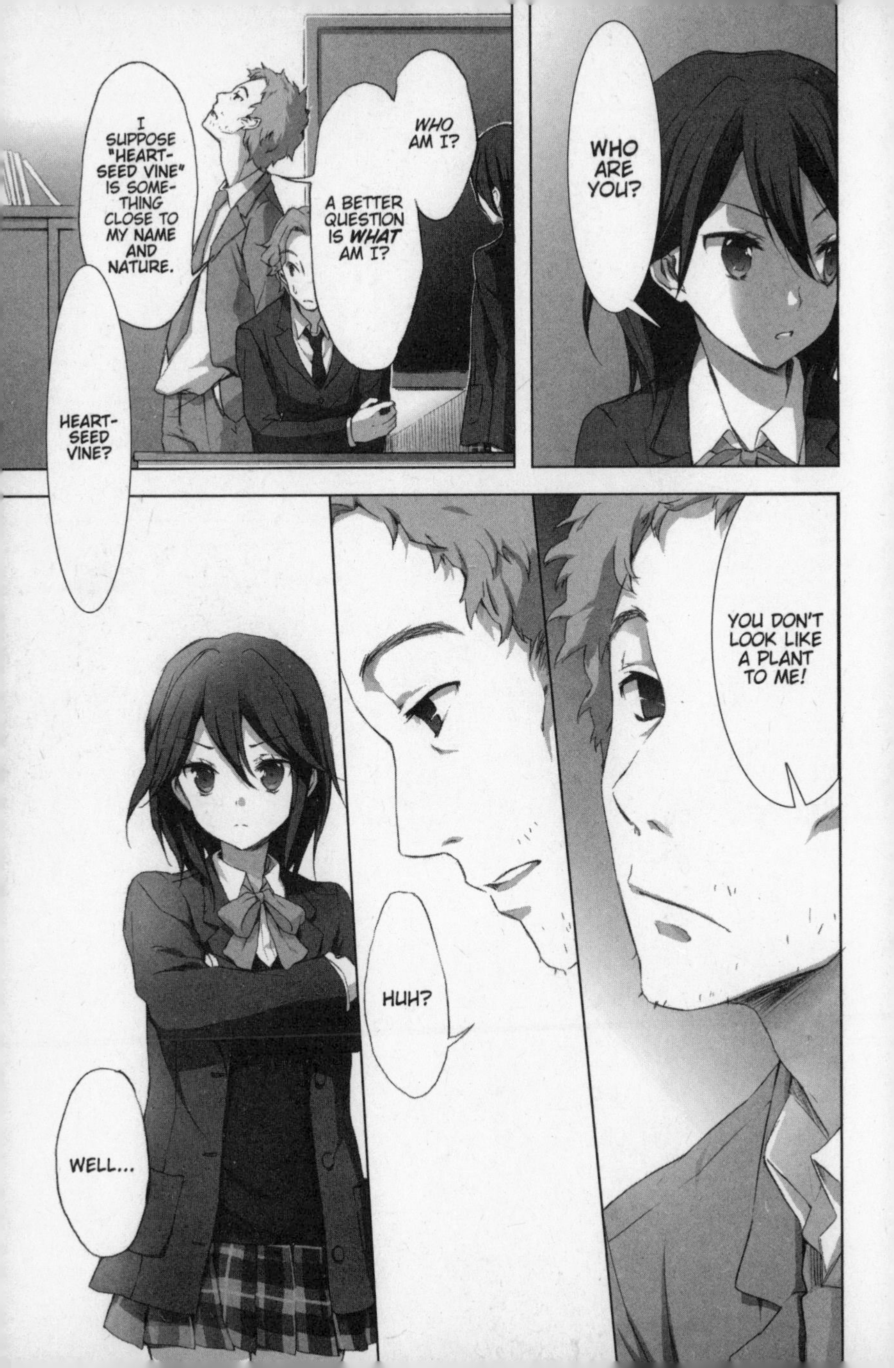
WHO ARE YOU?
WHO AM I?
A BETTER QUESTION IS *WHAT* AM I?
I SUPPOSE "HEART-SEED VINE" IS SOME-THING CLOSE TO MY NAME AND NATURE.
HEART-SEED VINE?
YOU DON'T LOOK LIKE A PLANT TO ME!
HUH?
WELL...

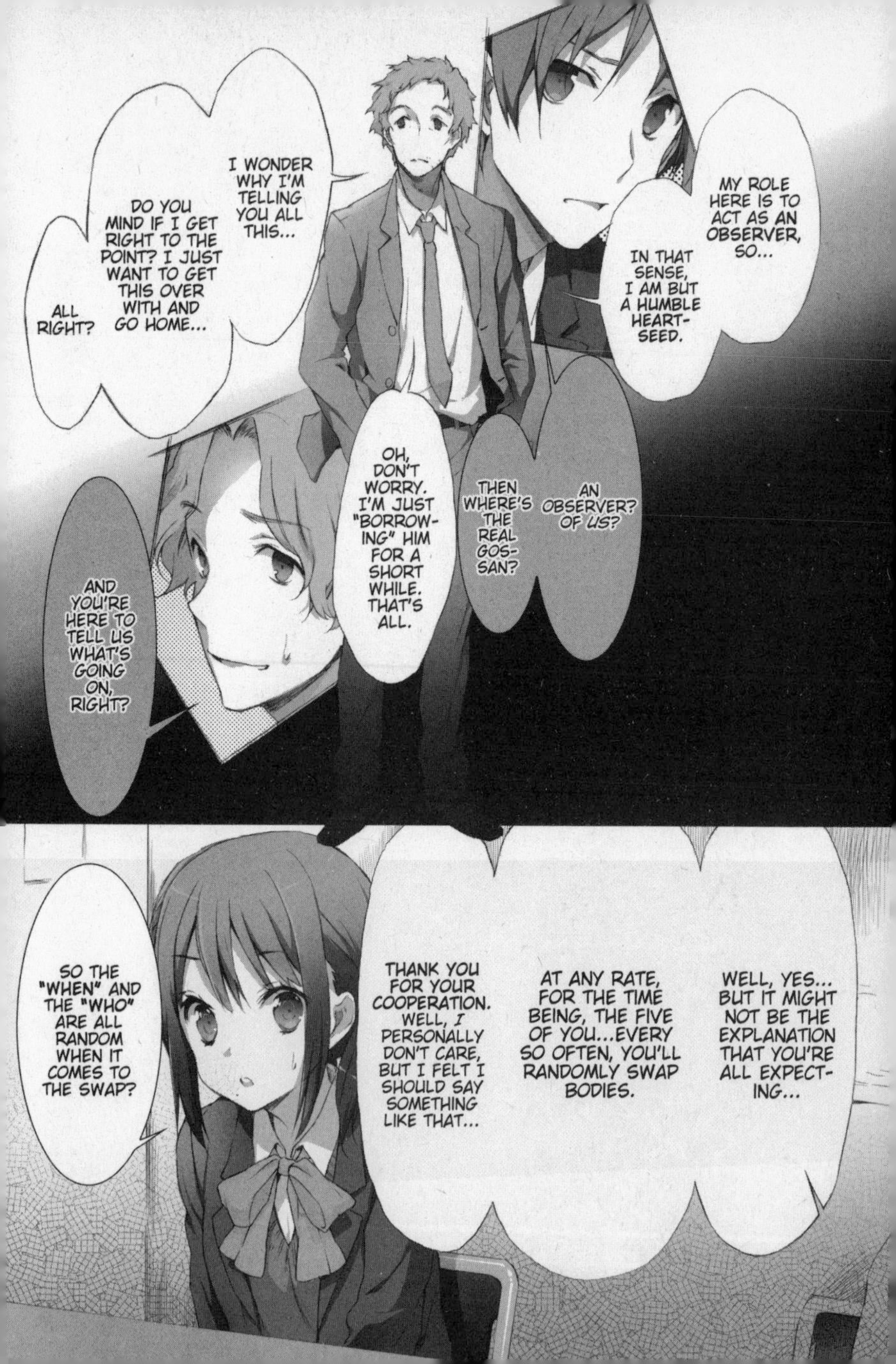
MY ROLE HERE IS TO ACT AS AN OBSERVER, SO...
IN THAT SENSE, I AM BUT A HUMBLE HEART-SEED.
I WONDER WHY I'M TELLING YOU ALL THIS...
DO YOU MIND IF I GET RIGHT TO THE POINT? I JUST WANT TO GET THIS OVER WITH AND GO HOME...
ALL RIGHT?
AN OBSERVER? OF US?
THEN WHERE'S THE REAL GOS-SAN?
OH, DON'T WORRY. I'M JUST "BORROWING" HIM FOR A SHORT WHILE. THAT'S ALL.
AND YOU'RE HERE TO TELL US WHAT'S GOING ON, RIGHT?
WELL, YES... BUT IT MIGHT NOT BE THE EXPLANATION THAT YOU'RE ALL EXPECTING...
AT ANY RATE, FOR THE TIME BEING, THE FIVE OF YOU...EVERY SO OFTEN, YOU'LL RANDOMLY SWAP BODIES.
THANK YOU FOR YOUR COOPERATION. WELL, *I* PERSONALLY DON'T CARE, BUT I FELT I SHOULD SAY SOMETHING LIKE THAT...
SO THE "WHEN" AND THE "WHO" ARE ALL RANDOM WHEN IT COMES TO THE SWAP?

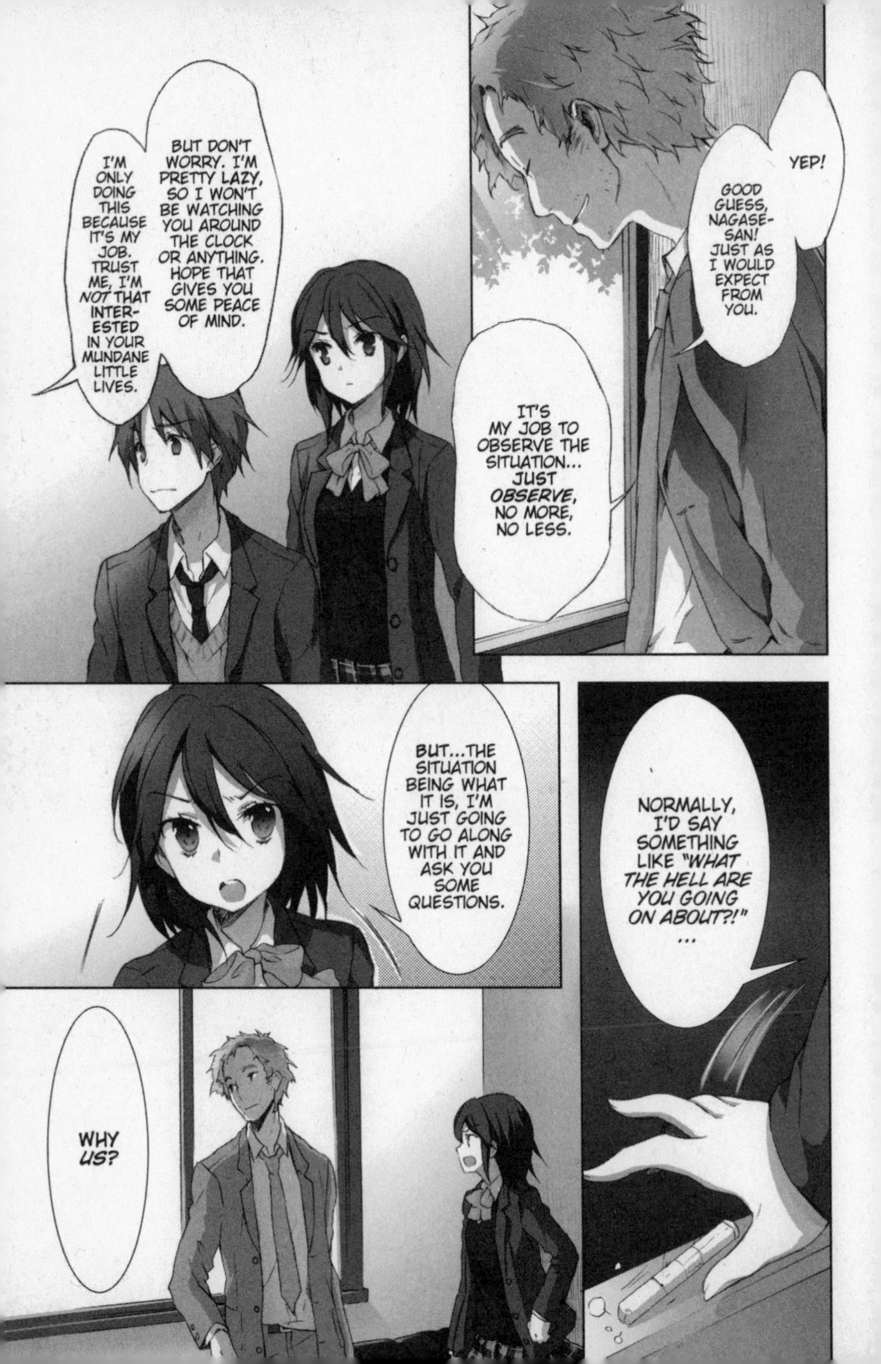
YEP!
GOOD GUESS, NAGASE-SAN! JUST AS I WOULD EXPECT FROM YOU.
IT'S MY JOB TO OBSERVE THE SITUATION... JUST *OBSERVE*, NO MORE, NO LESS.
BUT DON'T WORRY. I'M PRETTY LAZY, SO I WON'T BE WATCHING YOU AROUND THE CLOCK OR ANYTHING. HOPE THAT GIVES YOU SOME PEACE OF MIND.
I'M ONLY DOING THIS BECAUSE IT'S MY JOB. TRUST ME, I'M *NOT* THAT INTERESTED IN YOUR MUNDANE LITTLE LIVES.
NORMALLY, I'D SAY SOMETHING LIKE "*WHAT THE HELL ARE YOU GOING ON ABOUT?!*" ...
BUT...THE SITUATION BEING WHAT IT IS, I'M JUST GOING TO GO ALONG WITH IT AND ASK YOU SOME QUESTIONS.
WHY *US*?

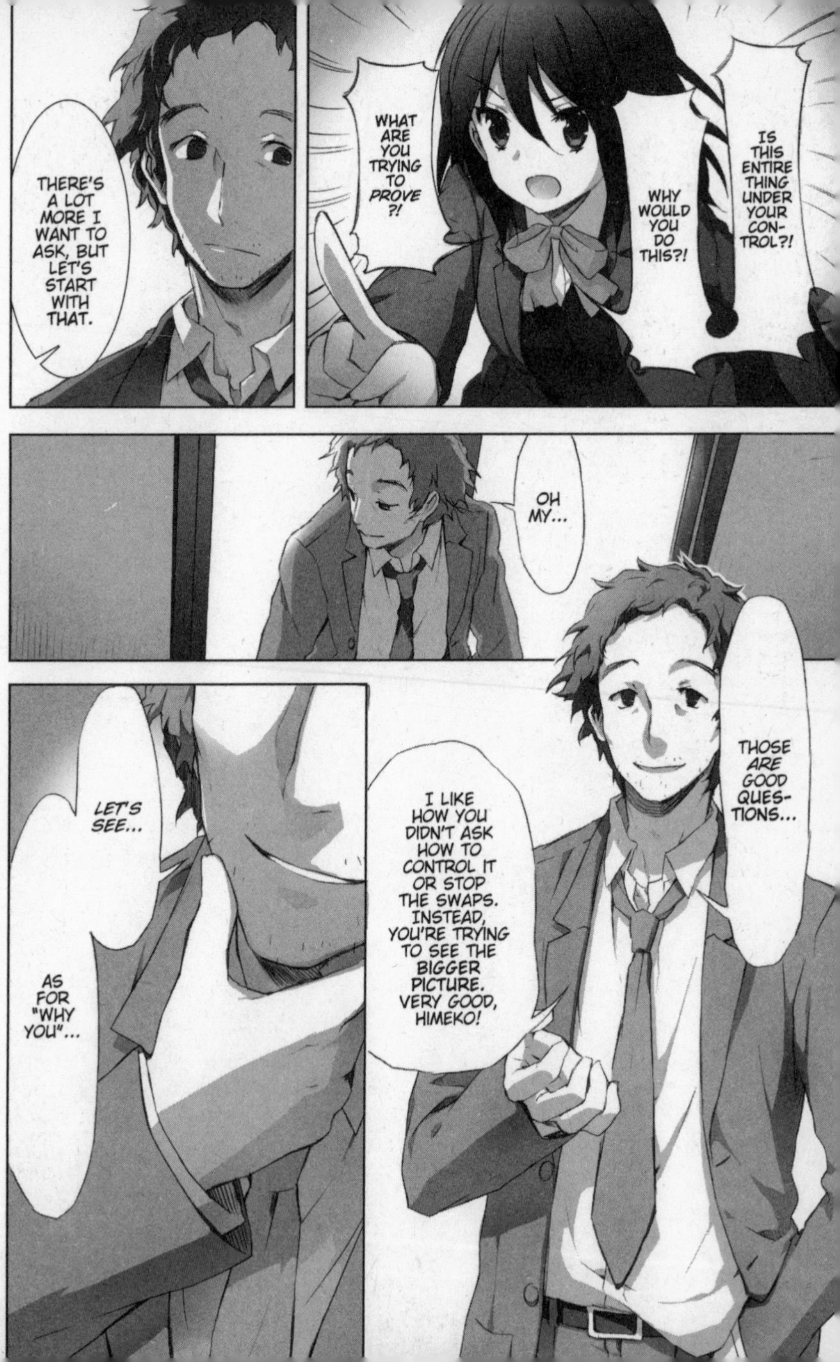
IS THIS ENTIRE THING UNDER YOUR CON-TROL?!
WHY WOULD YOU DO THIS?!
WHAT ARE YOU TRYING TO *PROVE* ?!
THERE'S A LOT MORE I WANT TO ASK, BUT LET'S START WITH THAT.
OH MY...
THOSE *ARE* GOOD QUES-TIONS...
I LIKE HOW YOU DIDN'T ASK HOW TO CONTROL IT OR STOP THE SWAPS. INSTEAD, YOU'RE TRYING TO SEE THE BIGGER PICTURE. VERY GOOD, HIMEKO!
LET'S SEE...
AS FOR "WHY YOU"...

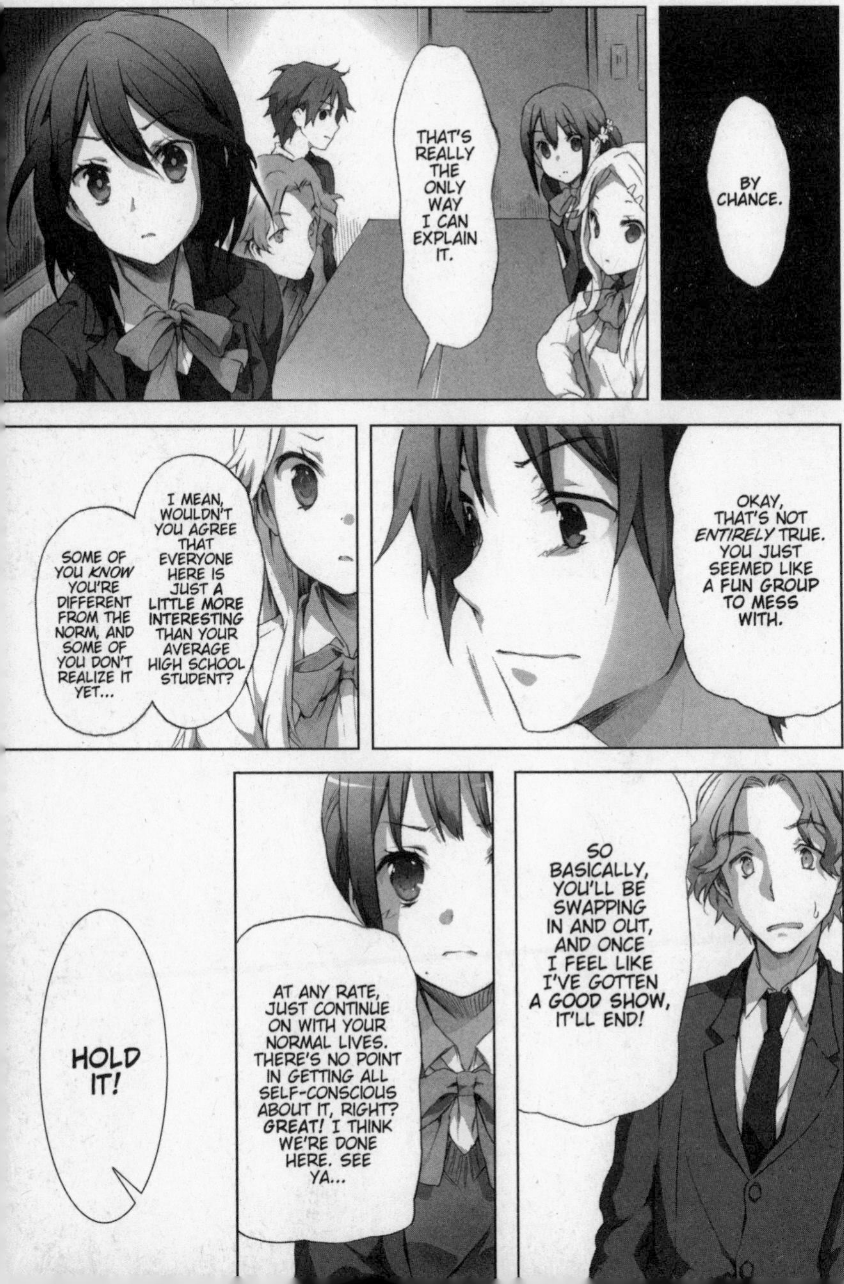
BY CHANCE.
THAT'S REALLY THE ONLY WAY I CAN EXPLAIN IT.
OKAY, THAT'S NOT *ENTIRELY* TRUE. YOU JUST SEEMED LIKE A FUN GROUP TO MESS WITH.
I MEAN, WOULDN'T YOU AGREE THAT EVERYONE HERE IS JUST A LITTLE MORE INTERESTING THAN YOUR AVERAGE HIGH SCHOOL STUDENT?
SOME OF YOU *KNOW* YOU'RE DIFFERENT FROM THE NORM, AND SOME OF YOU DON'T REALIZE IT YET...
SO BASICALLY, YOU'LL BE SWAPPING IN AND OUT, AND ONCE I FEEL LIKE I'VE GOTTEN A GOOD SHOW, IT'LL END!
AT ANY RATE, JUST CONTINUE ON WITH YOUR NORMAL LIVES. THERE'S NO POINT IN GETTING ALL SELF-CONSCIOUS ABOUT IT, RIGHT? GREAT! I THINK WE'RE DONE HERE. SEE YA...
HOLD IT!

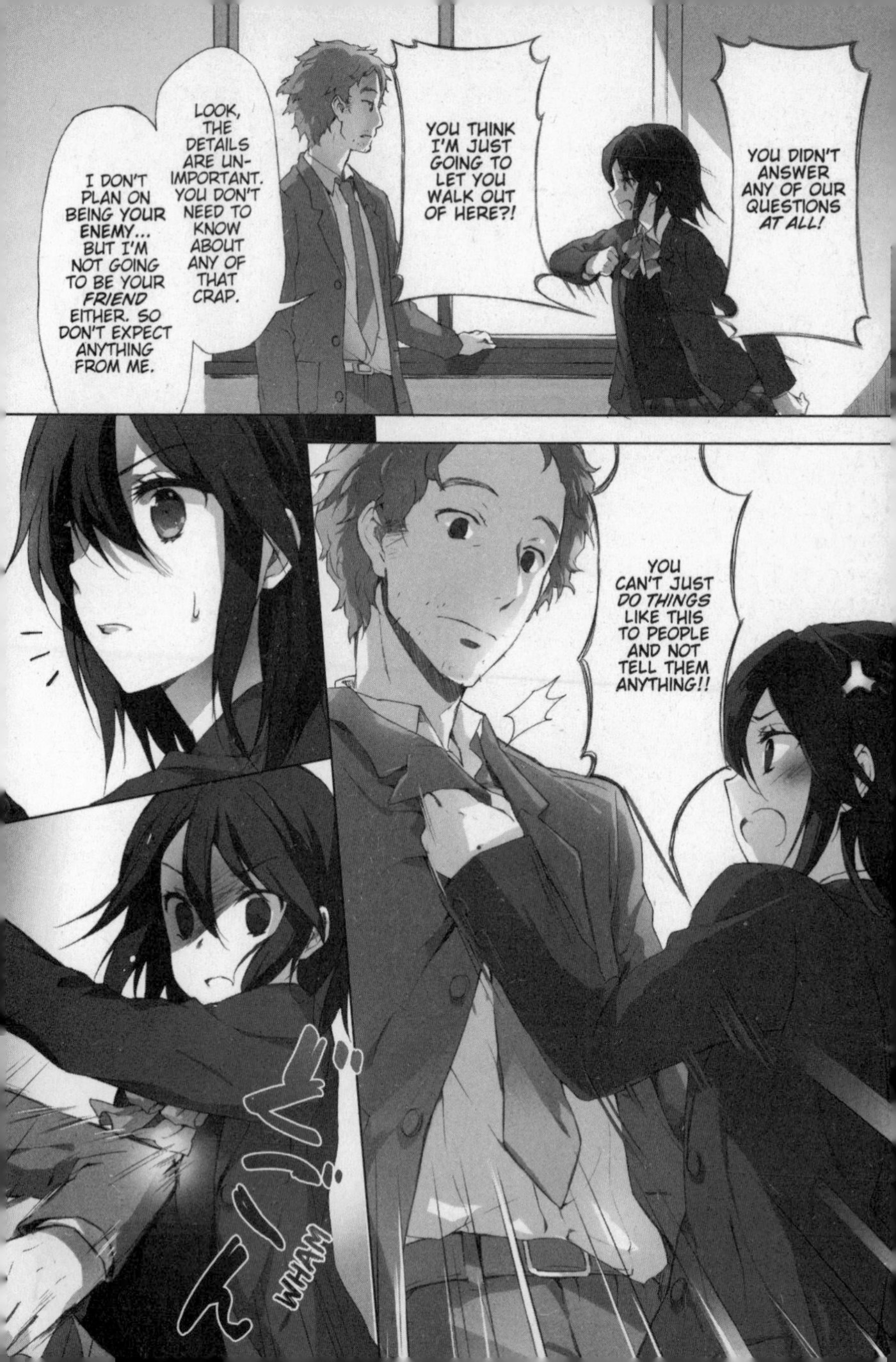
YOU DIDN'T ANSWER ANY OF OUR QUESTIONS AT ALL!
YOU THINK I'M JUST GOING TO LET YOU WALK OUT OF HERE?!
LOOK, THE DETAILS ARE UN-IMPORTANT. YOU DON'T NEED TO KNOW ABOUT ANY OF THAT CRAP.
I DON'T PLAN ON BEING YOUR ENEMY... BUT I'M NOT GOING TO BE YOUR FRIEND EITHER. SO DON'T EXPECT ANYTHING FROM ME.
YOU CAN'T JUST DO THINGS LIKE THIS TO PEOPLE AND NOT TELL THEM ANYTHING!!
WHAM

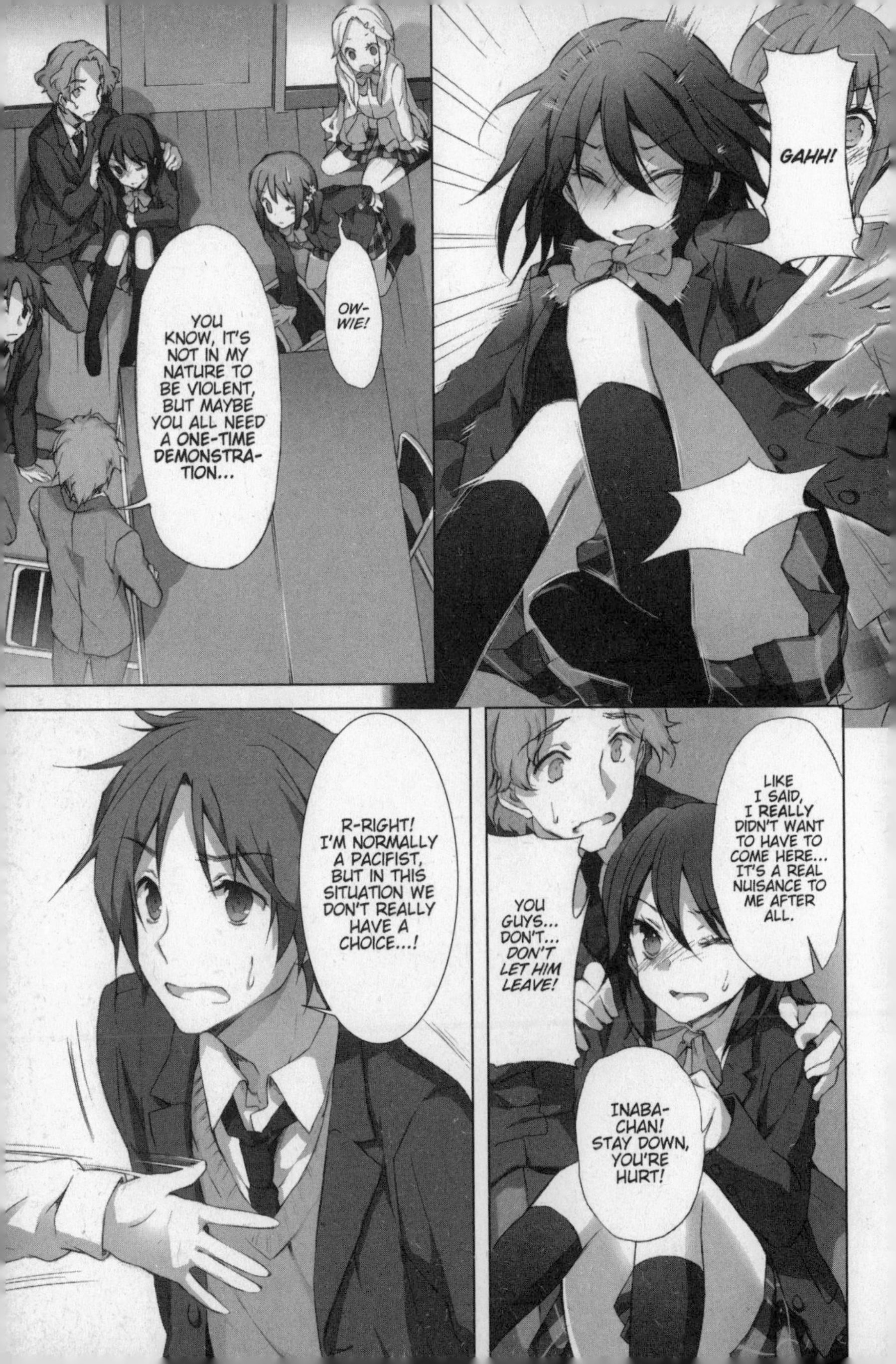
GAHH!
OW-WIE!
YOU KNOW, IT'S NOT IN MY NATURE TO BE VIOLENT, BUT MAYBE YOU ALL NEED A ONE-TIME DEMONSTRATION...
LIKE I SAID, I REALLY DIDN'T WANT TO HAVE TO COME HERE... IT'S A REAL NUISANCE TO ME AFTER ALL.
YOU GUYS... DON'T... DON'T LET HIM LEAVE!
INABA-CHAN! STAY DOWN, YOU'RE HURT!
R-RIGHT! I'M NORMALLY A PACIFIST, BUT IN THIS SITUATION WE DON'T REALLY HAVE A CHOICE...!

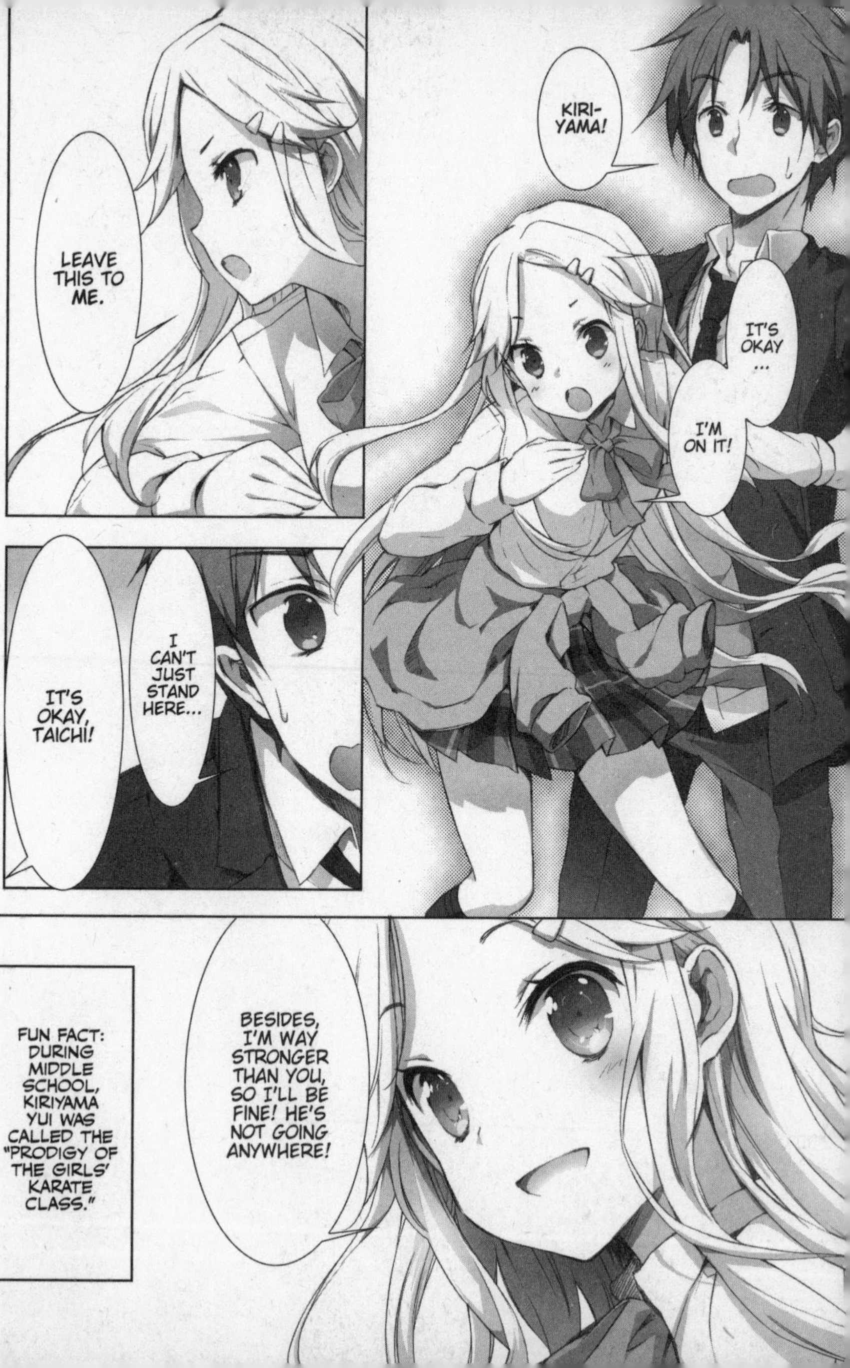
KIRI-YAMA!
IT'S OKAY ...
I'M ON IT!
LEAVE THIS TO ME.
I CAN'T JUST STAND HERE...
IT'S OKAY, TAICHI!
BESIDES, I'M WAY STRONGER THAN YOU, SO I'LL BE FINE! HE'S NOT GOING ANYWHERE!
FUN FACT: DURING MIDDLE SCHOOL, KIRIYAMA YUI WAS CALLED THE "PRODIGY OF THE GIRLS' KARATE CLASS."

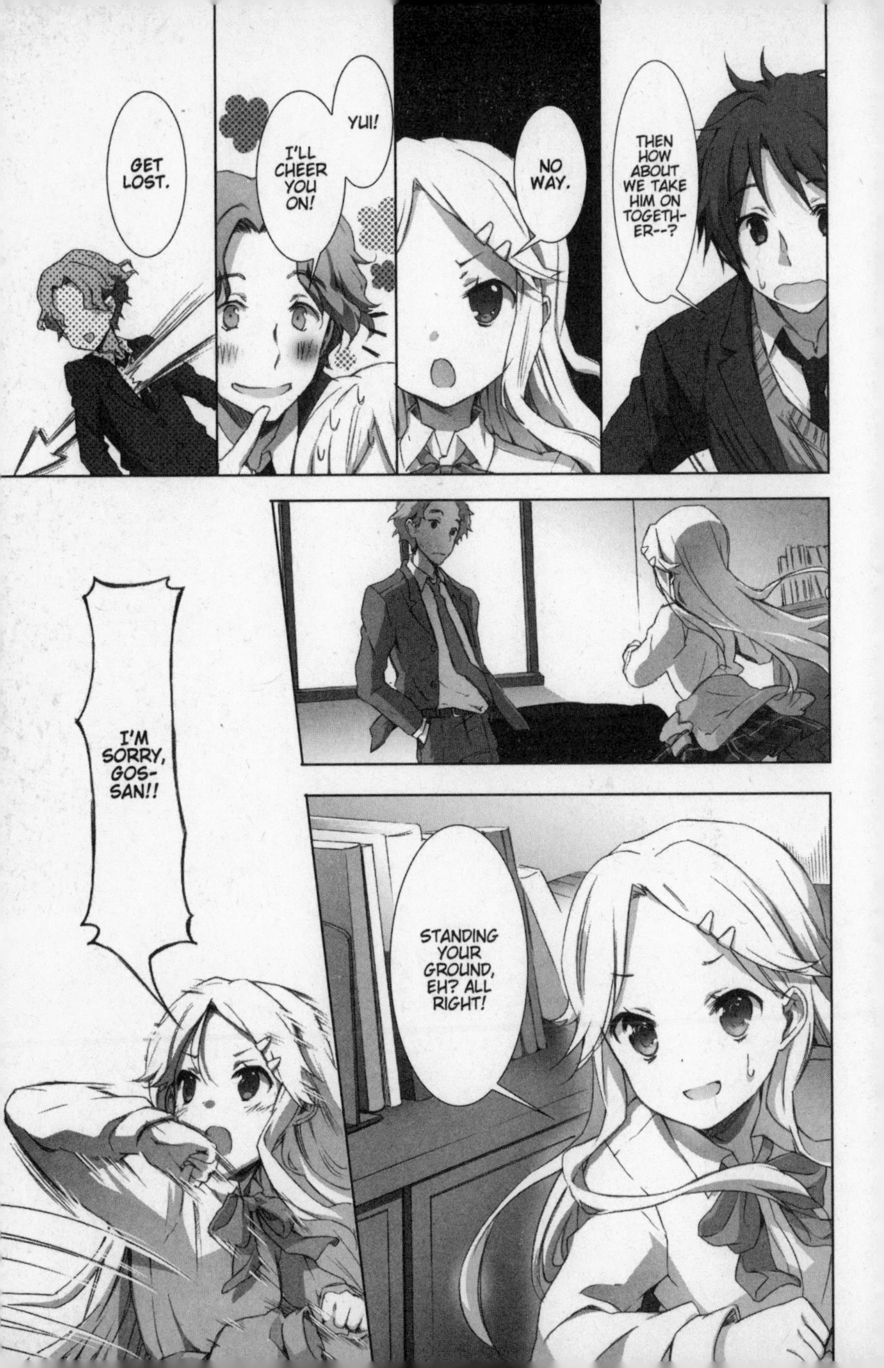
THEN HOW ABOUT WE TAKE HIM ON TOGETH-ER--?
NO WAY.
YUI!
I'LL CHEER YOU ON!
GET LOST.
STANDING YOUR GROUND, EH? ALL RIGHT!
I'M SORRY, GOS-SAN!!

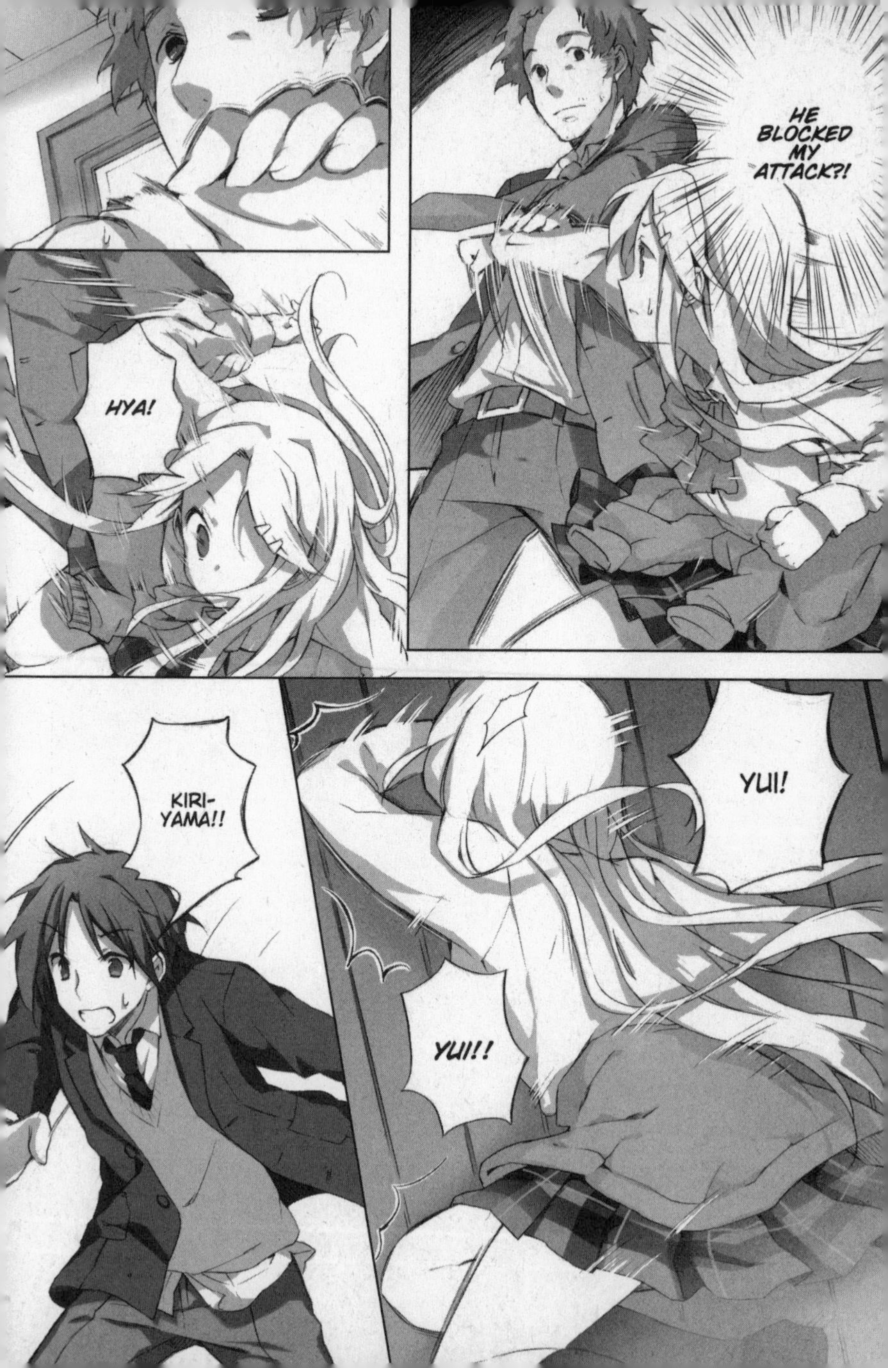
HE BLOCKED MY ATTACK?!
HYA!
YUI!
YUI!!
KIRI-YAMA!!

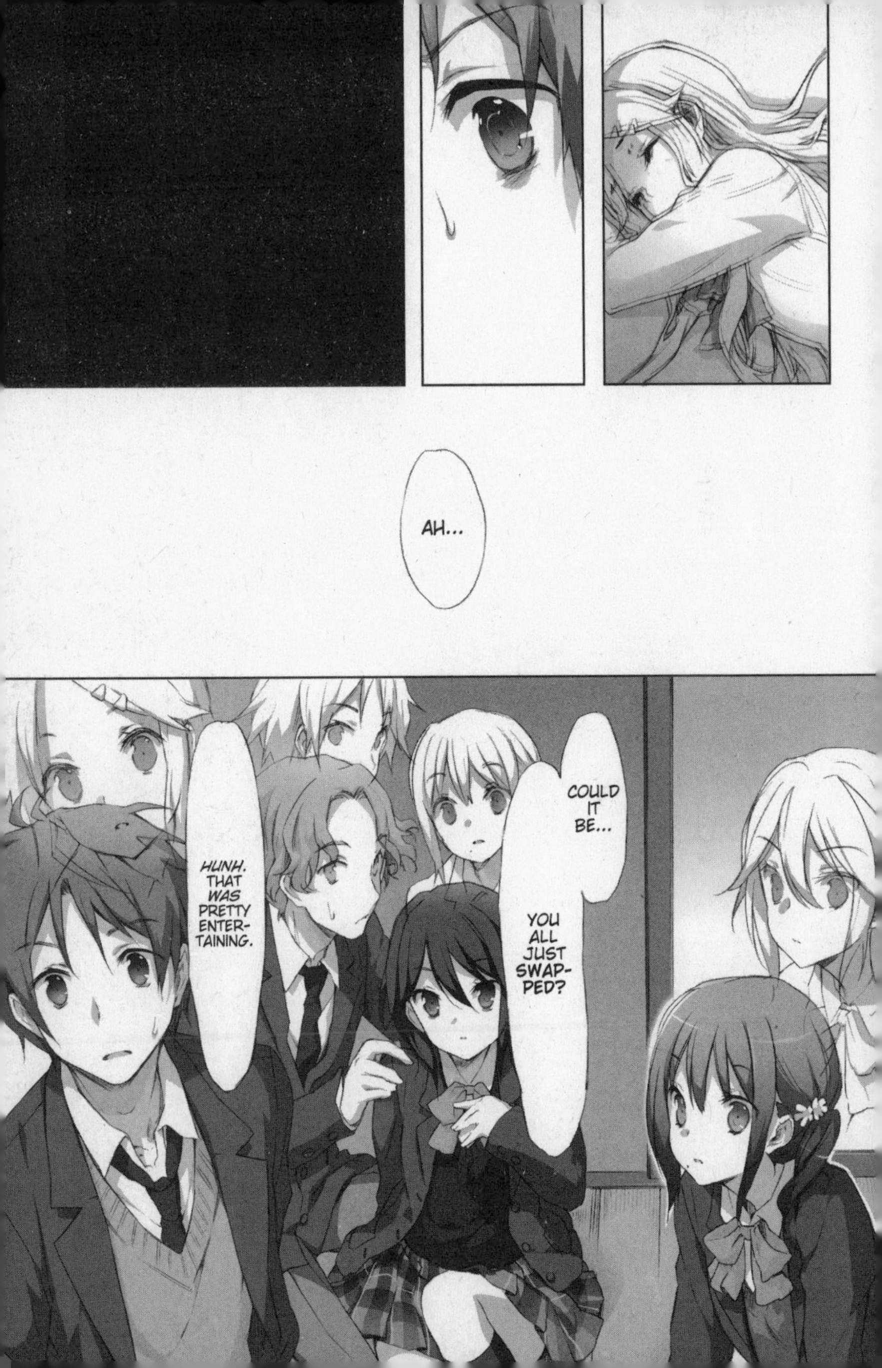
AH...
COULD IT BE...
YOU ALL JUST SWAP-PED?
HUNH. THAT WAS PRETTY ENTER-TAINING.

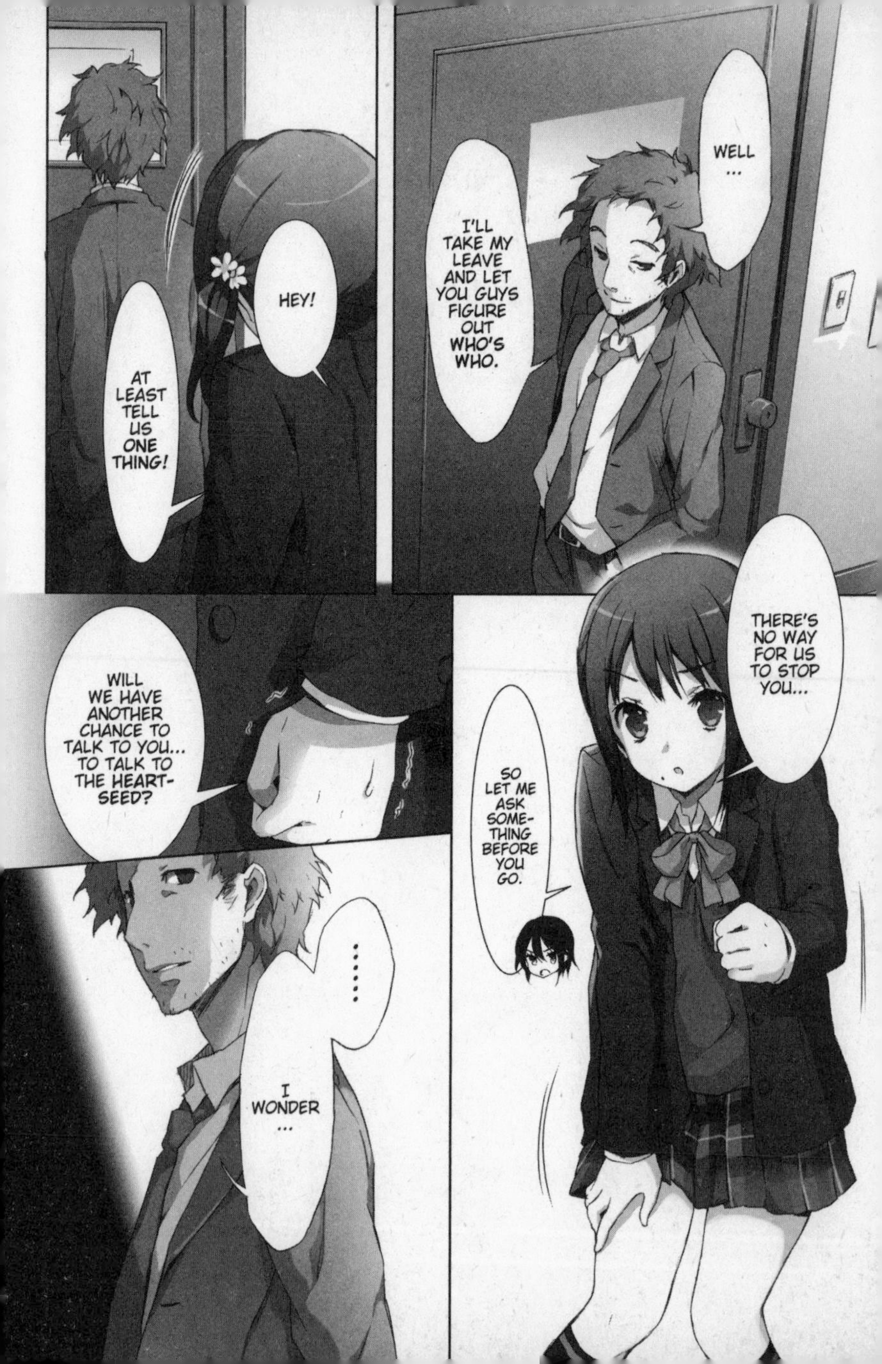
WELL ...
I'LL TAKE MY LEAVE AND LET YOU GUYS FIGURE OUT WHO'S WHO.
HEY!
AT LEAST TELL US ONE THING!
THERE'S NO WAY FOR US TO STOP YOU...
SO LET ME ASK SOMETHING BEFORE YOU GO.
WILL WE HAVE ANOTHER CHANCE TO TALK TO YOU... TO TALK TO THE HEART-SEED?
......
I WONDER ...

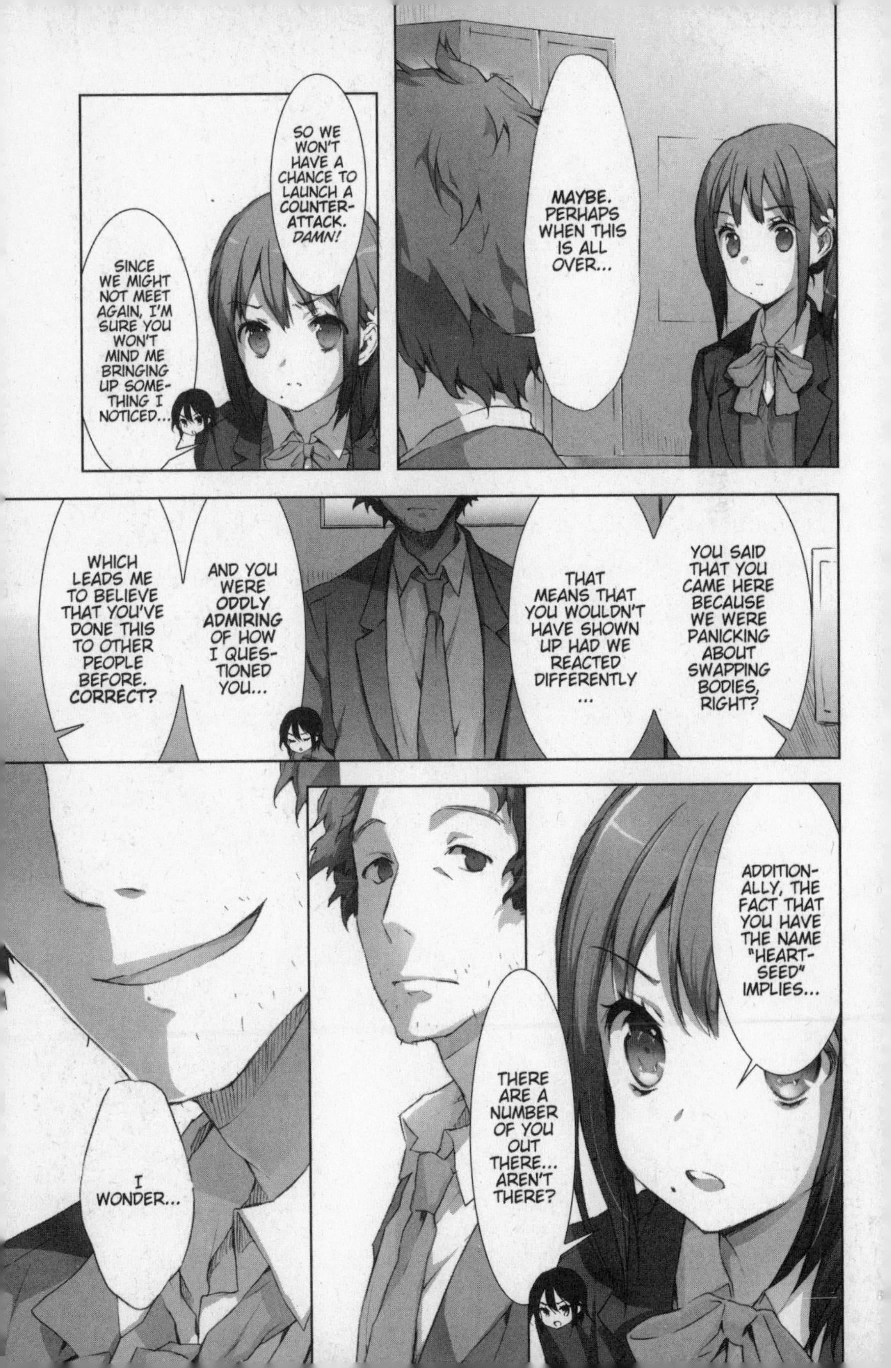
MAYBE. PERHAPS WHEN THIS IS ALL OVER...
SO WE WON'T HAVE A CHANCE TO LAUNCH A COUNTER-ATTACK. DAMN!
SINCE WE MIGHT NOT MEET AGAIN, I'M SURE YOU WON'T MIND ME BRINGING UP SOME-THING I NOTICED...
YOU SAID THAT YOU CAME HERE BECAUSE WE WERE PANICKING ABOUT SWAPPING BODIES, RIGHT?
THAT MEANS THAT YOU WOULDN'T HAVE SHOWN UP HAD WE REACTED DIFFERENTLY...
AND YOU WERE ODDLY ADMIRING OF HOW I QUES-TIONED YOU...
WHICH LEADS ME TO BELIEVE THAT YOU'VE DONE THIS TO OTHER PEOPLE BEFORE. CORRECT?
ADDITION-ALLY, THE FACT THAT YOU HAVE THE NAME "HEART-SEED" IMPLIES...
THERE ARE A NUMBER OF YOU OUT THERE... AREN'T THERE?
I WONDER...

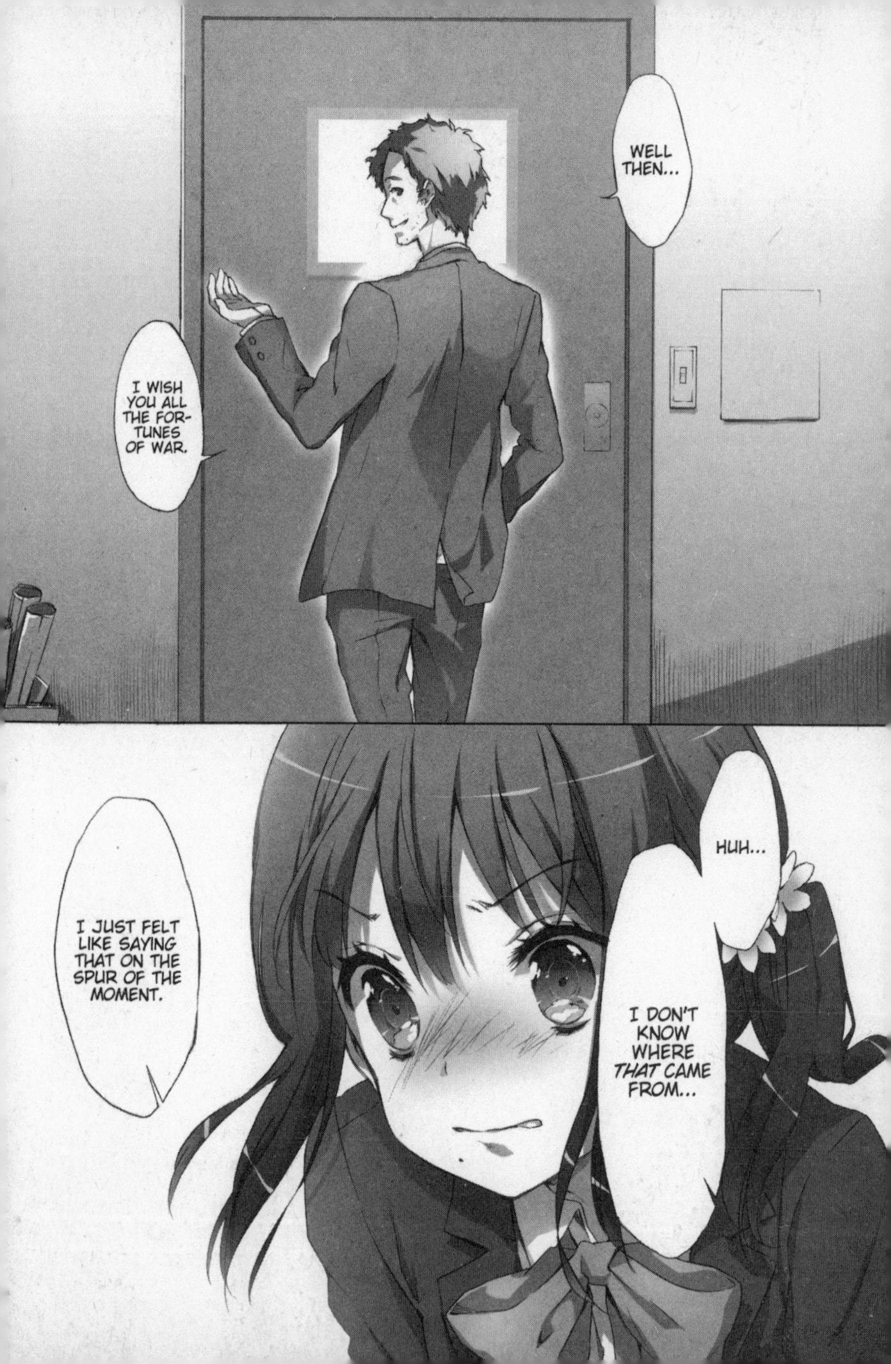
WELL THEN...
I WISH YOU ALL THE FORTUNES OF WAR.
HUH...
I DON'T KNOW WHERE *THAT* CAME FROM...
I JUST FELT LIKE SAYING THAT ON THE SPUR OF THE MOMENT.

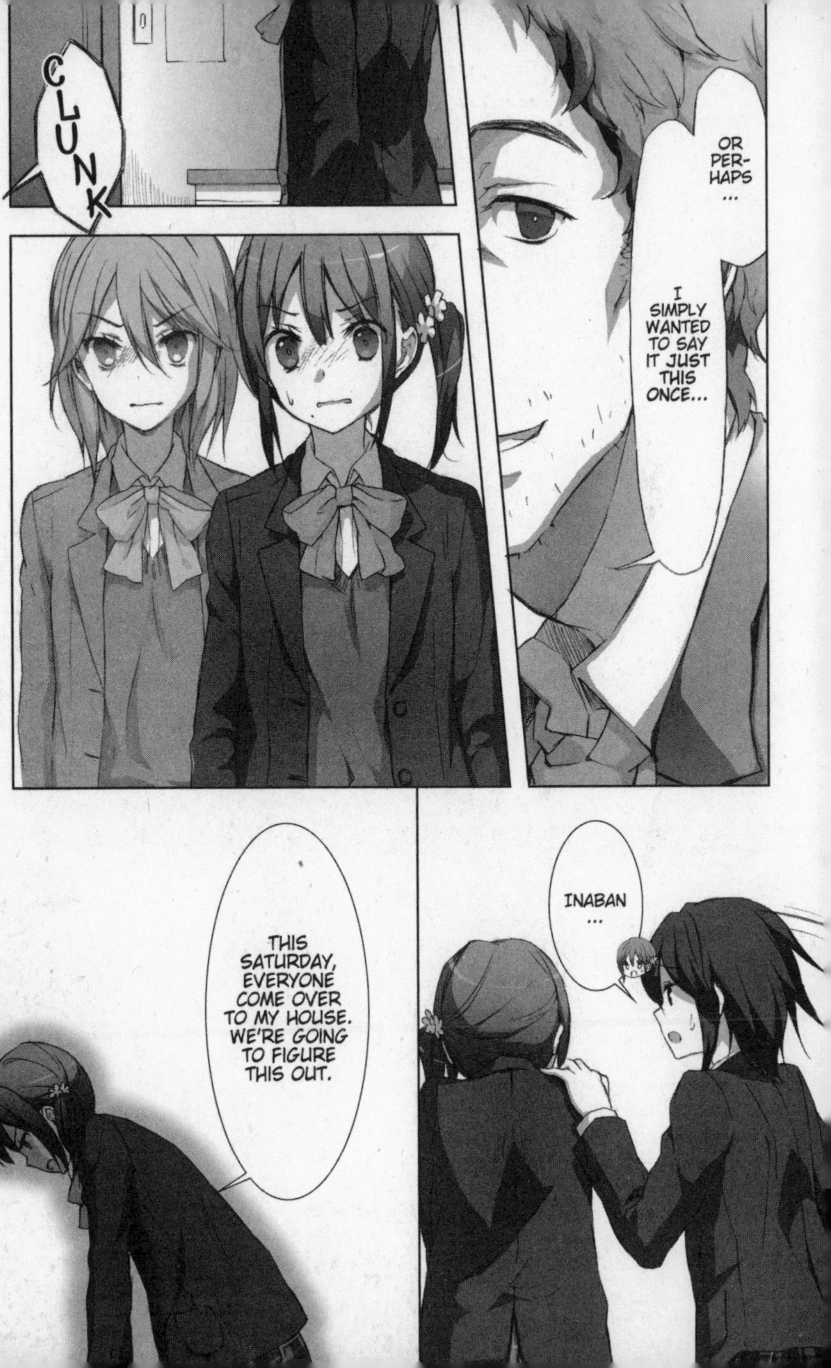
OR PER-HAPS ...
I SIMPLY WANTED TO SAY IT JUST THIS ONCE...
CLUNK
INABAN ...
THIS SATURDAY, EVERYONE COME OVER TO MY HOUSE. WE'RE GOING TO FIGURE THIS OUT.

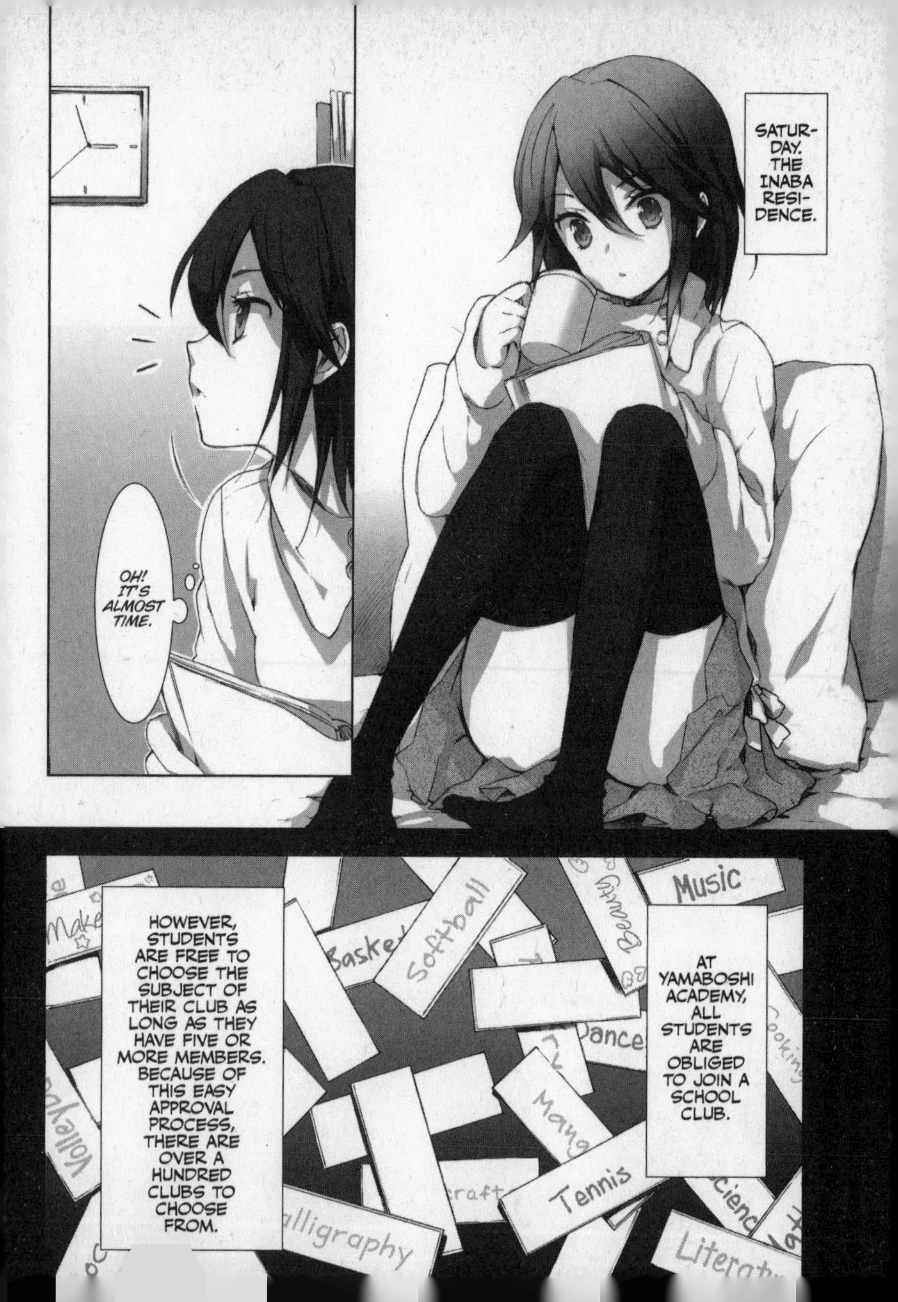
SATURDAY. THE INABA RESIDENCE.
OH! IT'S ALMOST TIME.
AT YAMABOSHI ACADEMY, ALL STUDENTS ARE OBLIGED TO JOIN A SCHOOL CLUB.
HOWEVER, STUDENTS ARE FREE TO CHOOSE THE SUBJECT OF THEIR CLUB AS LONG AS THEY HAVE FIVE OR MORE MEMBERS. BECAUSE OF THIS EASY APPROVAL PROCESS, THERE ARE OVER A HUNDRED CLUBS TO CHOOSE FROM.
Music
Beauty
Softball
Tennis

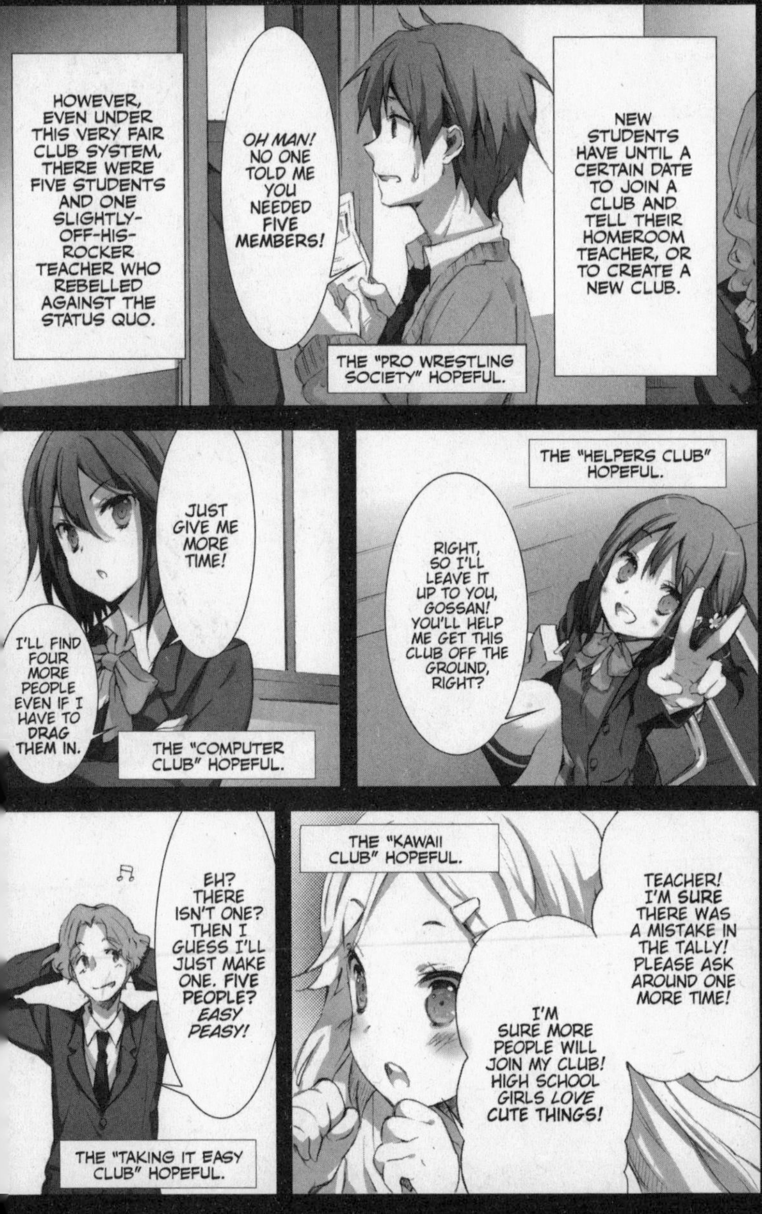
NEW STUDENTS HAVE UNTIL A CERTAIN DATE TO JOIN A CLUB AND TELL THEIR HOMEROOM TEACHER, OR TO CREATE A NEW CLUB.
HOWEVER, EVEN UNDER THIS VERY FAIR CLUB SYSTEM, THERE WERE FIVE STUDENTS AND ONE SLIGHTLY-OFF-HIS-ROCKER TEACHER WHO REBELLED AGAINST THE STATUS QUO.
OH MAN! NO ONE TOLD ME YOU NEEDED FIVE MEMBERS!
THE "PRO WRESTLING SOCIETY" HOPEFUL.
THE "HELPERS CLUB" HOPEFUL.
RIGHT, SO I'LL LEAVE IT UP TO YOU, GOSSAN! YOU'LL HELP ME GET THIS CLUB OFF THE GROUND, RIGHT?
JUST GIVE ME MORE TIME!
I'LL FIND FOUR MORE PEOPLE EVEN IF I HAVE TO DRAG THEM IN.
THE "COMPUTER CLUB" HOPEFUL.
THE "KAWAII CLUB" HOPEFUL.
TEACHER! I'M SURE THERE WAS A MISTAKE IN THE TALLY! PLEASE ASK AROUND ONE MORE TIME!
I'M SURE MORE PEOPLE WILL JOIN MY CLUB! HIGH SCHOOL GIRLS *LOVE* CUTE THINGS!
EH? THERE ISN'T ONE? THEN I GUESS I'LL JUST MAKE ONE. FIVE PEOPLE? *EASY PEASY!*
THE "TAKING IT EASY CLUB" HOPEFUL.

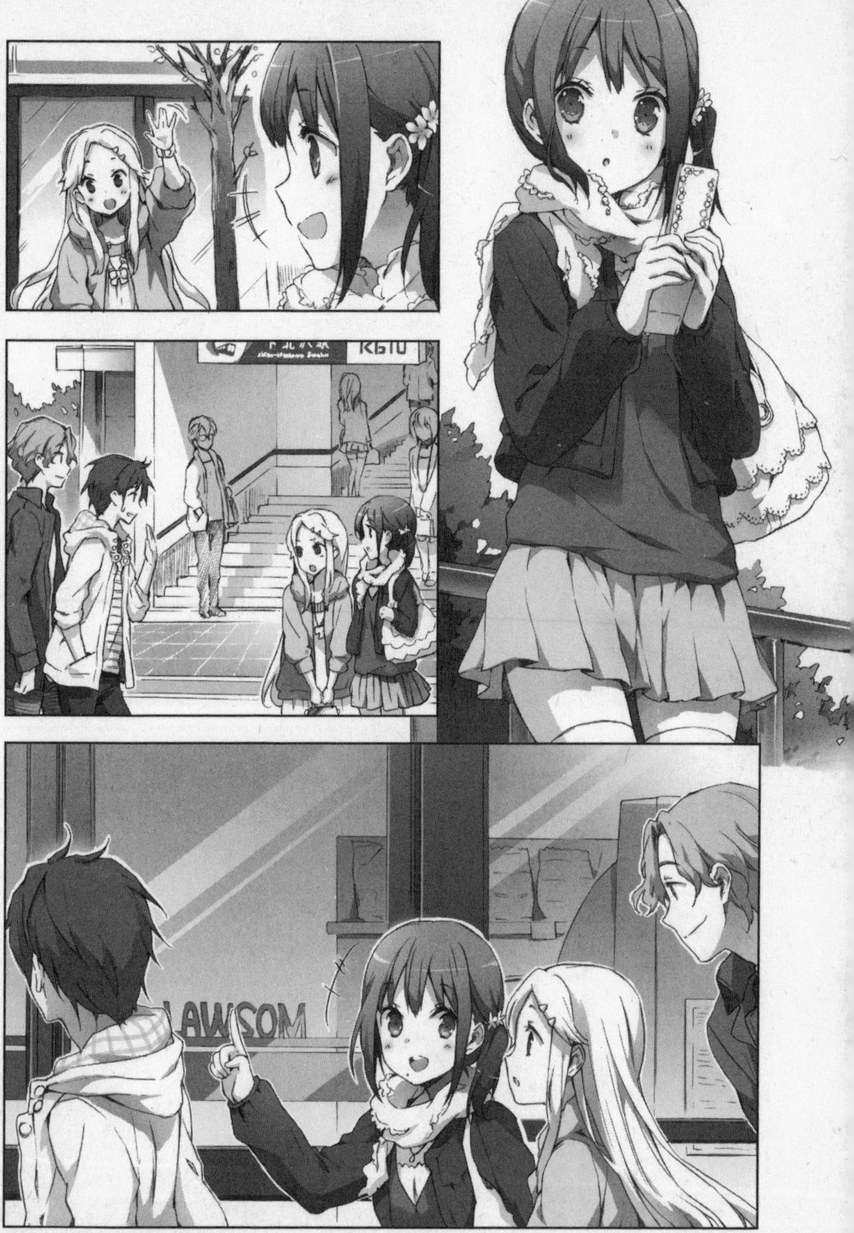

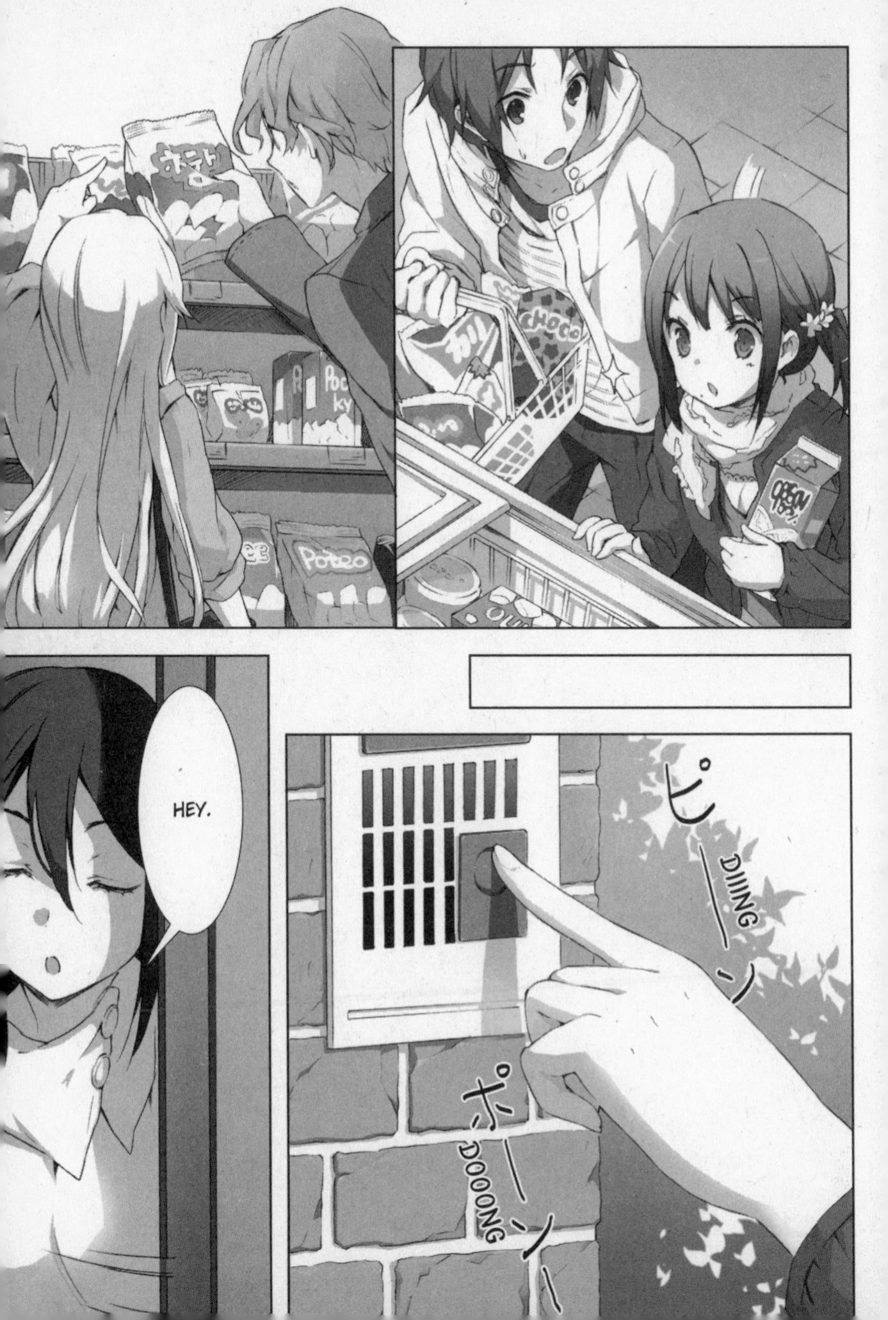
CHOCO
Pocky
ピーーン
DIIING
ポーーン
DOOONG
HEY.

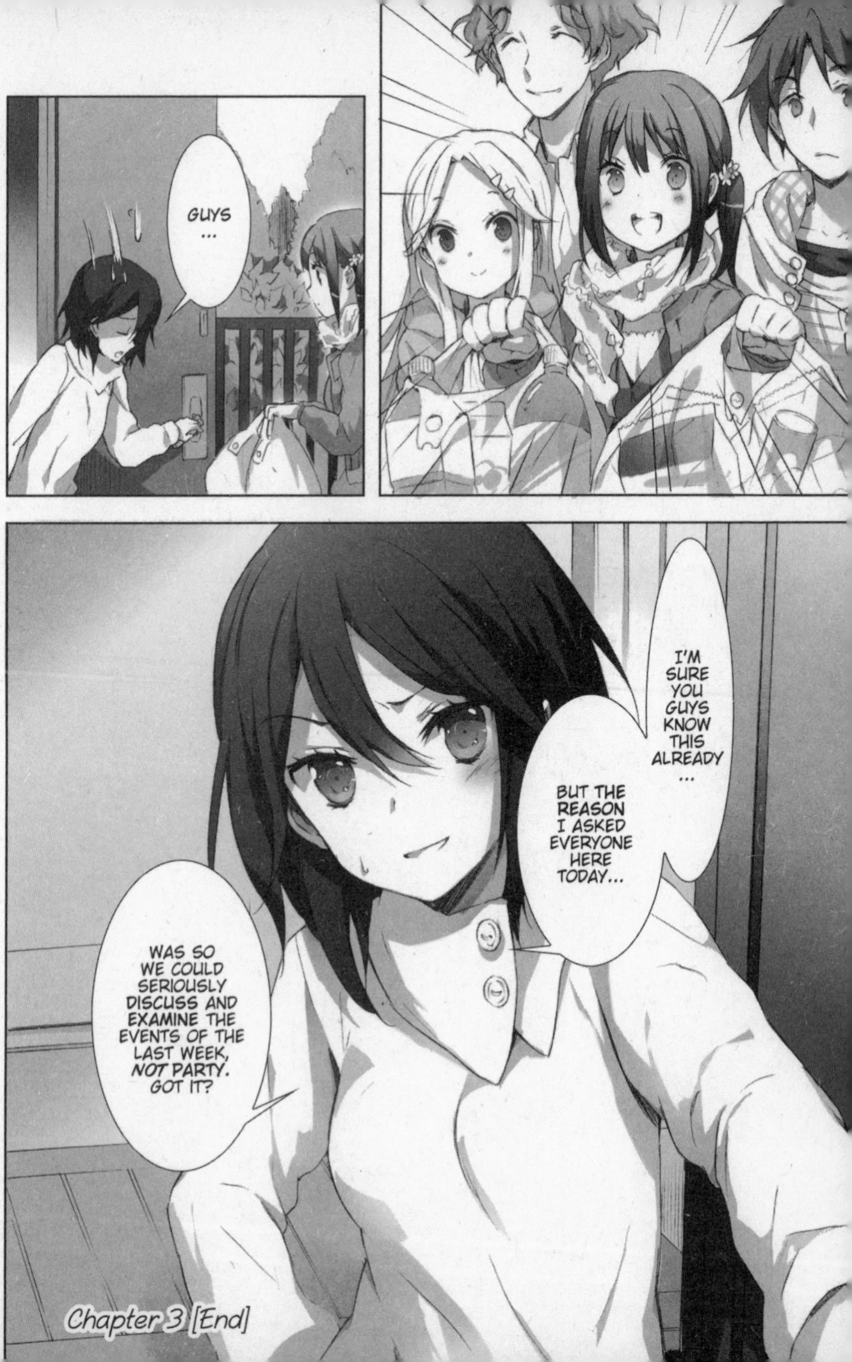
GUYS ...
I'M SURE YOU GUYS KNOW THIS ALREADY ...
BUT THE REASON I ASKED EVERYONE HERE TODAY...
WAS SO WE COULD SERIOUSLY DISCUSS AND EXAMINE THE EVENTS OF THE LAST WEEK, *NOT* PARTY. GOT IT?
Chapter 3 [End]

Make sure you
have plenty of
light when you're
reading!

KOKORO CONNECT

Chapter 4

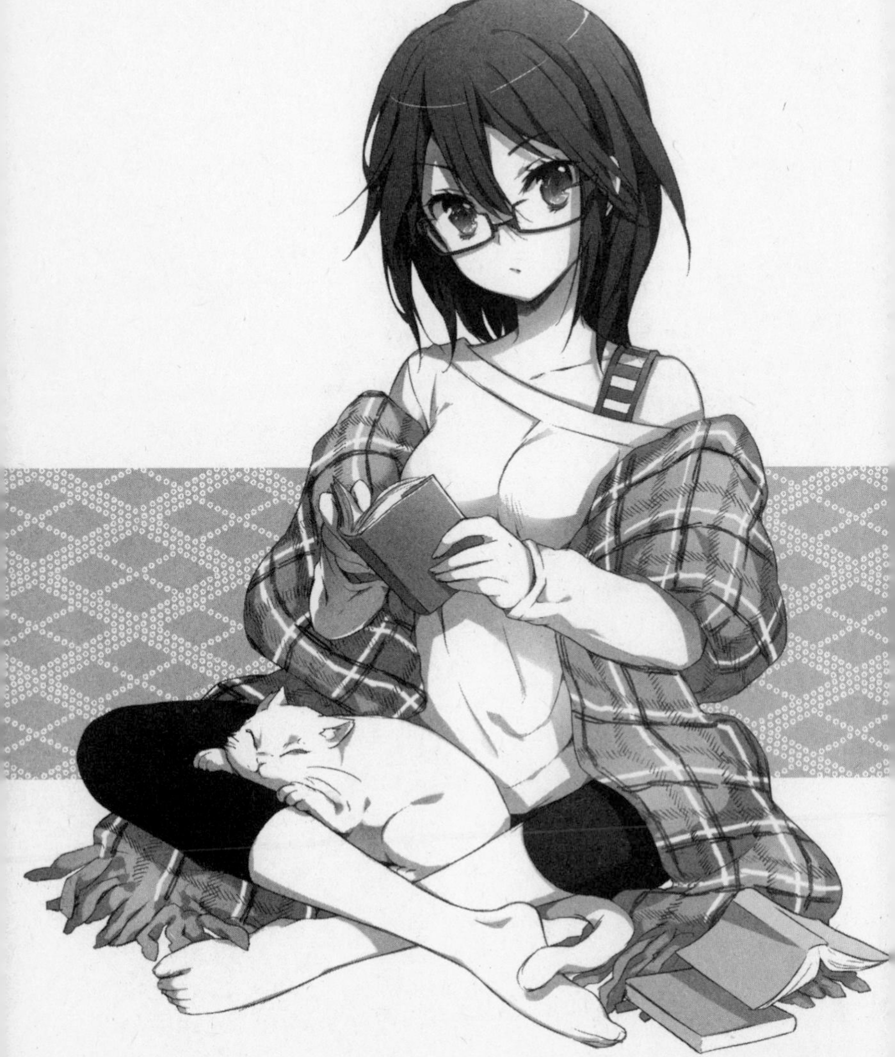

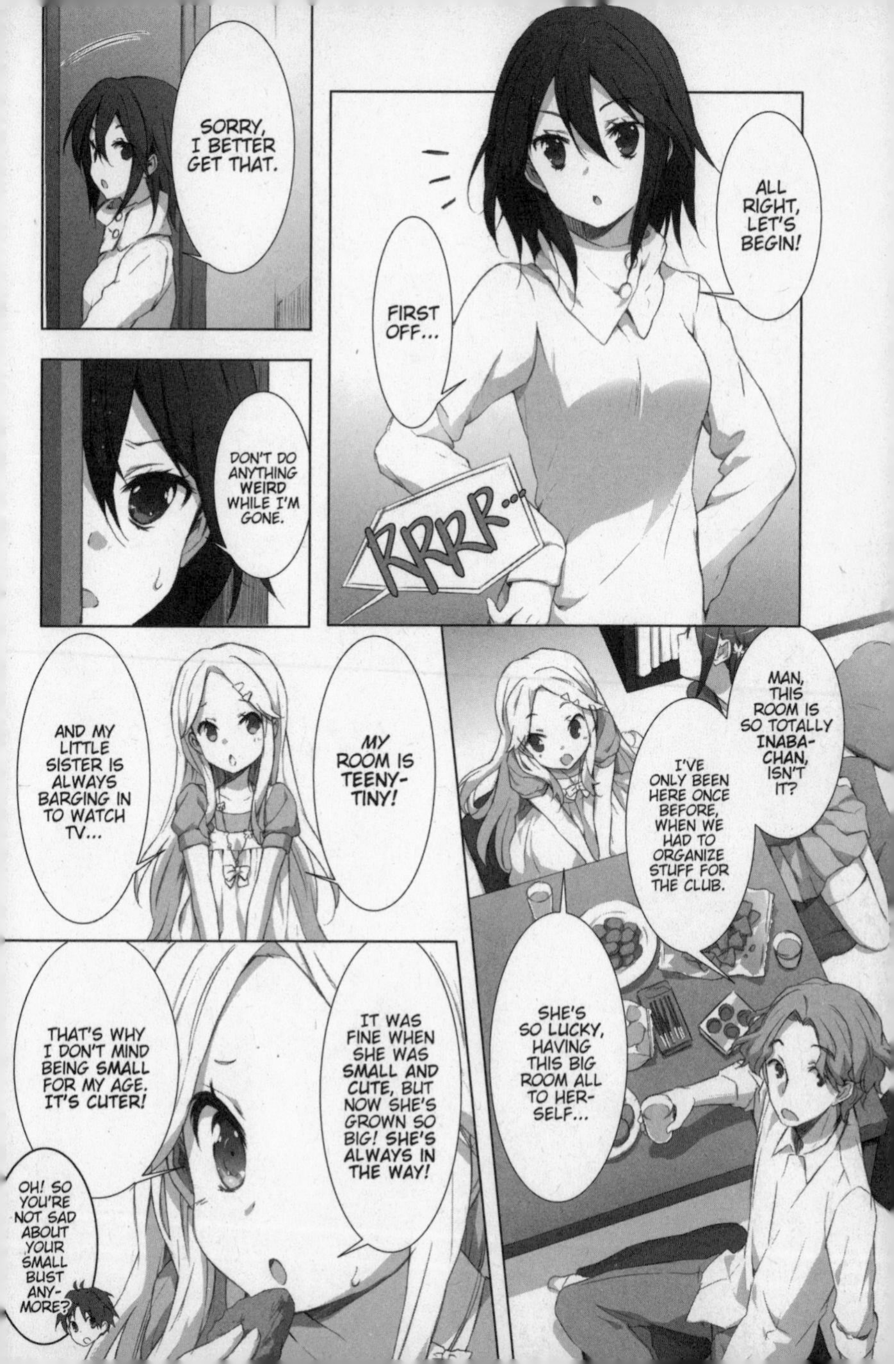
ALL RIGHT, LET'S BEGIN!
FIRST OFF...
RRRR...
SORRY, I BETTER GET THAT.
DON'T DO ANYTHING WEIRD WHILE I'M GONE.
MAN, THIS ROOM IS SO TOTALLY INABA-CHAN, ISN'T IT?
I'VE ONLY BEEN HERE ONCE BEFORE, WHEN WE HAD TO ORGANIZE STUFF FOR THE CLUB.
SHE'S SO LUCKY, HAVING THIS BIG ROOM ALL TO HER-SELF...
MY ROOM IS TEENY-TINY!
AND MY LITTLE SISTER IS ALWAYS BARGING IN TO WATCH TV...
IT WAS FINE WHEN SHE WAS SMALL AND CUTE, BUT NOW SHE'S GROWN SO BIG! SHE'S ALWAYS IN THE WAY!
THAT'S WHY I DON'T MIND BEING SMALL FOR MY AGE. IT'S CUTER!
OH! SO YOU'RE NOT SAD ABOUT YOUR SMALL BUST ANY-MORE?

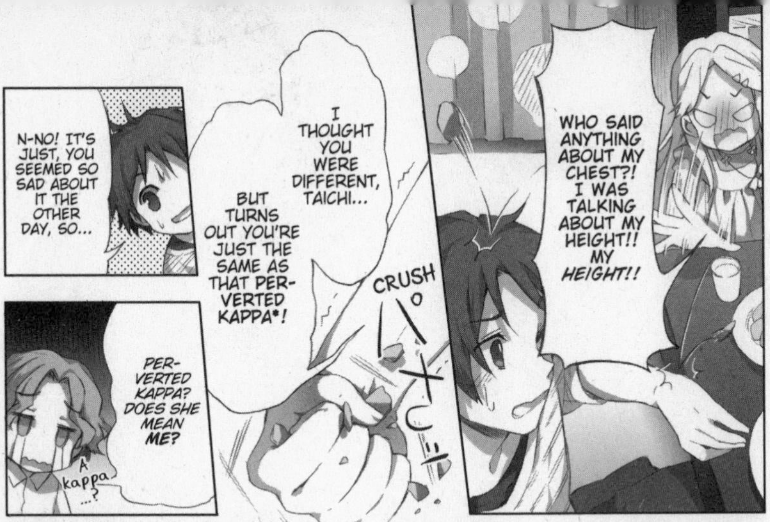
WHO SAID ANYTHING ABOUT MY CHEST?! I WAS TALKING ABOUT MY HEIGHT!! MY *HEIGHT*!!
CRUSH
I THOUGHT YOU WERE DIFFERENT, TAICHI...
BUT TURNS OUT YOU'RE JUST THE SAME AS THAT PER-VERTED KAPPA*!
N-NO! IT'S JUST, YOU SEEMED SO SAD ABOUT IT THE OTHER DAY, SO...
PER-VERTED KAPPA? DOES SHE MEAN **ME**?
A kappa ...?

*A kappa is a Japanese river monster (yokai).

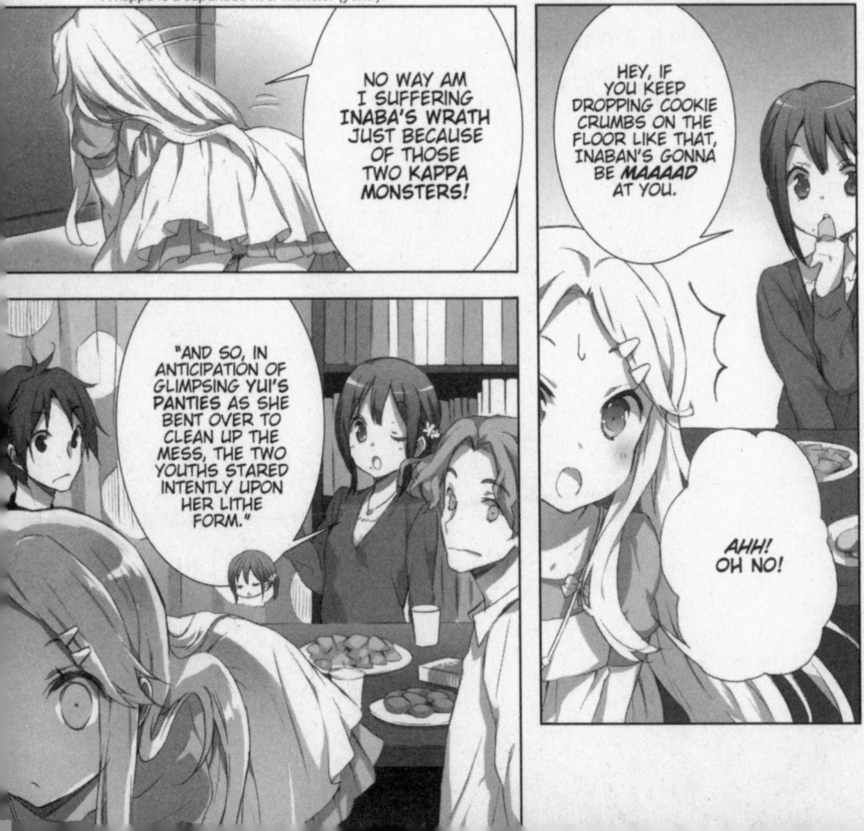
HEY, IF YOU KEEP DROPPING COOKIE CRUMBS ON THE FLOOR LIKE THAT, INABAN'S GONNA BE *MAAAAD* AT YOU.
AHH! OH NO!
NO WAY AM I SUFFERING **INABA'S WRATH** JUST BECAUSE OF THOSE TWO KAPPA MONSTERS!
"AND SO, IN ANTICIPATION OF GLIMPSING YUI'S PANTIES AS SHE BENT OVER TO CLEAN UP THE MESS, THE TWO YOUTHS STARED INTENTLY UPON HER LITHE FORM."

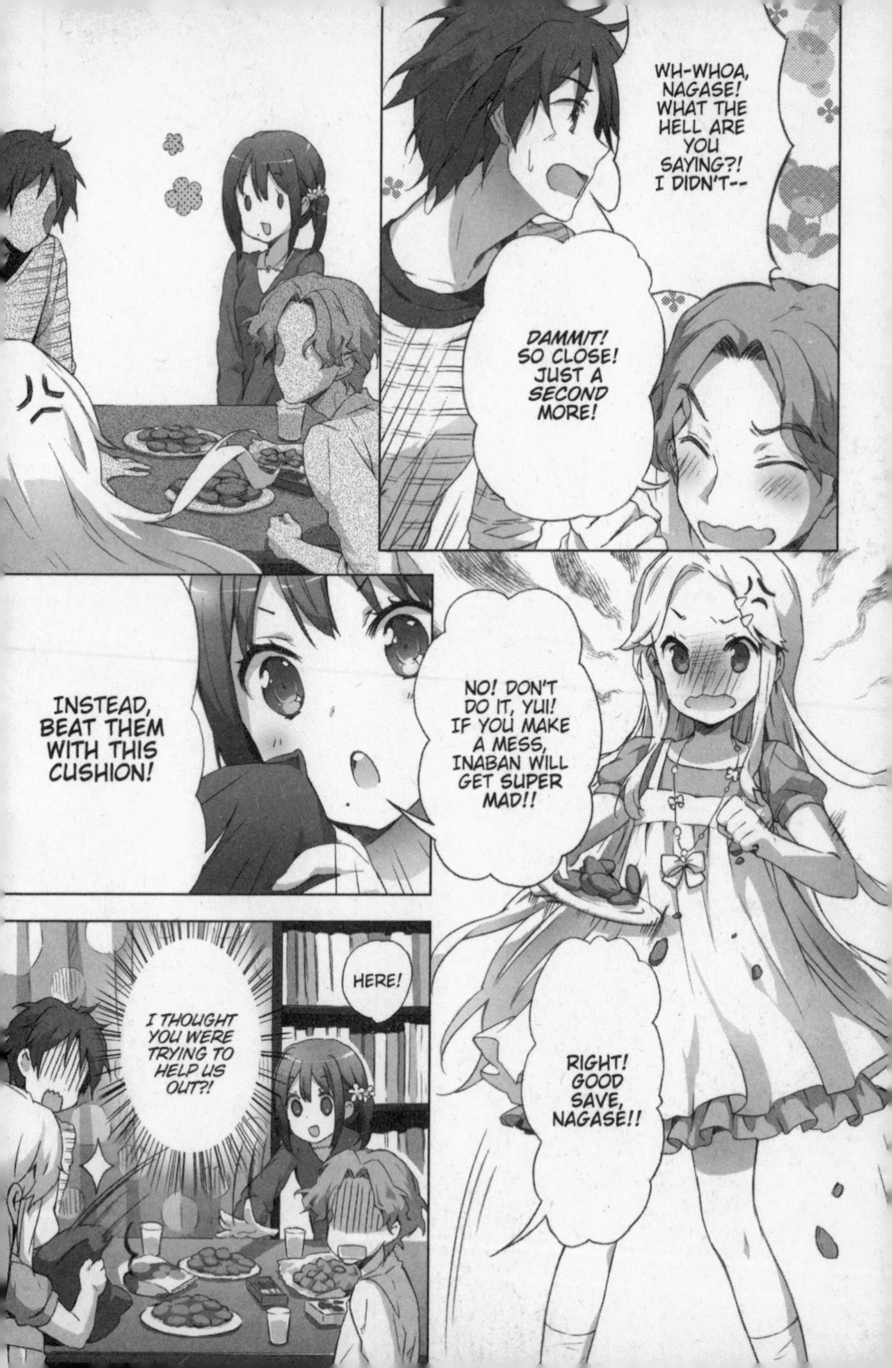
WH-WHOA, NAGASE! WHAT THE HELL ARE YOU SAYING?! I DIDN'T--
DAMMIT! SO CLOSE! JUST A SECOND MORE!
NO! DON'T DO IT, YUI! IF YOU MAKE A MESS, INABAN WILL GET SUPER MAD!!
RIGHT! GOOD SAVE, NAGASE!!
INSTEAD, BEAT THEM WITH THIS CUSHION!
HERE!
I THOUGHT YOU WERE TRYING TO HELP US OUT?!

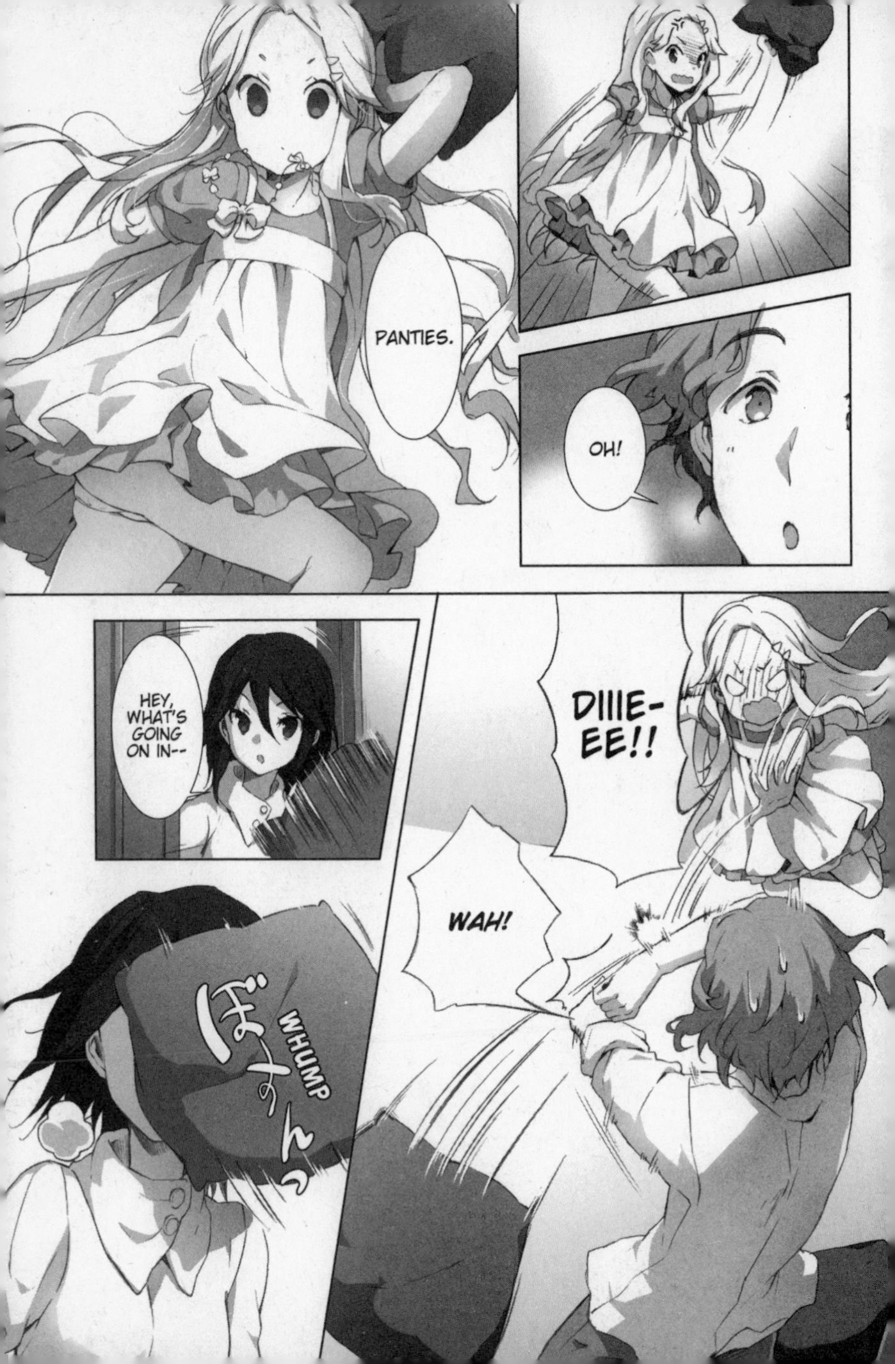
OH!
PANTIES.
DIIIE-EE!!
WAH!
HEY, WHAT'S GOING ON IN--
WHUMP
ぼふんっ

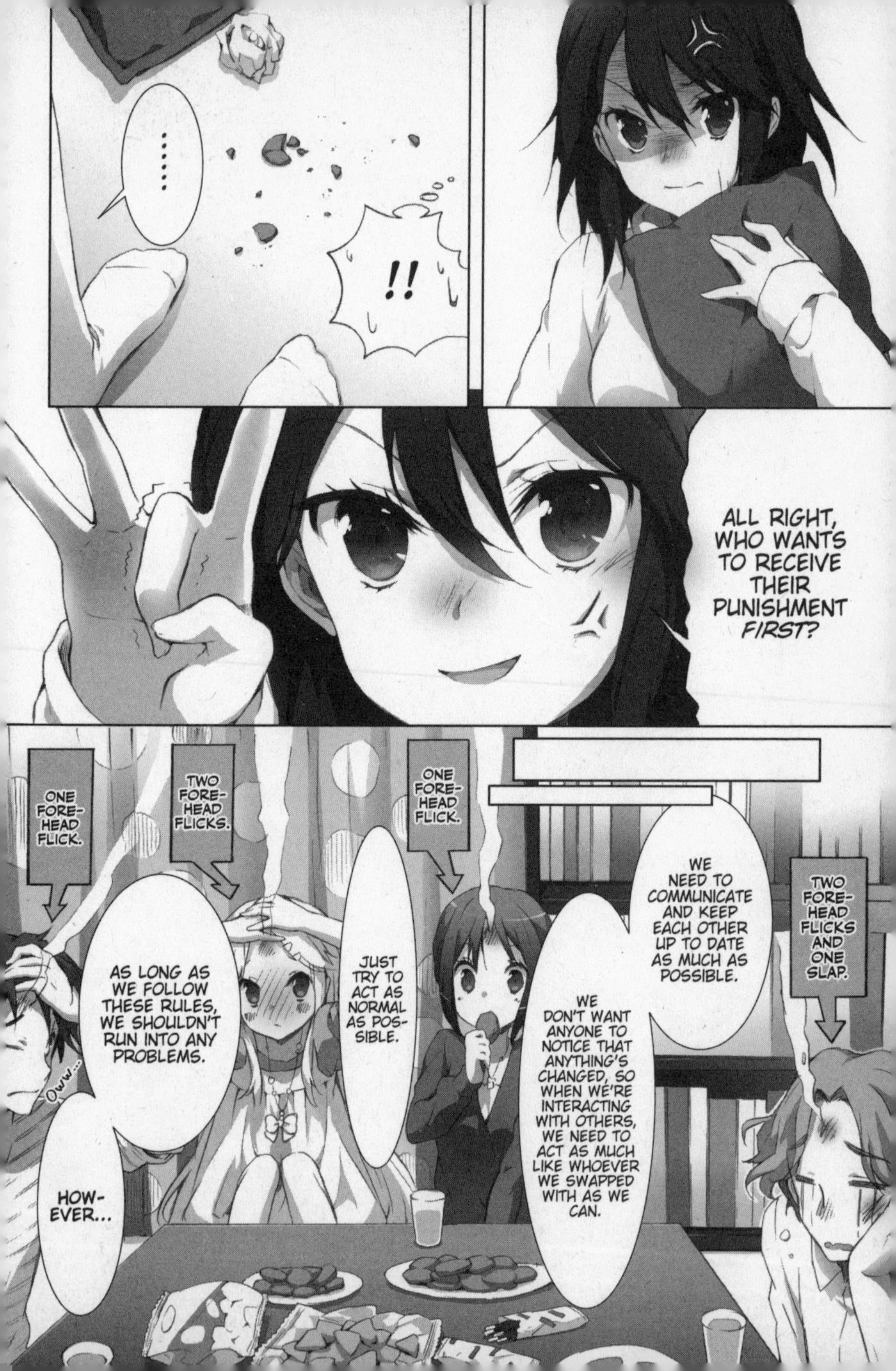
......
!!
ALL RIGHT, WHO WANTS TO RECEIVE THEIR PUNISHMENT *FIRST?*
TWO FORE-HEAD FLICKS AND ONE SLAP.
WE NEED TO COMMUNICATE AND KEEP EACH OTHER UP TO DATE AS MUCH AS POSSIBLE.
WE DON'T WANT ANYONE TO NOTICE THAT ANYTHING'S CHANGED, SO WHEN WE'RE INTERACTING WITH OTHERS, WE NEED TO ACT AS MUCH LIKE WHOEVER WE SWAPPED WITH AS WE CAN.
ONE FORE-HEAD FLICK.
JUST TRY TO ACT AS NORMAL AS POS-SIBLE.
TWO FORE-HEAD FLICKS.
AS LONG AS WE FOLLOW THESE RULES, WE SHOULDN'T RUN INTO ANY PROBLEMS.
ONE FORE-HEAD FLICK.
OWW...
HOW-EVER...

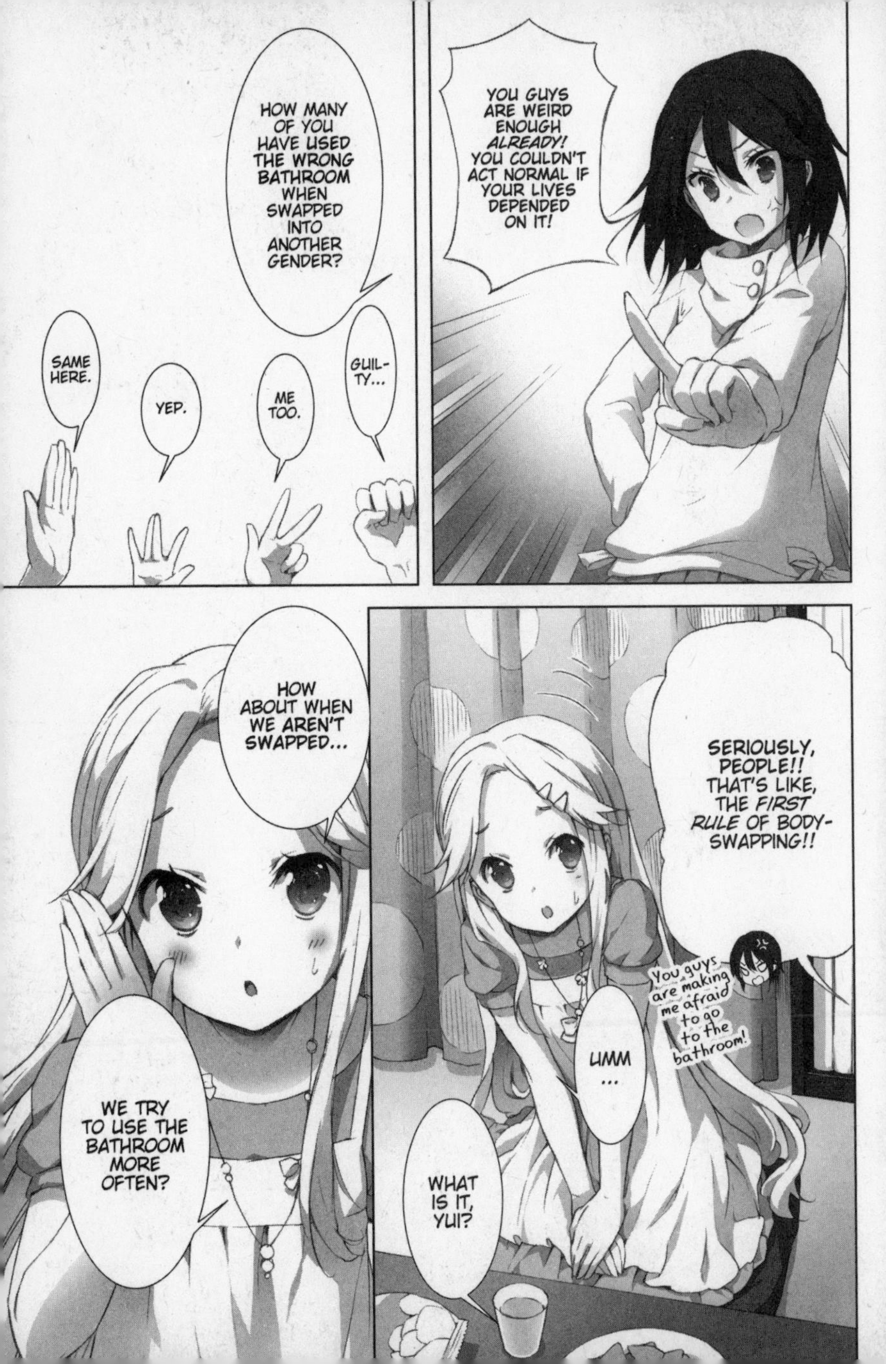
YOU GUYS ARE WEIRD ENOUGH *ALREADY!* YOU COULDN'T ACT NORMAL IF YOUR LIVES DEPENDED ON IT!
HOW MANY OF YOU HAVE USED THE WRONG BATHROOM WHEN SWAPPED INTO ANOTHER GENDER?
GUIL-TY...
ME TOO.
YEP.
SAME HERE.
SERIOUSLY, PEOPLE!! THAT'S LIKE, THE *FIRST RULE* OF BODY-SWAPPING!!
You guys are making me afraid to go to the bathroom!
UMM...
WHAT IS IT, YUI?
HOW ABOUT WHEN WE AREN'T SWAPPED...
WE TRY TO USE THE BATHROOM MORE OFTEN?

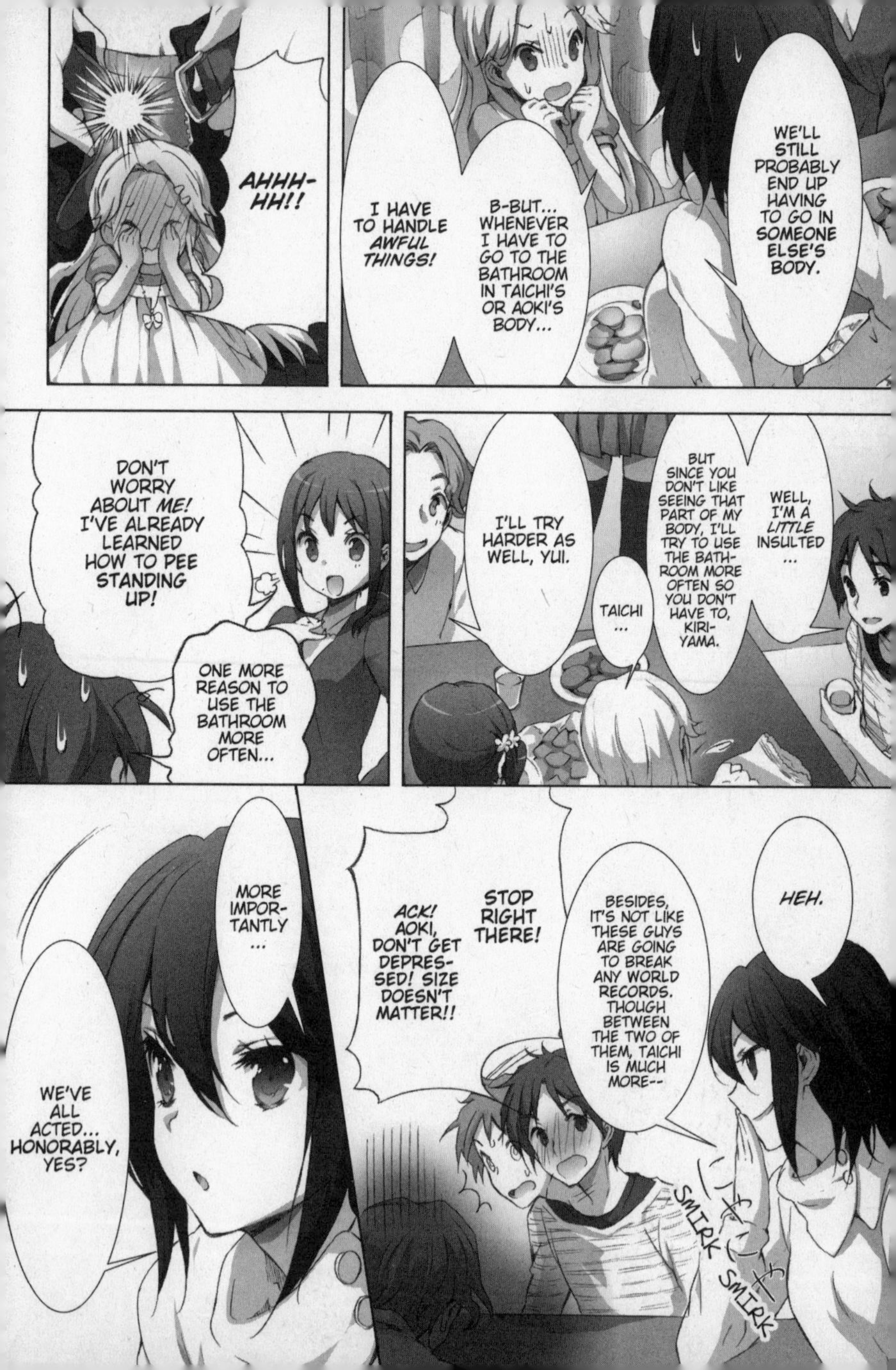
WE'LL STILL PROBABLY END UP HAVING TO GO IN SOMEONE ELSE'S BODY.
B-BUT... WHENEVER I HAVE TO GO TO THE BATHROOM IN TAICHI'S OR AOKI'S BODY...
I HAVE TO HANDLE *AWFUL THINGS!*
AHHHH-HH!!
WELL, I'M A *LITTLE* INSULTED ...
BUT SINCE YOU DON'T LIKE SEEING THAT PART OF MY BODY, I'LL TRY TO USE THE BATH-ROOM MORE OFTEN SO YOU DON'T HAVE TO, KIRI-YAMA.
TAICHI ...
I'LL TRY HARDER AS WELL, YUI.
DON'T WORRY ABOUT *ME!* I'VE ALREADY LEARNED HOW TO PEE STANDING UP!
ONE MORE REASON TO USE THE BATHROOM MORE OFTEN...
HEH.
BESIDES, IT'S NOT LIKE THESE GUYS ARE GOING TO BREAK ANY WORLD RECORDS. THOUGH BETWEEN THE TWO OF THEM, TAICHI IS MUCH MORE--
SMIRK SMIRK
STOP RIGHT THERE!
ACK! AOKI, DON'T GET DEPRES-SED! SIZE DOESN'T MATTER!!
MORE IMPOR-TANTLY ...
WE'VE ALL ACTED... HONORABLY, YES?

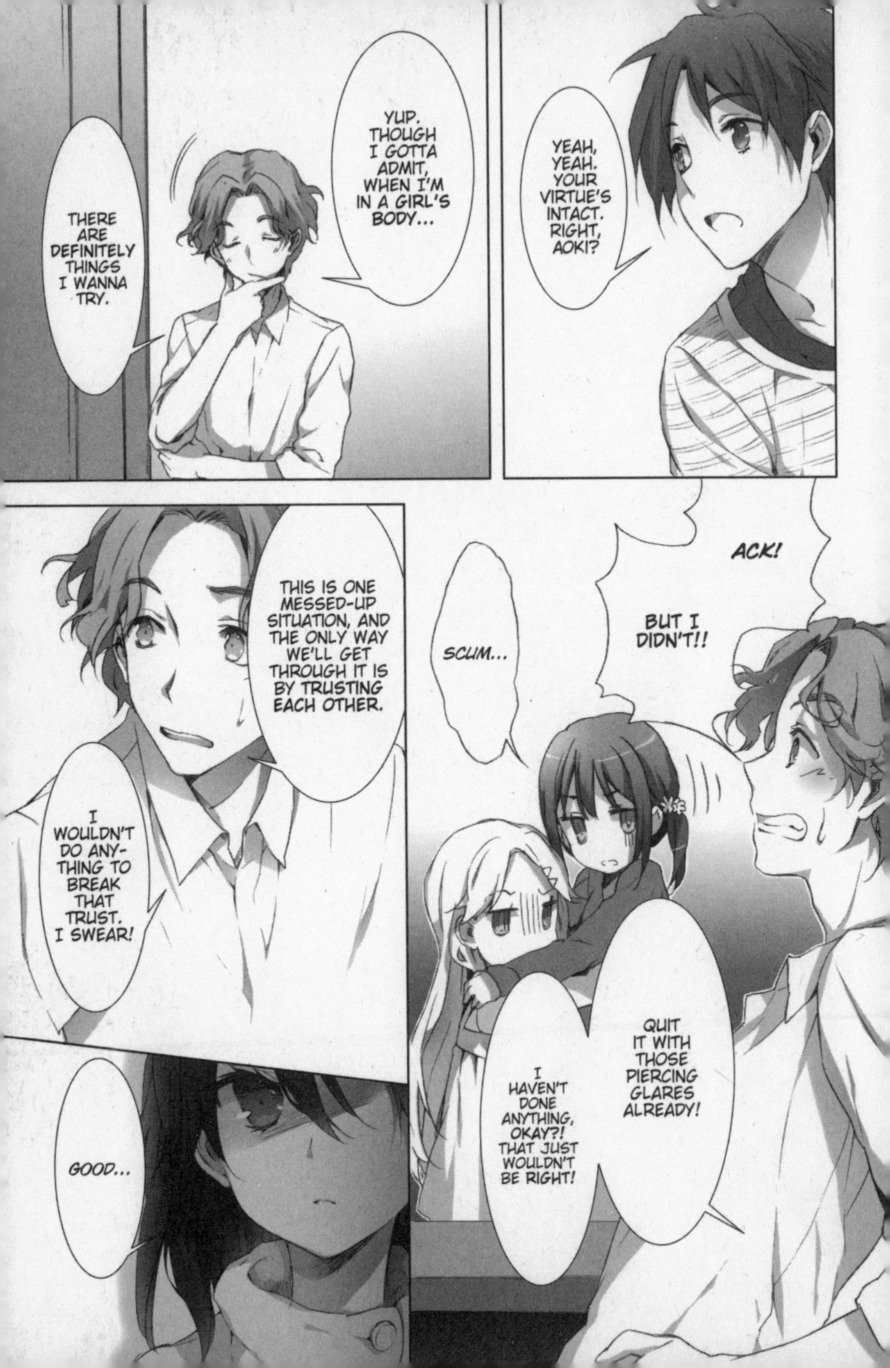
YEAH, YEAH. YOUR VIRTUE'S INTACT. RIGHT, AOKI?
YUP. THOUGH I GOTTA ADMIT, WHEN I'M IN A GIRL'S BODY...
THERE ARE DEFINITELY THINGS I WANNA TRY.
ACK!
BUT I DIDN'T!!
SCUM...
QUIT IT WITH THOSE PIERCING GLARES ALREADY!
I HAVEN'T DONE ANYTHING, OKAY?! THAT JUST WOULDN'T BE RIGHT!
THIS IS ONE MESSED-UP SITUATION, AND THE ONLY WAY WE'LL GET THROUGH IT IS BY TRUSTING EACH OTHER.
I WOULDN'T DO ANY-THING TO BREAK THAT TRUST. I SWEAR!
GOOD...

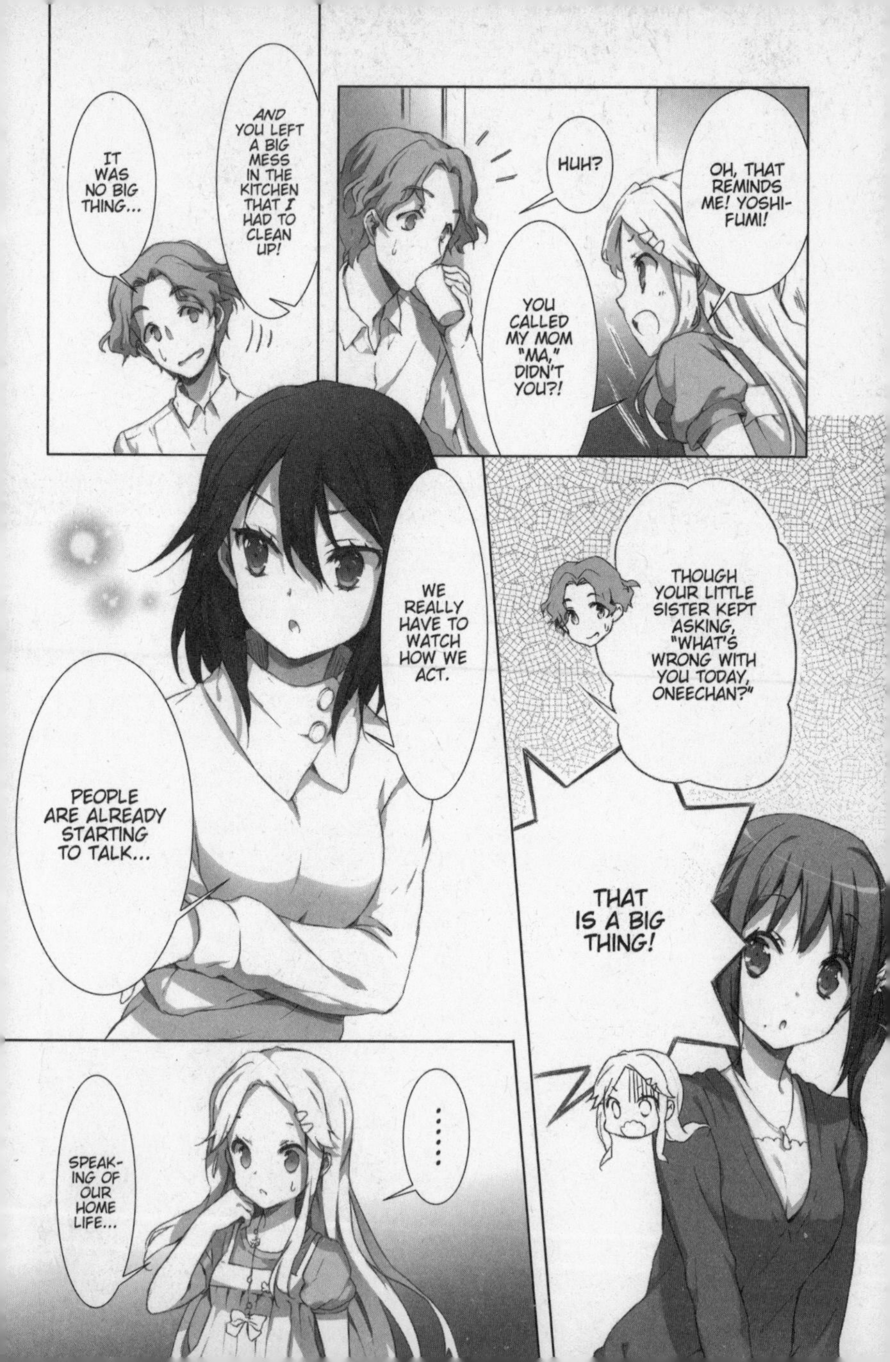
OH, THAT REMINDS ME! YOSHI-FUMI!
HUH?
YOU CALLED MY MOM "MA," DIDN'T YOU?!
AND YOU LEFT A BIG MESS IN THE KITCHEN THAT *I* HAD TO CLEAN UP!
IT WAS NO BIG THING...
THOUGH YOUR LITTLE SISTER KEPT ASKING, "WHAT'S WRONG WITH YOU TODAY, ONEECHAN?"
THAT IS A BIG THING!
WE REALLY HAVE TO WATCH HOW WE ACT.
PEOPLE ARE ALREADY STARTING TO TALK...
......
SPEAK-ING OF OUR HOME LIFE...

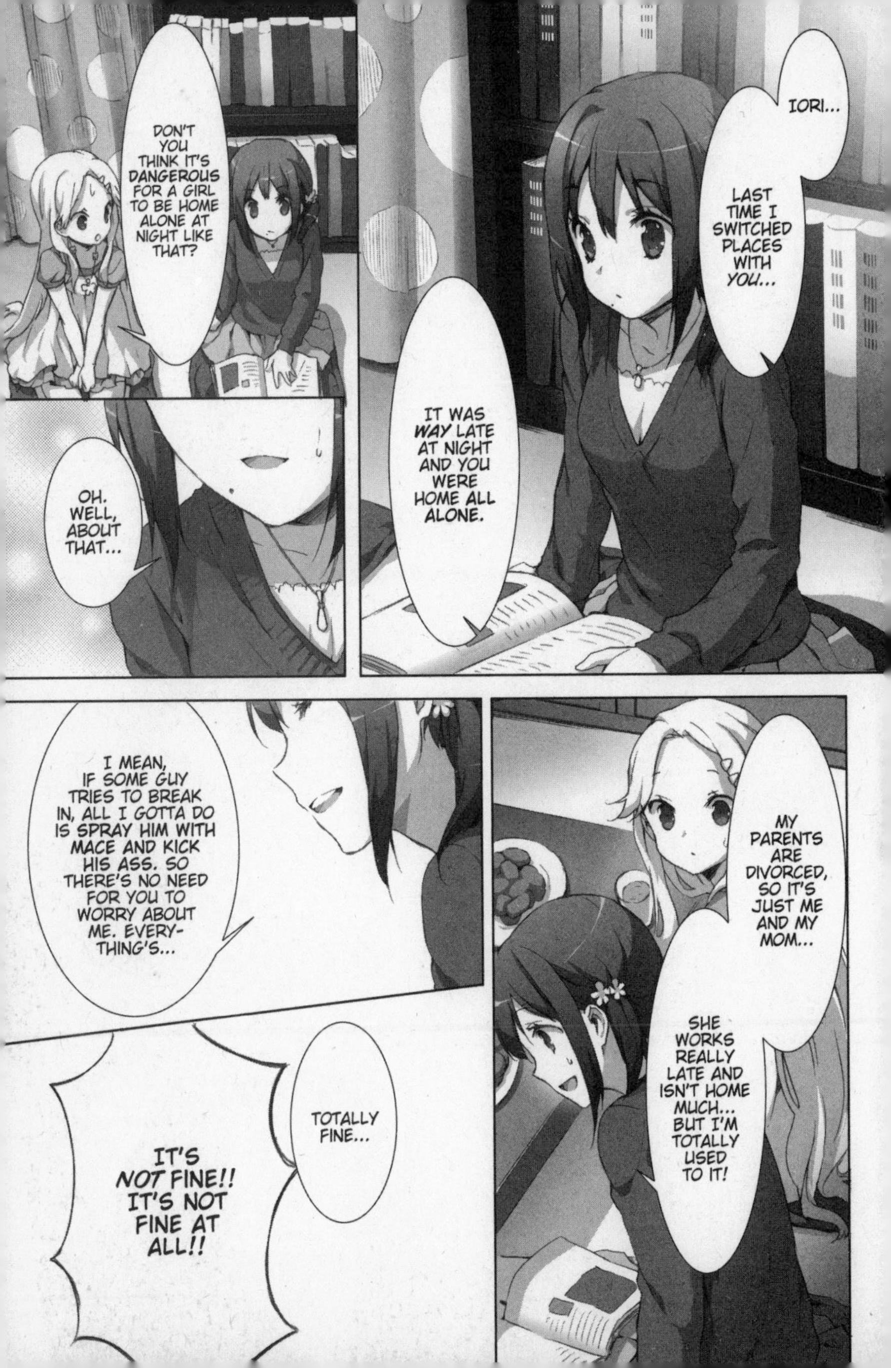
IORI...
LAST TIME I SWITCHED PLACES WITH *YOU*...
IT WAS *WAY* LATE AT NIGHT AND YOU WERE HOME ALL ALONE.
DON'T YOU THINK IT'S DANGEROUS FOR A GIRL TO BE HOME ALONE AT NIGHT LIKE THAT?
OH. WELL, ABOUT THAT...
MY PARENTS ARE DIVORCED, SO IT'S JUST ME AND MY MOM...
SHE WORKS REALLY LATE AND ISN'T HOME MUCH... BUT I'M TOTALLY USED TO IT!
I MEAN, IF SOME GUY TRIES TO BREAK IN, ALL I GOTTA DO IS SPRAY HIM WITH MACE AND KICK HIS ASS. SO THERE'S NO NEED FOR YOU TO WORRY ABOUT ME. EVERY-THING'S...
TOTALLY FINE...
IT'S *NOT* FINE!! IT'S NOT FINE AT ALL!!

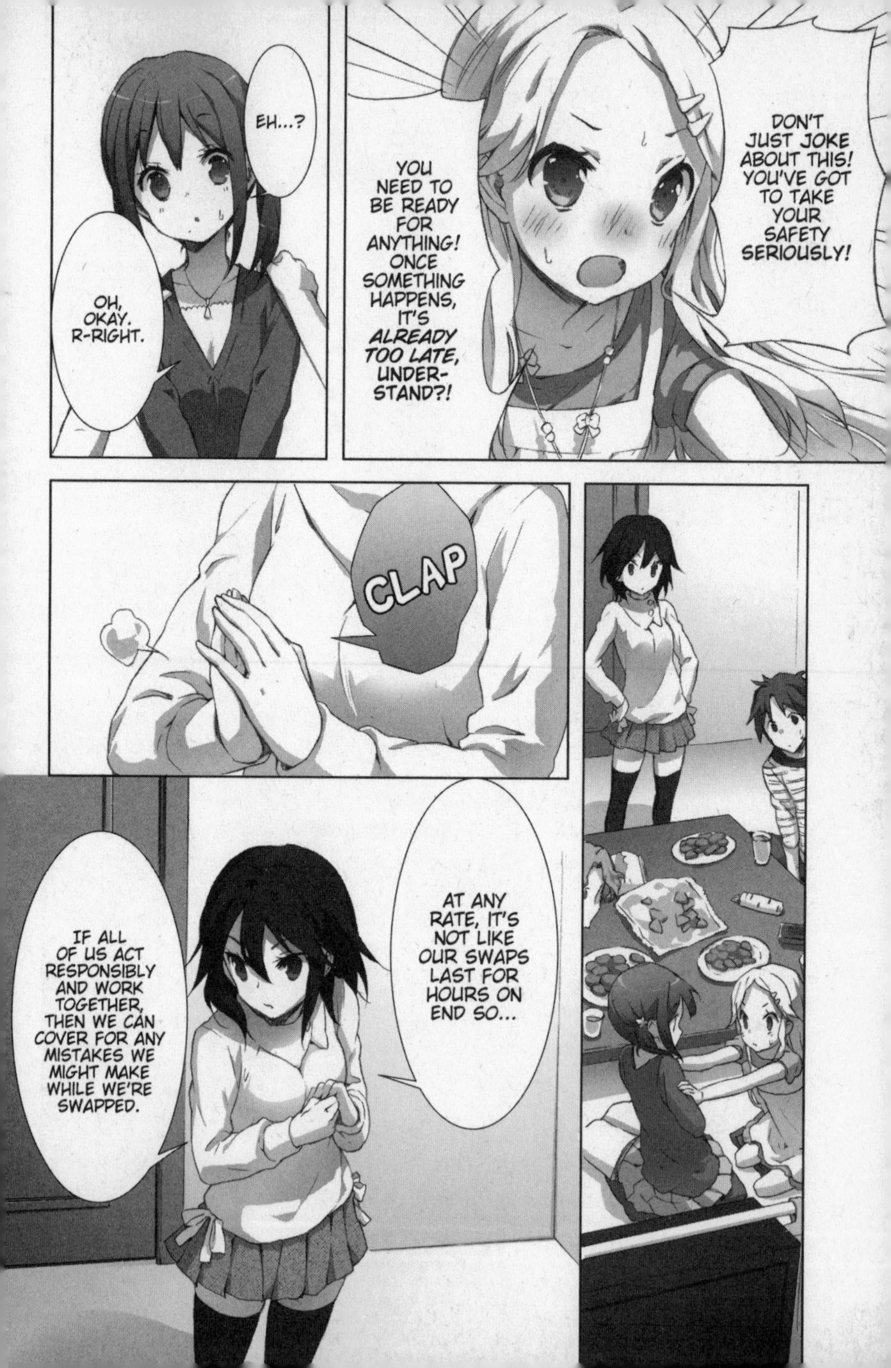
DON'T JUST JOKE ABOUT THIS! YOU'VE GOT TO TAKE YOUR SAFETY SERIOUSLY!
YOU NEED TO BE READY FOR ANYTHING! ONCE SOMETHING HAPPENS, IT'S *ALREADY TOO LATE*, UNDER-STAND?!
EH...?
OH, OKAY. R-RIGHT.
CLAP
AT ANY RATE, IT'S NOT LIKE OUR SWAPS LAST FOR HOURS ON END SO...
IF ALL OF US ACT RESPONSIBLY AND WORK TOGETHER, THEN WE CAN COVER FOR ANY MISTAKES WE MIGHT MAKE WHILE WE'RE SWAPPED.

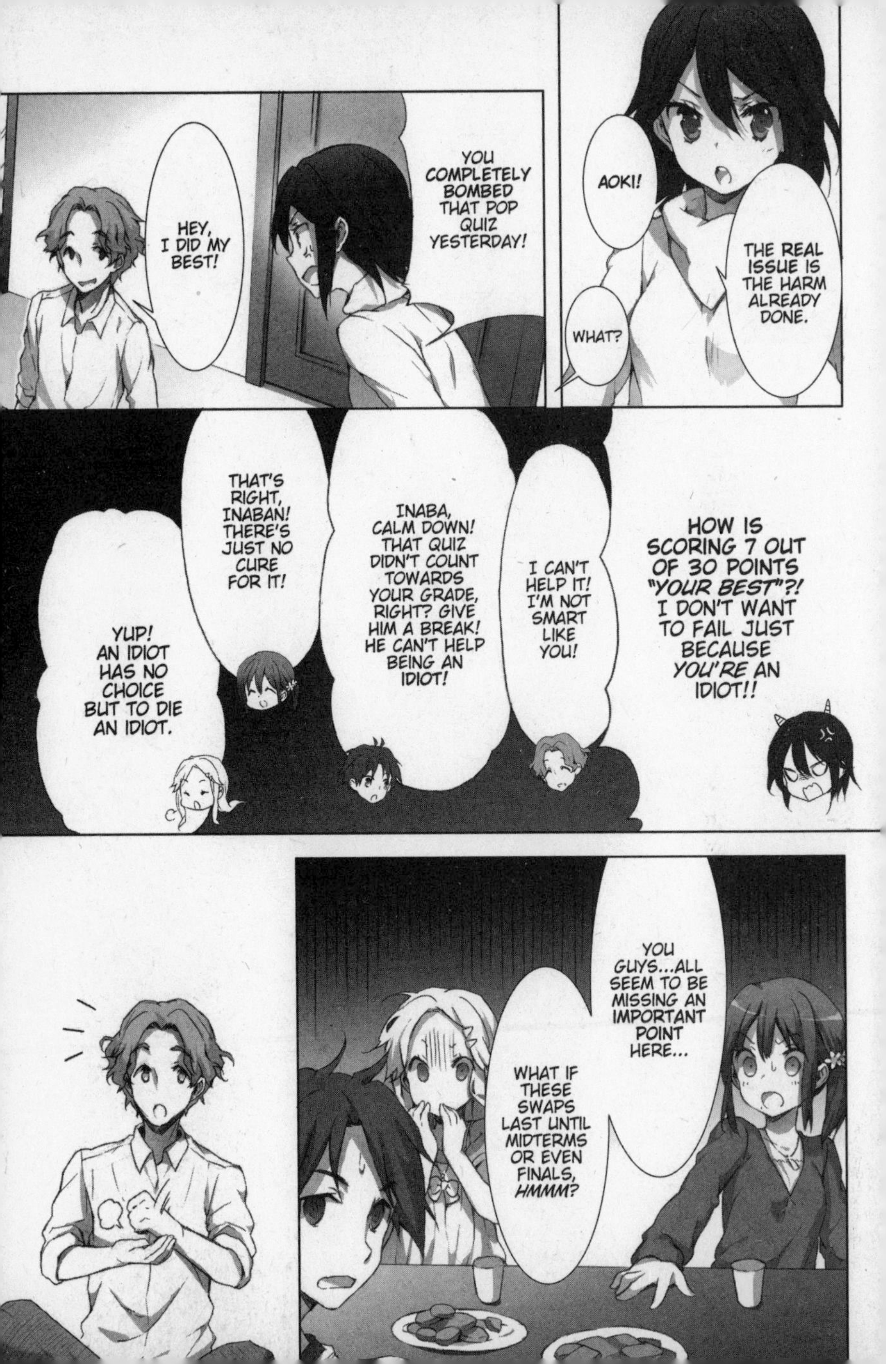
AOKI!
THE REAL ISSUE IS THE HARM ALREADY DONE.
WHAT?
YOU COMPLETELY BOMBED THAT POP QUIZ YESTERDAY!
HEY, I DID MY BEST!
HOW IS SCORING 7 OUT OF 30 POINTS *"YOUR BEST"*?! I DON'T WANT TO FAIL JUST BECAUSE *YOU'RE* AN IDIOT!!
I CAN'T HELP IT! I'M NOT SMART LIKE YOU!
INABA, CALM DOWN! THAT QUIZ DIDN'T COUNT TOWARDS YOUR GRADE, RIGHT? GIVE HIM A BREAK! HE CAN'T HELP BEING AN IDIOT!
THAT'S RIGHT, INABAN! THERE'S JUST NO CURE FOR IT!
YUP! AN IDIOT HAS NO CHOICE BUT TO DIE AN IDIOT.
YOU GUYS...ALL SEEM TO BE MISSING AN IMPORTANT POINT HERE...
WHAT IF THESE SWAPS LAST UNTIL MIDTERMS OR EVEN FINALS, *HMMM*?

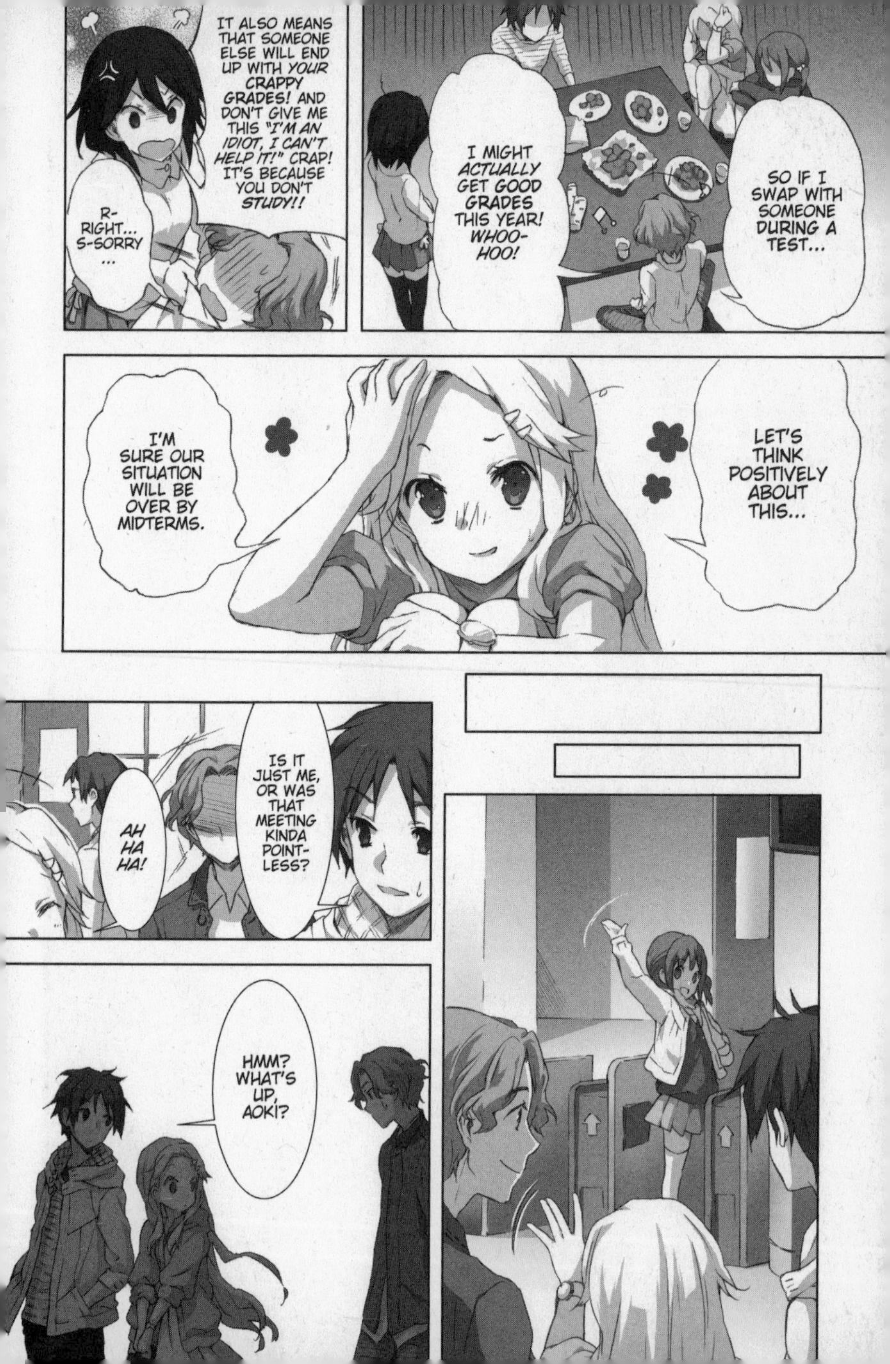
SO IF I SWAP WITH SOMEONE DURING A TEST...
I MIGHT *ACTUALLY* GET GOOD GRADES THIS YEAR! *WHOO-HOO!*
IT ALSO MEANS THAT SOMEONE ELSE WILL END UP WITH *YOUR* CRAPPY GRADES! AND DON'T GIVE ME THIS *"I'M AN IDIOT, I CAN'T HELP IT!"* CRAP! IT'S BECAUSE YOU DON'T *STUDY!!*
R-RIGHT... S-SORRY...
LET'S THINK POSITIVELY ABOUT THIS...
I'M SURE OUR SITUATION WILL BE OVER BY MIDTERMS.
IS IT JUST ME, OR WAS THAT MEETING KINDA POINTLESS?
AH HA HA!
HMM? WHAT'S UP, AOKI?

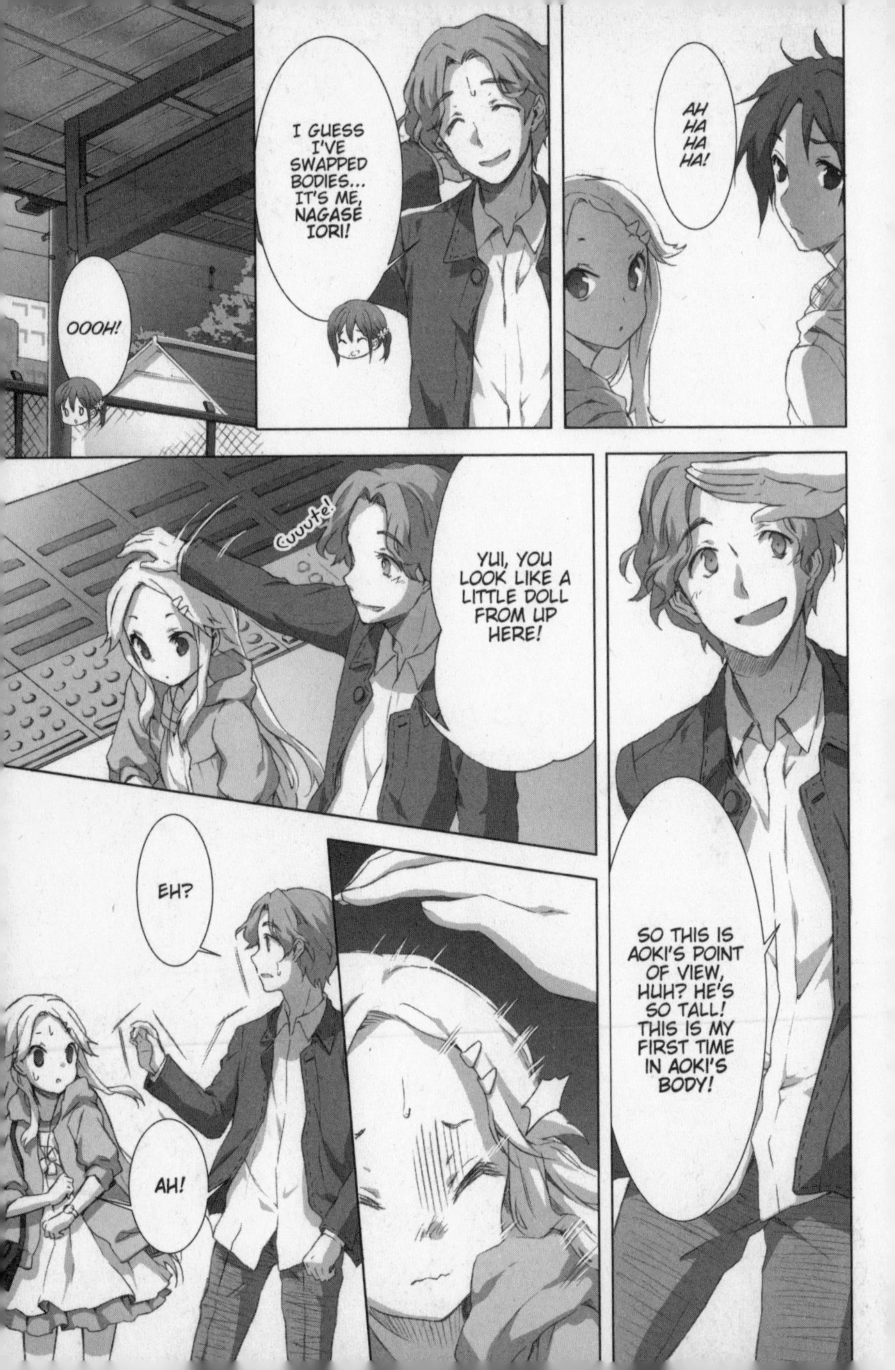
AH HA HA HA!
I GUESS I'VE SWAPPED BODIES... IT'S ME, NAGASE IORI!
OOOH!
SO THIS IS AOKI'S POINT OF VIEW, HUH? HE'S SO TALL! THIS IS MY FIRST TIME IN AOKI'S BODY!
YUI, YOU LOOK LIKE A LITTLE DOLL FROM UP HERE!
Cuuute!
EH?
AH!

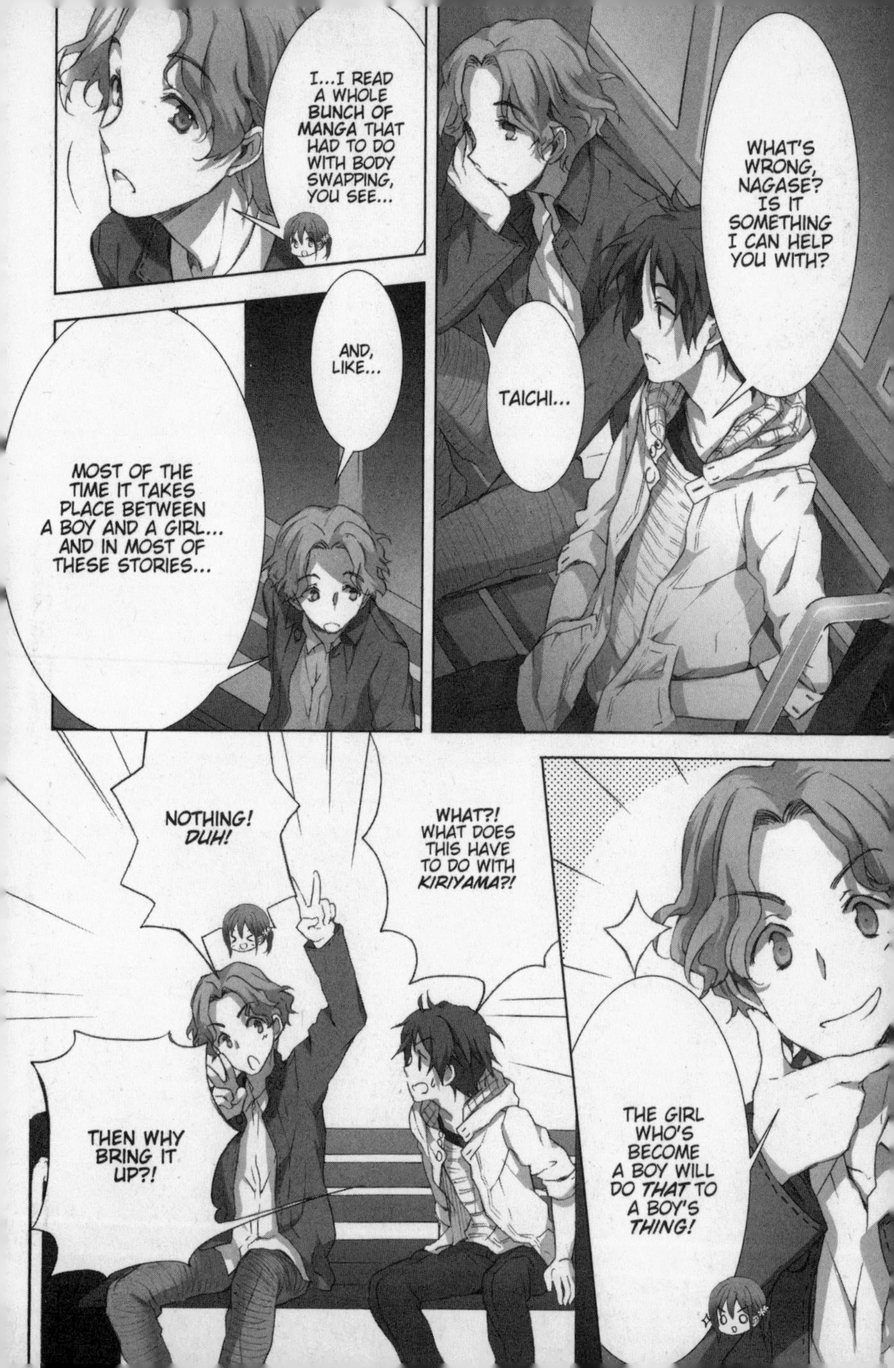
WHAT'S WRONG, NAGASE? IS IT SOMETHING I CAN HELP YOU WITH?
TAICHI...
I...I READ A WHOLE BUNCH OF MANGA THAT HAD TO DO WITH BODY SWAPPING, YOU SEE...
AND, LIKE...
MOST OF THE TIME IT TAKES PLACE BETWEEN A BOY AND A GIRL... AND IN MOST OF THESE STORIES...
THE GIRL WHO'S BECOME A BOY WILL DO *THAT* TO A BOY'S *THING*!
WHAT?! WHAT DOES THIS HAVE TO DO WITH *KIRIYAMA*?!
NOTHING! *DUH!*
THEN WHY BRING IT UP?!

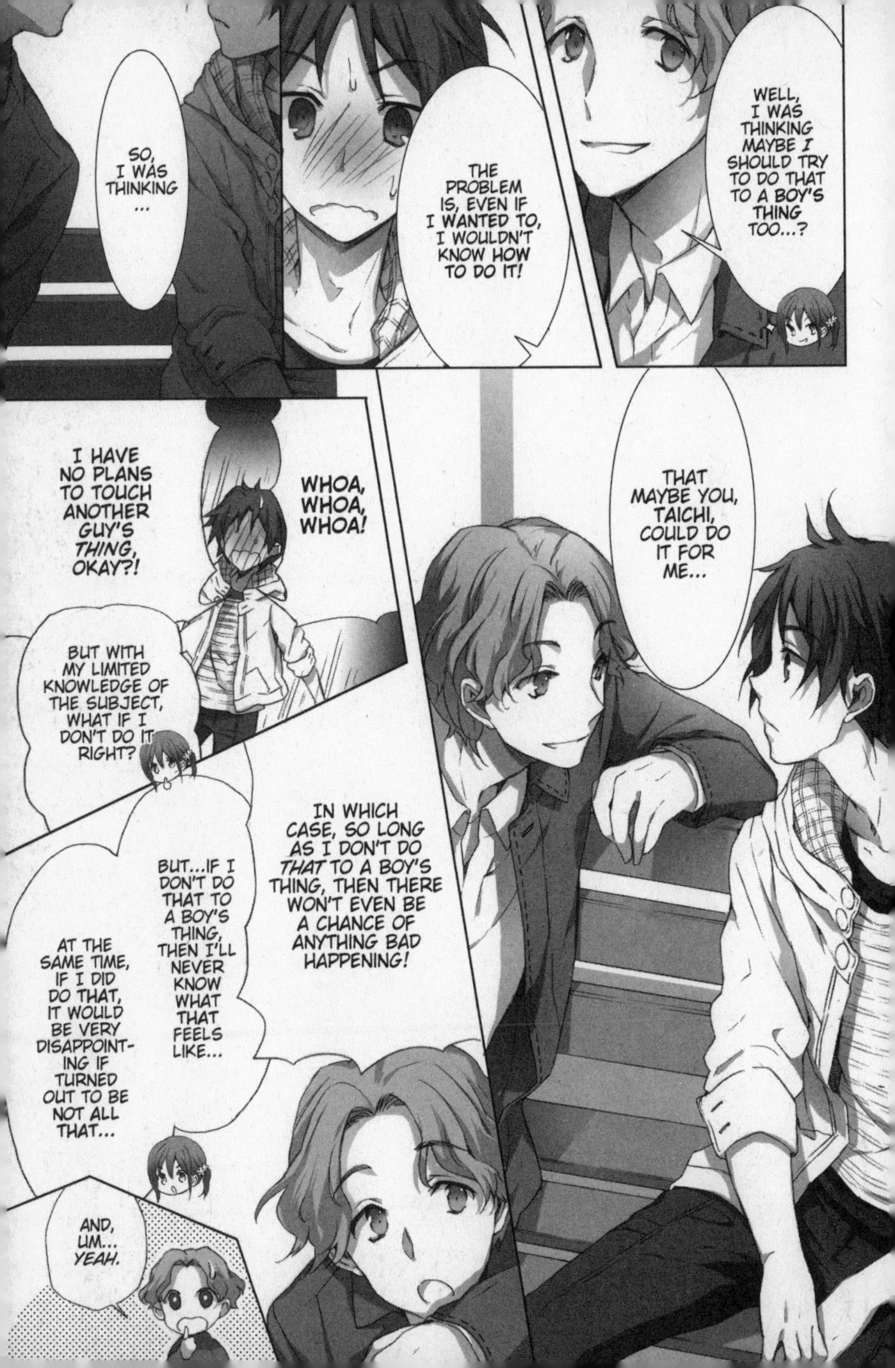
WELL, I WAS THINKING MAYBE *I* SHOULD TRY TO DO THAT TO A BOY'S THING TOO...?
THE PROBLEM IS, EVEN IF I WANTED TO, I WOULDN'T KNOW HOW TO DO IT!
SO, I WAS THINKING ...
THAT MAYBE YOU, TAICHI, COULD DO IT FOR ME...
WHOA, WHOA, WHOA!
I HAVE NO PLANS TO TOUCH ANOTHER GUY'S *THING*, OKAY?!
BUT WITH MY LIMITED KNOWLEDGE OF THE SUBJECT, WHAT IF I DON'T DO IT RIGHT?
IN WHICH CASE, SO LONG AS I DON'T DO *THAT* TO A BOY'S THING, THEN THERE WON'T EVEN BE A CHANCE OF ANYTHING BAD HAPPENING!
BUT...IF I DON'T DO THAT TO A BOY'S THING, THEN I'LL NEVER KNOW WHAT THAT FEELS LIKE...
AT THE SAME TIME, IF I DID DO THAT, IT WOULD BE VERY DISAPPOINT-ING IF TURNED OUT TO BE NOT ALL THAT...
AND, UM... *YEAH.*

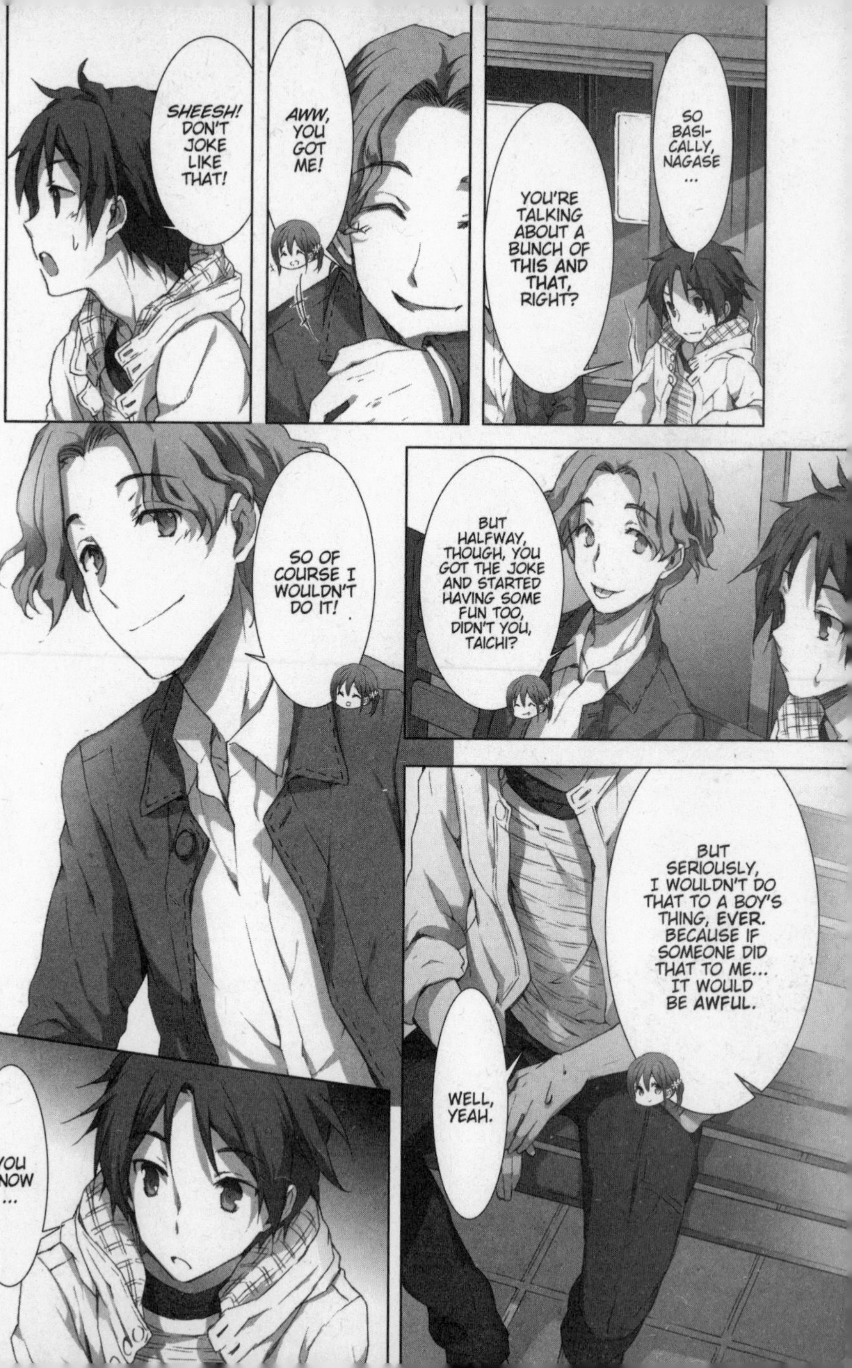
SO BASI-CALLY, NAGASE ...
YOU'RE TALKING ABOUT A BUNCH OF THIS AND THAT, RIGHT?
AWW, YOU GOT ME!
SHEESH! DON'T JOKE LIKE THAT!
BUT HALFWAY, THOUGH, YOU GOT THE JOKE AND STARTED HAVING SOME FUN TOO, DIDN'T YOU, TAICHI?
BUT SERIOUSLY, I WOULDN'T DO THAT TO A BOY'S THING, EVER. BECAUSE IF SOMEONE DID THAT TO ME... IT WOULD BE AWFUL.
WELL, YEAH.
SO OF COURSE I WOULDN'T DO IT!
YOU KNOW ...

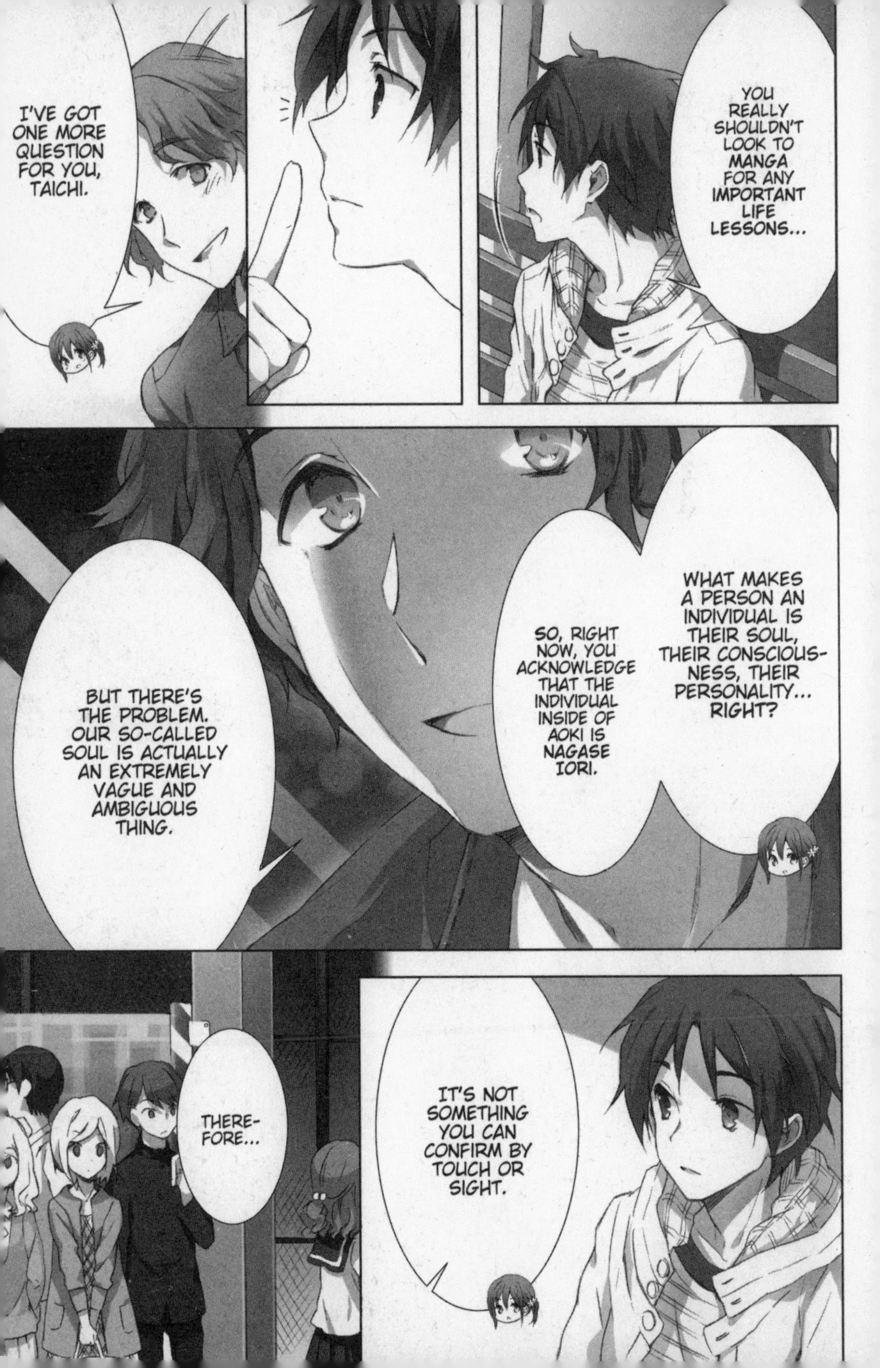
YOU REALLY SHOULDN'T LOOK TO MANGA FOR ANY IMPORTANT LIFE LESSONS...
I'VE GOT ONE MORE QUESTION FOR YOU, TAICHI.
WHAT MAKES A PERSON AN INDIVIDUAL IS THEIR SOUL, THEIR CONSCIOUS-NESS, THEIR PERSONALITY... RIGHT?
SO, RIGHT NOW, YOU ACKNOWLEDGE THAT THE INDIVIDUAL INSIDE OF AOKI IS NAGASE IORI.
BUT THERE'S THE PROBLEM. OUR SO-CALLED SOUL IS ACTUALLY AN EXTREMELY VAGUE AND AMBIGUOUS THING.
IT'S NOT SOMETHING YOU CAN CONFIRM BY TOUCH OR SIGHT.
THERE-FORE...

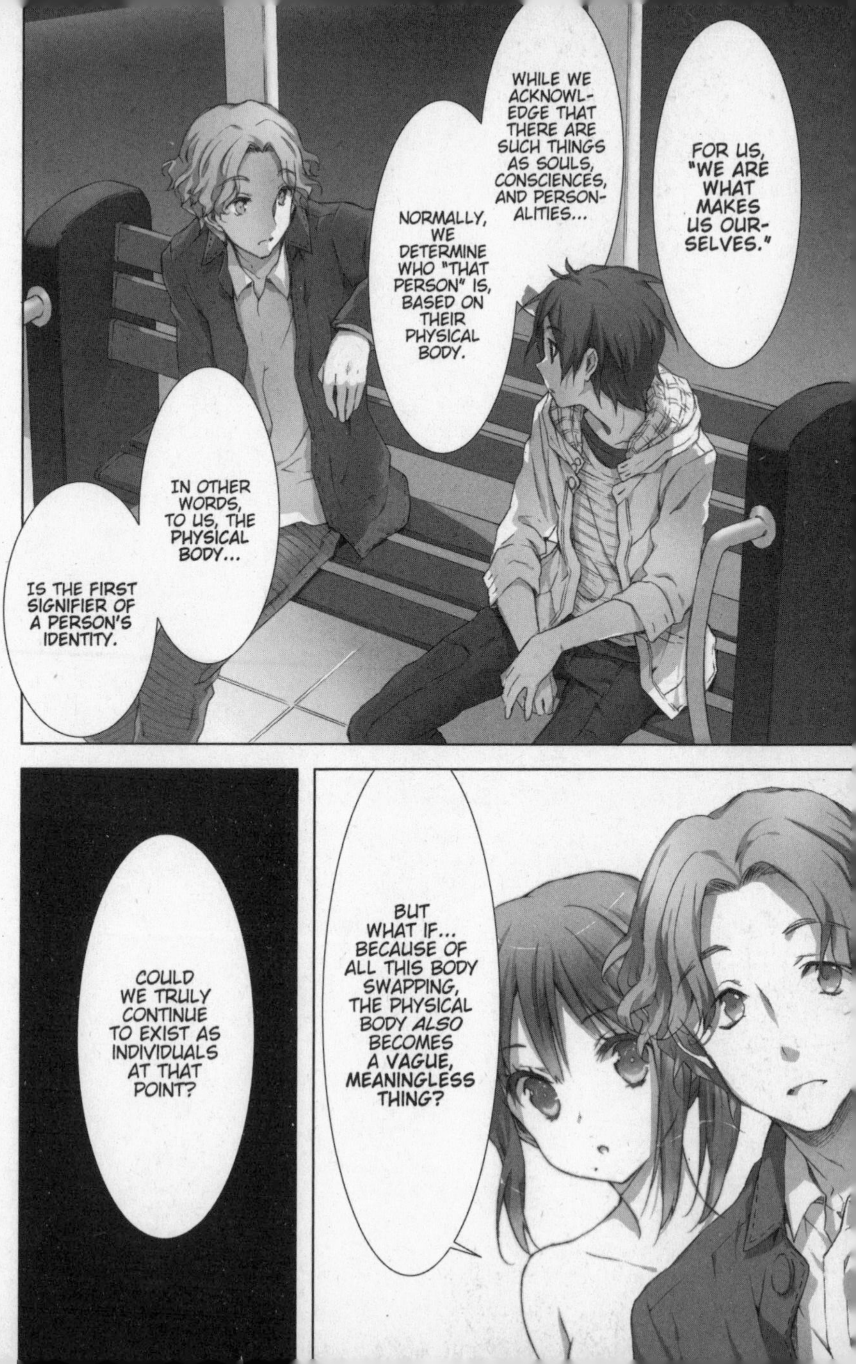
FOR US, "WE ARE WHAT MAKES US OURSELVES."
WHILE WE ACKNOWLEDGE THAT THERE ARE SUCH THINGS AS SOULS, CONSCIENCES, AND PERSONALITIES...
NORMALLY, WE DETERMINE WHO "THAT PERSON" IS, BASED ON THEIR PHYSICAL BODY.
IN OTHER WORDS, TO US, THE PHYSICAL BODY...
IS THE FIRST SIGNIFIER OF A PERSON'S IDENTITY.
BUT WHAT IF... BECAUSE OF ALL THIS BODY SWAPPING, THE PHYSICAL BODY *ALSO* BECOMES A VAGUE, MEANINGLESS THING?
COULD WE TRULY CONTINUE TO EXIST AS INDIVIDUALS AT THAT POINT?

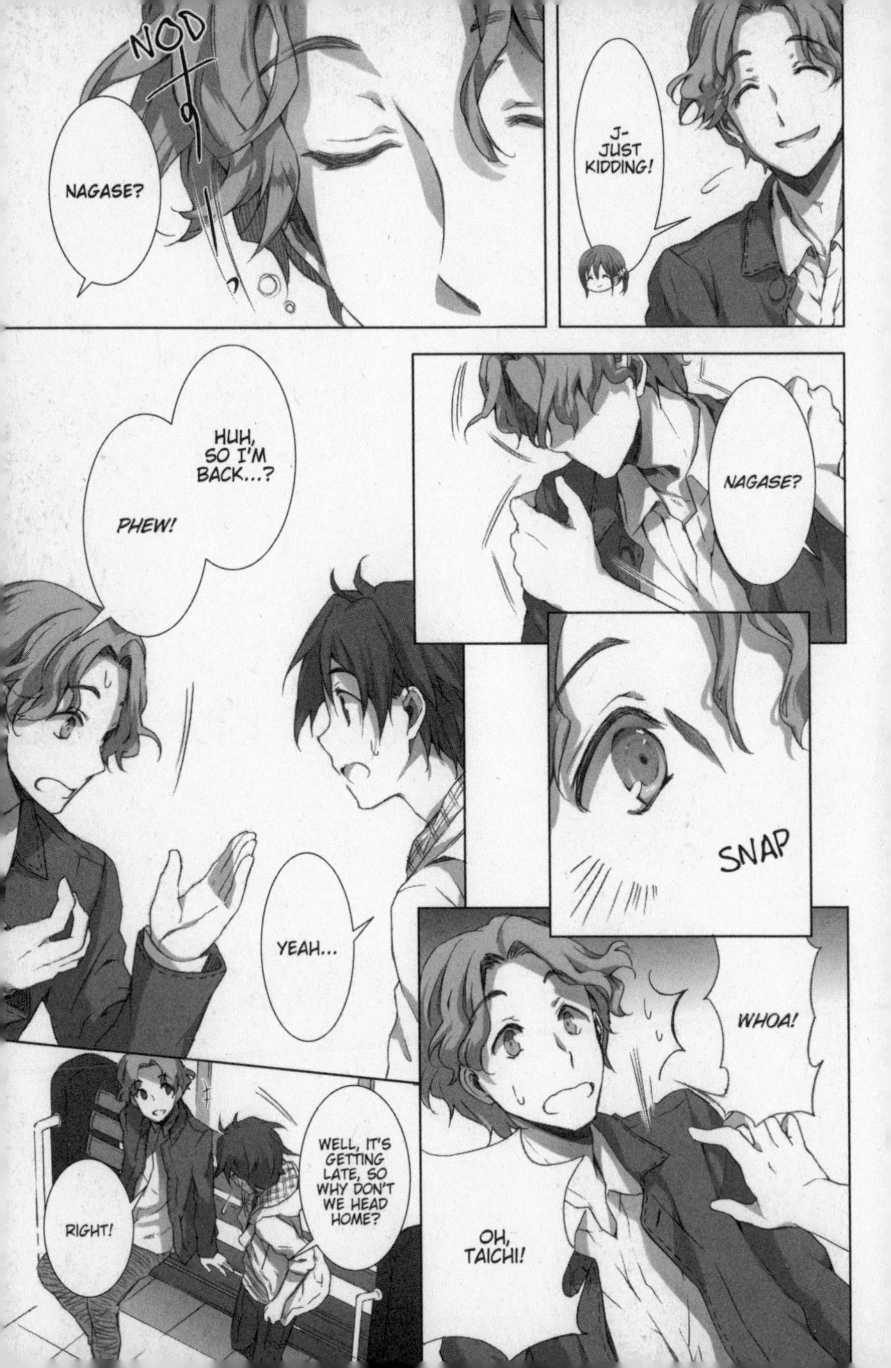
J-
JUST
KIDDING!
NOD
NAGASE?
NAGASE?
SNAP
WHOA!
OH,
TAICHI!
HUH,
SO I'M
BACK...?
PHEW!
YEAH...
WELL, IT'S
GETTING
LATE, SO
WHY DON'T
WE HEAD
HOME?
RIGHT!

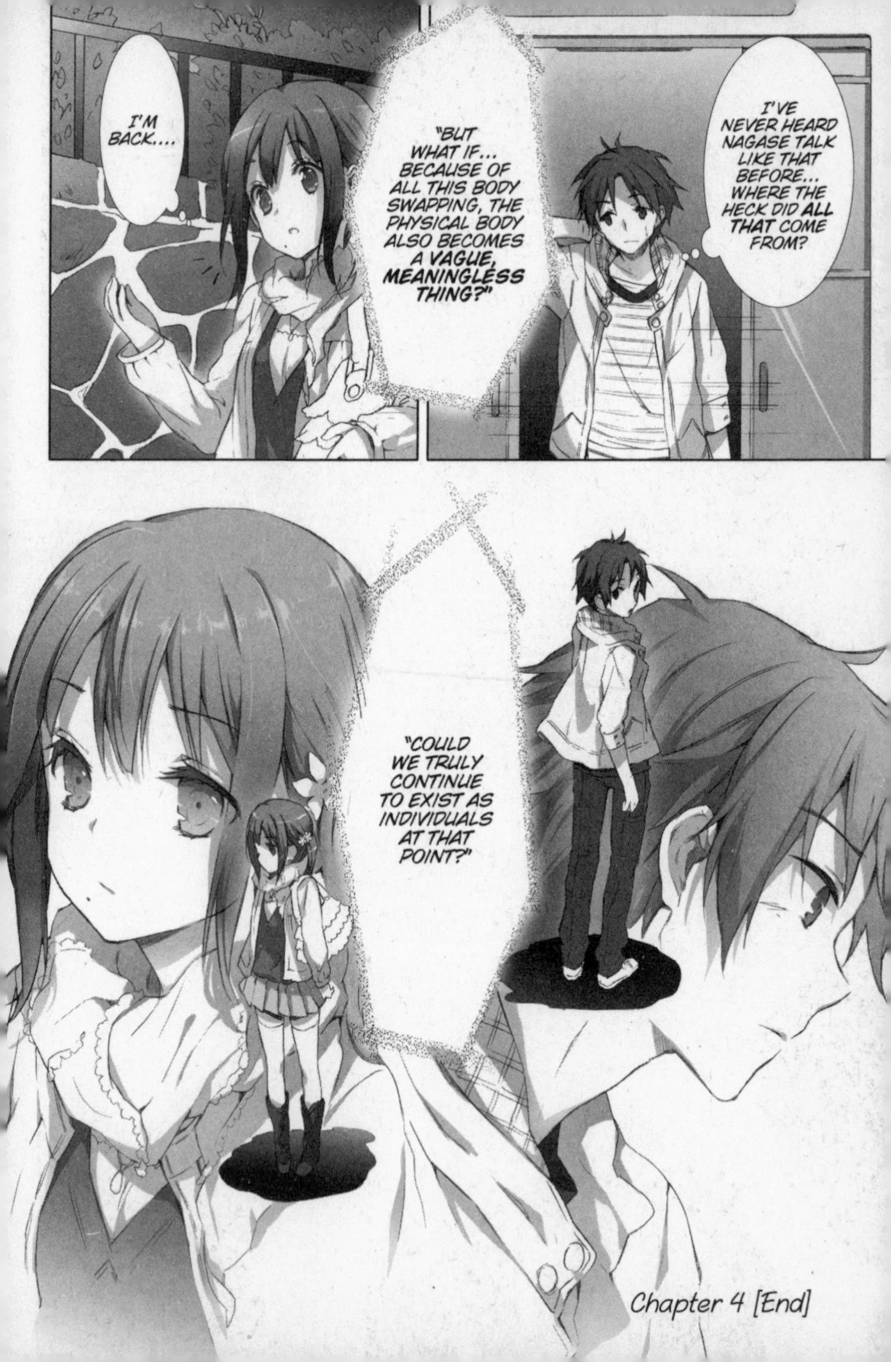
I'VE NEVER HEARD NAGASE TALK LIKE THAT BEFORE... WHERE THE HECK DID ALL THAT COME FROM?
"BUT WHAT IF... BECAUSE OF ALL THIS BODY SWAPPING, THE PHYSICAL BODY ALSO BECOMES A VAGUE, MEANINGLESS THING?"
I'M BACK....
"COULD WE TRULY CONTINUE TO EXIST AS INDIVIDUALS AT THAT POINT?"
Chapter 4 [End]

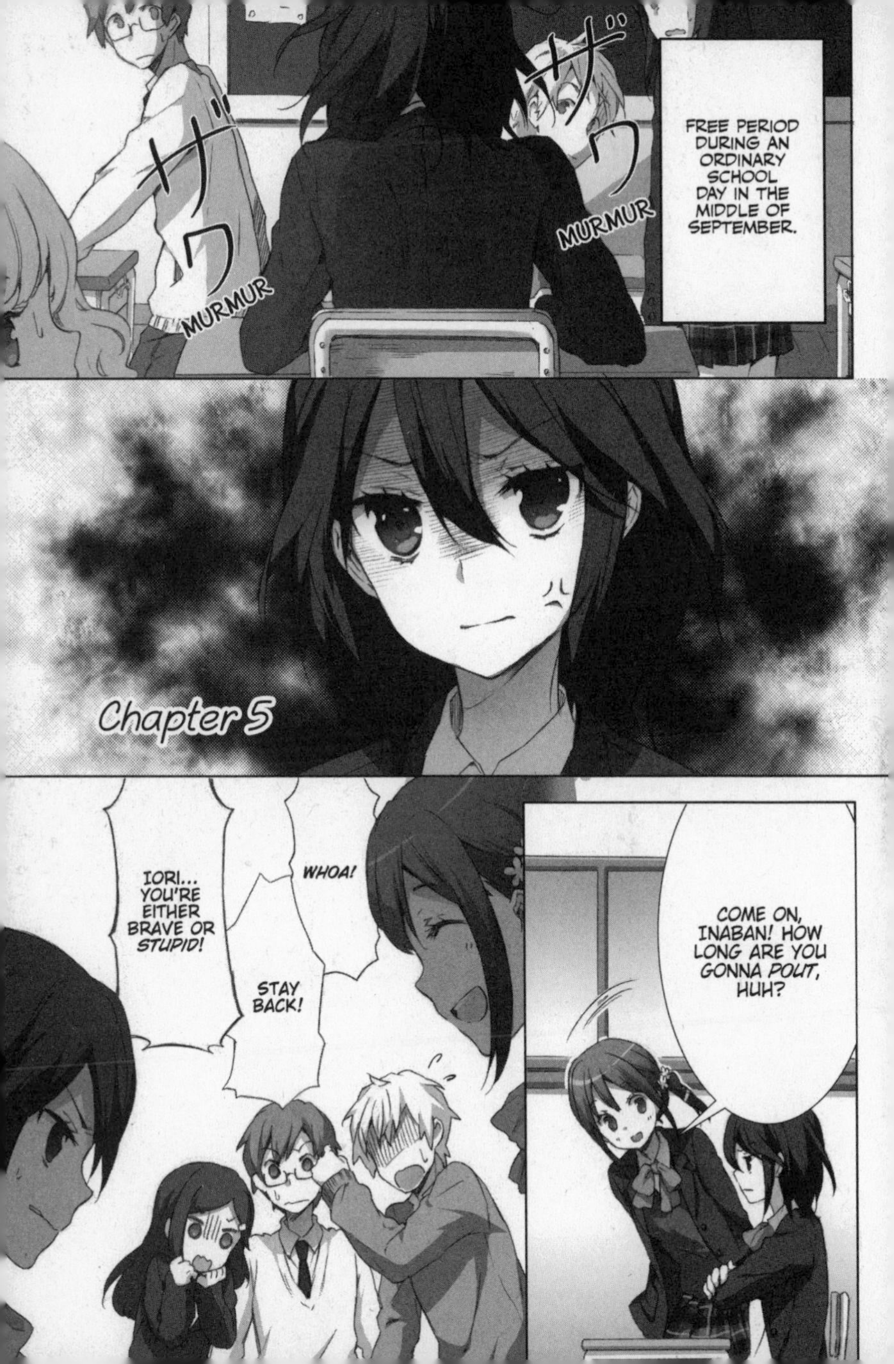

FREE PERIOD DURING AN ORDINARY SCHOOL DAY IN THE MIDDLE OF SEPTEMBER.
ザワ
MURMUR
ザワ
MURMUR
Chapter 5
COME ON, INABAN! HOW LONG ARE YOU GONNA *POUT*, HUH?
WHOA!
IORI... YOU'RE EITHER BRAVE OR *STUPID!*
STAY BACK!

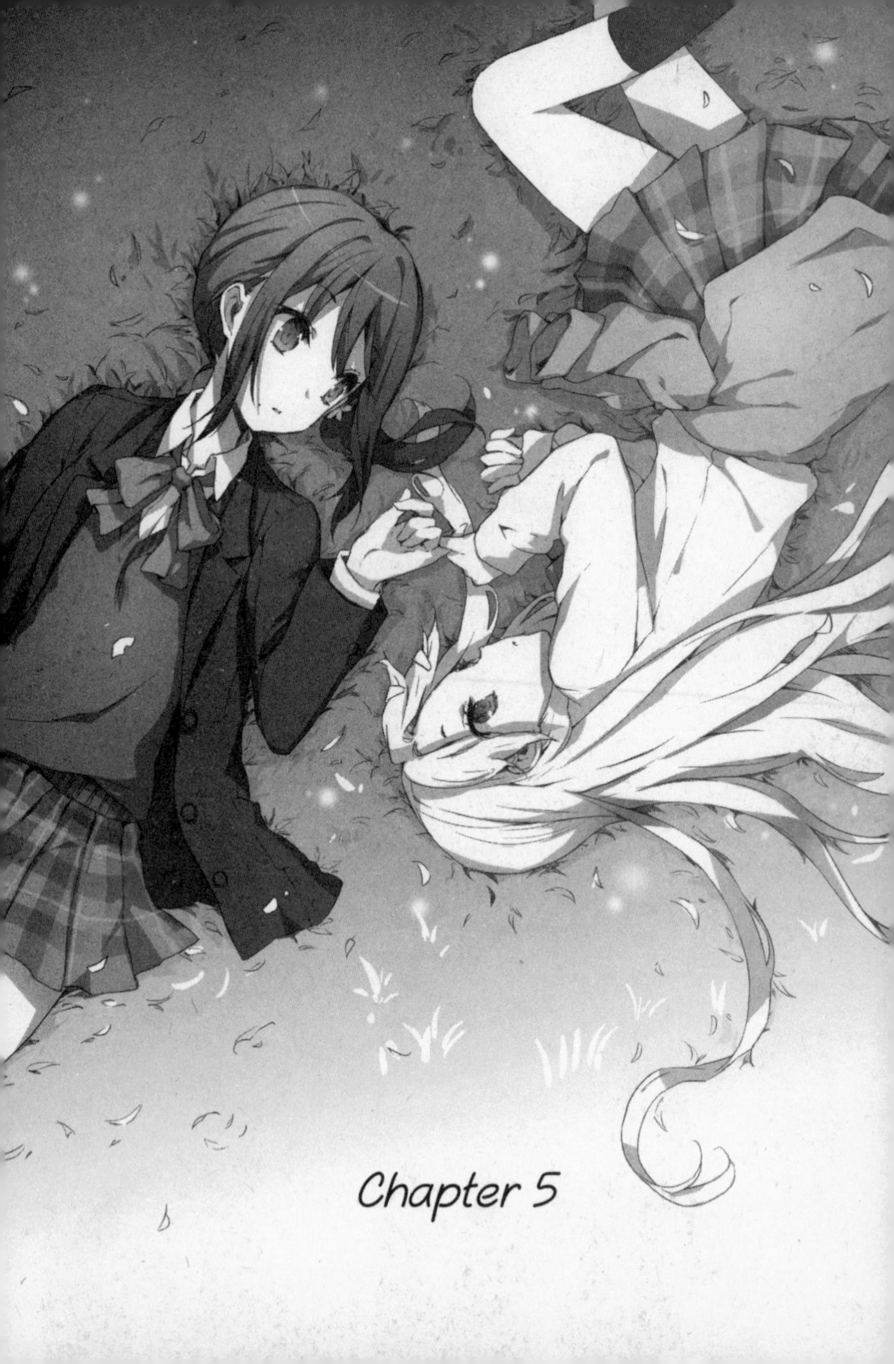
Chapter 5

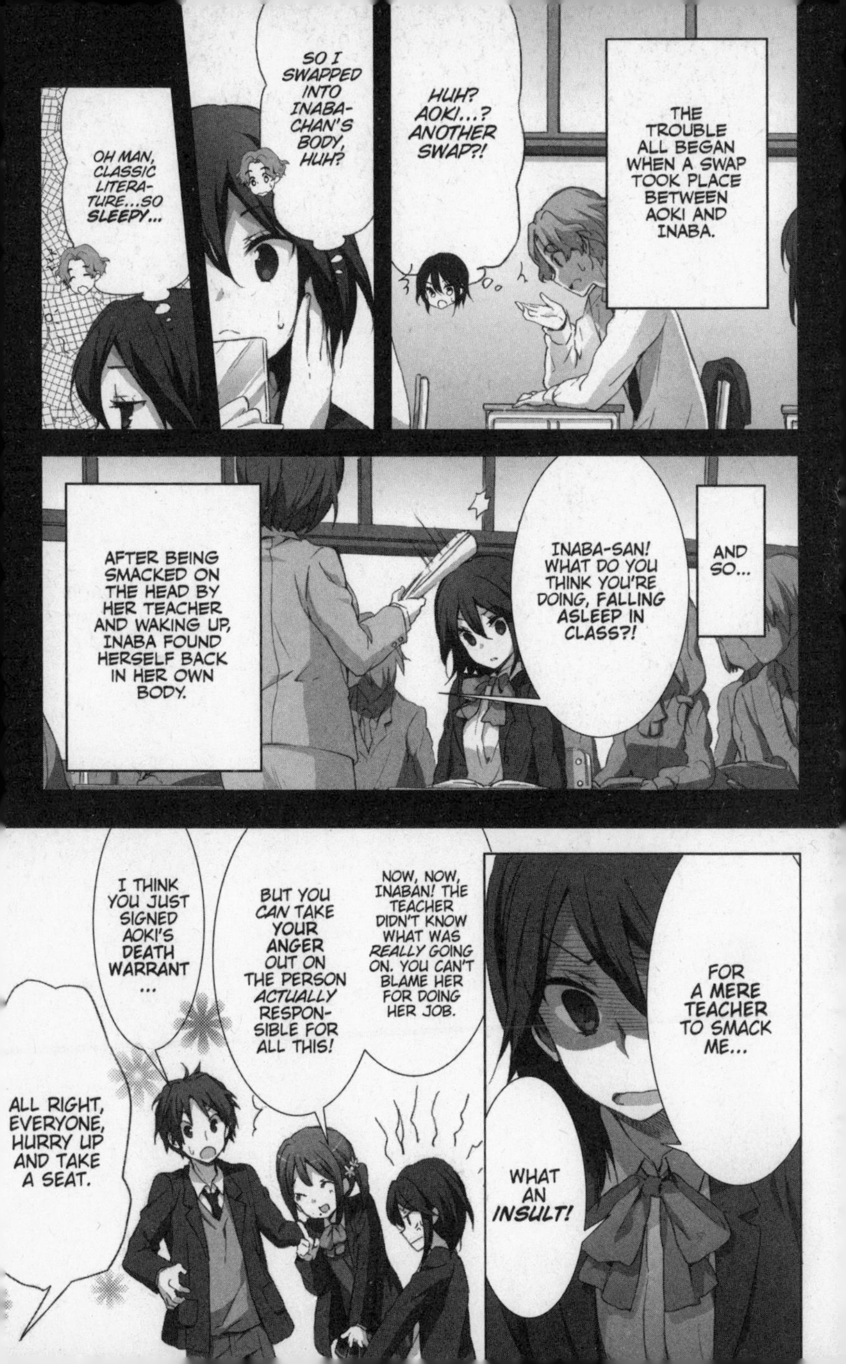
THE TROUBLE ALL BEGAN WHEN A SWAP TOOK PLACE BETWEEN AOKI AND INABA.
HUH? AOKI...? ANOTHER SWAP?!
SO I SWAPPED INTO INABA-CHAN'S BODY, HUH?
OH MAN, CLASSIC LITERA-TURE...SO SLEEPY...
AND SO...
INABA-SAN! WHAT DO YOU THINK YOU'RE DOING, FALLING ASLEEP IN CLASS?!
AFTER BEING SMACKED ON THE HEAD BY HER TEACHER AND WAKING UP, INABA FOUND HERSELF BACK IN HER OWN BODY.
FOR A MERE TEACHER TO SMACK ME...
WHAT AN INSULT!
NOW, NOW, INABAN! THE TEACHER DIDN'T KNOW WHAT WAS REALLY GOING ON. YOU CAN'T BLAME HER FOR DOING HER JOB.
BUT YOU CAN TAKE YOUR ANGER OUT ON THE PERSON ACTUALLY RESPON-SIBLE FOR ALL THIS!
I THINK YOU JUST SIGNED AOKI'S DEATH WARRANT...
ALL RIGHT, EVERYONE, HURRY UP AND TAKE A SEAT.

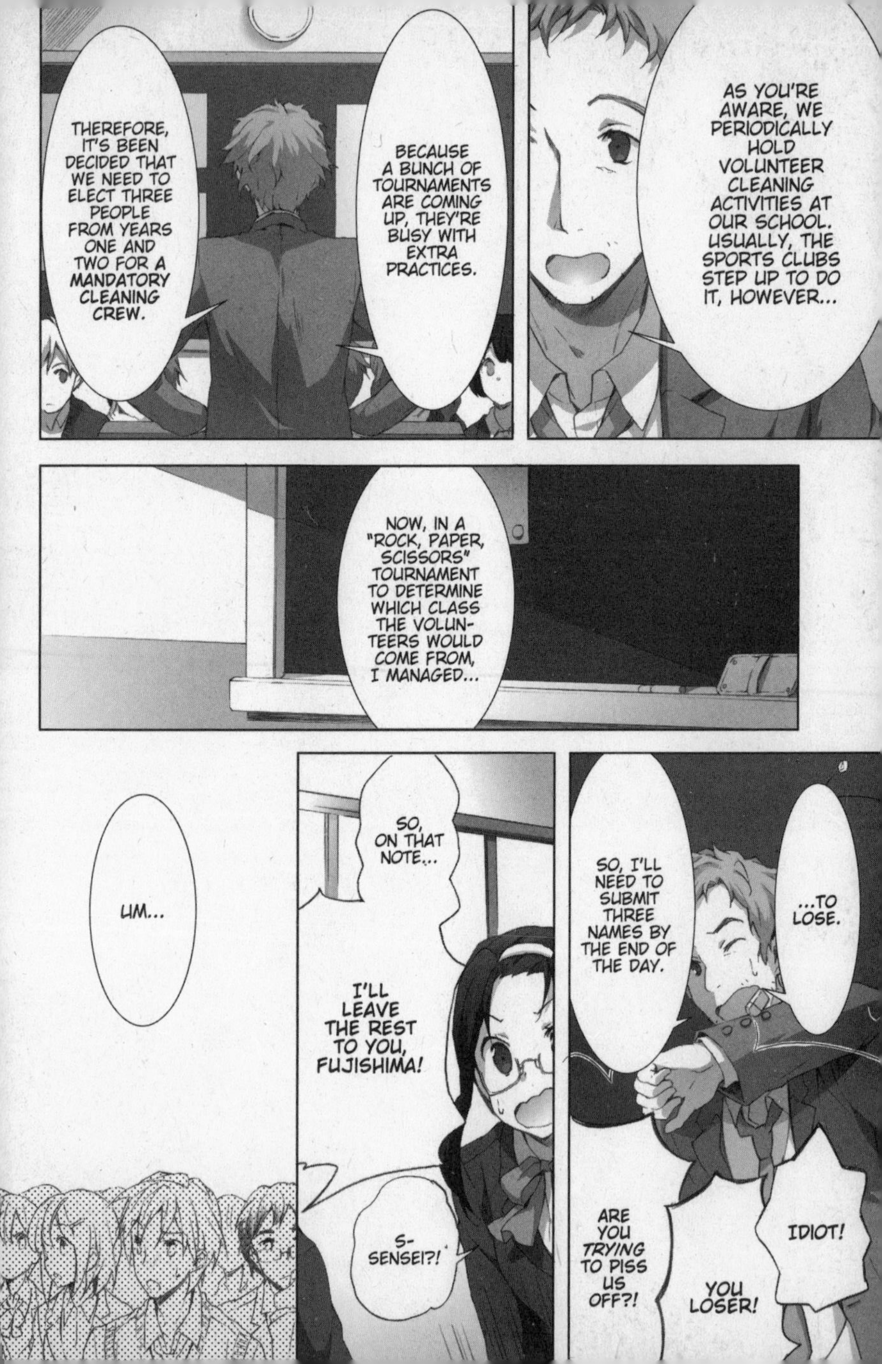
AS YOU'RE AWARE, WE PERIODICALLY HOLD VOLUNTEER CLEANING ACTIVITIES AT OUR SCHOOL. USUALLY, THE SPORTS CLUBS STEP UP TO DO IT, HOWEVER...
BECAUSE A BUNCH OF TOURNAMENTS ARE COMING UP, THEY'RE BUSY WITH EXTRA PRACTICES.
THEREFORE, IT'S BEEN DECIDED THAT WE NEED TO ELECT THREE PEOPLE FROM YEARS ONE AND TWO FOR A MANDATORY CLEANING CREW.
NOW, IN A "ROCK, PAPER, SCISSORS" TOURNAMENT TO DETERMINE WHICH CLASS THE VOLUNTEERS WOULD COME FROM, I MANAGED...
...TO LOSE.
SO, I'LL NEED TO SUBMIT THREE NAMES BY THE END OF THE DAY.
IDIOT!
YOU LOSER!
ARE YOU *TRYING* TO PISS US OFF?!
SO, ON THAT NOTE...
I'LL LEAVE THE REST TO YOU, FUJISHIMA!
S-SENSEI?!
UM...

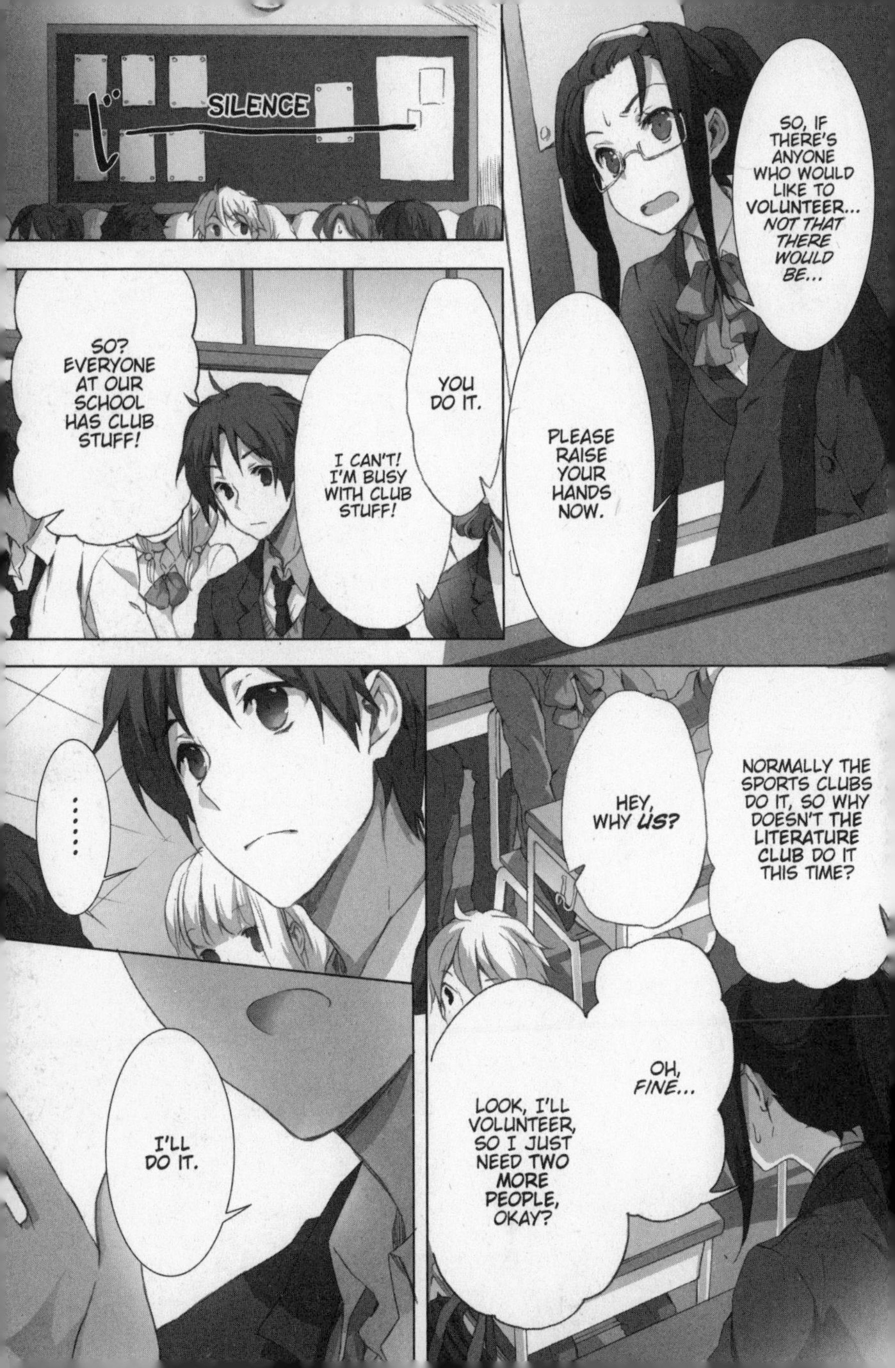
SO, IF THERE'S ANYONE WHO WOULD LIKE TO VOLUNTEER... *NOT THAT THERE WOULD BE...*
PLEASE RAISE YOUR HANDS NOW.
SILENCE
YOU DO IT.
I CAN'T! I'M BUSY WITH CLUB STUFF!
SO? EVERYONE AT OUR SCHOOL HAS CLUB STUFF!
NORMALLY THE SPORTS CLUBS DO IT, SO WHY DOESN'T THE LITERATURE CLUB DO IT THIS TIME?
HEY, WHY *US?*
OH, *FINE...*
LOOK, I'LL VOLUNTEER, SO I JUST NEED TWO MORE PEOPLE, OKAY?
......
I'LL DO IT.

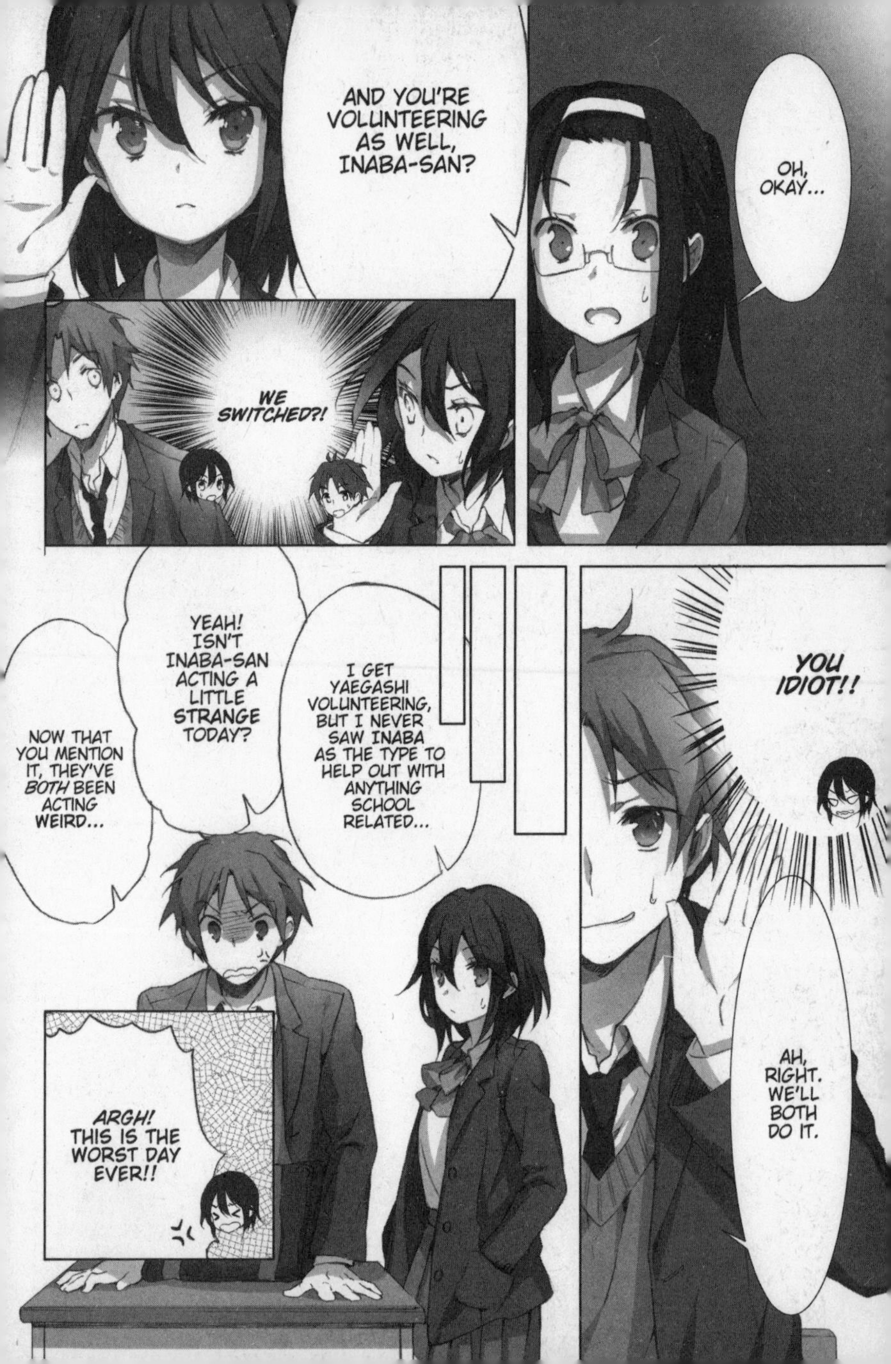
OH, OKAY...
AND YOU'RE VOLUNTEERING AS WELL, INABA-SAN?
WE SWITCHED?!
YOU IDIOT!!
AH, RIGHT. WE'LL BOTH DO IT.
I GET YAEGASHI VOLUNTEERING, BUT I NEVER SAW INABA AS THE TYPE TO HELP OUT WITH ANYTHING SCHOOL RELATED...
YEAH! ISN'T INABA-SAN ACTING A LITTLE STRANGE TODAY?
NOW THAT YOU MENTION IT, THEY'VE *BOTH* BEEN ACTING WEIRD...
ARGH! THIS IS THE WORST DAY EVER!!

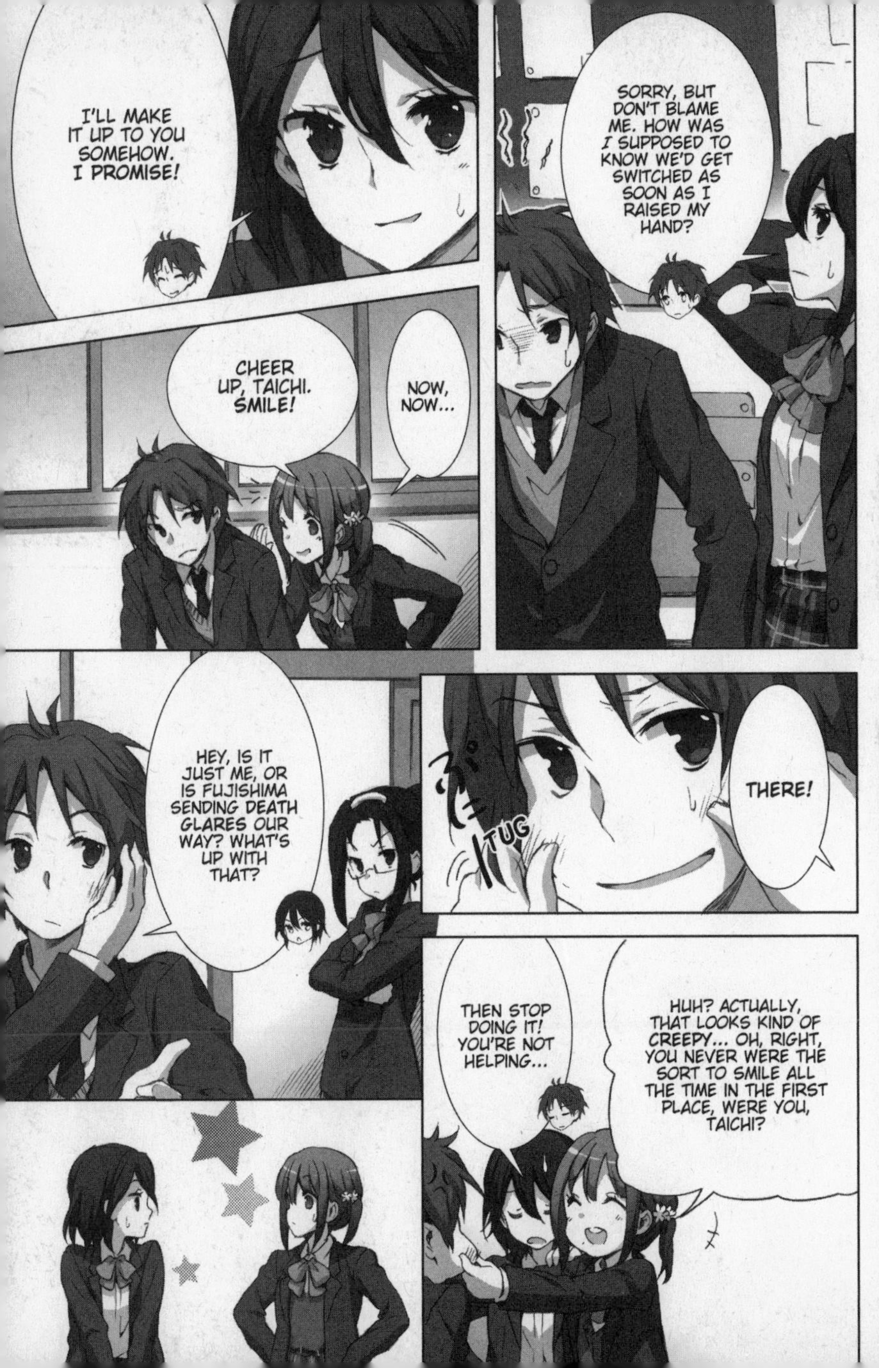
SORRY, BUT DON'T BLAME ME. HOW WAS I SUPPOSED TO KNOW WE'D GET SWITCHED AS SOON AS I RAISED MY HAND?
I'LL MAKE IT UP TO YOU SOMEHOW. I PROMISE!
NOW, NOW...
CHEER UP, TAICHI. SMILE!
TUG
THERE!
HUH? ACTUALLY, THAT LOOKS KIND OF CREEPY... OH, RIGHT, YOU NEVER WERE THE SORT TO SMILE ALL THE TIME IN THE FIRST PLACE, WERE YOU, TAICHI?
THEN STOP DOING IT! YOU'RE NOT HELPING...
HEY, IS IT JUST ME, OR IS FUJISHIMA SENDING DEATH GLARES OUR WAY? WHAT'S UP WITH THAT?

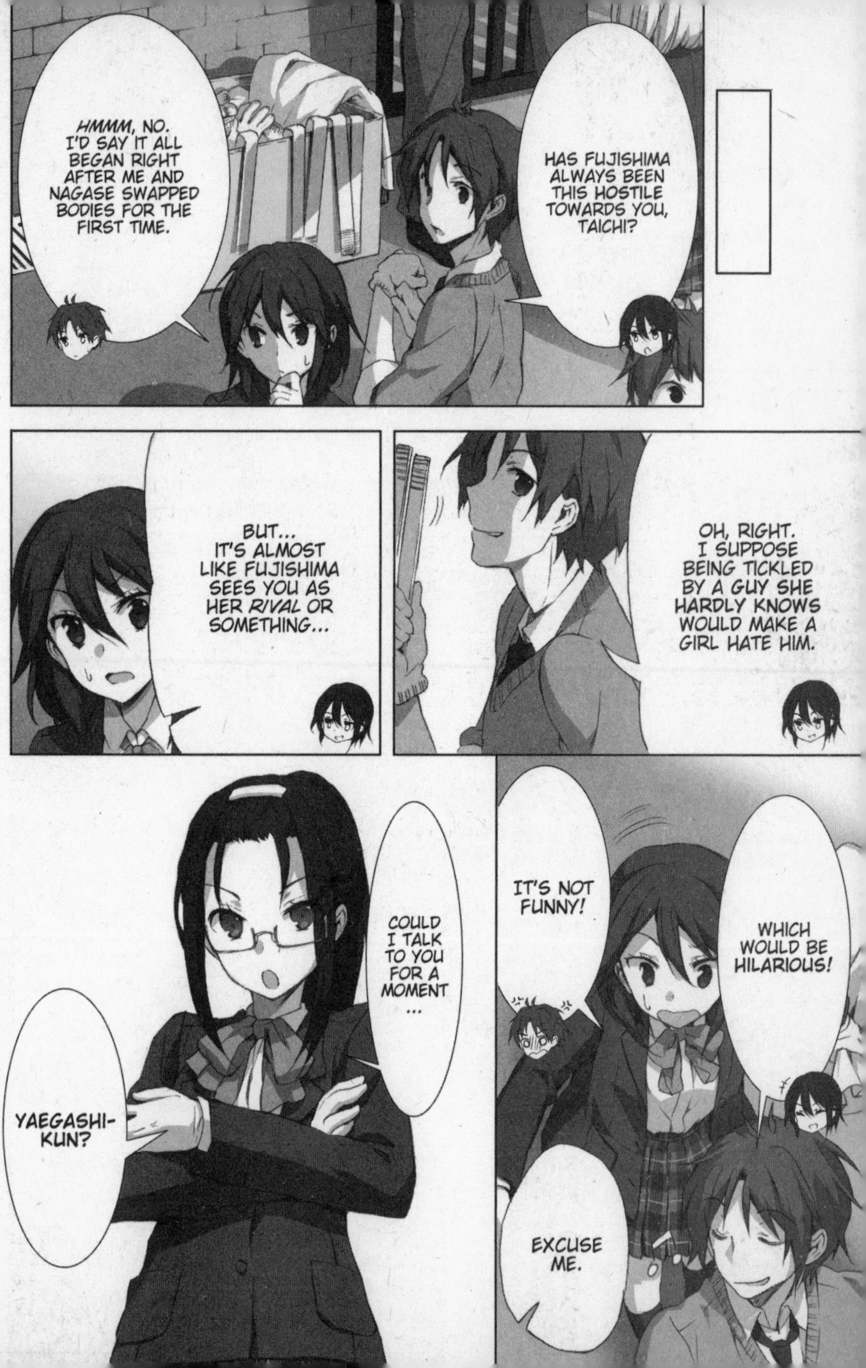
HAS FUJISHIMA ALWAYS BEEN THIS HOSTILE TOWARDS YOU, TAICHI?
HMMM, NO. I'D SAY IT ALL BEGAN RIGHT AFTER ME AND NAGASE SWAPPED BODIES FOR THE FIRST TIME.
OH, RIGHT. I SUPPOSE BEING TICKLED BY A GUY SHE HARDLY KNOWS WOULD MAKE A GIRL HATE HIM.
BUT... IT'S ALMOST LIKE FUJISHIMA SEES YOU AS HER *RIVAL* OR SOMETHING...
WHICH WOULD BE HILARIOUS!
IT'S NOT FUNNY!
EXCUSE ME.
COULD I TALK TO YOU FOR A MOMENT ...
YAEGASHI-KUN?

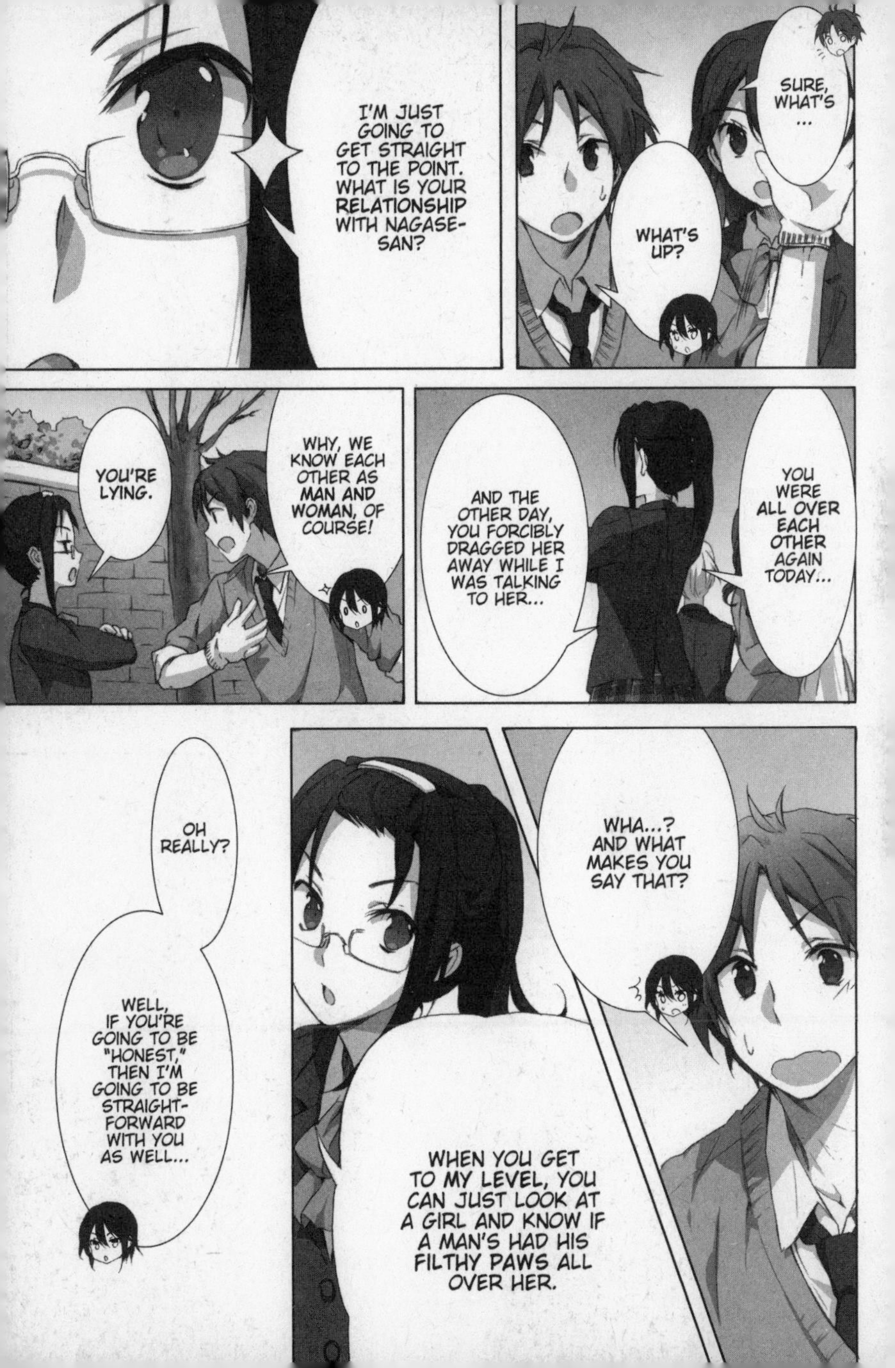
SURE, WHAT'S ...
WHAT'S UP?
I'M JUST GOING TO GET STRAIGHT TO THE POINT. WHAT IS YOUR RELATIONSHIP WITH NAGASE-SAN?
YOU WERE ALL OVER EACH OTHER AGAIN TODAY...
AND THE OTHER DAY, YOU FORCIBLY DRAGGED HER AWAY WHILE I WAS TALKING TO HER...
WHY, WE KNOW EACH OTHER AS MAN AND WOMAN, OF COURSE!
YOU'RE LYING.
WHA...? AND WHAT MAKES YOU SAY THAT?
WHEN YOU GET TO MY LEVEL, YOU CAN JUST LOOK AT A GIRL AND KNOW IF A MAN'S HAD HIS FILTHY PAWS ALL OVER HER.
OH REALLY?
WELL, IF YOU'RE GOING TO BE "HONEST," THEN I'M GOING TO BE STRAIGHT-FORWARD WITH YOU AS WELL...

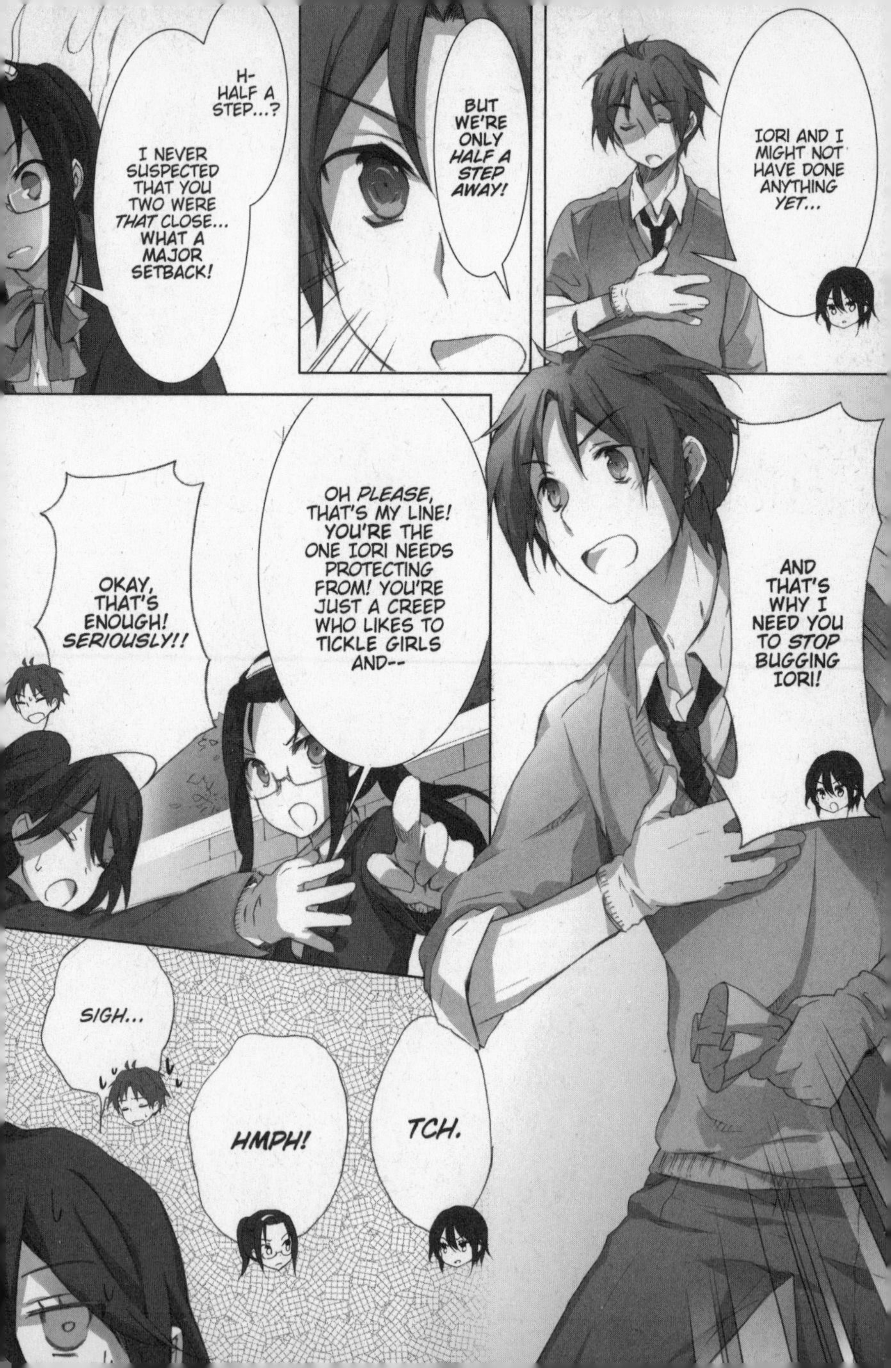
IORI AND I MIGHT NOT HAVE DONE ANYTHING *YET*...
BUT WE'RE ONLY *HALF A STEP AWAY!*
H- HALF A STEP...?
I NEVER SUSPECTED THAT YOU TWO WERE *THAT* CLOSE... WHAT A MAJOR SETBACK!
AND THAT'S WHY I NEED YOU TO *STOP* BUGGING IORI!
OH *PLEASE*, THAT'S MY LINE! YOU'RE THE ONE IORI NEEDS PROTECTING FROM! YOU'RE JUST A CREEP WHO LIKES TO TICKLE GIRLS AND--
OKAY, THAT'S ENOUGH! *SERIOUSLY!!*
TCH.
HMPH!
SIGH...

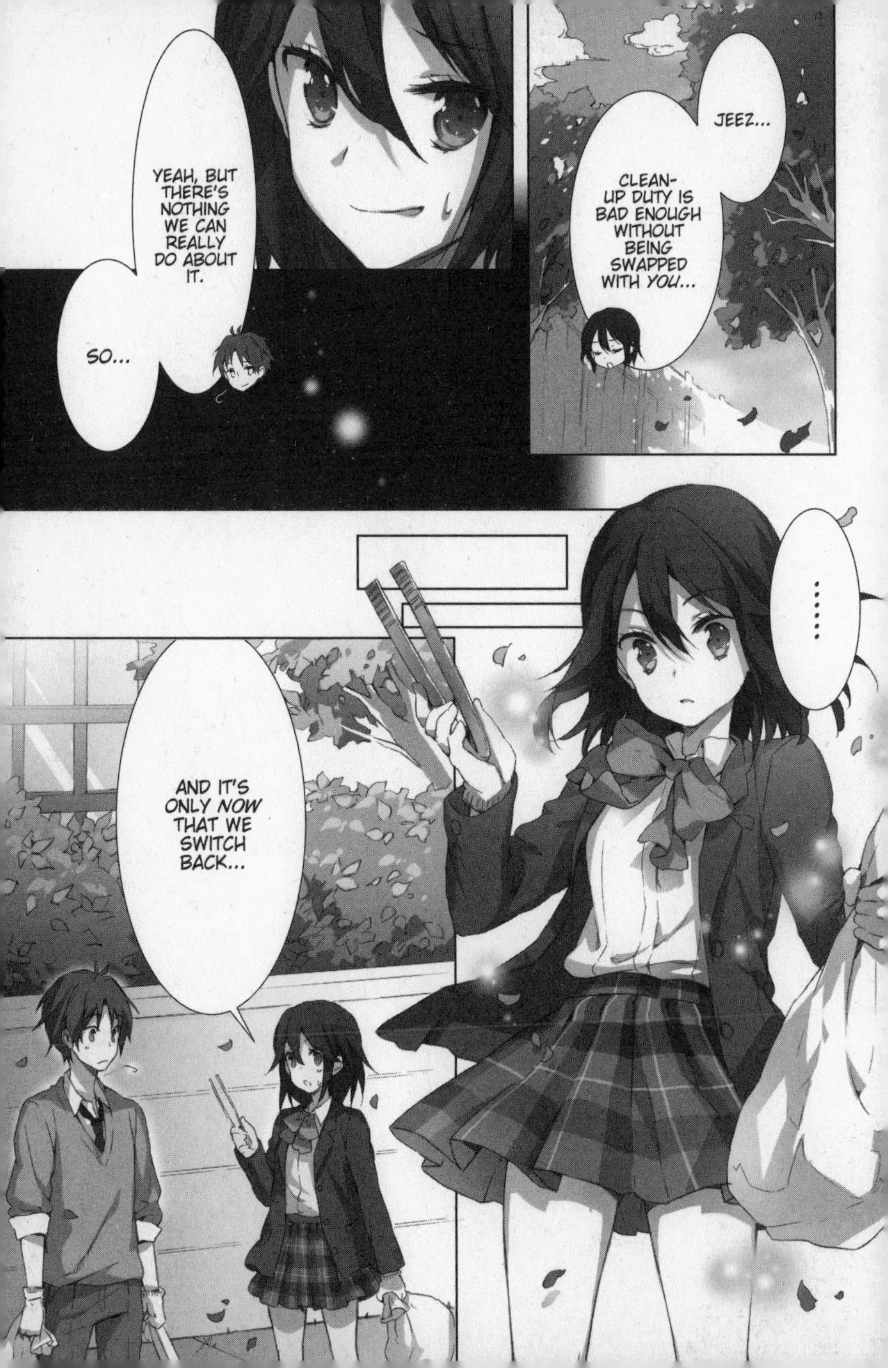
JEEZ...
CLEAN-UP DUTY IS BAD ENOUGH WITHOUT BEING SWAPPED WITH *YOU*...
YEAH, BUT THERE'S NOTHING WE CAN REALLY DO ABOUT IT.
SO...
......
AND IT'S ONLY *NOW* THAT WE SWITCH BACK...

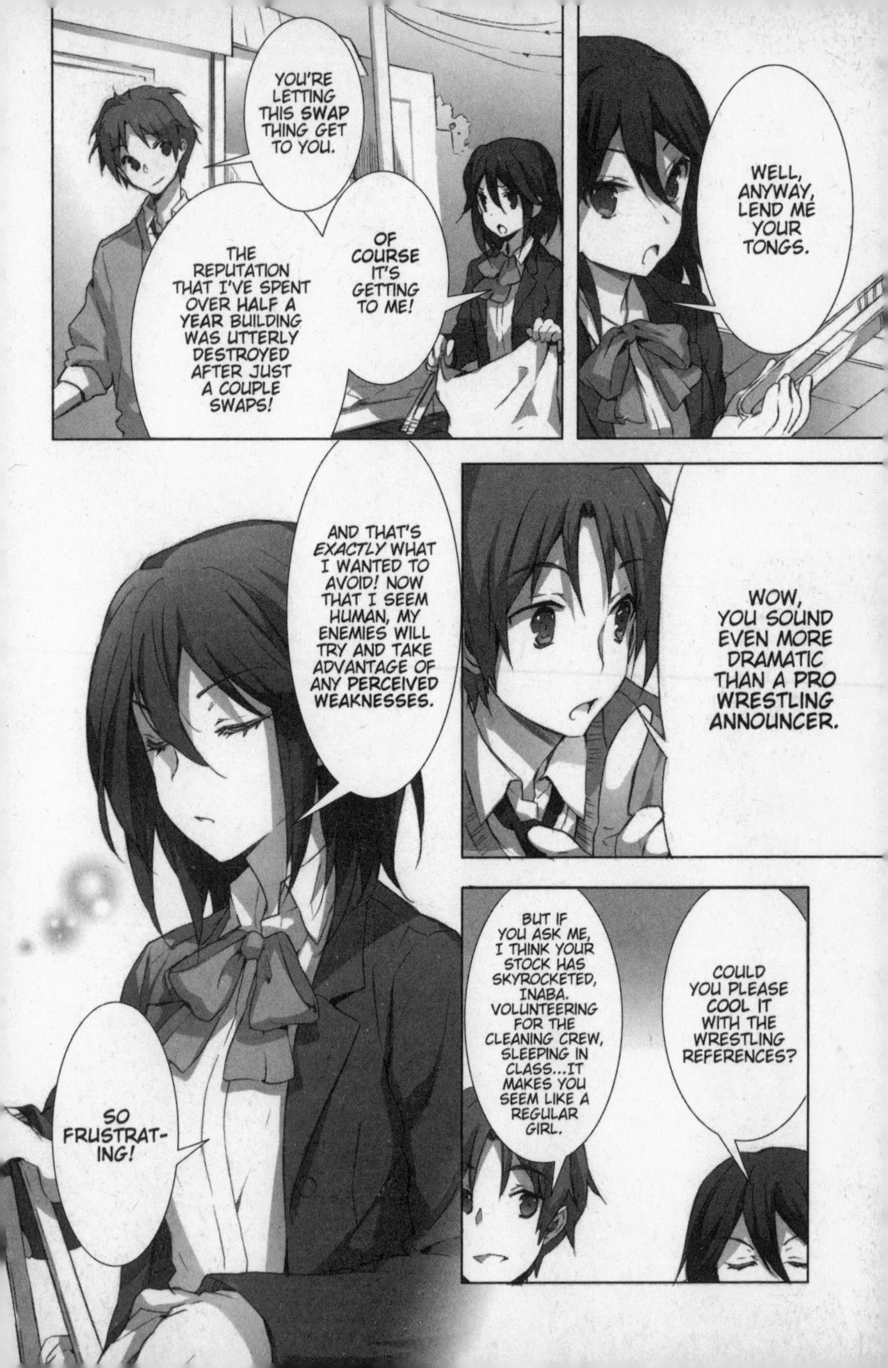
WELL, ANYWAY, LEND ME YOUR TONGS.
YOU'RE LETTING THIS SWAP THING GET TO YOU.
OF COURSE IT'S GETTING TO ME!
THE REPUTATION THAT I'VE SPENT OVER HALF A YEAR BUILDING WAS UTTERLY DESTROYED AFTER JUST A COUPLE SWAPS!
WOW, YOU SOUND EVEN MORE DRAMATIC THAN A PRO WRESTLING ANNOUNCER.
COULD YOU PLEASE COOL IT WITH THE WRESTLING REFERENCES?
BUT IF YOU ASK ME, I THINK YOUR STOCK HAS SKYROCKETED, INABA. VOLUNTEERING FOR THE CLEANING CREW, SLEEPING IN CLASS...IT MAKES YOU SEEM LIKE A REGULAR GIRL.
AND THAT'S *EXACTLY* WHAT I WANTED TO AVOID! NOW THAT I SEEM HUMAN, MY ENEMIES WILL TRY AND TAKE ADVANTAGE OF ANY PERCEIVED WEAKNESSES.
SO FRUSTRAT-ING!

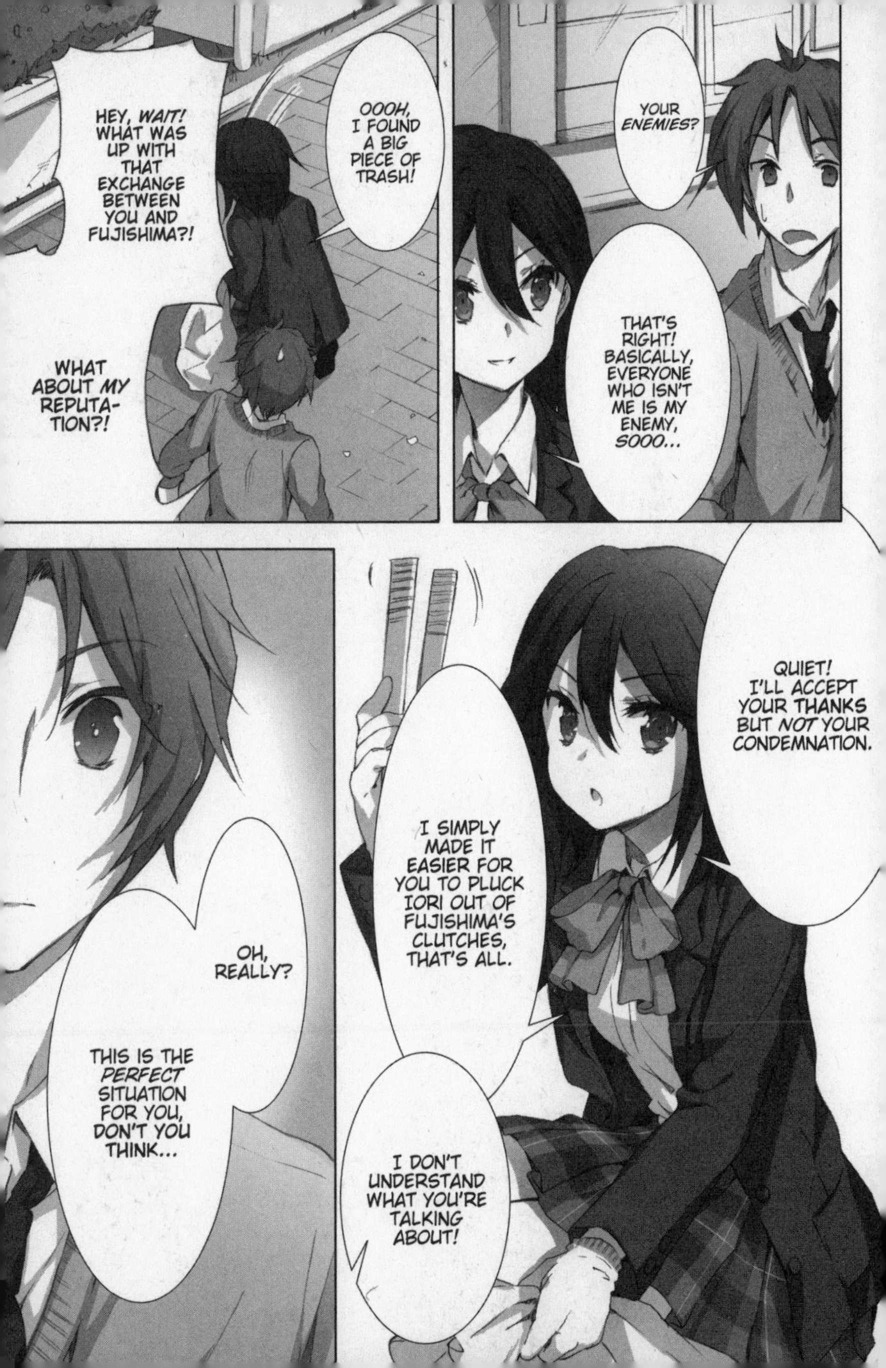
YOUR *ENEMIES*?
THAT'S RIGHT! BASICALLY, EVERYONE WHO ISN'T ME IS MY ENEMY, *SOOO*...
OOOH, I FOUND A BIG PIECE OF TRASH!
HEY, *WAIT!* WHAT WAS UP WITH THAT EXCHANGE BETWEEN YOU AND FUJISHIMA?!
WHAT ABOUT *MY* REPUTATION?!
QUIET! I'LL ACCEPT YOUR THANKS BUT *NOT* YOUR CONDEMNATION.
I SIMPLY MADE IT EASIER FOR YOU TO PLUCK IORI OUT OF FUJISHIMA'S CLUTCHES, THAT'S ALL.
I DON'T UNDERSTAND WHAT YOU'RE TALKING ABOUT!
OH, REALLY?
THIS IS THE *PERFECT* SITUATION FOR YOU, DON'T YOU THINK...

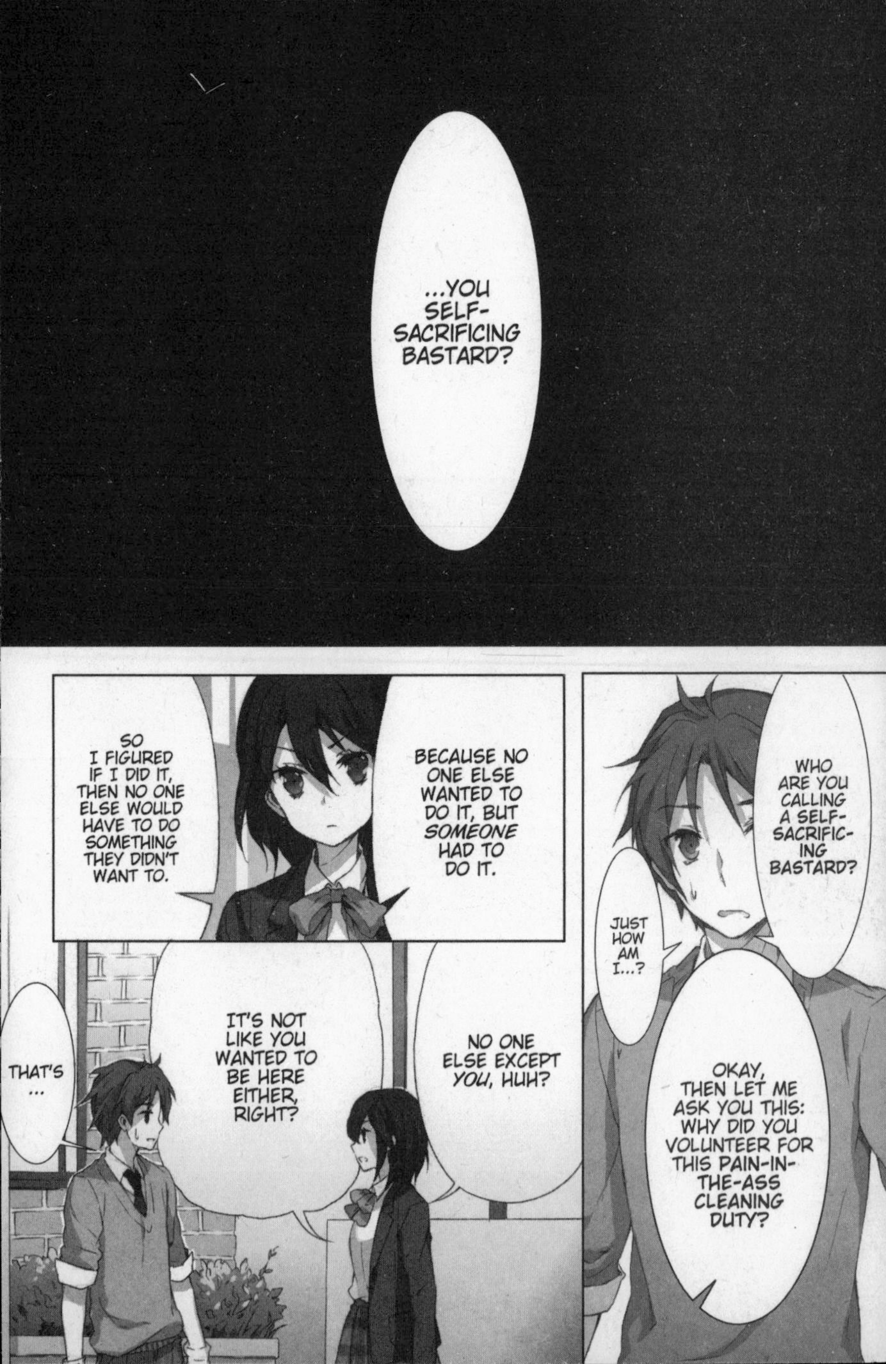
...YOU SELF-SACRIFICING BASTARD?
WHO ARE YOU CALLING A SELF-SACRIFICING BASTARD?
JUST HOW AM I...?
OKAY, THEN LET ME ASK YOU THIS: WHY DID YOU VOLUNTEER FOR THIS PAIN-IN-THE-ASS CLEANING DUTY?
BECAUSE NO ONE ELSE WANTED TO DO IT, BUT *SOMEONE* HAD TO DO IT.
SO I FIGURED IF I DID IT, THEN NO ONE ELSE WOULD HAVE TO DO SOMETHING THEY DIDN'T WANT TO.
NO ONE ELSE EXCEPT *YOU*, HUH?
IT'S NOT LIKE YOU WANTED TO BE HERE EITHER, RIGHT?
THAT'S ...

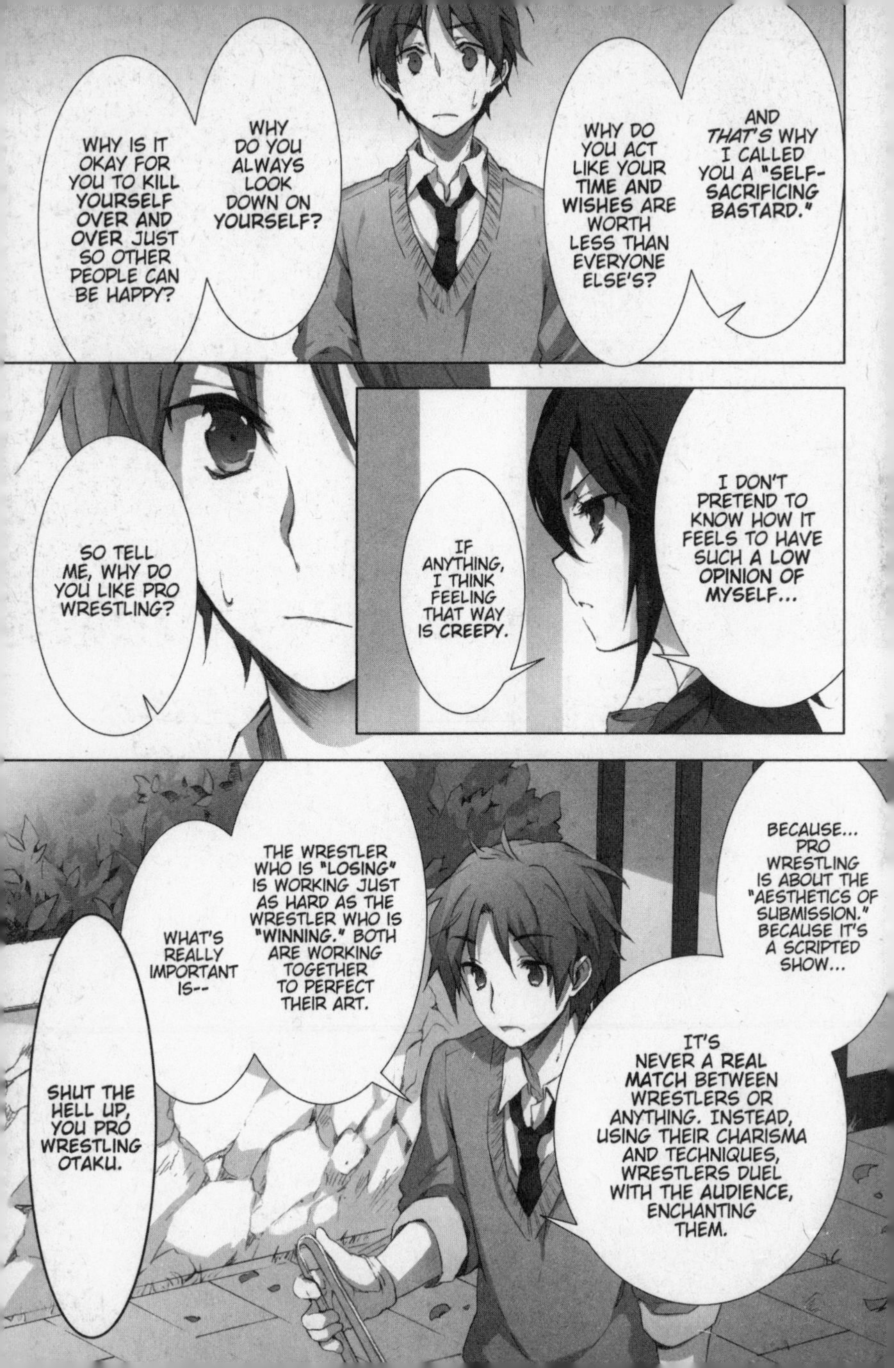
AND *THAT'S* WHY I CALLED YOU A "SELF-SACRIFICING BASTARD."
WHY DO YOU ACT LIKE YOUR TIME AND WISHES ARE WORTH LESS THAN EVERYONE ELSE'S?
WHY DO YOU ALWAYS LOOK DOWN ON YOURSELF?
WHY IS IT OKAY FOR YOU TO KILL YOURSELF OVER AND OVER JUST SO OTHER PEOPLE CAN BE HAPPY?
I DON'T PRETEND TO KNOW HOW IT FEELS TO HAVE SUCH A LOW OPINION OF MYSELF...
IF ANYTHING, I THINK FEELING THAT WAY IS CREEPY.
SO TELL ME, WHY DO YOU LIKE PRO WRESTLING?
BECAUSE... PRO WRESTLING IS ABOUT THE "AESTHETICS OF SUBMISSION." BECAUSE IT'S A SCRIPTED SHOW...
IT'S NEVER A REAL MATCH BETWEEN WRESTLERS OR ANYTHING. INSTEAD, USING THEIR CHARISMA AND TECHNIQUES, WRESTLERS DUEL WITH THE AUDIENCE, ENCHANTING THEM.
THE WRESTLER WHO IS "LOSING" IS WORKING JUST AS HARD AS THE WRESTLER WHO IS "WINNING." BOTH ARE WORKING TOGETHER TO PERFECT THEIR ART.
WHAT'S REALLY IMPORTANT IS--
SHUT THE HELL UP, YOU PRO WRESTLING OTAKU.

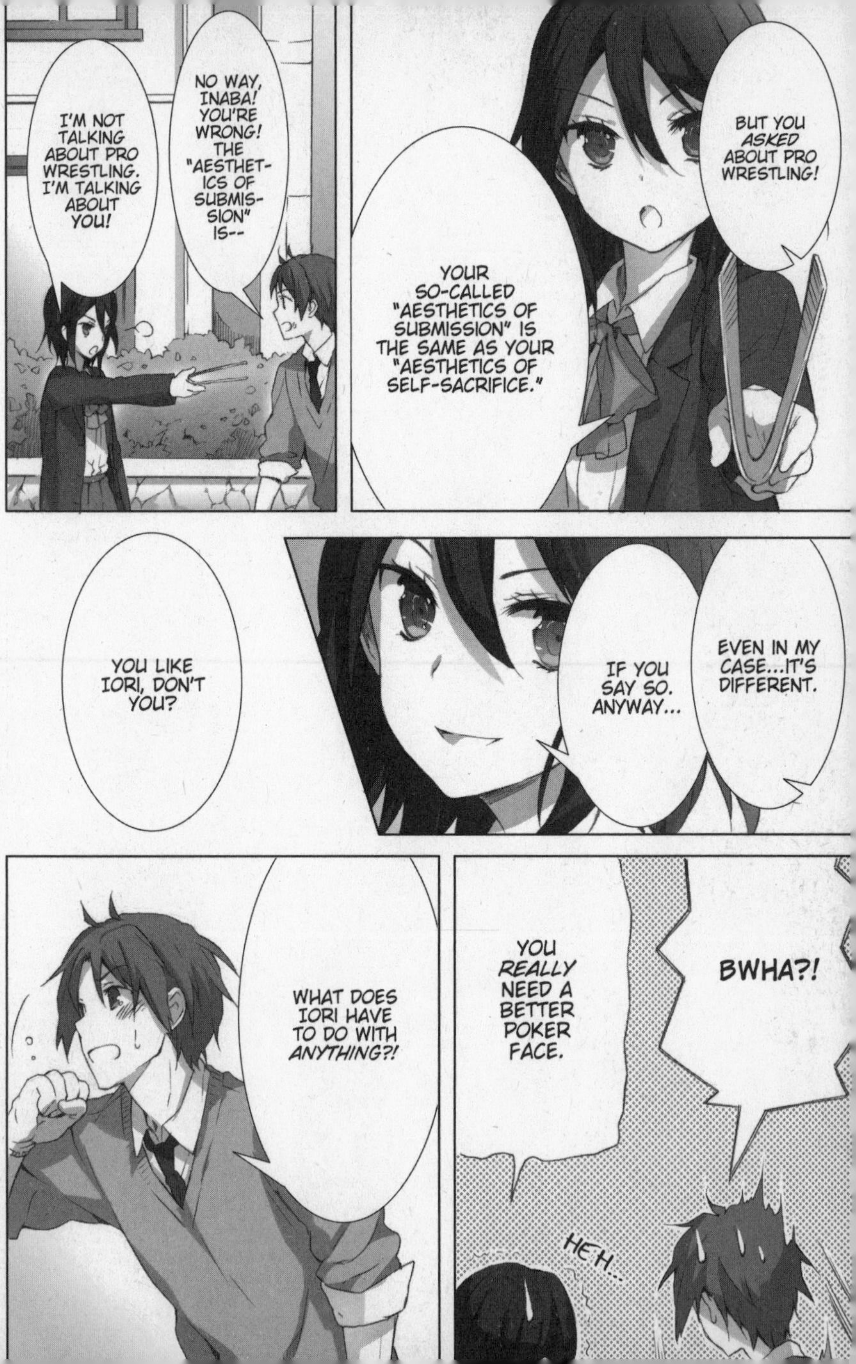
BUT YOU *ASKED* ABOUT PRO WRESTLING!
YOUR SO-CALLED "AESTHETICS OF SUBMISSION" IS THE SAME AS YOUR "AESTHETICS OF SELF-SACRIFICE."
NO WAY, INABA! YOU'RE WRONG! THE "AESTHETICS OF SUBMISSION" IS--
I'M NOT TALKING ABOUT PRO WRESTLING. I'M TALKING ABOUT YOU!
EVEN IN MY CASE...IT'S DIFFERENT.
IF YOU SAY SO. ANYWAY...
YOU LIKE IORI, DON'T YOU?
BWHA?!
YOU *REALLY* NEED A BETTER POKER FACE.
HEH...
WHAT DOES IORI HAVE TO DO WITH *ANYTHING*?!

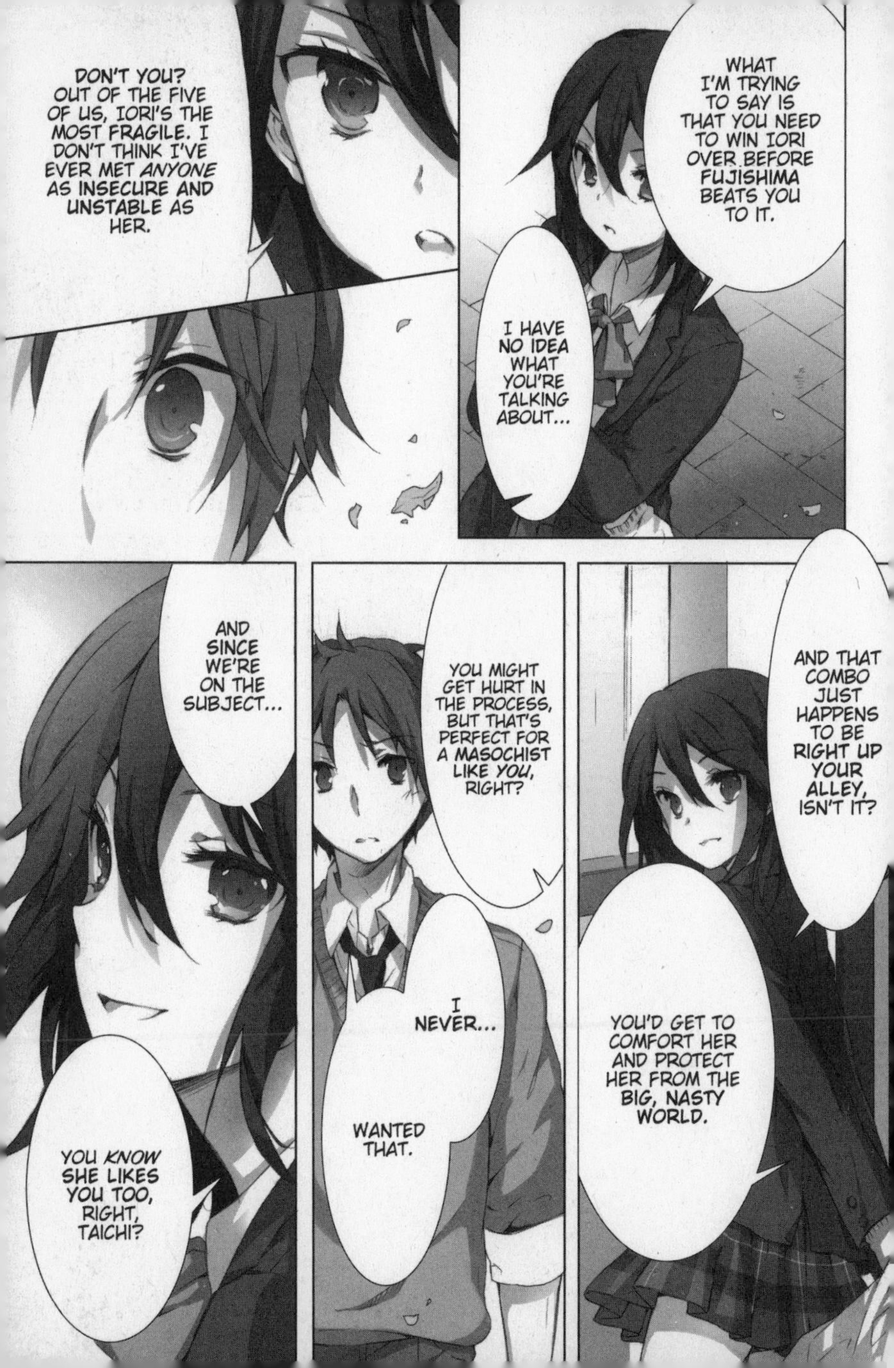
WHAT I'M TRYING TO SAY IS THAT YOU NEED TO WIN IORI OVER BEFORE FUJISHIMA BEATS YOU TO IT.
I HAVE NO IDEA WHAT YOU'RE TALKING ABOUT...
DON'T YOU? OUT OF THE FIVE OF US, IORI'S THE MOST FRAGILE. I DON'T THINK I'VE EVER MET *ANYONE* AS INSECURE AND UNSTABLE AS HER.
AND THAT COMBO JUST HAPPENS TO BE RIGHT UP YOUR ALLEY, ISN'T IT?
YOU'D GET TO COMFORT HER AND PROTECT HER FROM THE BIG, NASTY WORLD.
YOU MIGHT GET HURT IN THE PROCESS, BUT THAT'S PERFECT FOR A MASOCHIST LIKE *YOU*, RIGHT?
I NEVER...
WANTED THAT.
AND SINCE WE'RE ON THE SUBJECT...
YOU *KNOW* SHE LIKES YOU TOO, RIGHT, TAICHI?

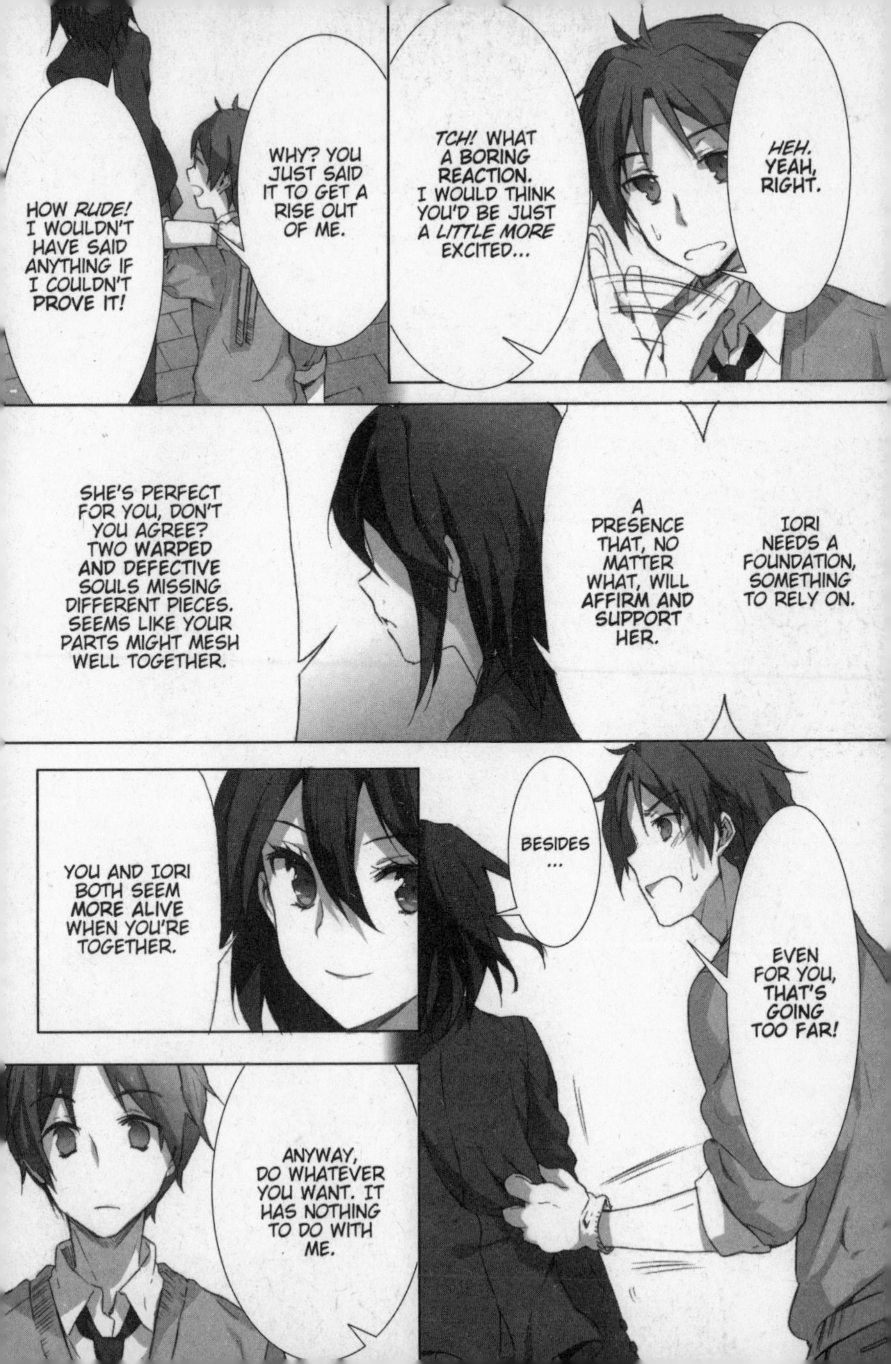
HEH. YEAH, RIGHT.
TCH! WHAT A BORING REACTION. I WOULD THINK YOU'D BE JUST A LITTLE MORE EXCITED...
WHY? YOU JUST SAID IT TO GET A RISE OUT OF ME.
HOW RUDE! I WOULDN'T HAVE SAID ANYTHING IF I COULDN'T PROVE IT!
IORI NEEDS A FOUNDATION, SOMETHING TO RELY ON.
A PRESENCE THAT, NO MATTER WHAT, WILL AFFIRM AND SUPPORT HER.
SHE'S PERFECT FOR YOU, DON'T YOU AGREE? TWO WARPED AND DEFECTIVE SOULS MISSING DIFFERENT PIECES. SEEMS LIKE YOUR PARTS MIGHT MESH WELL TOGETHER.
BESIDES...
YOU AND IORI BOTH SEEM MORE ALIVE WHEN YOU'RE TOGETHER.
EVEN FOR YOU, THAT'S GOING TOO FAR!
ANYWAY, DO WHATEVER YOU WANT. IT HAS NOTHING TO DO WITH ME.

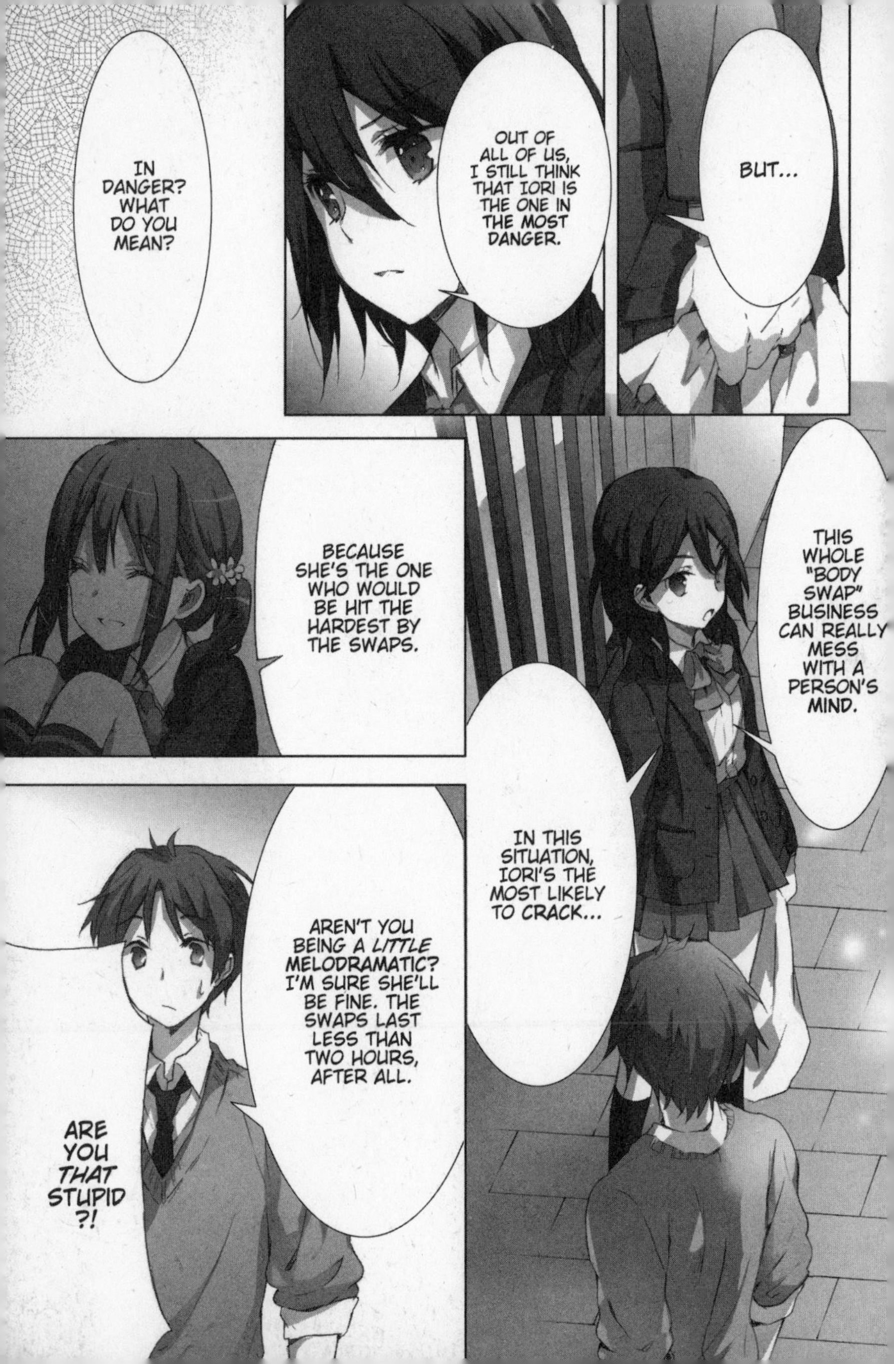
BUT...
OUT OF ALL OF US, I STILL THINK THAT IORI IS THE ONE IN THE MOST DANGER.
IN DANGER? WHAT DO YOU MEAN?
BECAUSE SHE'S THE ONE WHO WOULD BE HIT THE HARDEST BY THE SWAPS.
THIS WHOLE "BODY SWAP" BUSINESS CAN REALLY MESS WITH A PERSON'S MIND.
IN THIS SITUATION, IORI'S THE MOST LIKELY TO CRACK...
AREN'T YOU BEING A *LITTLE* MELODRAMATIC? I'M SURE SHE'LL BE FINE. THE SWAPS LAST LESS THAN TWO HOURS, AFTER ALL.
ARE YOU *THAT* STUPID ?!

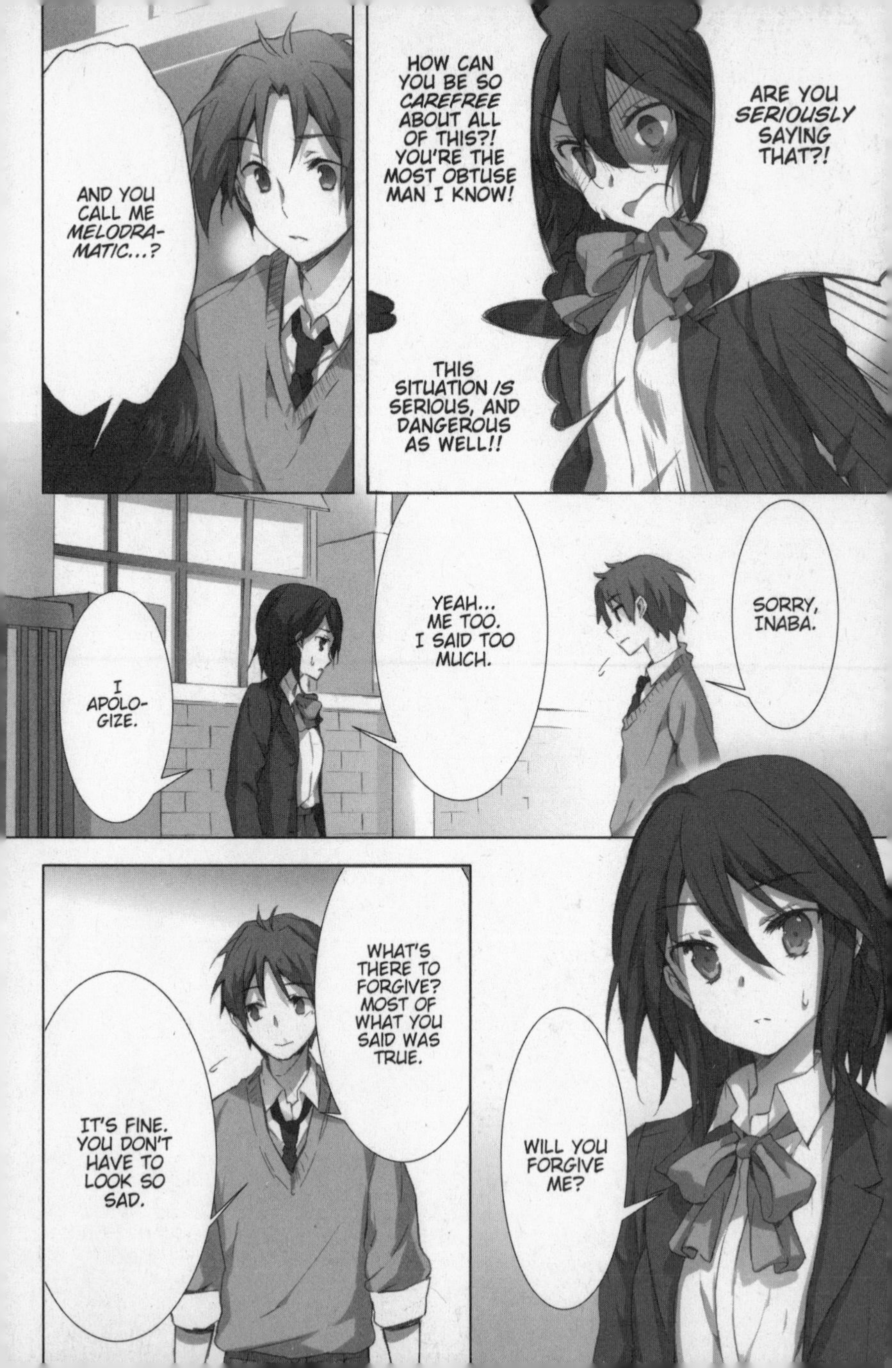
ARE YOU SERIOUSLY SAYING THAT?!
HOW CAN YOU BE SO CAREFREE ABOUT ALL OF THIS?! YOU'RE THE MOST OBTUSE MAN I KNOW!
THIS SITUATION IS SERIOUS, AND DANGEROUS AS WELL!!
AND YOU CALL ME MELODRAMATIC...?
SORRY, INABA.
YEAH... ME TOO. I SAID TOO MUCH.
I APOLOGIZE.
WILL YOU FORGIVE ME?
WHAT'S THERE TO FORGIVE? MOST OF WHAT YOU SAID WAS TRUE.
IT'S FINE. YOU DON'T HAVE TO LOOK SO SAD.

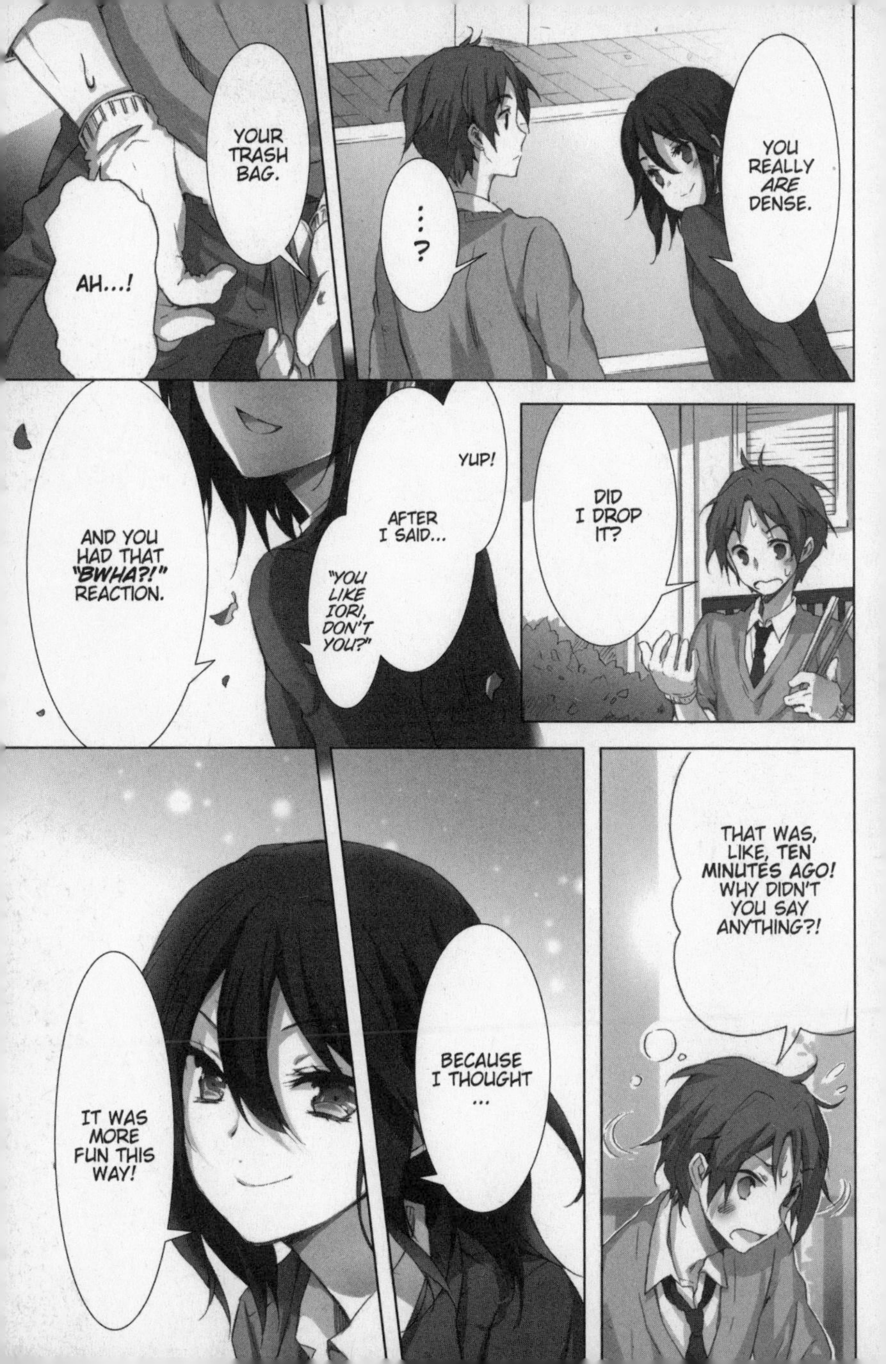
YOU REALLY ARE DENSE.
...?
YOUR TRASH BAG.
AH...!
DID I DROP IT?
YUP!
AFTER I SAID...
"YOU LIKE IORI, DON'T YOU?"
AND YOU HAD THAT "BWHA?!" REACTION.
THAT WAS, LIKE, TEN MINUTES AGO! WHY DIDN'T YOU SAY ANYTHING?!
BECAUSE I THOUGHT ...
IT WAS MORE FUN THIS WAY!

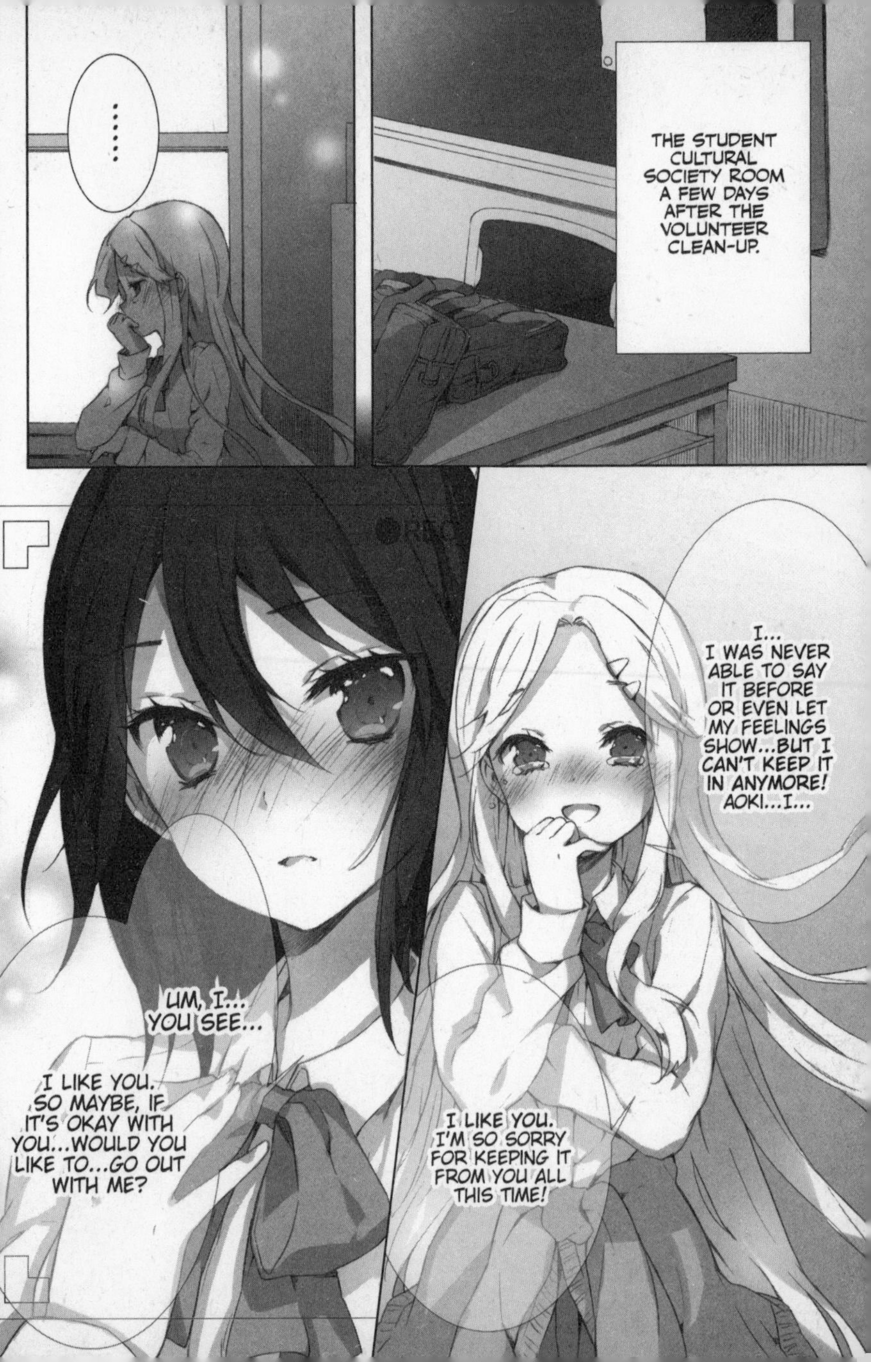
THE STUDENT CULTURAL SOCIETY ROOM A FEW DAYS AFTER THE VOLUNTEER CLEAN-UP.
......
I... I WAS NEVER ABLE TO SAY IT BEFORE OR EVEN LET MY FEELINGS SHOW...BUT I CAN'T KEEP IT IN ANYMORE! AOKI...I...
I LIKE YOU. I'M SO SORRY FOR KEEPING IT FROM YOU ALL THIS TIME!
UM, I... YOU SEE...
I LIKE YOU. SO MAYBE, IF IT'S OKAY WITH YOU...WOULD YOU LIKE TO...GO OUT WITH ME?

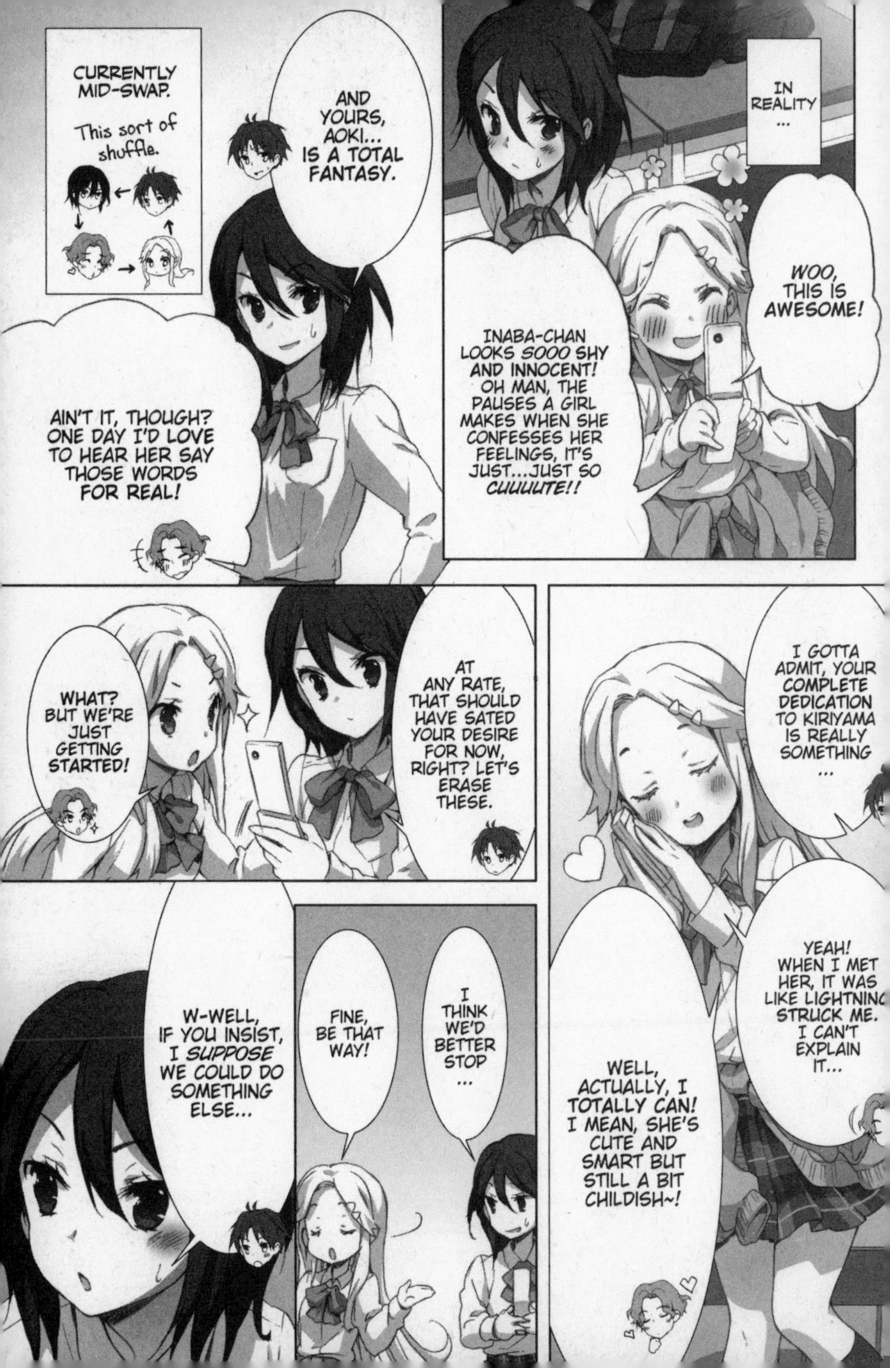
IN REALITY ...
WOO, THIS IS AWESOME!
INABA-CHAN LOOKS SOOO SHY AND INNOCENT! OH MAN, THE PAUSES A GIRL MAKES WHEN SHE CONFESSES HER FEELINGS, IT'S JUST...JUST SO CUUUUTE!!
CURRENTLY MID-SWAP.
This sort of shuffle.
AND YOURS, AOKI... IS A TOTAL FANTASY.
AIN'T IT, THOUGH? ONE DAY I'D LOVE TO HEAR HER SAY THOSE WORDS FOR REAL!
I GOTTA ADMIT, YOUR COMPLETE DEDICATION TO KIRIYAMA IS REALLY SOMETHING ...
YEAH! WHEN I MET HER, IT WAS LIKE LIGHTNING STRUCK ME. I CAN'T EXPLAIN IT...
WELL, ACTUALLY, I TOTALLY CAN! I MEAN, SHE'S CUTE AND SMART BUT STILL A BIT CHILDISH~!
AT ANY RATE, THAT SHOULD HAVE SATED YOUR DESIRE FOR NOW, RIGHT? LET'S ERASE THESE.
WHAT? BUT WE'RE JUST GETTING STARTED!
I THINK WE'D BETTER STOP ...
FINE, BE THAT WAY!
W-WELL, IF YOU INSIST, I SUPPOSE WE COULD DO SOMETHING ELSE...

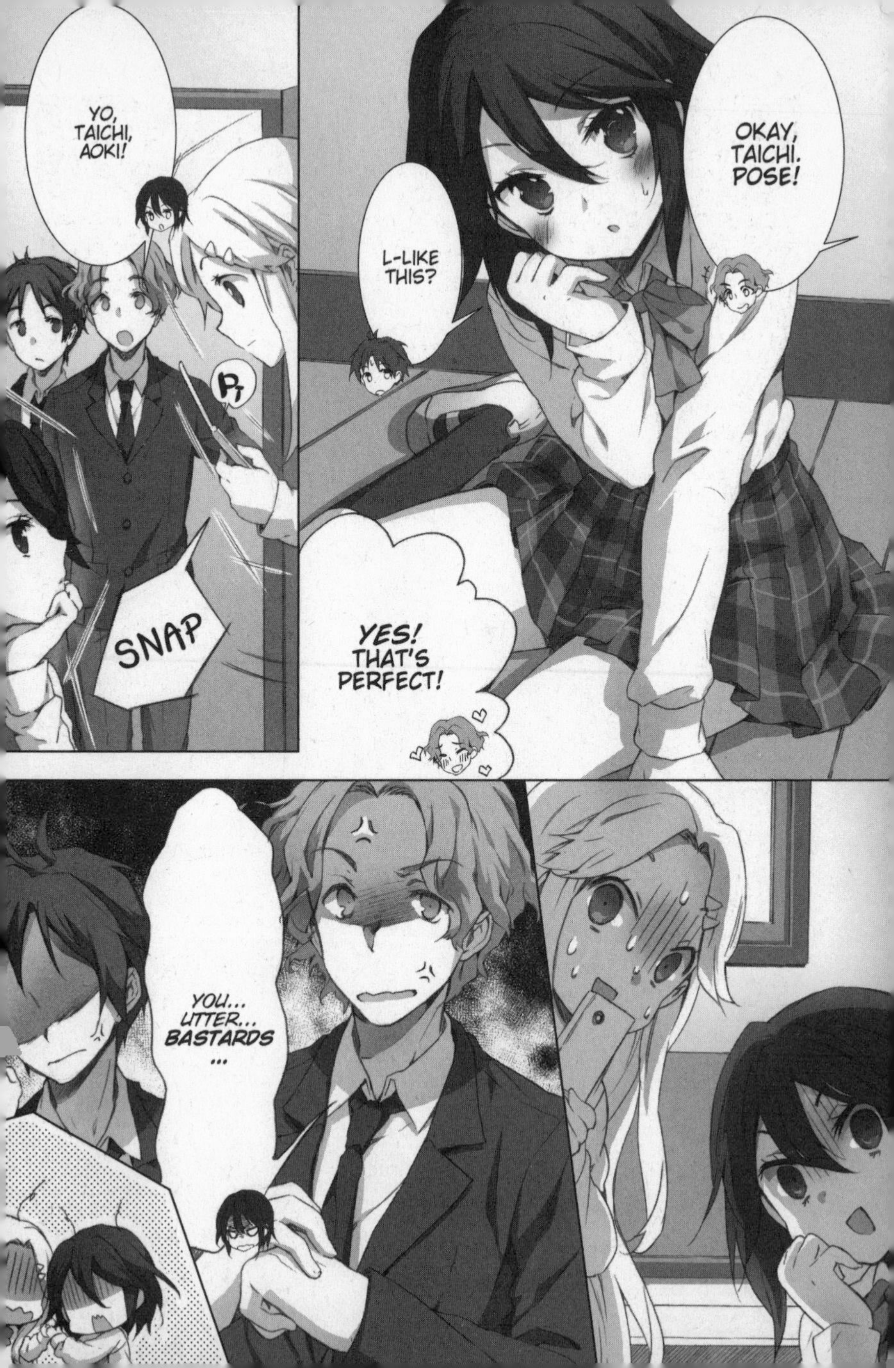
OKAY, TAICHI. POSE!
L-LIKE THIS?
YES! THAT'S PERFECT!
YO, TAICHI, AOKI!
Pi
SNAP
YOU... UTTER... BASTARDS ...

Chapter 6

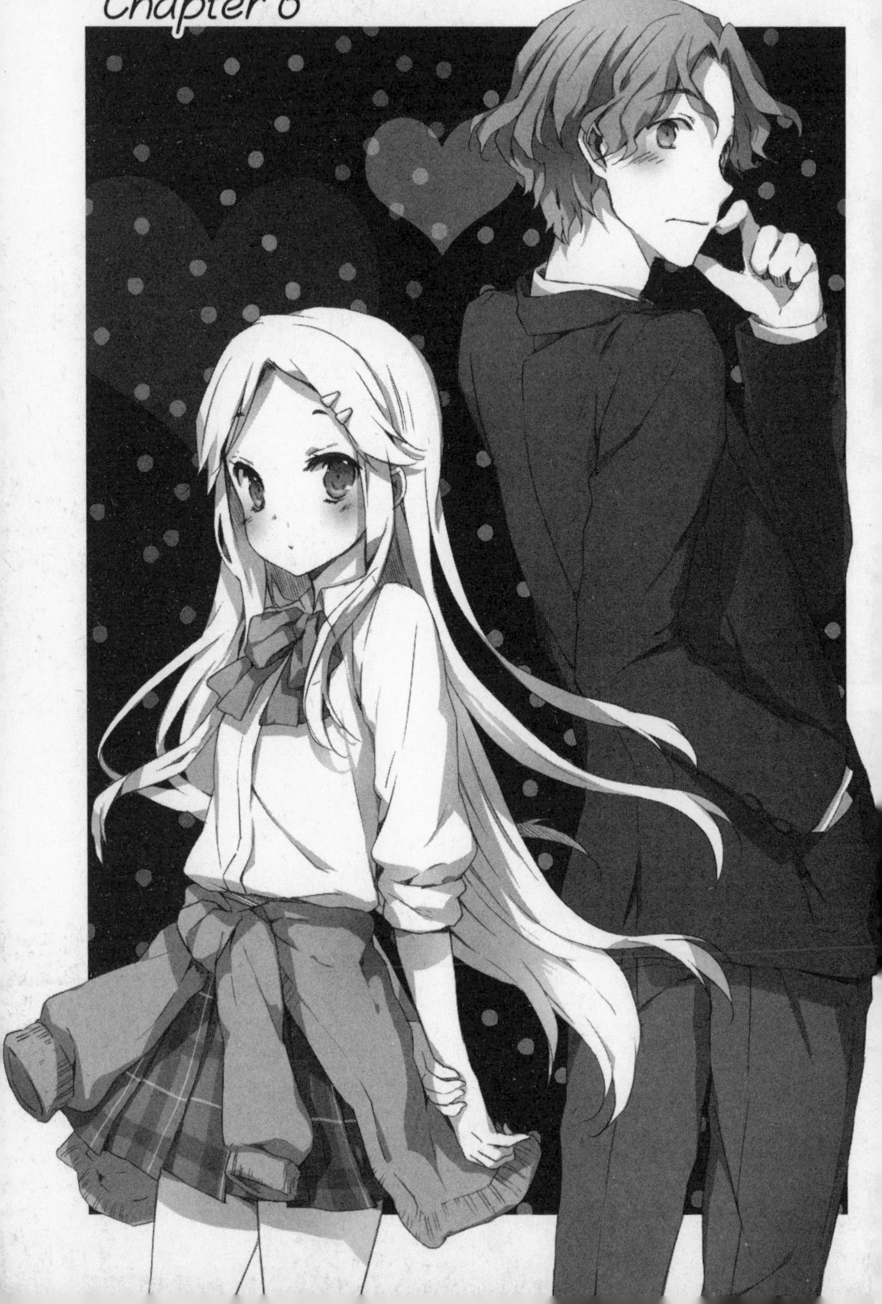

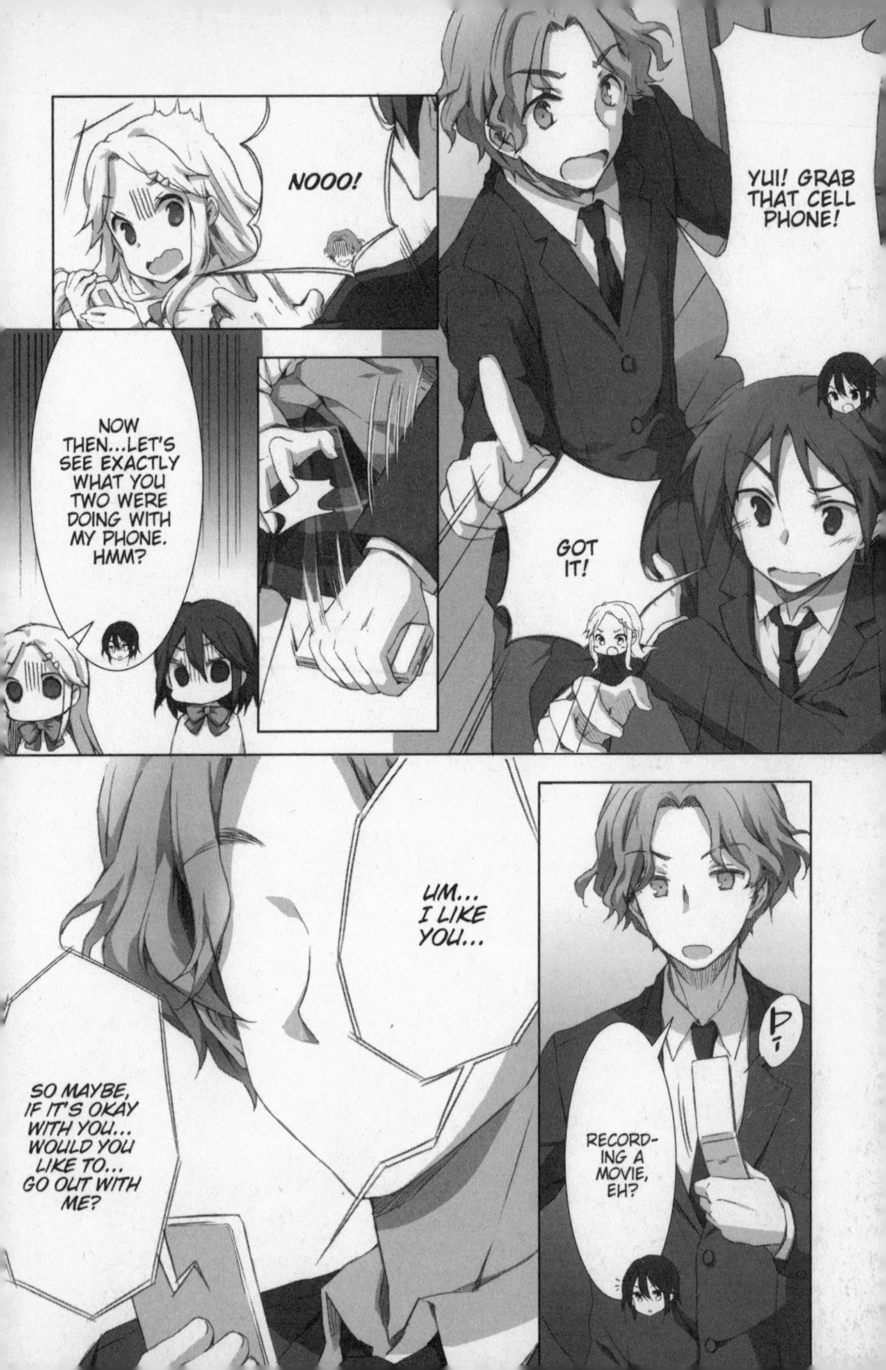
YUI! GRAB THAT CELL PHONE!
GOT IT!
NOOO!
NOW THEN...LET'S SEE EXACTLY WHAT YOU TWO WERE DOING WITH MY PHONE. HMM?
RECORD-ING A MOVIE, EH?
UM... I LIKE YOU...
SO MAYBE, IF IT'S OKAY WITH YOU... WOULD YOU LIKE TO... GO OUT WITH ME?

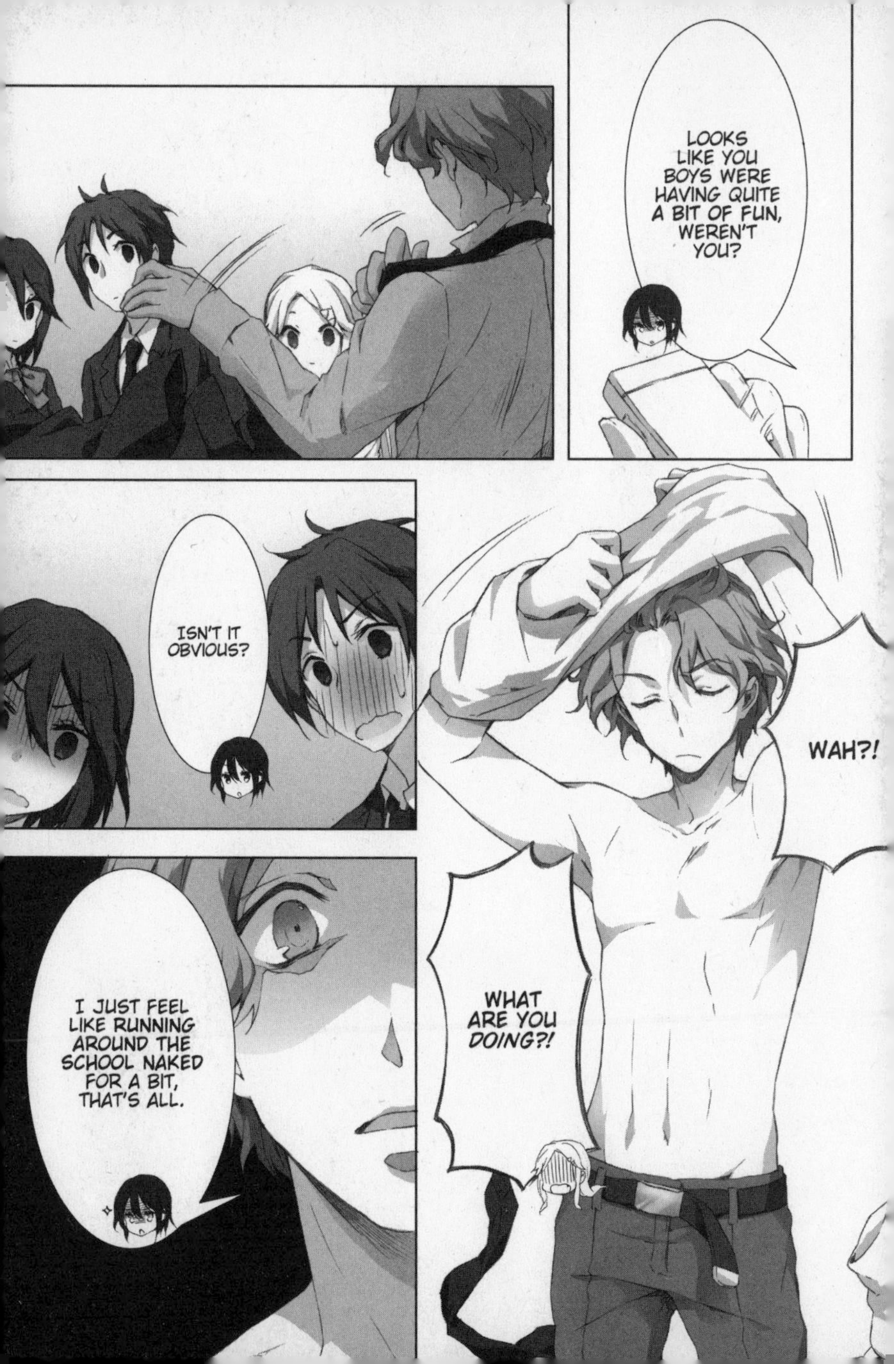
LOOKS LIKE YOU BOYS WERE HAVING QUITE A BIT OF FUN, WEREN'T YOU?
WAH?!
WHAT ARE YOU DOING?!
ISN'T IT OBVIOUS?
I JUST FEEL LIKE RUNNING AROUND THE SCHOOL NAKED FOR A BIT, THAT'S ALL.

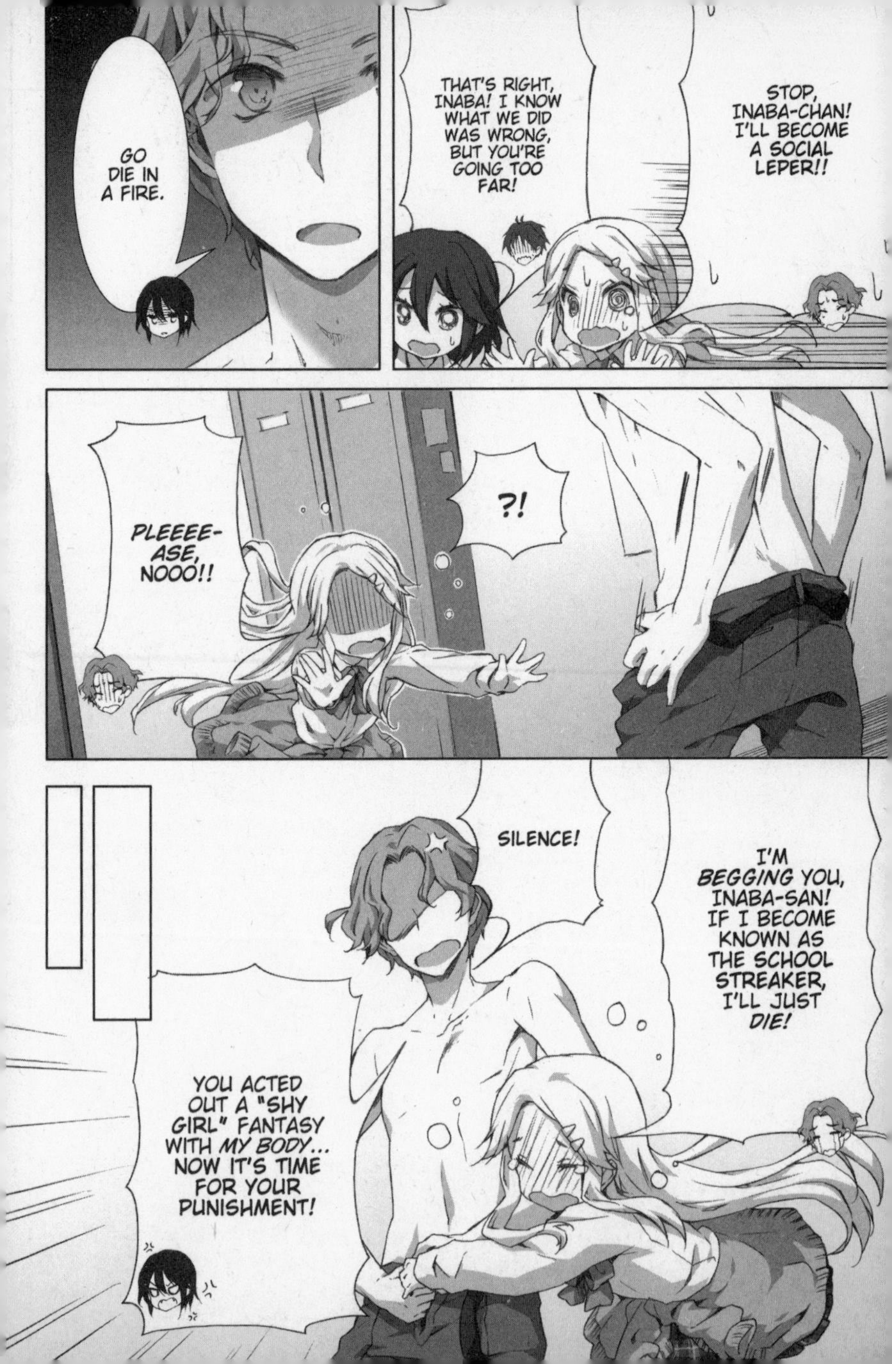
STOP, INABA-CHAN! I'LL BECOME A SOCIAL LEPER!!
THAT'S RIGHT, INABA! I KNOW WHAT WE DID WAS WRONG, BUT YOU'RE GOING TOO FAR!
GO DIE IN A FIRE.
?!
PLEEEE-ASE, NOOO!!
I'M BEGGING YOU, INABA-SAN! IF I BECOME KNOWN AS THE SCHOOL STREAKER, I'LL JUST DIE!
SILENCE!
YOU ACTED OUT A "SHY GIRL" FANTASY WITH MY BODY... NOW IT'S TIME FOR YOUR PUNISHMENT!

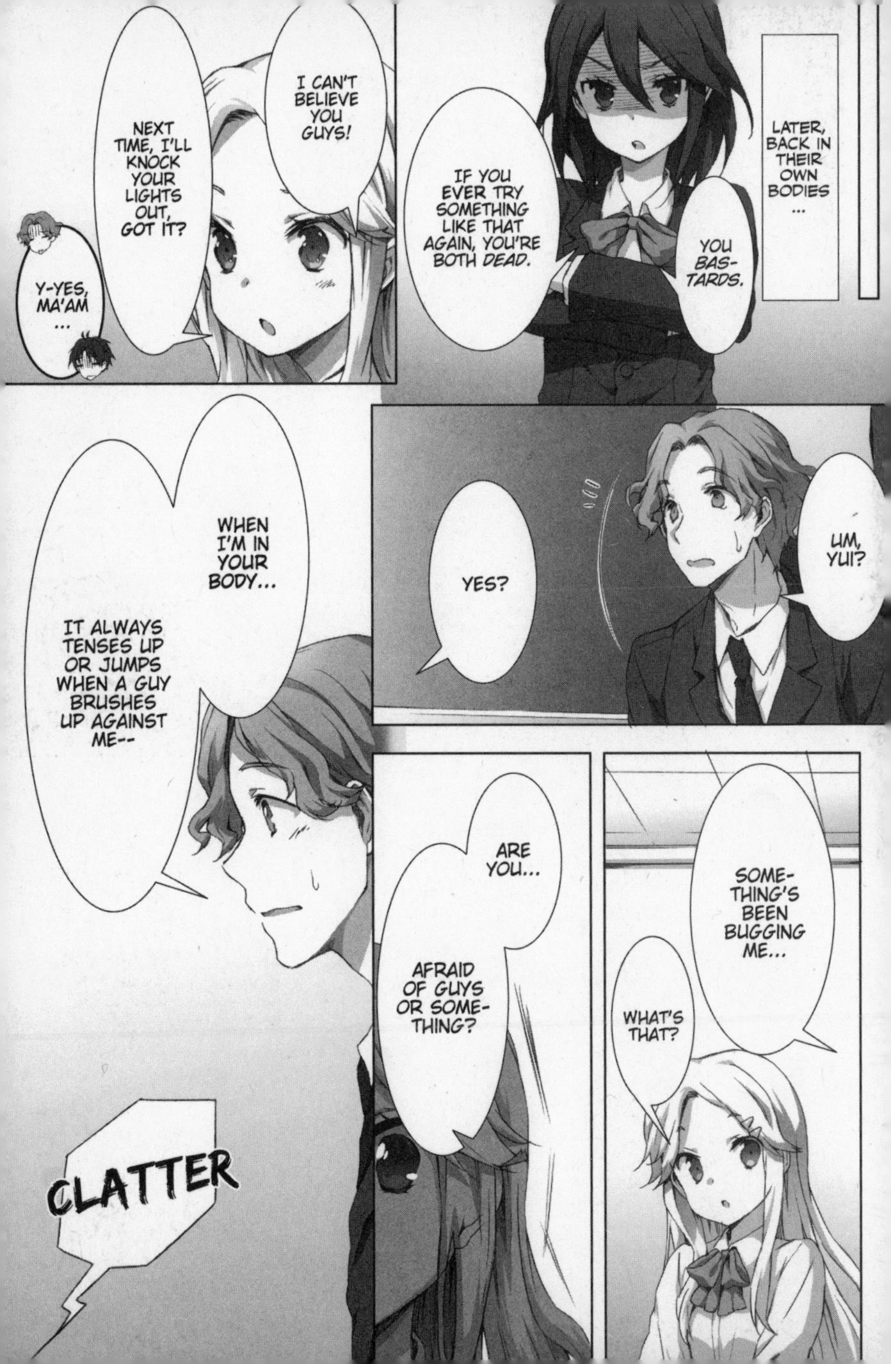
LATER, BACK IN THEIR OWN BODIES ...
YOU BASTARDS.
IF YOU EVER TRY SOMETHING LIKE THAT AGAIN, YOU'RE BOTH *DEAD*.
I CAN'T BELIEVE YOU GUYS!
NEXT TIME, I'LL KNOCK YOUR LIGHTS OUT, GOT IT?
Y-YES, MA'AM ...
UM, YUI?
YES?
SOME-THING'S BEEN BUGGING ME...
WHAT'S THAT?
ARE YOU...
AFRAID OF GUYS OR SOME-THING?
WHEN I'M IN YOUR BODY...
IT ALWAYS TENSES UP OR JUMPS WHEN A GUY BRUSHES UP AGAINST ME--
CLATTER

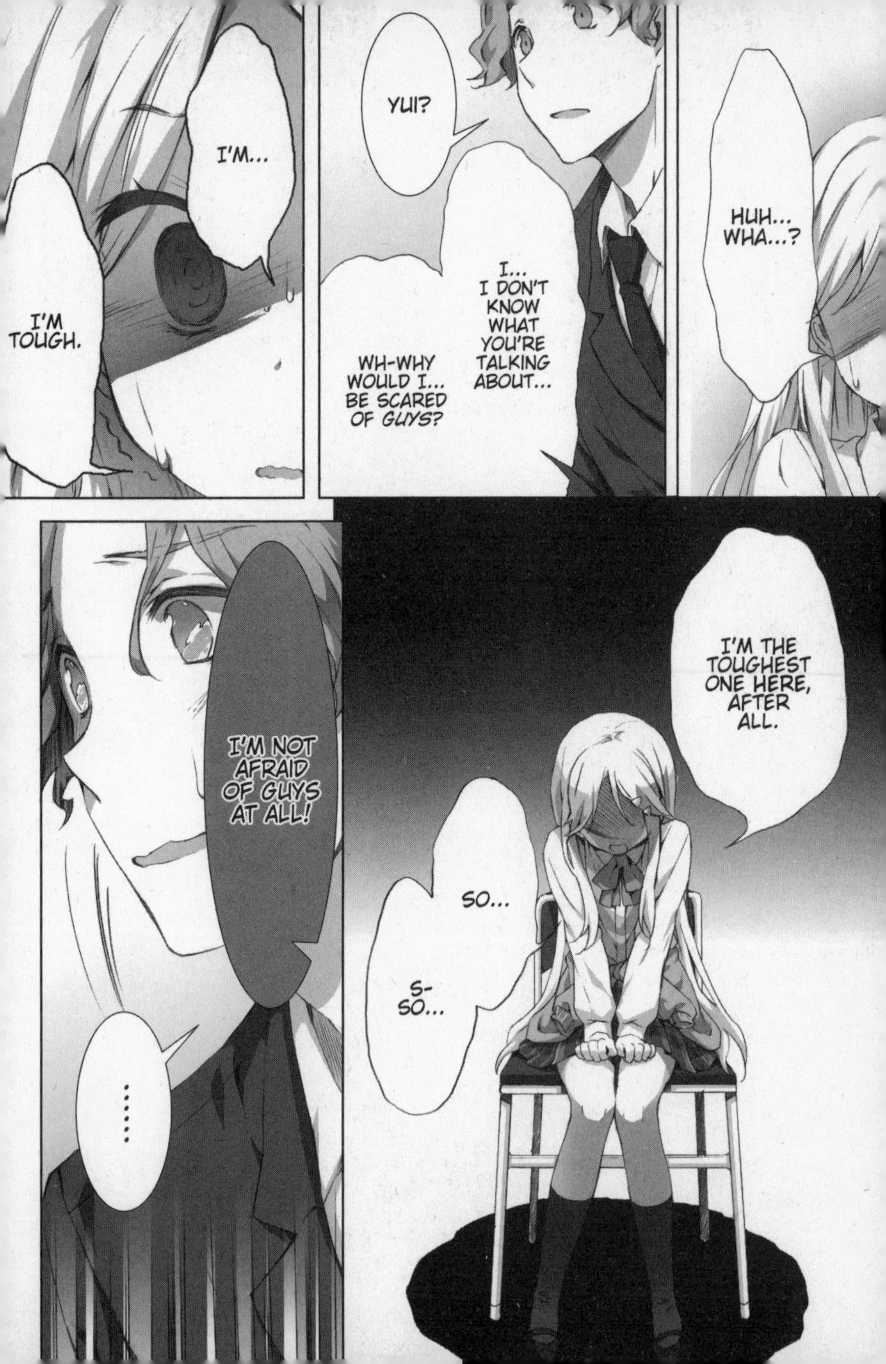
HUH... WHA...?
YUI?
I... I DON'T KNOW WHAT YOU'RE TALKING ABOUT...
WH-WHY WOULD I... BE SCARED OF GUYS?
I'M...
I'M TOUGH.
I'M THE TOUGHEST ONE HERE, AFTER ALL.
SO...
S- SO...
I'M NOT AFRAID OF GUYS AT ALL!
......

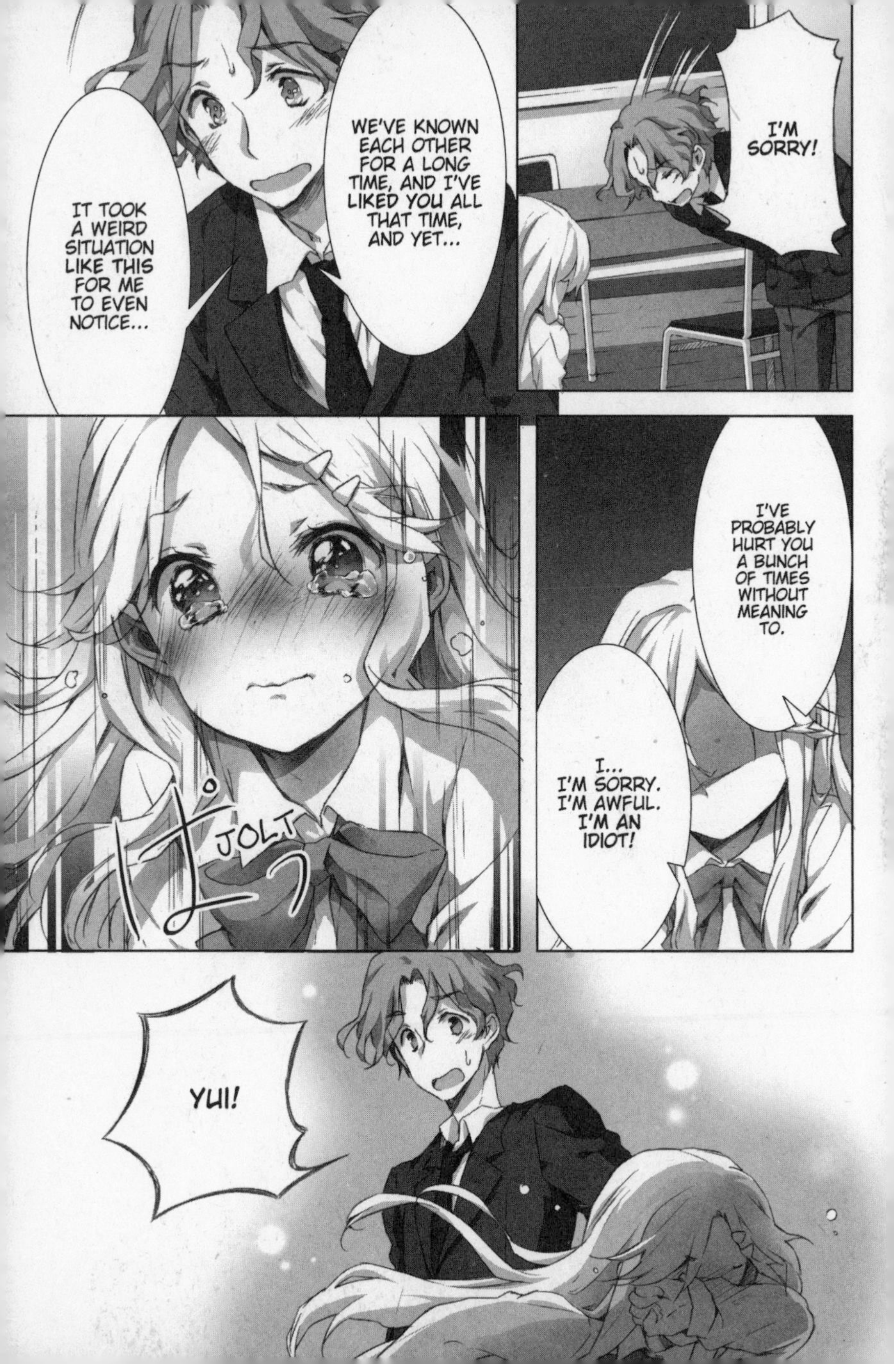
I'M SORRY!
WE'VE KNOWN EACH OTHER FOR A LONG TIME, AND I'VE LIKED YOU ALL THAT TIME, AND YET...
IT TOOK A WEIRD SITUATION LIKE THIS FOR ME TO EVEN NOTICE...
I'VE PROBABLY HURT YOU A BUNCH OF TIMES WITHOUT MEANING TO.
I... I'M SORRY. I'M AWFUL. I'M AN IDIOT!
JOLT
YUI!

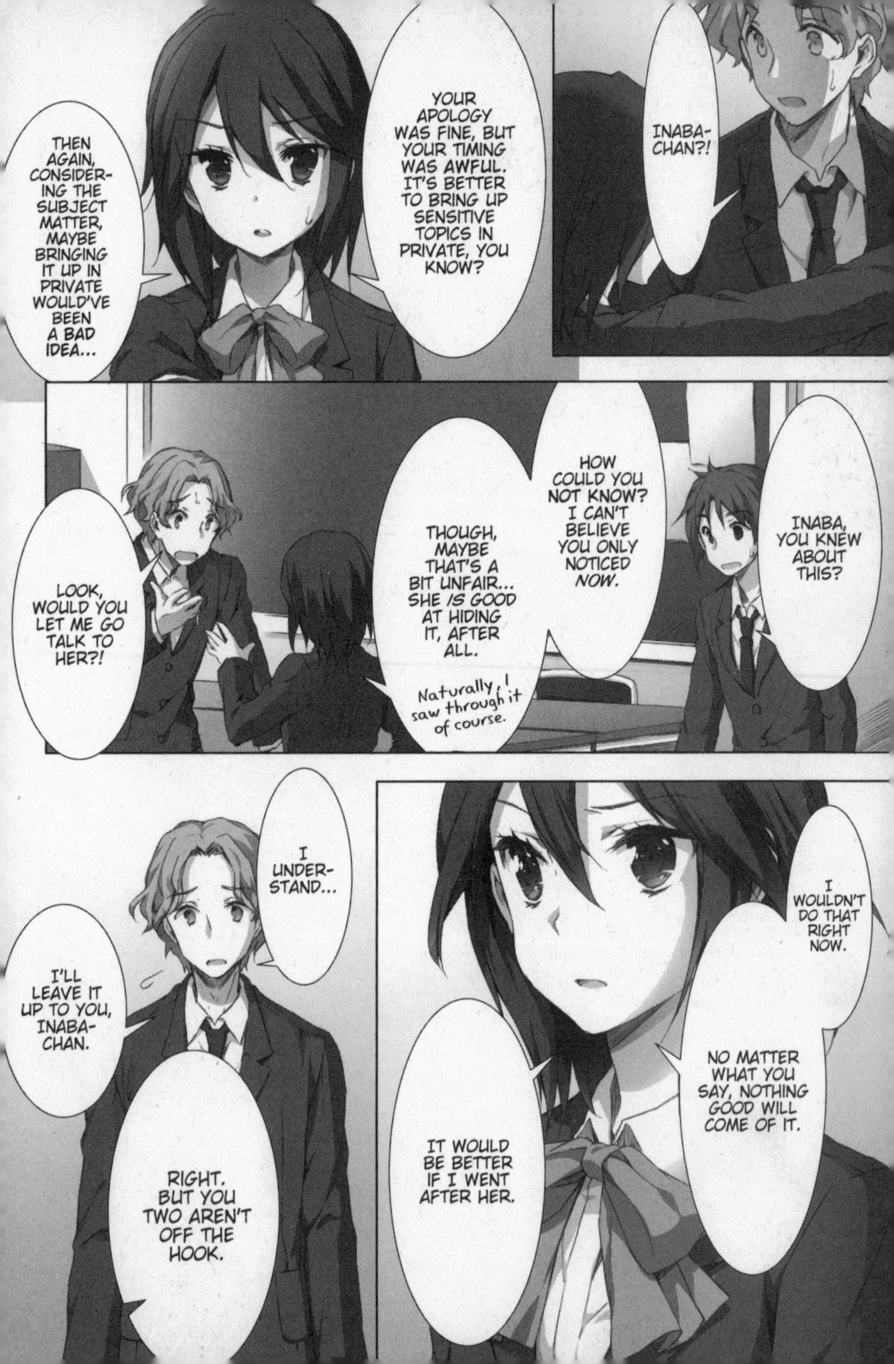
INABA-CHAN?!
YOUR APOLOGY WAS FINE, BUT YOUR TIMING WAS AWFUL. IT'S BETTER TO BRING UP SENSITIVE TOPICS IN PRIVATE, YOU KNOW?
THEN AGAIN, CONSIDERING THE SUBJECT MATTER, MAYBE BRINGING IT UP IN PRIVATE WOULD'VE BEEN A BAD IDEA...
INABA, YOU KNEW ABOUT THIS?
HOW COULD YOU NOT KNOW? I CAN'T BELIEVE YOU ONLY NOTICED *NOW*.
THOUGH, MAYBE THAT'S A BIT UNFAIR... SHE *IS* GOOD AT HIDING IT, AFTER ALL.
Naturally, I saw through it of course.
LOOK, WOULD YOU LET ME GO TALK TO HER?!
I WOULDN'T DO THAT RIGHT NOW.
NO MATTER WHAT YOU SAY, NOTHING GOOD WILL COME OF IT.
IT WOULD BE BETTER IF I WENT AFTER HER.
I UNDERSTAND...
I'LL LEAVE IT UP TO YOU, INABA-CHAN.
RIGHT. BUT YOU TWO AREN'T OFF THE HOOK.

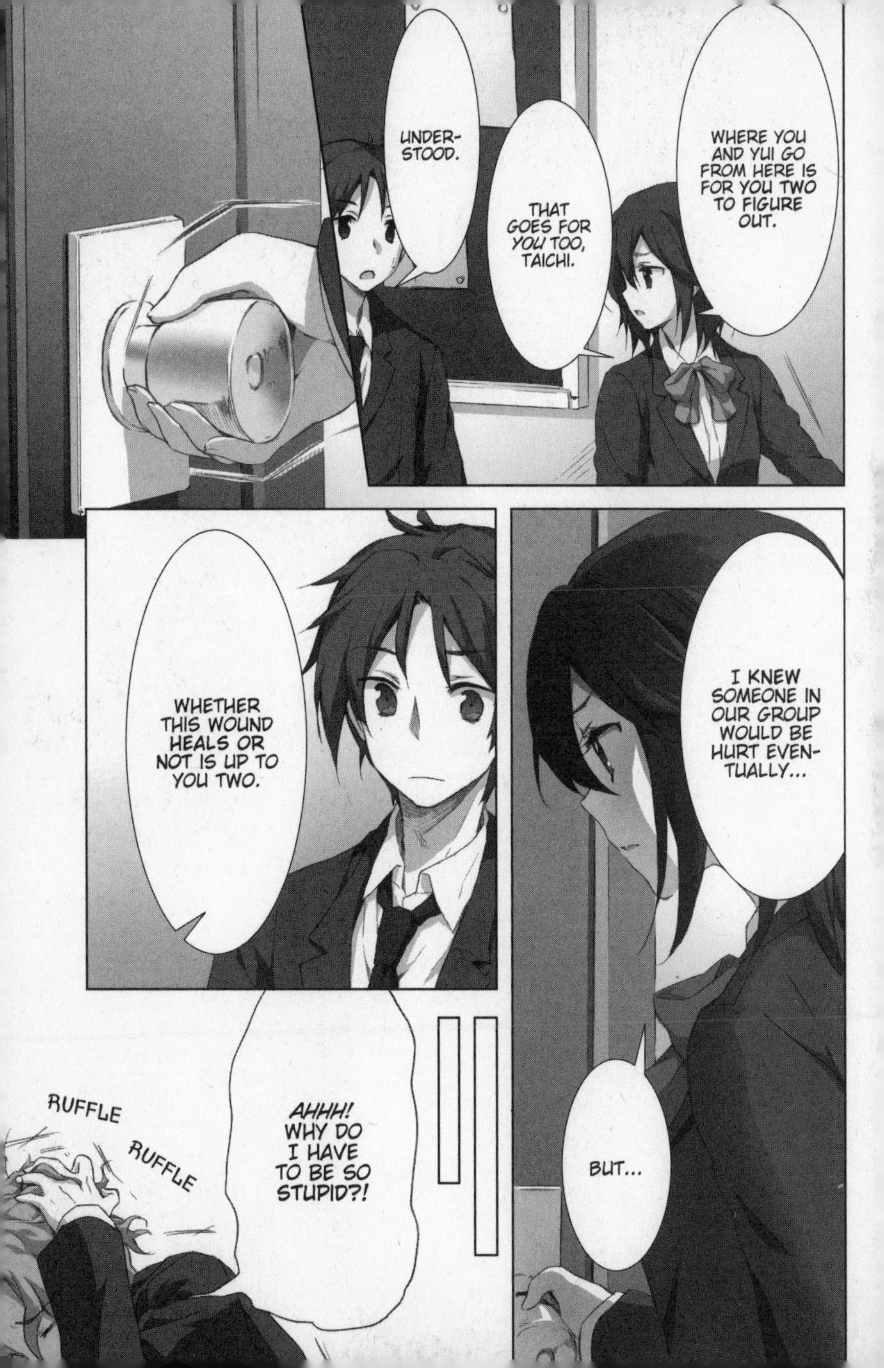
WHERE YOU AND YUI GO FROM HERE IS FOR YOU TWO TO FIGURE OUT.
THAT GOES FOR *YOU* TOO, TAICHI.
UNDER-STOOD.
I KNEW SOMEONE IN OUR GROUP WOULD BE HURT EVEN-TUALLY...
BUT...
WHETHER THIS WOUND HEALS OR NOT IS UP TO YOU TWO.
AHHH! WHY DO I HAVE TO BE SO STUPID?!
RUFFLE
RUFFLE

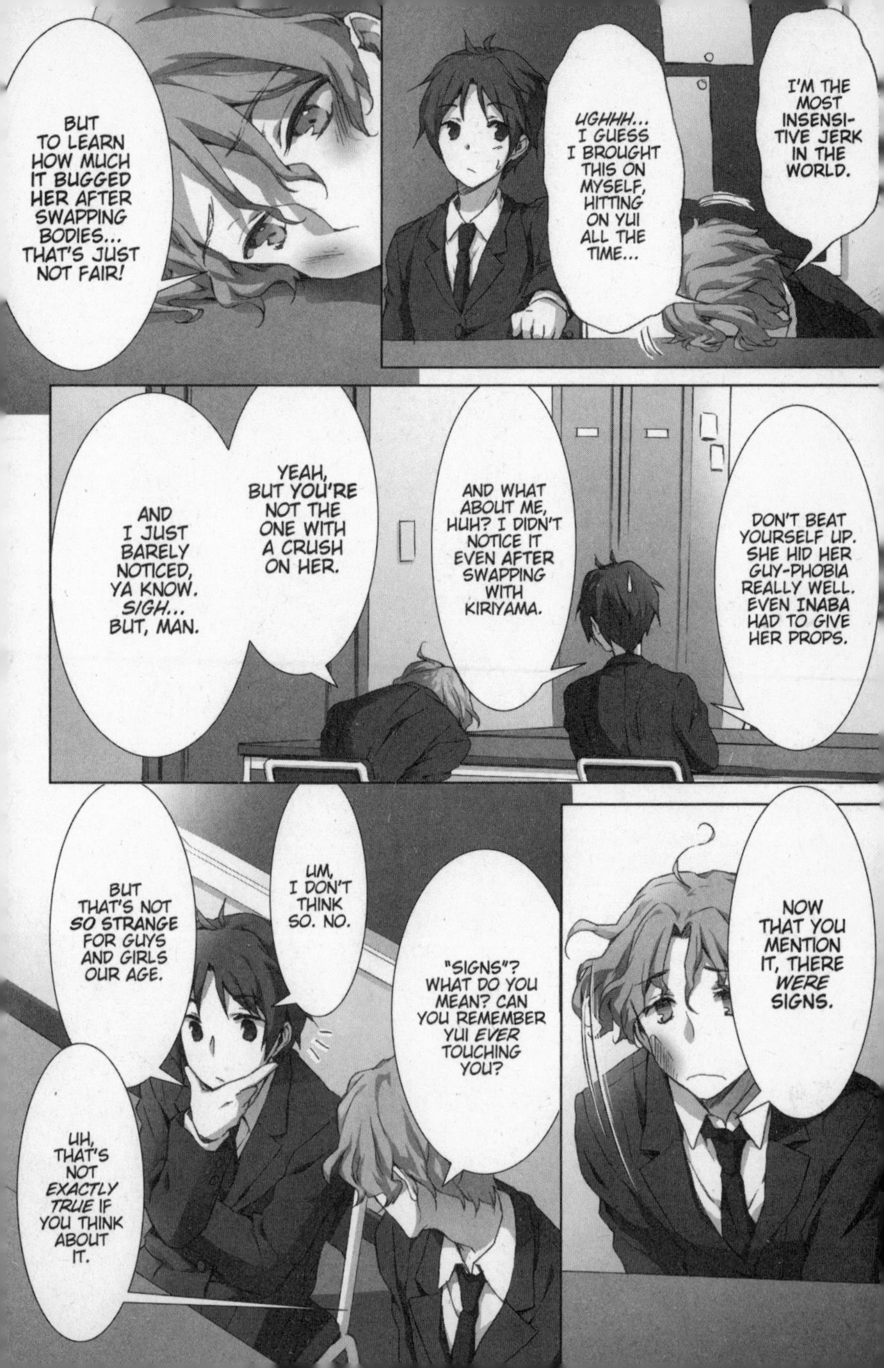
I'M THE MOST INSENSITIVE JERK IN THE WORLD.
UGHHH... I GUESS I BROUGHT THIS ON MYSELF, HITTING ON YUI ALL THE TIME...
BUT TO LEARN HOW MUCH IT BUGGED HER AFTER SWAPPING BODIES... THAT'S JUST NOT FAIR!
DON'T BEAT YOURSELF UP. SHE HID HER GUY-PHOBIA REALLY WELL. EVEN INABA HAD TO GIVE HER PROPS.
AND WHAT ABOUT ME, HUH? I DIDN'T NOTICE IT EVEN AFTER SWAPPING WITH KIRIYAMA.
YEAH, BUT *YOU'RE* NOT THE ONE WITH A CRUSH ON HER.
AND I JUST BARELY NOTICED, YA KNOW. *SIGH...* BUT, MAN.
NOW THAT YOU MENTION IT, THERE *WERE* SIGNS.
"SIGNS"? WHAT DO YOU MEAN? CAN YOU REMEMBER YUI *EVER* TOUCHING YOU?
UM, I DON'T THINK SO. NO.
BUT THAT'S NOT *SO* STRANGE FOR GUYS AND GIRLS OUR AGE.
UH, THAT'S NOT *EXACTLY TRUE* IF YOU THINK ABOUT IT.

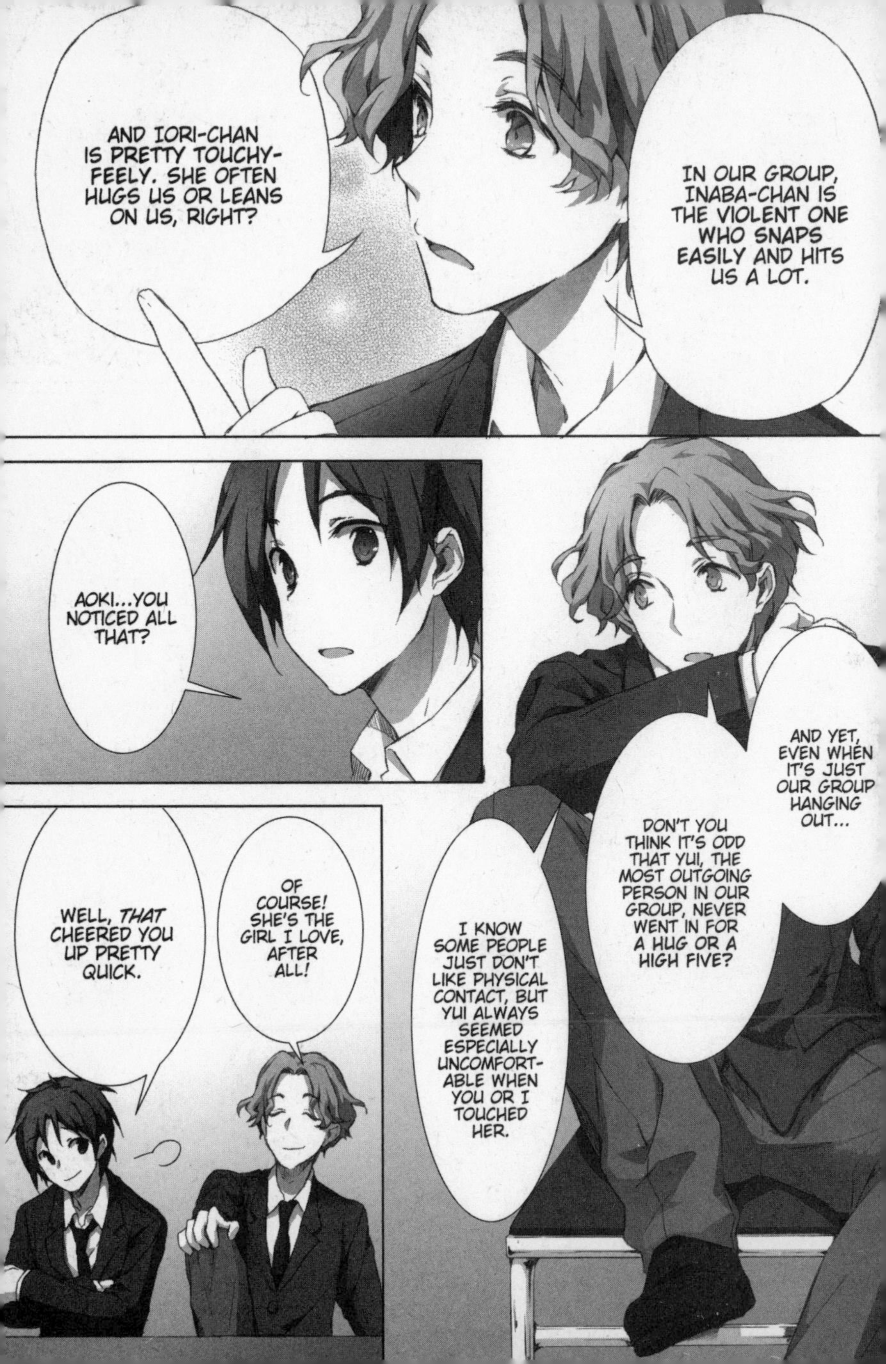
IN OUR GROUP, INABA-CHAN IS THE VIOLENT ONE WHO SNAPS EASILY AND HITS US A LOT.
AND IORI-CHAN IS PRETTY TOUCHY-FEELY. SHE OFTEN HUGS US OR LEANS ON US, RIGHT?
AND YET, EVEN WHEN IT'S JUST OUR GROUP HANGING OUT...
DON'T YOU THINK IT'S ODD THAT YUI, THE MOST OUTGOING PERSON IN OUR GROUP, NEVER WENT IN FOR A HUG OR A HIGH FIVE?
I KNOW SOME PEOPLE JUST DON'T LIKE PHYSICAL CONTACT, BUT YUI ALWAYS SEEMED ESPECIALLY UNCOMFORT-ABLE WHEN YOU OR I TOUCHED HER.
AOKI...YOU NOTICED ALL THAT?
WELL, *THAT* CHEERED YOU UP PRETTY QUICK.
OF COURSE! SHE'S THE GIRL I LOVE, AFTER ALL!

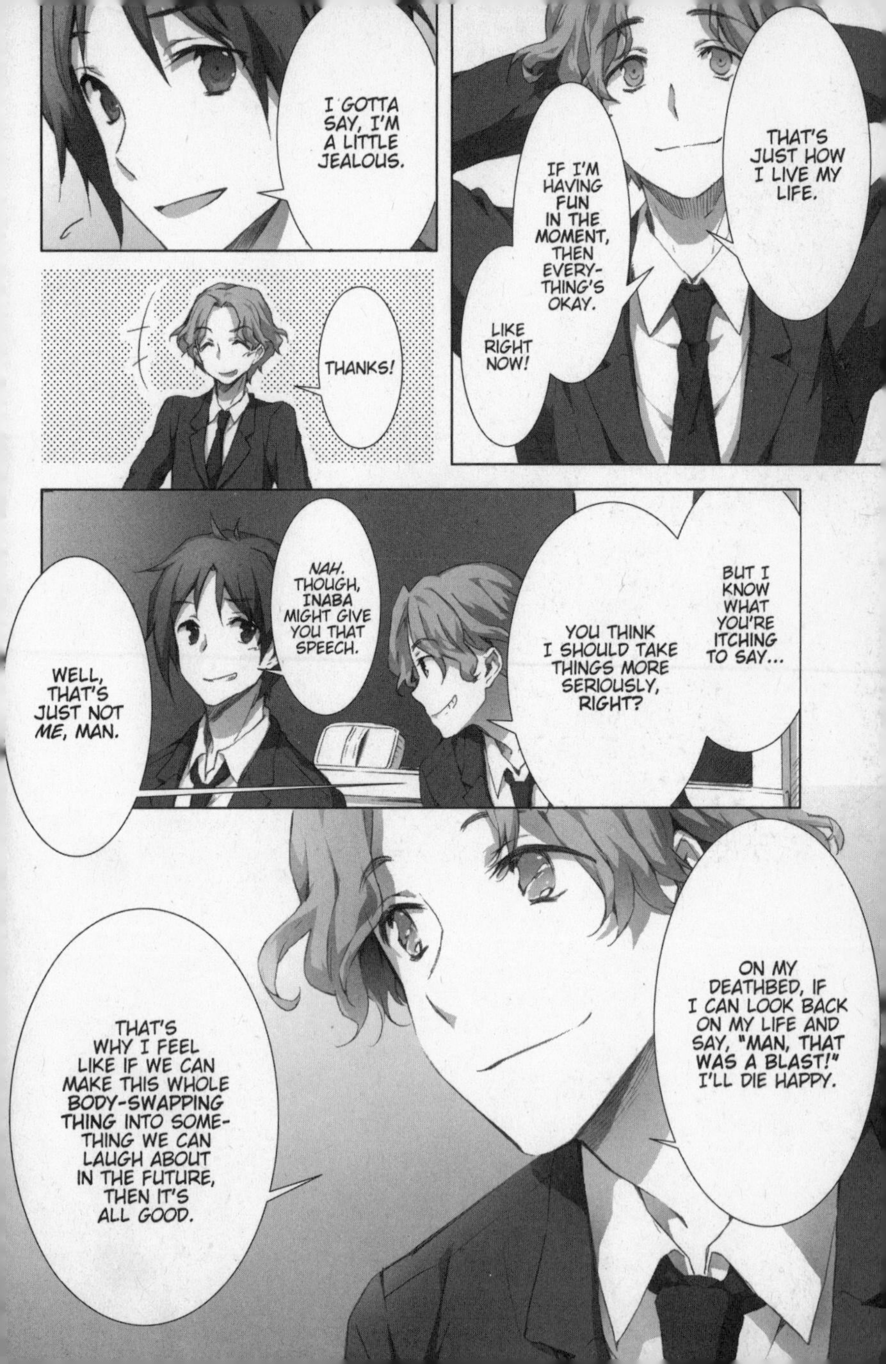
THAT'S JUST HOW I LIVE MY LIFE.
IF I'M HAVING FUN IN THE MOMENT, THEN EVERYTHING'S OKAY.
LIKE RIGHT NOW!
I GOTTA SAY, I'M A LITTLE JEALOUS.
THANKS!
BUT I KNOW WHAT YOU'RE ITCHING TO SAY...
YOU THINK I SHOULD TAKE THINGS MORE SERIOUSLY, RIGHT?
NAH. THOUGH, INABA MIGHT GIVE YOU THAT SPEECH.
WELL, THAT'S JUST NOT ME, MAN.
ON MY DEATHBED, IF I CAN LOOK BACK ON MY LIFE AND SAY, "MAN, THAT WAS A BLAST!" I'LL DIE HAPPY.
THAT'S WHY I FEEL LIKE IF WE CAN MAKE THIS WHOLE BODY-SWAPPING THING INTO SOMETHING WE CAN LAUGH ABOUT IN THE FUTURE, THEN IT'S ALL GOOD.

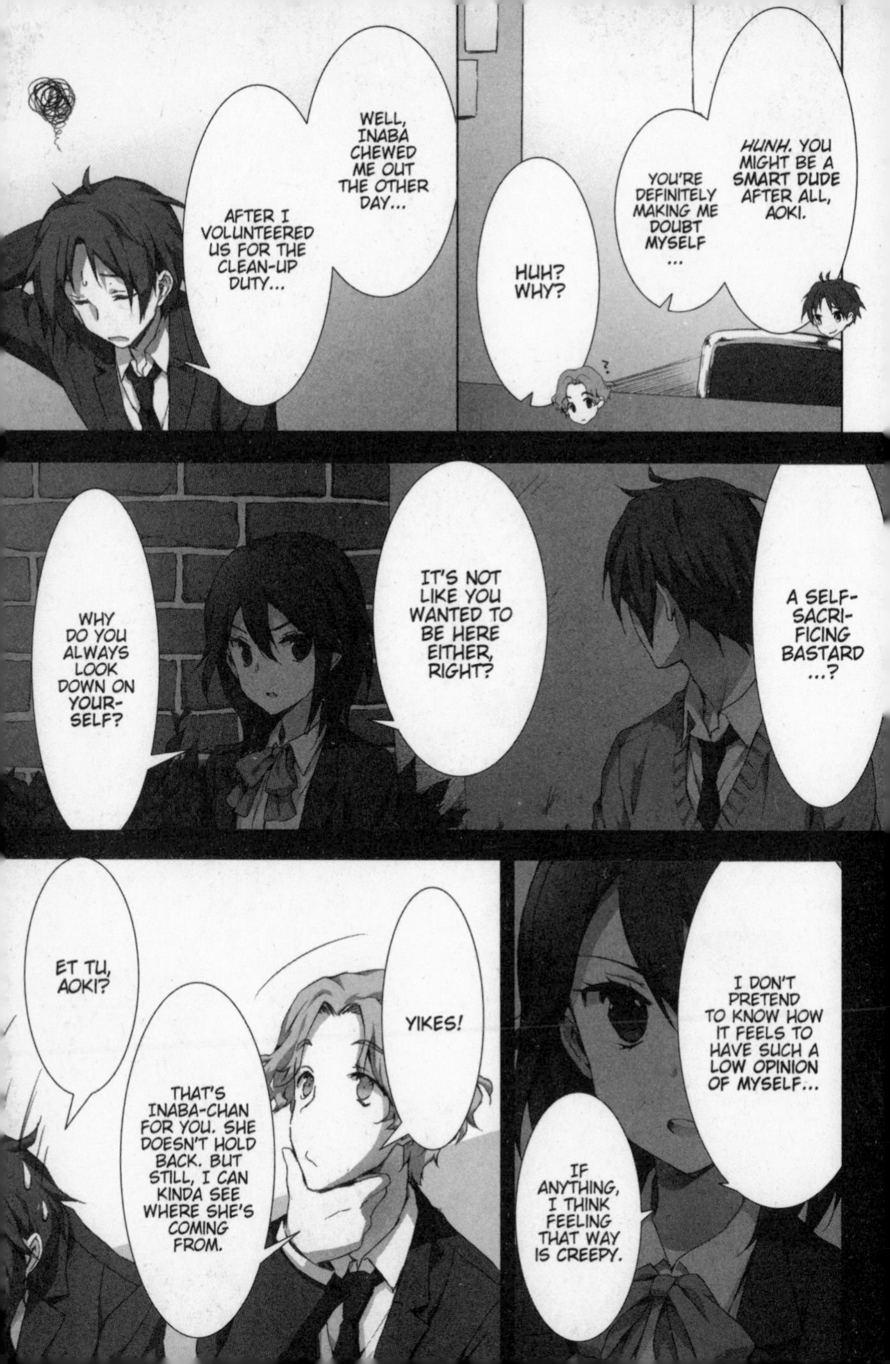
HUNH. YOU MIGHT BE A SMART DUDE AFTER ALL, AOKI.
YOU'RE DEFINITELY MAKING ME DOUBT MYSELF ...
HUH? WHY?
WELL, INABA CHEWED ME OUT THE OTHER DAY...
AFTER I VOLUNTEERED US FOR THE CLEAN-UP DUTY...
A SELF-SACRIFICING BASTARD ...?
IT'S NOT LIKE YOU WANTED TO BE HERE EITHER, RIGHT?
WHY DO YOU ALWAYS LOOK DOWN ON YOURSELF?
I DON'T PRETEND TO KNOW HOW IT FEELS TO HAVE SUCH A LOW OPINION OF MYSELF...
IF ANYTHING, I THINK FEELING THAT WAY IS CREEPY.
YIKES!
THAT'S INABA-CHAN FOR YOU. SHE DOESN'T HOLD BACK. BUT STILL, I CAN KINDA SEE WHERE SHE'S COMING FROM.
ET TU, AOKI?

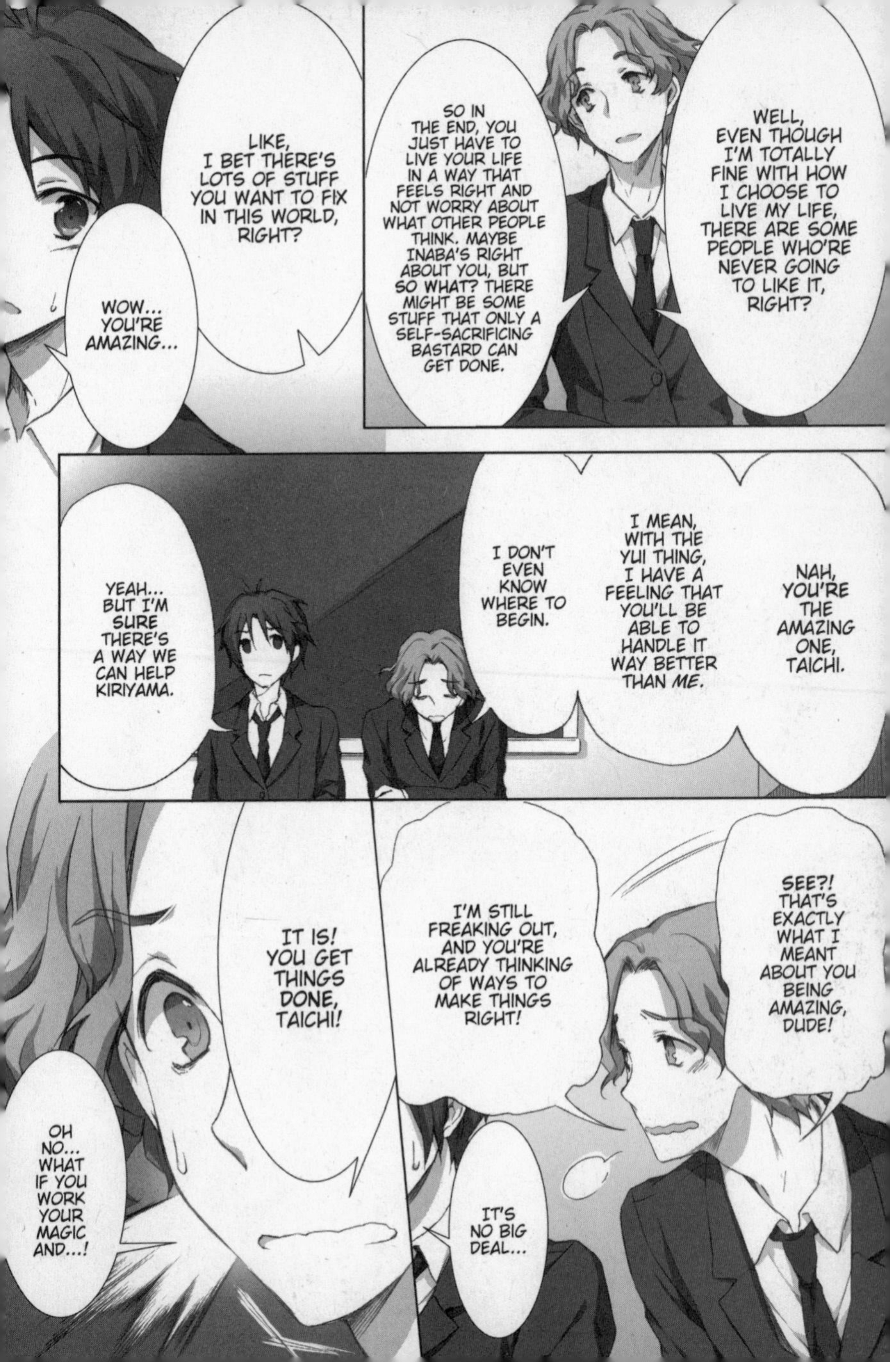
WELL, EVEN THOUGH I'M TOTALLY FINE WITH HOW I CHOOSE TO LIVE MY LIFE, THERE ARE SOME PEOPLE WHO'RE NEVER GOING TO LIKE IT, RIGHT?
SO IN THE END, YOU JUST HAVE TO LIVE YOUR LIFE IN A WAY THAT FEELS RIGHT AND NOT WORRY ABOUT WHAT OTHER PEOPLE THINK. MAYBE INABA'S RIGHT ABOUT YOU, BUT SO WHAT? THERE MIGHT BE SOME STUFF THAT ONLY A SELF-SACRIFICING BASTARD CAN GET DONE.
LIKE, I BET THERE'S LOTS OF STUFF YOU WANT TO FIX IN THIS WORLD, RIGHT?
WOW... YOU'RE AMAZING...
NAH, YOU'RE THE AMAZING ONE, TAICHI.
I MEAN, WITH THE YUI THING, I HAVE A FEELING THAT YOU'LL BE ABLE TO HANDLE IT WAY BETTER THAN *ME*.
I DON'T EVEN KNOW WHERE TO BEGIN.
YEAH... BUT I'M SURE THERE'S A WAY WE CAN HELP KIRIYAMA.
SEE?! THAT'S EXACTLY WHAT I MEANT ABOUT YOU BEING AMAZING, DUDE!
I'M STILL FREAKING OUT, AND YOU'RE ALREADY THINKING OF WAYS TO MAKE THINGS RIGHT!
IT'S NO BIG DEAL...
IT IS! YOU GET THINGS DONE, TAICHI!
OH NO... WHAT IF YOU WORK YOUR MAGIC AND...!

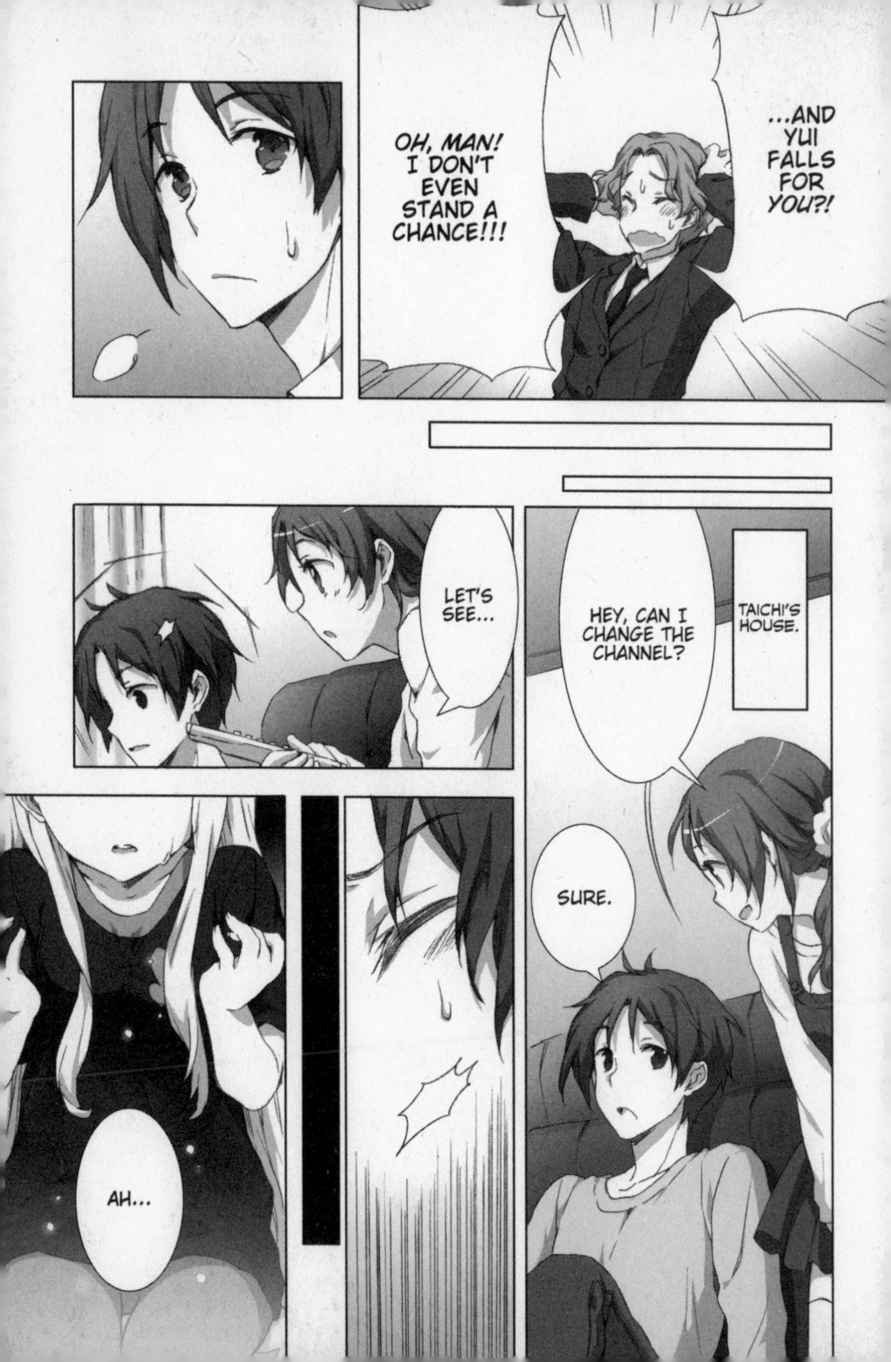
...AND YUI FALLS FOR YOU?!
OH, MAN! I DON'T EVEN STAND A CHANCE!!!
TAICHI'S HOUSE.
HEY, CAN I CHANGE THE CHANNEL?
SURE.
LET'S SEE...
AH...

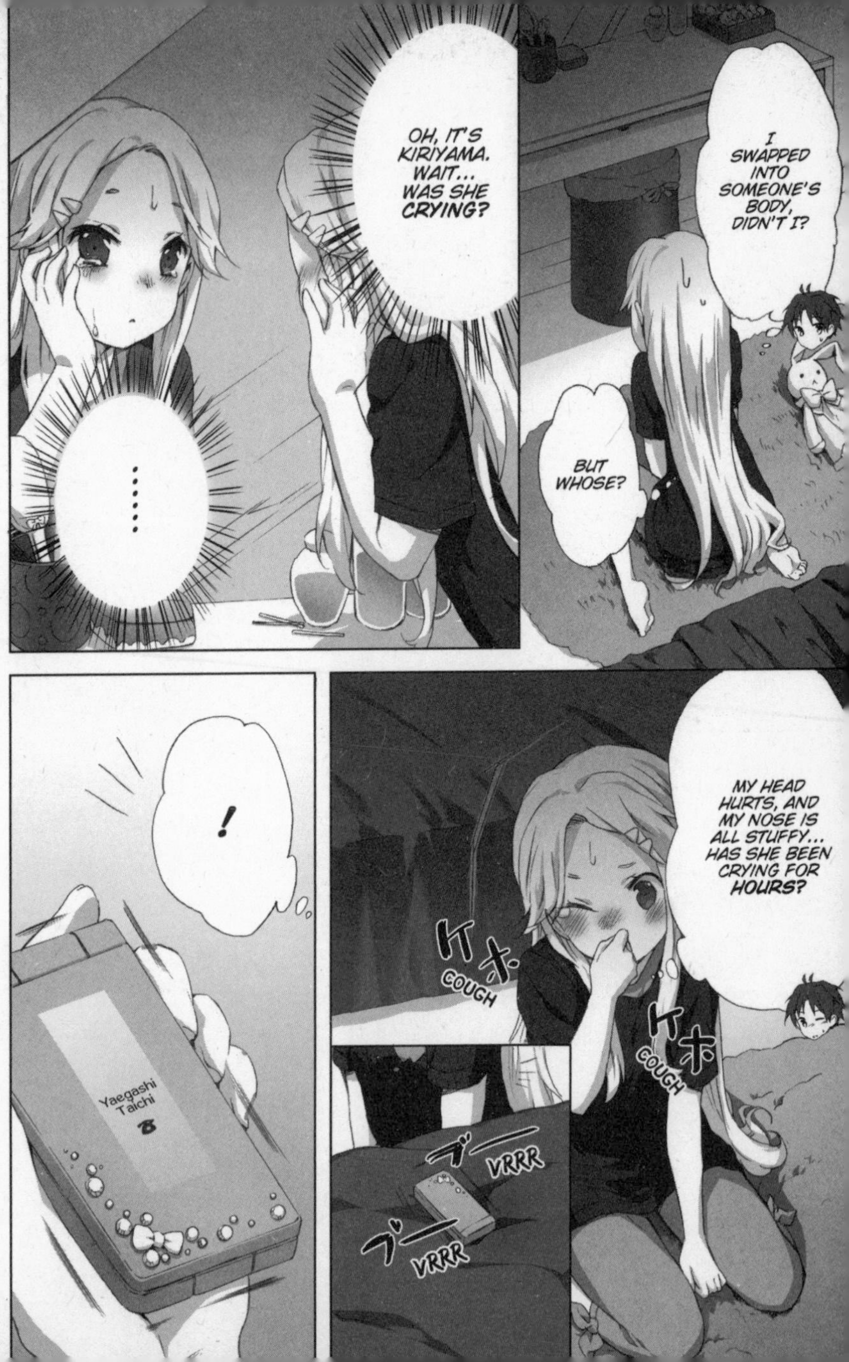
I SWAPPED INTO SOMEONE'S BODY, DIDN'T I?
BUT WHOSE?
OH, IT'S KIRIYAMA. WAIT... WAS SHE CRYING?
......
MY HEAD HURTS, AND MY NOSE IS ALL STUFFY... HAS SHE BEEN CRYING FOR HOURS?
ケホ COUGH
ケホ COUGH
ブー VRRR
ブー VRRR
!
Yaegashi Taichi

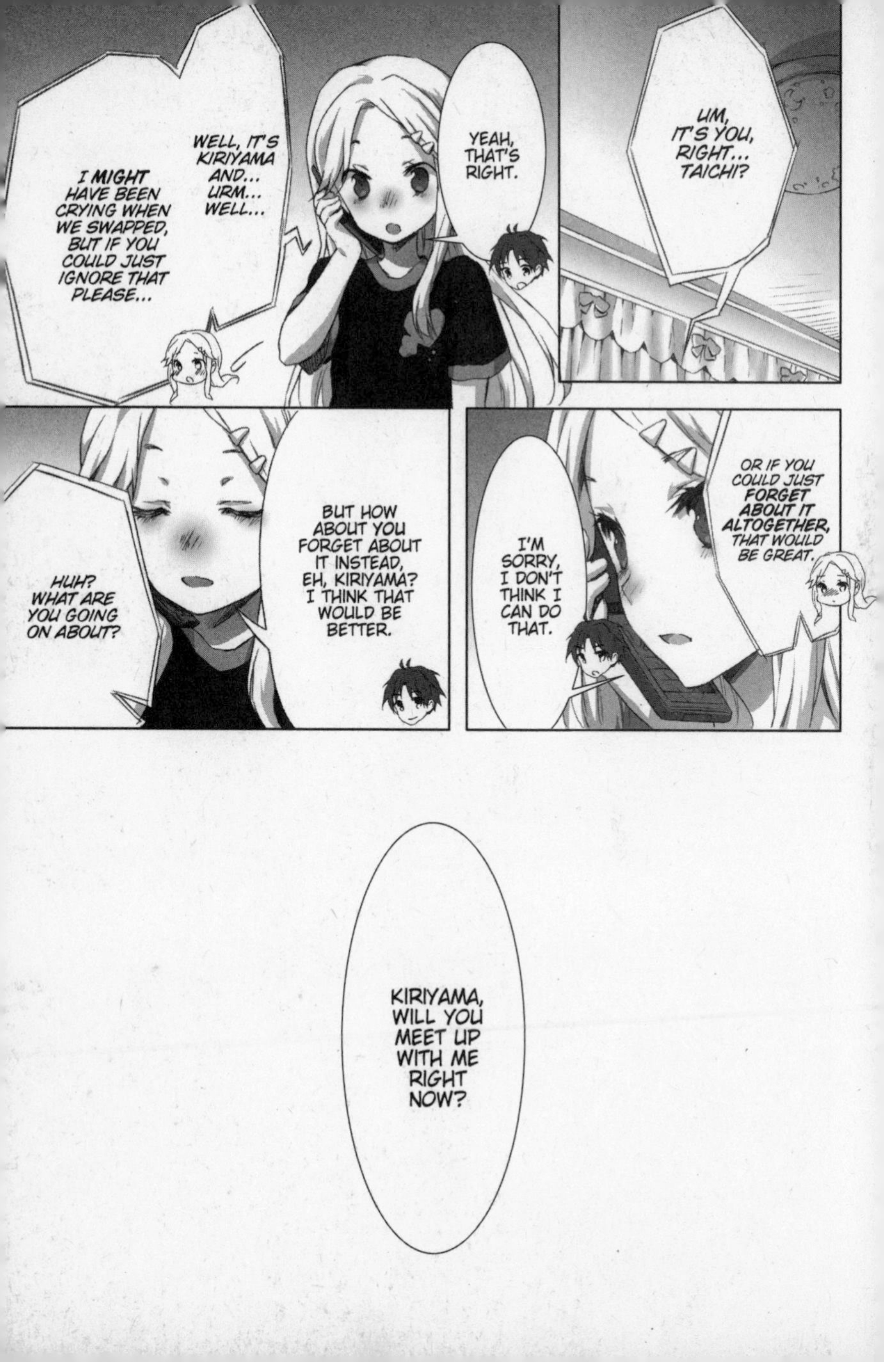
UM, IT'S YOU, RIGHT... TAICHI?
YEAH, THAT'S RIGHT.
WELL, IT'S KIRIYAMA AND... URM... WELL...
I MIGHT HAVE BEEN CRYING WHEN WE SWAPPED, BUT IF YOU COULD JUST IGNORE THAT PLEASE...
OR IF YOU COULD JUST FORGET ABOUT IT ALTOGETHER, THAT WOULD BE GREAT.
I'M SORRY, I DON'T THINK I CAN DO THAT.
BUT HOW ABOUT YOU FORGET ABOUT IT INSTEAD, EH, KIRIYAMA? I THINK THAT WOULD BE BETTER.
HUH? WHAT ARE YOU GOING ON ABOUT?
KIRIYAMA, WILL YOU MEET UP WITH ME RIGHT NOW?

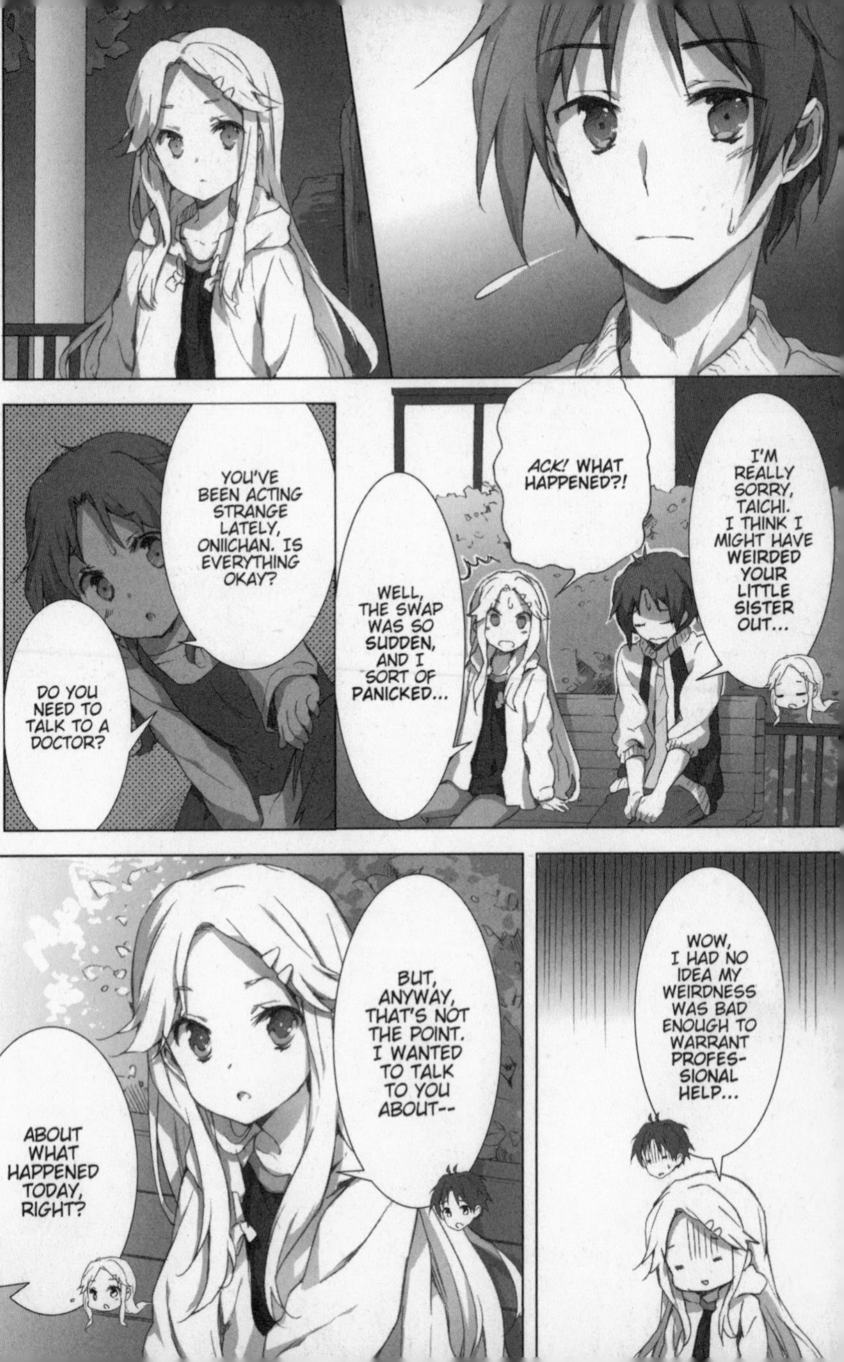
I'M REALLY SORRY, TAICHI. I THINK I MIGHT HAVE WEIRDED YOUR LITTLE SISTER OUT...
ACK! WHAT HAPPENED?!
WELL, THE SWAP WAS SO SUDDEN, AND I SORT OF PANICKED...
YOU'VE BEEN ACTING STRANGE LATELY, ONIICHAN. IS EVERYTHING OKAY?
DO YOU NEED TO TALK TO A DOCTOR?
WOW, I HAD NO IDEA MY WEIRDNESS WAS BAD ENOUGH TO WARRANT PROFES-SIONAL HELP...
BUT, ANYWAY, THAT'S NOT THE POINT. I WANTED TO TALK TO YOU ABOUT--
ABOUT WHAT HAPPENED TODAY, RIGHT?

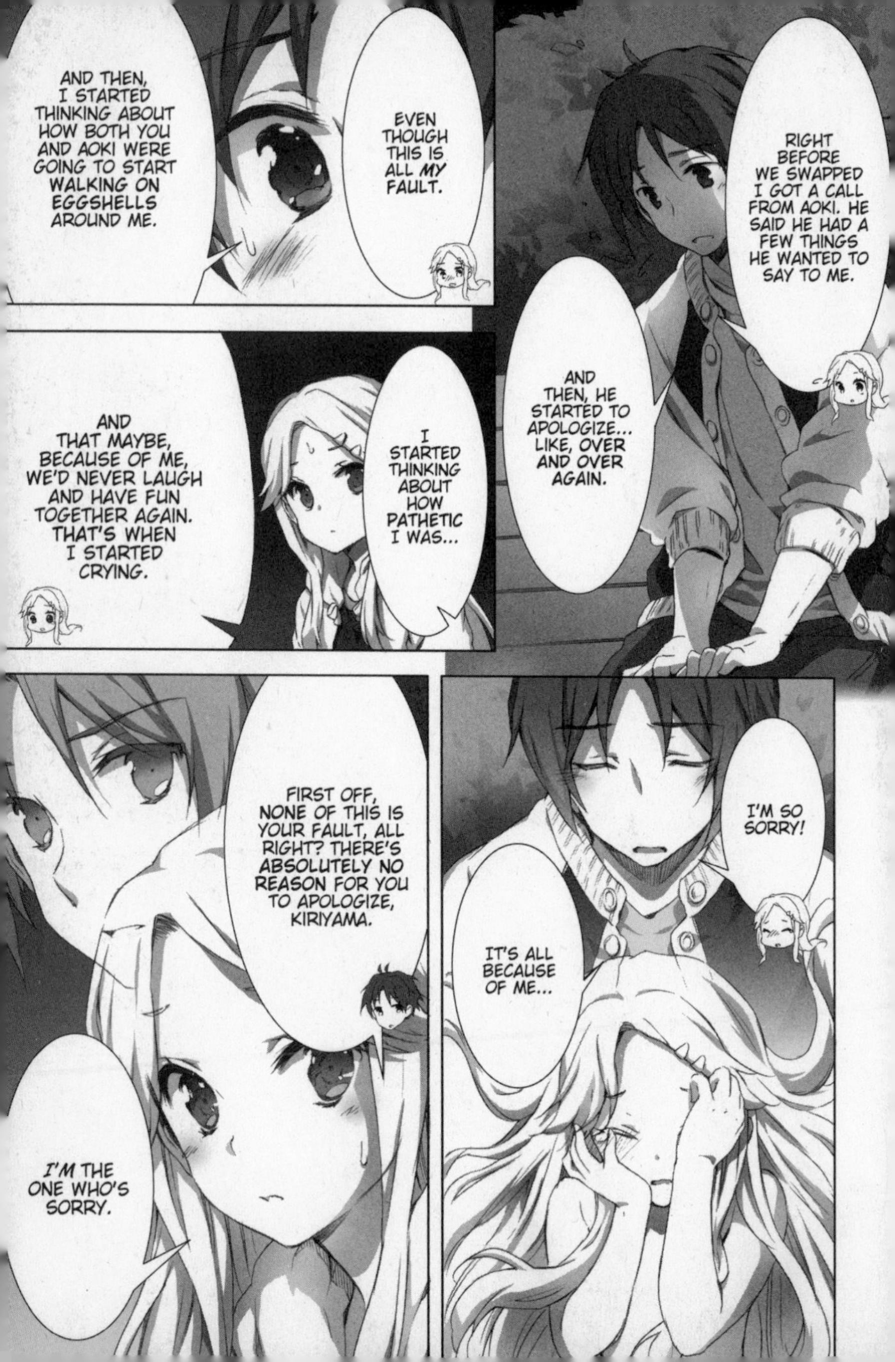
RIGHT BEFORE WE SWAPPED I GOT A CALL FROM AOKI. HE SAID HE HAD A FEW THINGS HE WANTED TO SAY TO ME.
AND THEN, HE STARTED TO APOLOGIZE... LIKE, OVER AND OVER AGAIN.
EVEN THOUGH THIS IS ALL *MY* FAULT.
AND THEN, I STARTED THINKING ABOUT HOW BOTH YOU AND AOKI WERE GOING TO START WALKING ON EGGSHELLS AROUND ME.
I STARTED THINKING ABOUT HOW PATHETIC I WAS...
AND THAT MAYBE, BECAUSE OF ME, WE'D NEVER LAUGH AND HAVE FUN TOGETHER AGAIN. THAT'S WHEN I STARTED CRYING.
I'M SO SORRY!
IT'S ALL BECAUSE OF ME...
FIRST OFF, NONE OF THIS IS YOUR FAULT, ALL RIGHT? THERE'S ABSOLUTELY NO REASON FOR YOU TO APOLOGIZE, KIRIYAMA.
I'M THE ONE WHO'S SORRY.

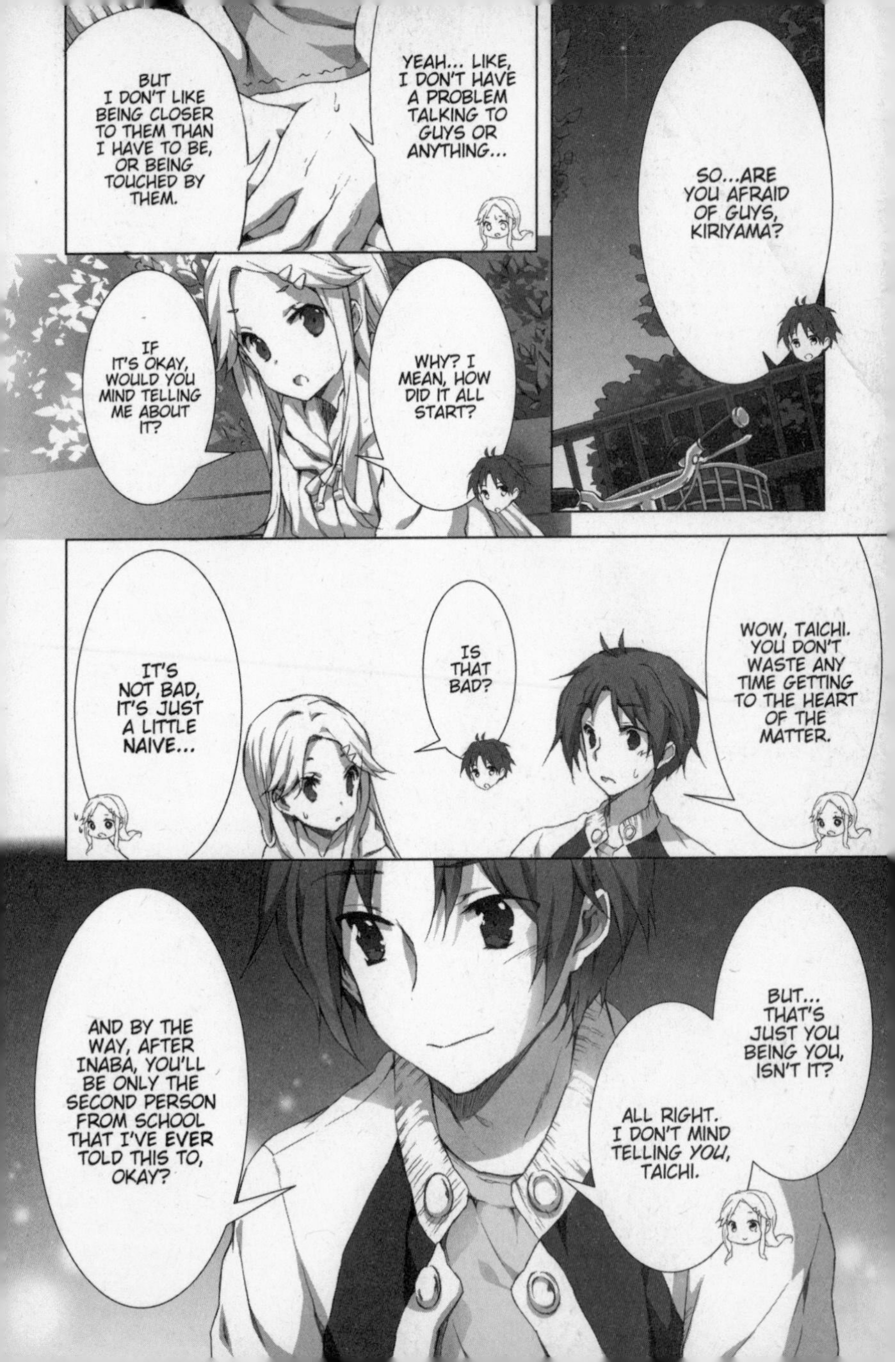

SO...ARE YOU AFRAID OF GUYS, KIRIYAMA?
YEAH... LIKE, I DON'T HAVE A PROBLEM TALKING TO GUYS OR ANYTHING...
BUT I DON'T LIKE BEING CLOSER TO THEM THAN I HAVE TO BE, OR BEING TOUCHED BY THEM.
WHY? I MEAN, HOW DID IT ALL START?
IF IT'S OKAY, WOULD YOU MIND TELLING ME ABOUT IT?
WOW, TAICHI. YOU DON'T WASTE ANY TIME GETTING TO THE HEART OF THE MATTER.
IS THAT BAD?
IT'S NOT BAD, IT'S JUST A LITTLE NAIVE...
BUT... THAT'S JUST YOU BEING YOU, ISN'T IT?
ALL RIGHT. I DON'T MIND TELLING *YOU*, TAICHI.
AND BY THE WAY, AFTER INABA, YOU'LL BE ONLY THE SECOND PERSON FROM SCHOOL THAT I'VE EVER TOLD THIS TO, OKAY?

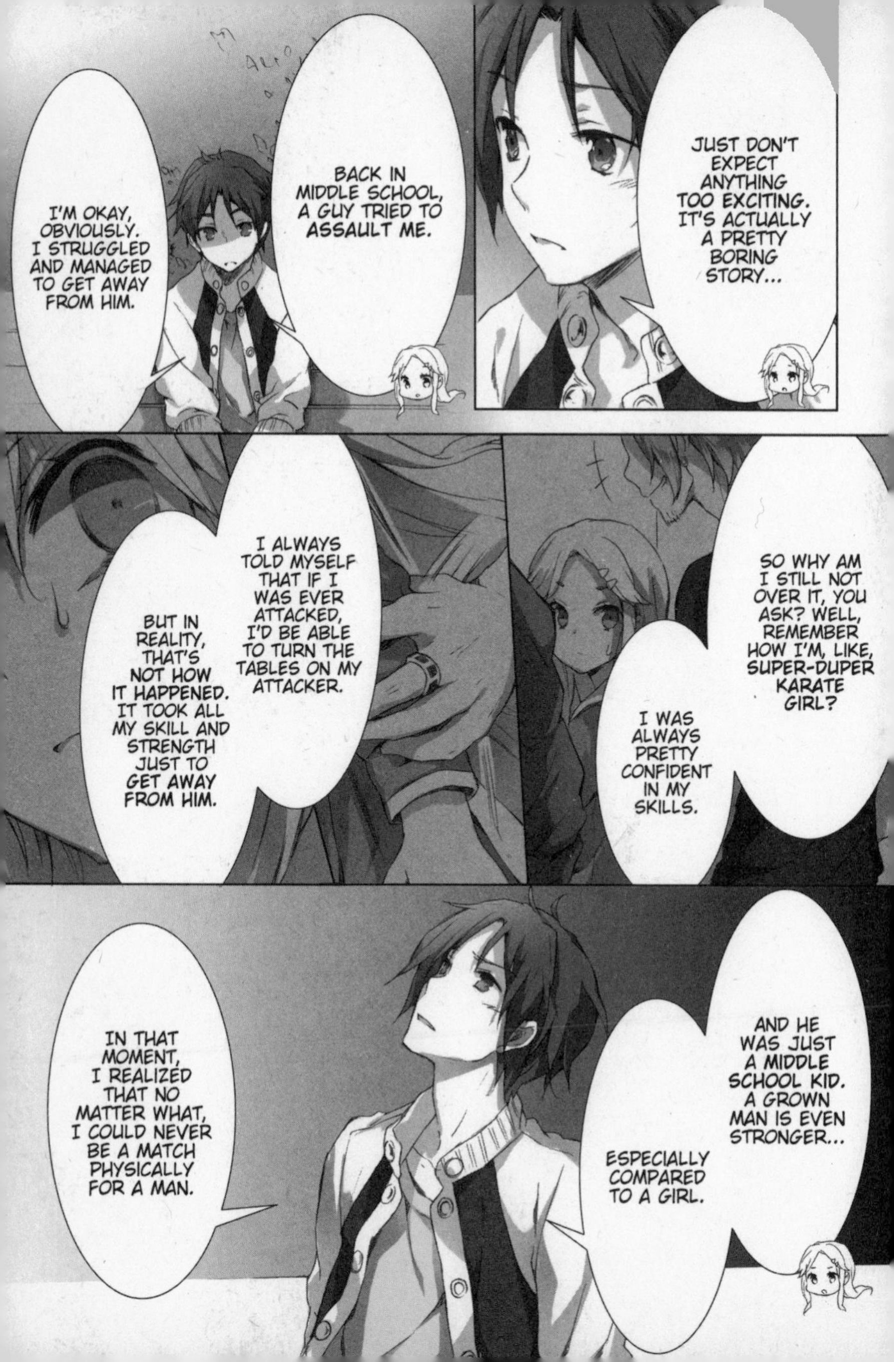
JUST DON'T EXPECT ANYTHING TOO EXCITING. IT'S ACTUALLY A PRETTY BORING STORY...
BACK IN MIDDLE SCHOOL, A GUY TRIED TO ASSAULT ME.
I'M OKAY, OBVIOUSLY. I STRUGGLED AND MANAGED TO GET AWAY FROM HIM.
SO WHY AM I STILL NOT OVER IT, YOU ASK? WELL, REMEMBER HOW I'M, LIKE, SUPER-DUPER KARATE GIRL?
I WAS ALWAYS PRETTY CONFIDENT IN MY SKILLS.
I ALWAYS TOLD MYSELF THAT IF I WAS EVER ATTACKED, I'D BE ABLE TO TURN THE TABLES ON MY ATTACKER.
BUT IN REALITY, THAT'S NOT HOW IT HAPPENED. IT TOOK ALL MY SKILL AND STRENGTH JUST TO GET AWAY FROM HIM.
AND HE WAS JUST A MIDDLE SCHOOL KID. A GROWN MAN IS EVEN STRONGER...
ESPECIALLY COMPARED TO A GIRL.
IN THAT MOMENT, I REALIZED THAT NO MATTER WHAT, I COULD NEVER BE A MATCH PHYSICALLY FOR A MAN.

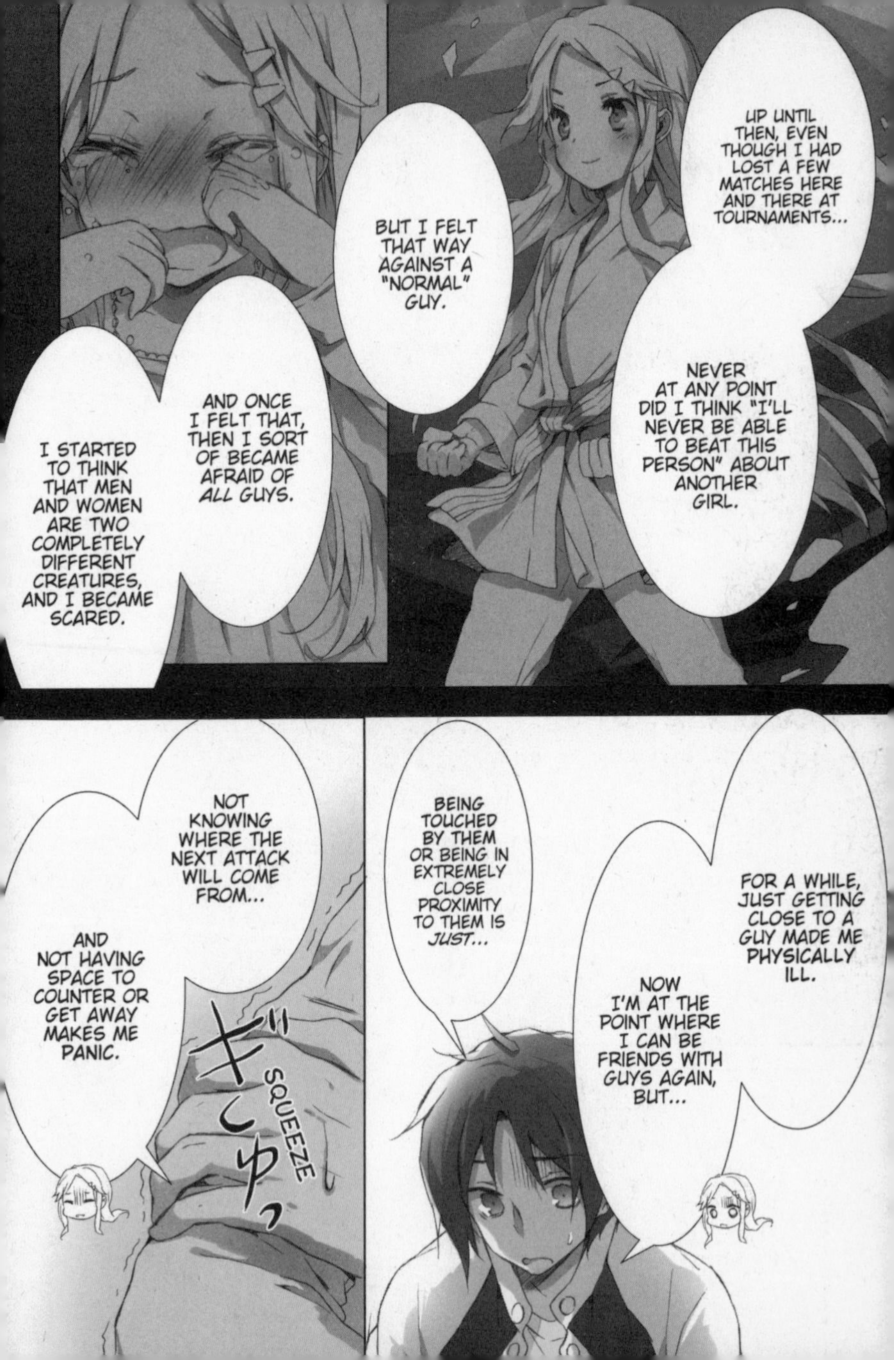
UP UNTIL THEN, EVEN THOUGH I HAD LOST A FEW MATCHES HERE AND THERE AT TOURNAMENTS...
NEVER AT ANY POINT DID I THINK "I'LL NEVER BE ABLE TO BEAT THIS PERSON" ABOUT ANOTHER GIRL.
BUT I FELT THAT WAY AGAINST A "NORMAL" GUY.
AND ONCE I FELT THAT, THEN I SORT OF BECAME AFRAID OF *ALL* GUYS.
I STARTED TO THINK THAT MEN AND WOMEN ARE TWO COMPLETELY DIFFERENT CREATURES, AND I BECAME SCARED.
FOR A WHILE, JUST GETTING CLOSE TO A GUY MADE ME PHYSICALLY ILL.
NOW I'M AT THE POINT WHERE I CAN BE FRIENDS WITH GUYS AGAIN, BUT...
BEING TOUCHED BY THEM OR BEING IN EXTREMELY CLOSE PROXIMITY TO THEM IS *JUST*...
NOT KNOWING WHERE THE NEXT ATTACK WILL COME FROM...
AND NOT HAVING SPACE TO COUNTER OR GET AWAY MAKES ME PANIC.
ぎゅっ
SQUEEZE

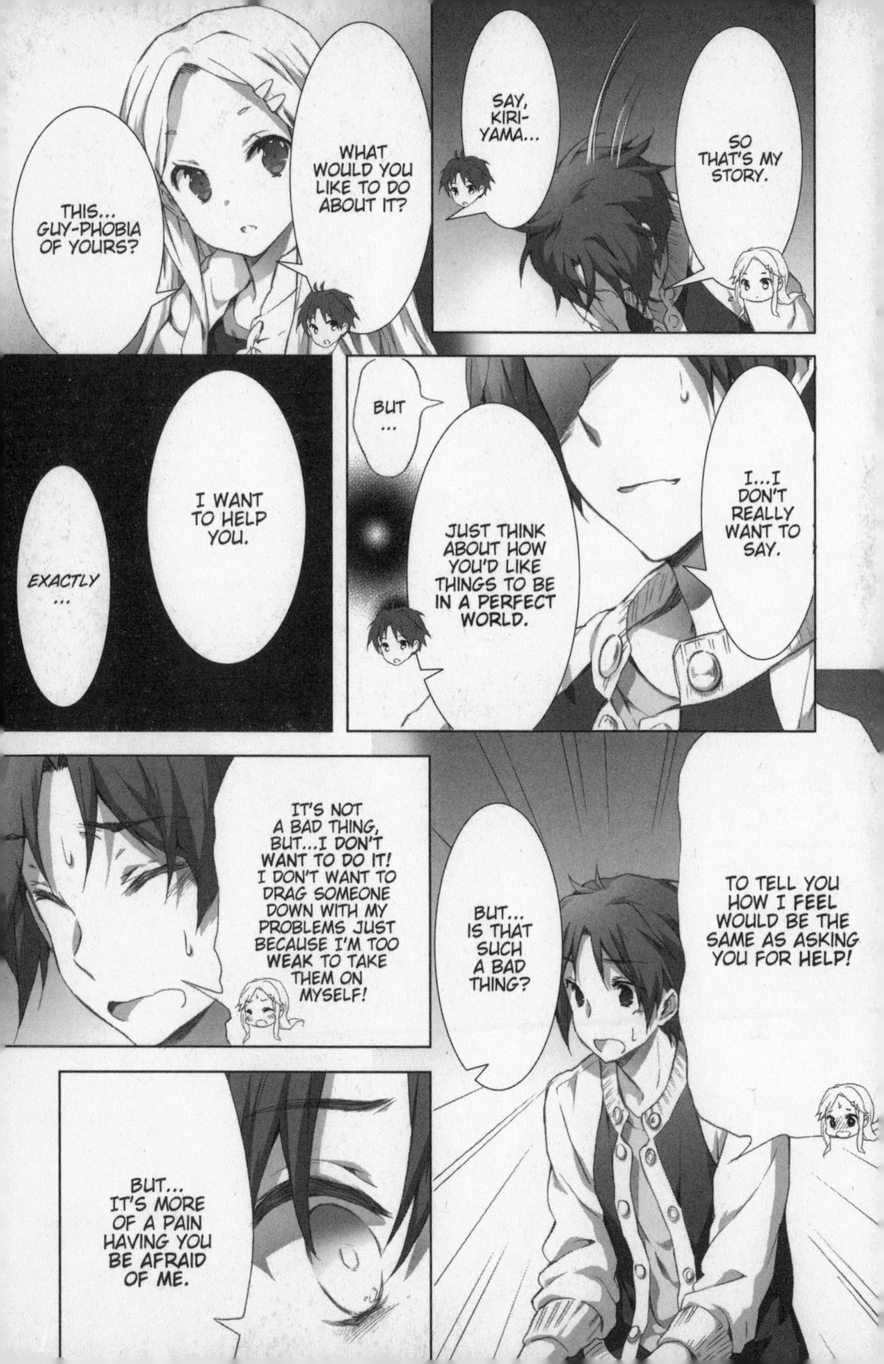

SO THAT'S MY STORY.
SAY, KIRI-YAMA...
WHAT WOULD YOU LIKE TO DO ABOUT IT?
THIS... GUY-PHOBIA OF YOURS?
I...I DON'T REALLY WANT TO SAY.
JUST THINK ABOUT HOW YOU'D LIKE THINGS TO BE IN A PERFECT WORLD.
BUT ...
I WANT TO HELP YOU.
EXACTLY ...
TO TELL YOU HOW I FEEL WOULD BE THE SAME AS ASKING YOU FOR HELP!
BUT... IS THAT SUCH A BAD THING?
IT'S NOT A BAD THING, BUT...I DON'T WANT TO DO IT! I DON'T WANT TO DRAG SOMEONE DOWN WITH MY PROBLEMS JUST BECAUSE I'M TOO WEAK TO TAKE THEM ON MYSELF!
BUT... IT'S MORE OF A PAIN HAVING YOU BE AFRAID OF ME.

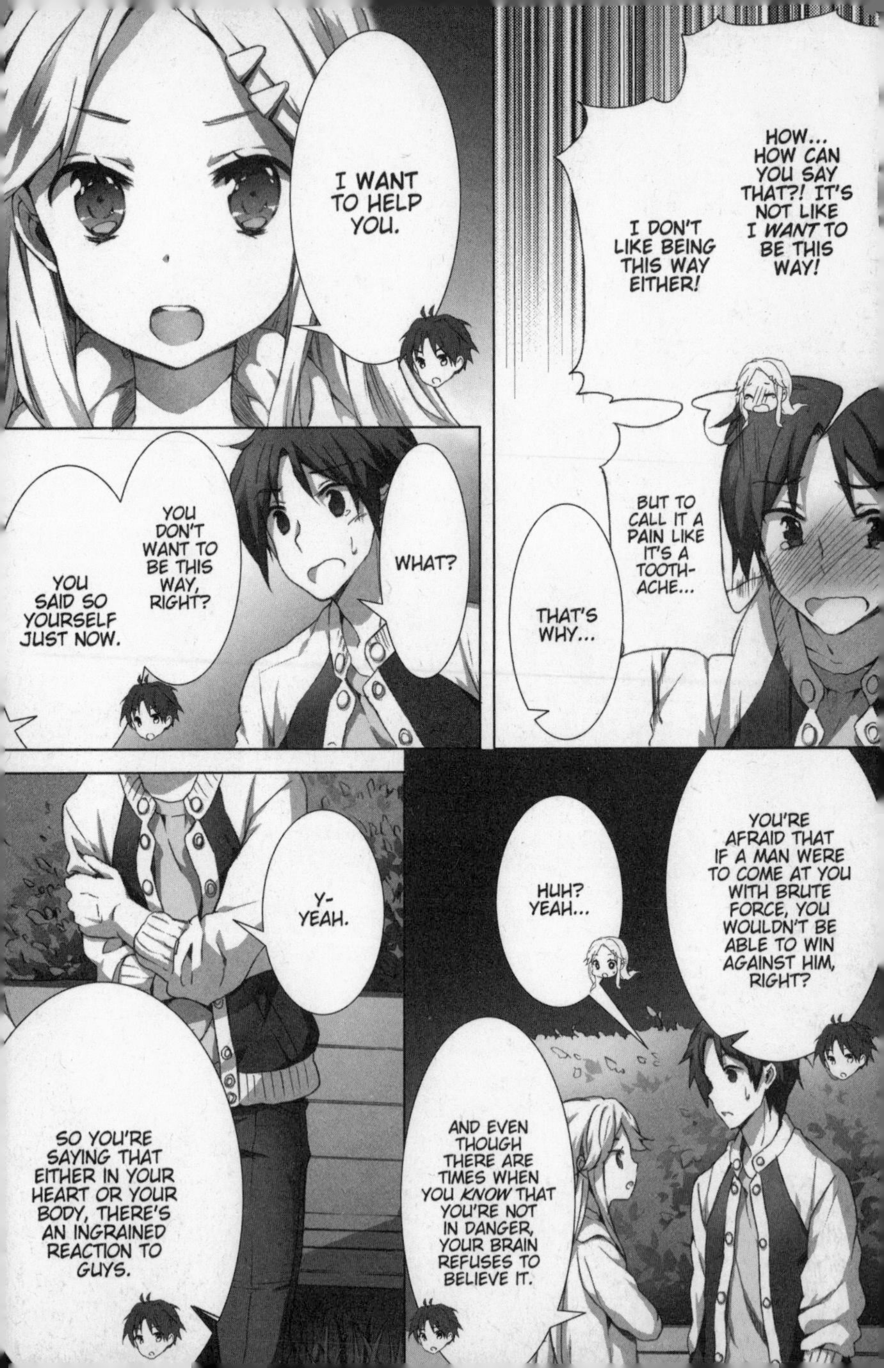
HOW... HOW CAN YOU SAY THAT?! IT'S NOT LIKE I *WANT* TO BE THIS WAY!
I DON'T LIKE BEING THIS WAY EITHER!
BUT TO CALL IT A PAIN LIKE IT'S A TOOTH-ACHE...
THAT'S WHY...
I WANT TO HELP YOU.
WHAT?
YOU DON'T WANT TO BE THIS WAY, RIGHT?
YOU SAID SO YOURSELF JUST NOW.
YOU'RE AFRAID THAT IF A MAN WERE TO COME AT YOU WITH BRUTE FORCE, YOU WOULDN'T BE ABLE TO WIN AGAINST HIM, RIGHT?
HUH? YEAH...
AND EVEN THOUGH THERE ARE TIMES WHEN YOU *KNOW* THAT YOU'RE NOT IN DANGER, YOUR BRAIN REFUSES TO BELIEVE IT.
Y-YEAH.
SO YOU'RE SAYING THAT EITHER IN YOUR HEART OR YOUR BODY, THERE'S AN INGRAINED REACTION TO GUYS.

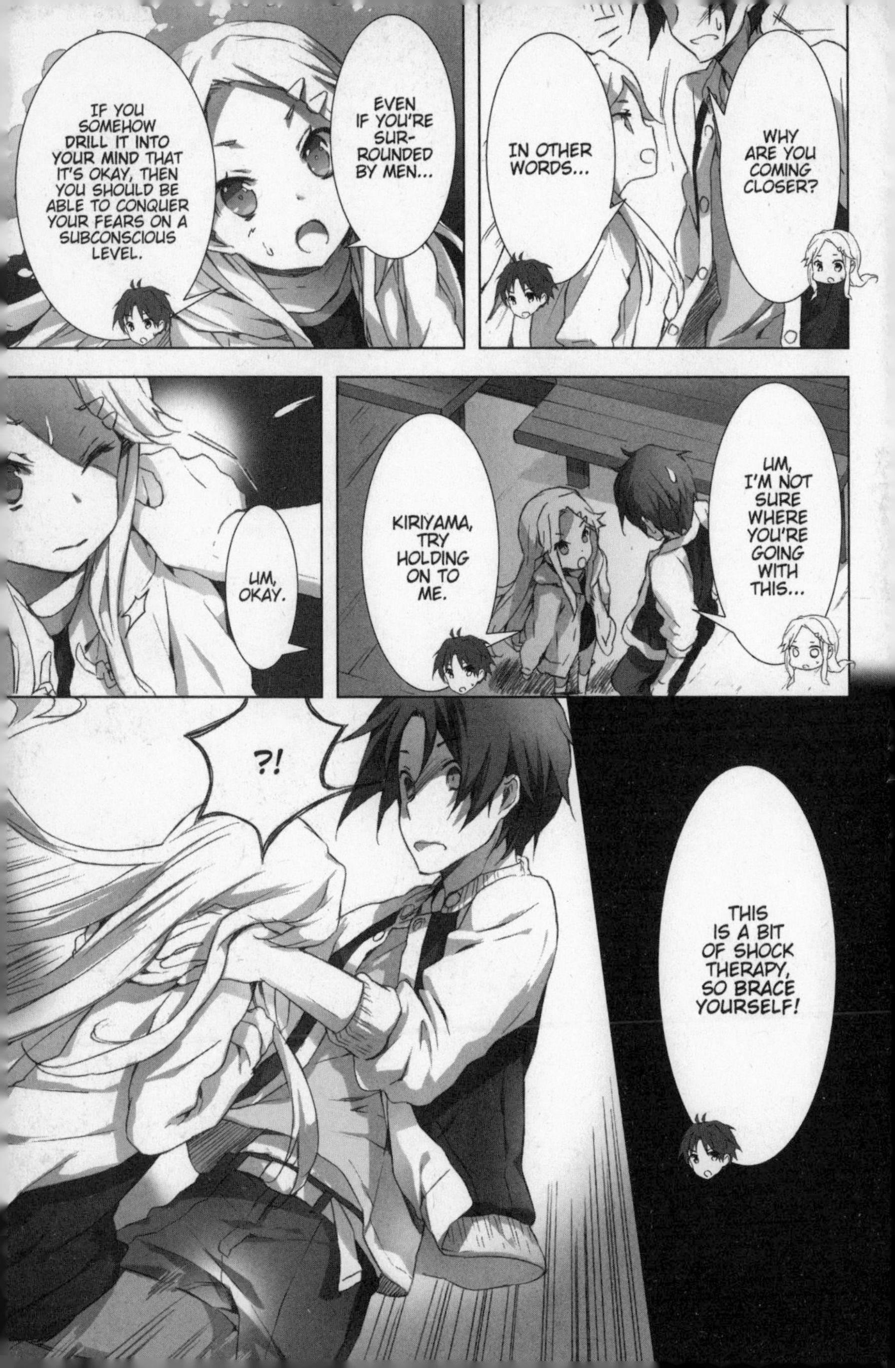
WHY ARE YOU COMING CLOSER?
IN OTHER WORDS...
EVEN IF YOU'RE SUR-ROUNDED BY MEN...
IF YOU SOMEHOW DRILL IT INTO YOUR MIND THAT IT'S OKAY, THEN YOU SHOULD BE ABLE TO CONQUER YOUR FEARS ON A SUBCONSCIOUS LEVEL.
UM, I'M NOT SURE WHERE YOU'RE GOING WITH THIS...
KIRIYAMA, TRY HOLDING ON TO ME.
UM, OKAY.
THIS IS A BIT OF SHOCK THERAPY, SO BRACE YOURSELF!
?!

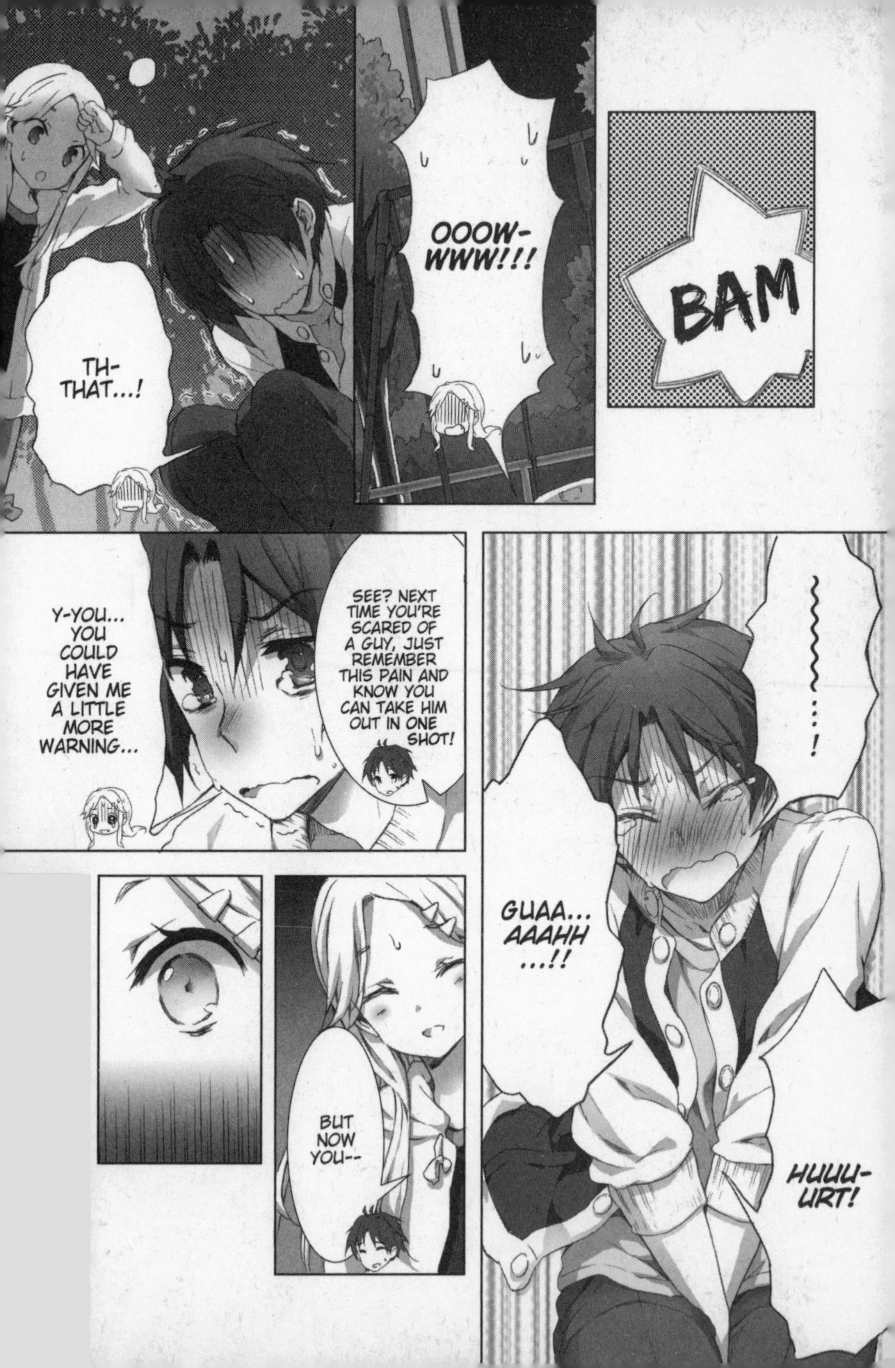
BAM
OOOW-WWW!!!
TH-THAT...!
...!
GUAA... AAAHH ...!!
HUUU-URT!
SEE? NEXT TIME YOU'RE SCARED OF A GUY, JUST REMEMBER THIS PAIN AND KNOW YOU CAN TAKE HIM OUT IN ONE SHOT!
Y-YOU... YOU COULD HAVE GIVEN ME A LITTLE MORE WARNING...
BUT NOW YOU--

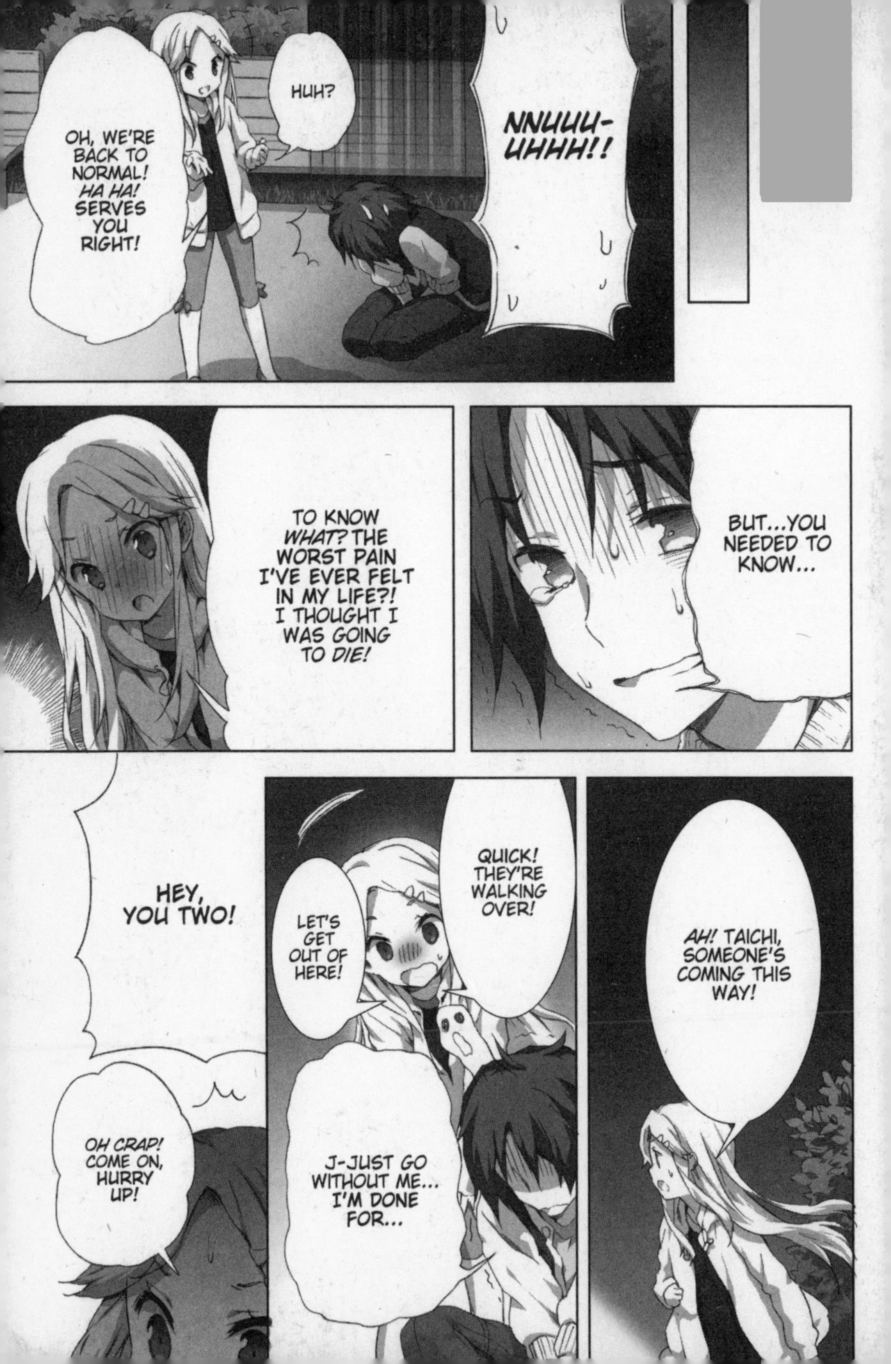
NNUUU-UHHH!!
HUH?
OH, WE'RE BACK TO NORMAL! HA HA! SERVES YOU RIGHT!
BUT...YOU NEEDED TO KNOW...
TO KNOW WHAT? THE WORST PAIN I'VE EVER FELT IN MY LIFE?! I THOUGHT I WAS GOING TO DIE!
AH! TAICHI, SOMEONE'S COMING THIS WAY!
QUICK! THEY'RE WALKING OVER!
LET'S GET OUT OF HERE!
J-JUST GO WITHOUT ME... I'M DONE FOR...
HEY, YOU TWO!
OH CRAP! COME ON, HURRY UP!

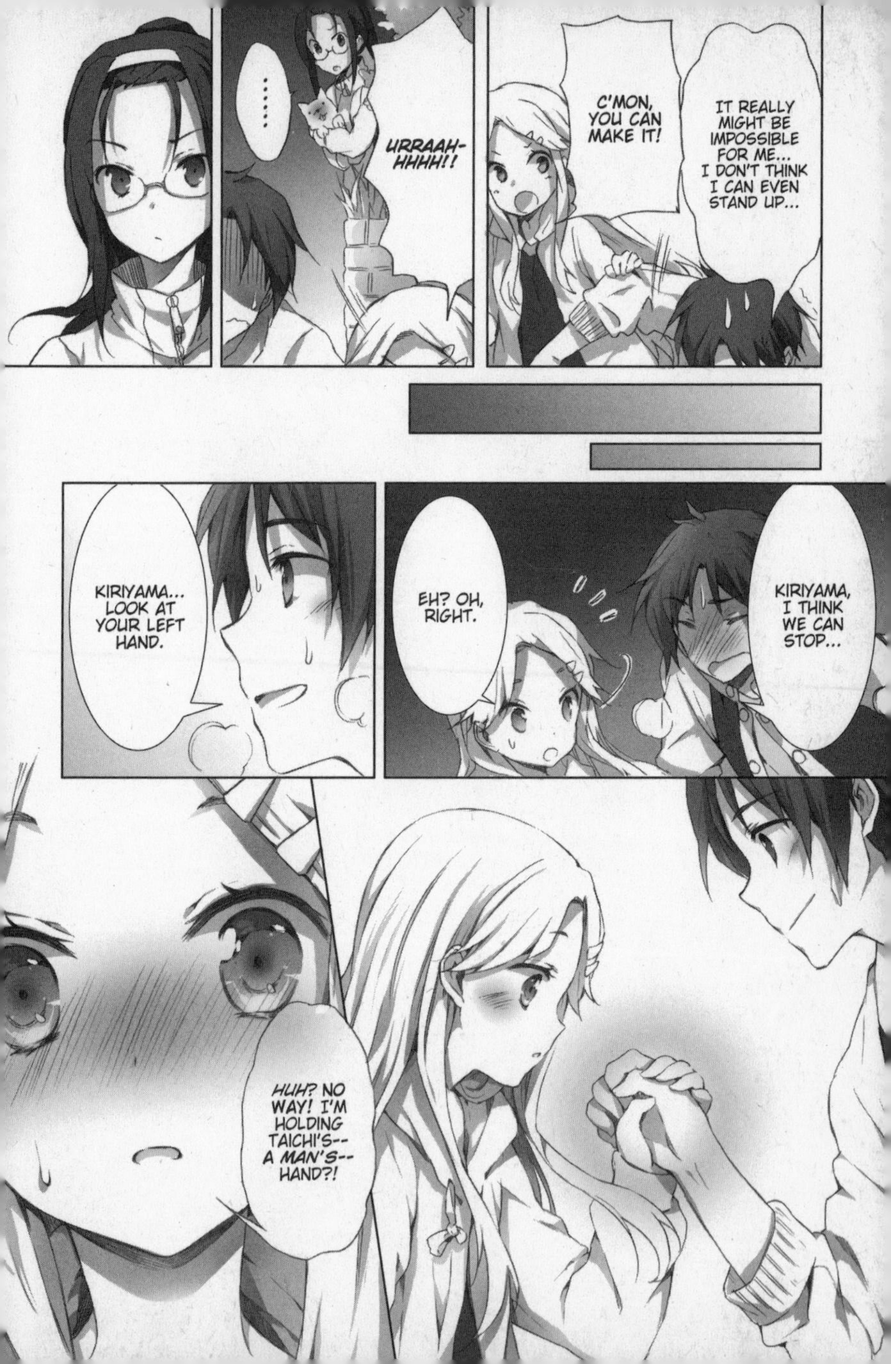
IT REALLY MIGHT BE IMPOSSIBLE FOR ME... I DON'T THINK I CAN EVEN STAND UP...
C'MON, YOU CAN MAKE IT!
......
URRAAH-HHHH!!
KIRIYAMA, I THINK WE CAN STOP...
EH? OH, RIGHT.
KIRIYAMA... LOOK AT YOUR LEFT HAND.
HUH? NO WAY! I'M HOLDING TAICHI'S-- A MAN'S-- HAND?!

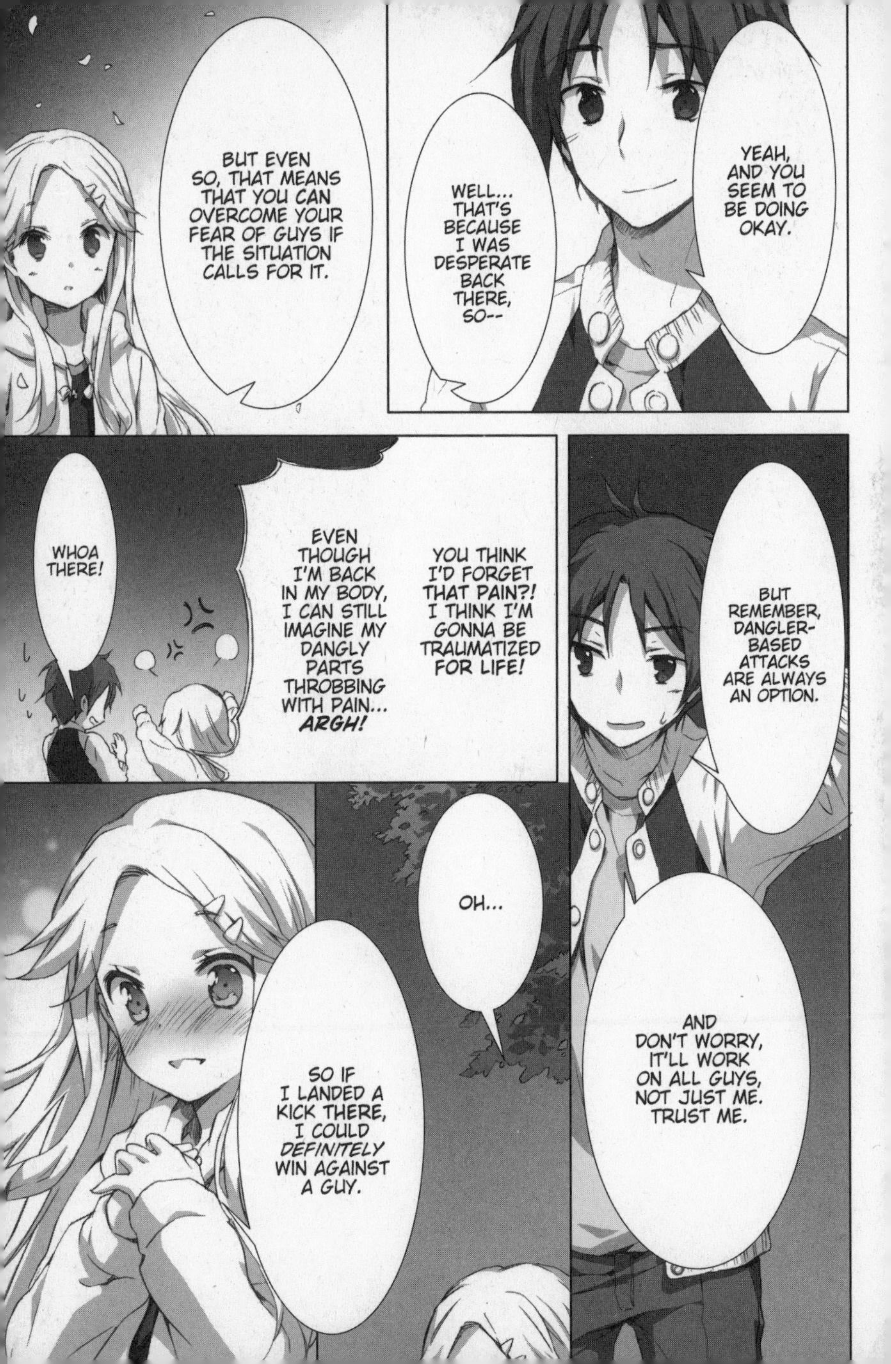
YEAH, AND YOU SEEM TO BE DOING OKAY.
WELL... THAT'S BECAUSE I WAS DESPERATE BACK THERE, SO--
BUT EVEN SO, THAT MEANS THAT YOU CAN OVERCOME YOUR FEAR OF GUYS IF THE SITUATION CALLS FOR IT.
BUT REMEMBER, DANGLER-BASED ATTACKS ARE ALWAYS AN OPTION.
AND DON'T WORRY, IT'LL WORK ON ALL GUYS, NOT JUST ME. TRUST ME.
YOU THINK I'D FORGET THAT PAIN?! I THINK I'M GONNA BE TRAUMATIZED FOR LIFE!
EVEN THOUGH I'M BACK IN MY BODY, I CAN STILL IMAGINE MY DANGLY PARTS THROBBING WITH PAIN... *ARGH!*
WHOA THERE!
OH...
SO IF I LANDED A KICK THERE, I COULD *DEFINITELY* WIN AGAINST A GUY.

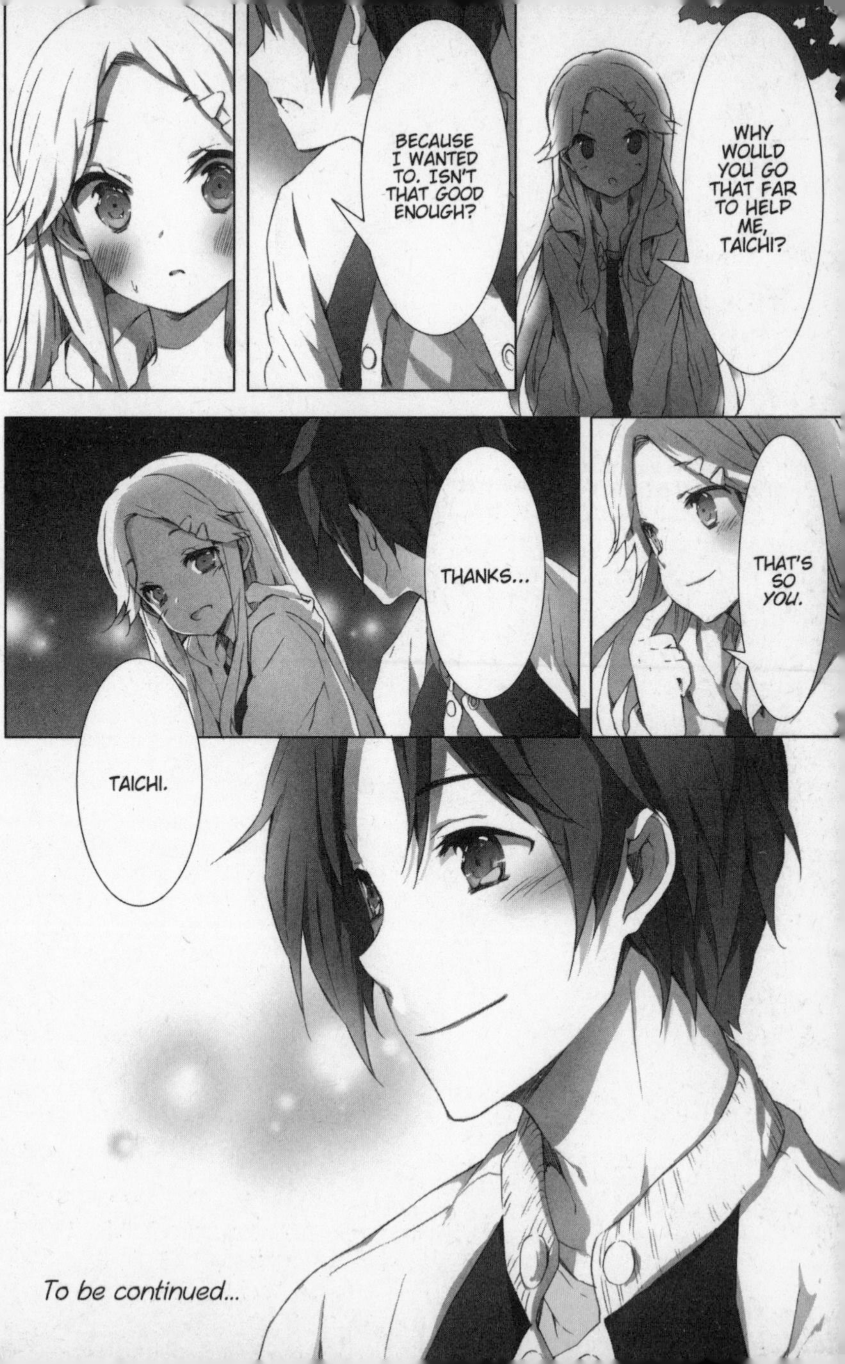
WHY WOULD YOU GO THAT FAR TO HELP ME, TAICHI?
BECAUSE I WANTED TO. ISN'T THAT GOOD ENOUGH?
THAT'S SO *YOU*.
THANKS...
TAICHI.
To be continued...

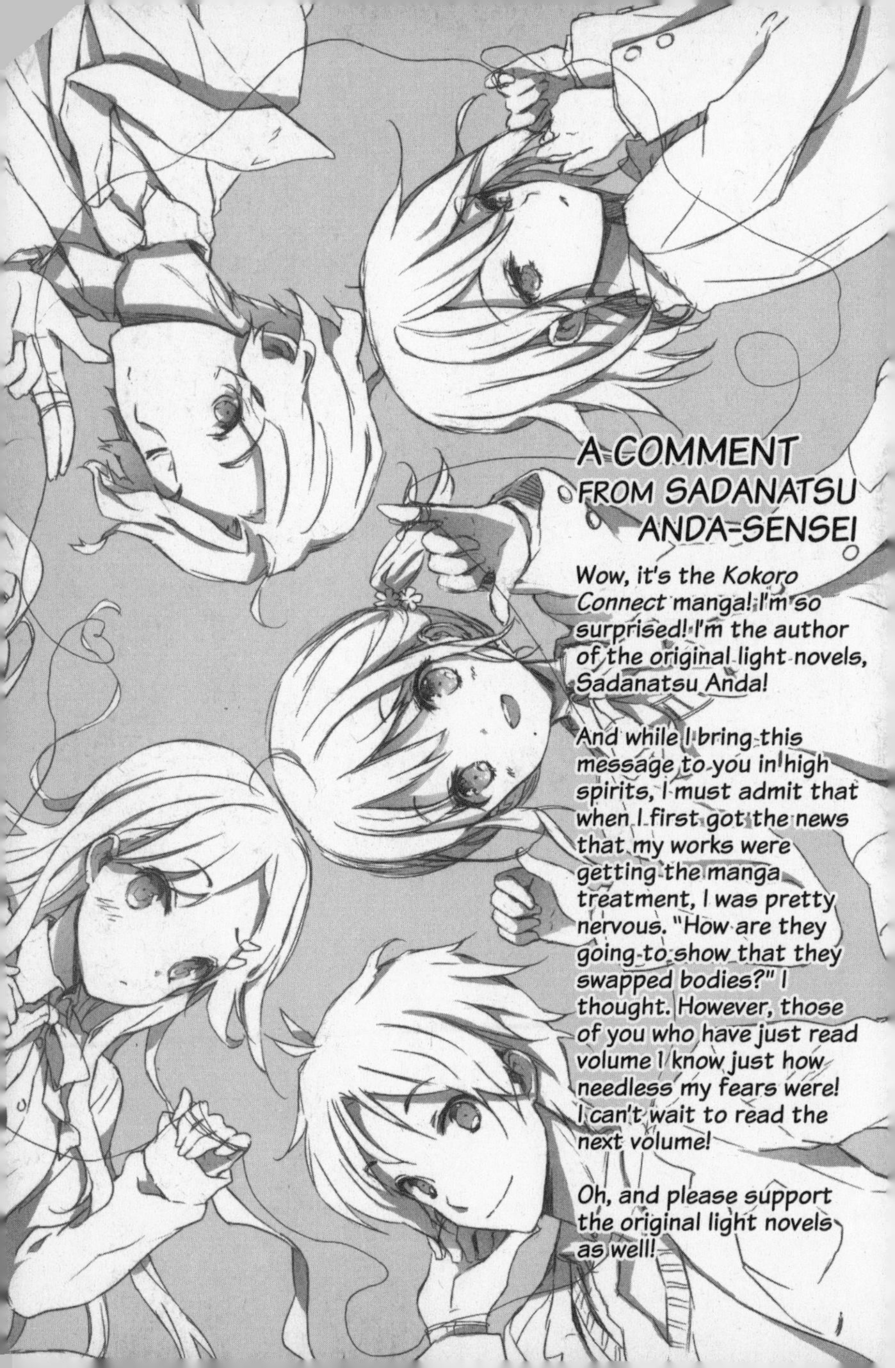

A COMMENT FROM SADANATSU ANDA-SENSEI

Wow, it's the *Kokoro Connect* manga! I'm so surprised! I'm the author of the original light novels, Sadanatsu Anda!

And while I bring this message to you in high spirits, I must admit that when I first got the news that my works were getting the manga treatment, I was pretty nervous. "How are they going to show that they swapped bodies?" I thought. However, those of you who have just read volume 1 know just how needless my fears were! I can't wait to read the next volume!

Oh, and please support the original light novels as well!

SPECIAL ILLUSTRATION & COMMENT

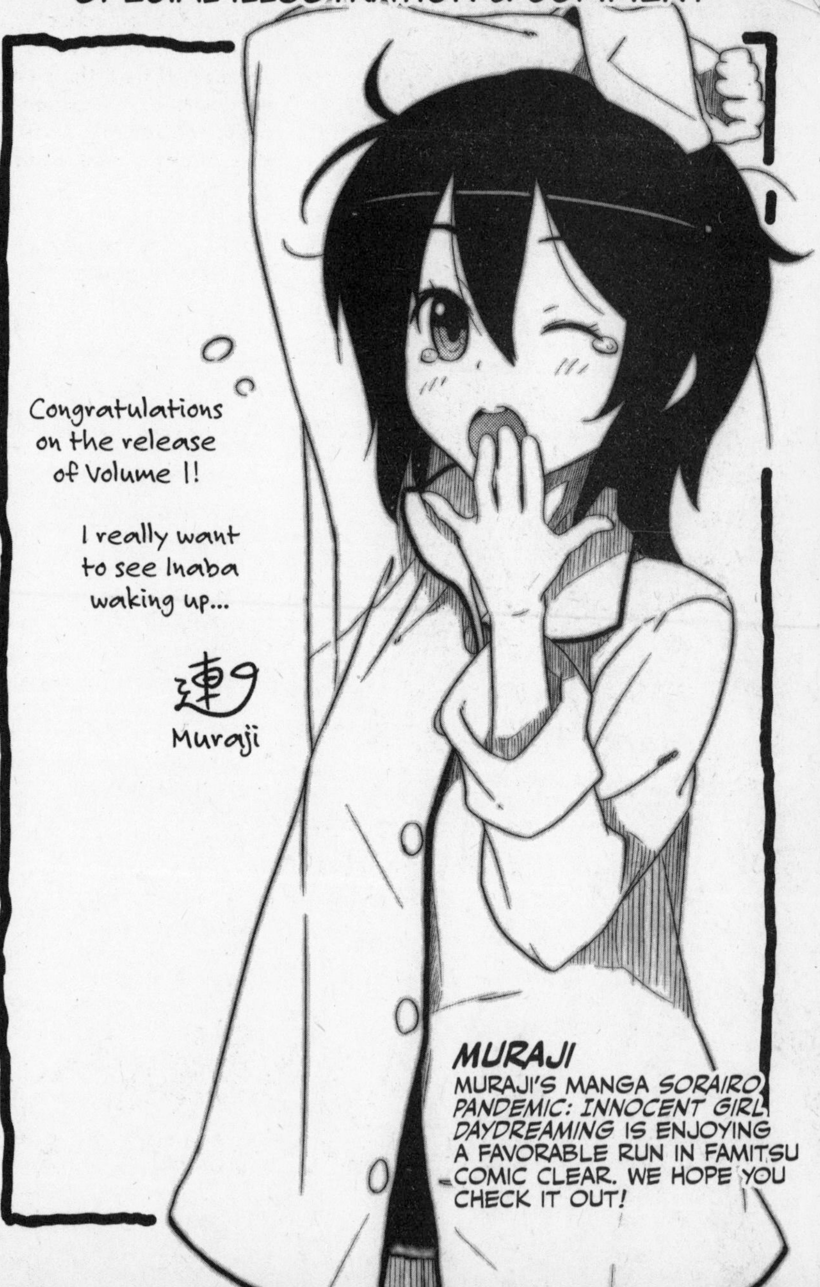
Congratulations on the release of Volume 1!
I really want to see Inaba waking up...
Muraji

MURAJI

MURAJI'S MANGA *SORAIRO PANDEMIC: INNOCENT GIRL DAYDREAMING* IS ENJOYING A FAVORABLE RUN IN FAMITSU COMIC CLEAR. WE HOPE YOU CHECK IT OUT!

It's volume 1 of Kokoro Connect! High school students are so much fun! When I look at the five members of the Student Cultural Society, I can't help but feel such fondness for them!

Thank you all so very much for reading!!

CuteG
2011.04

+Special thanks+

Sadanatsu Anda
Shiromizakana-san
My handlers F-san S-san
Nari-chan
Mirin-chan

CUTEG COMMENT

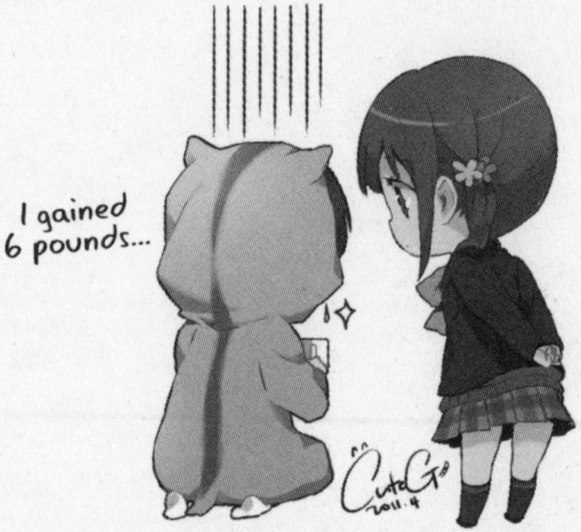
I gained
6 pounds...
CuteG
2011.4

BORN JANUARY 6TH.

BLOOD TYPE A.

CURRENTLY ENJOYING LIFE IN MY OWN SPECIAL WAY BY DRAWING ILLUSTRATIONS AND MANGA.

BIGGEST WEAKNESS: "BOY MEETS GIRL" STORIES (AND SWEET THINGS).

I WISH I COULD GO VIEW THE CHERRY BLOSSOMS...

KOKORO CONNECT

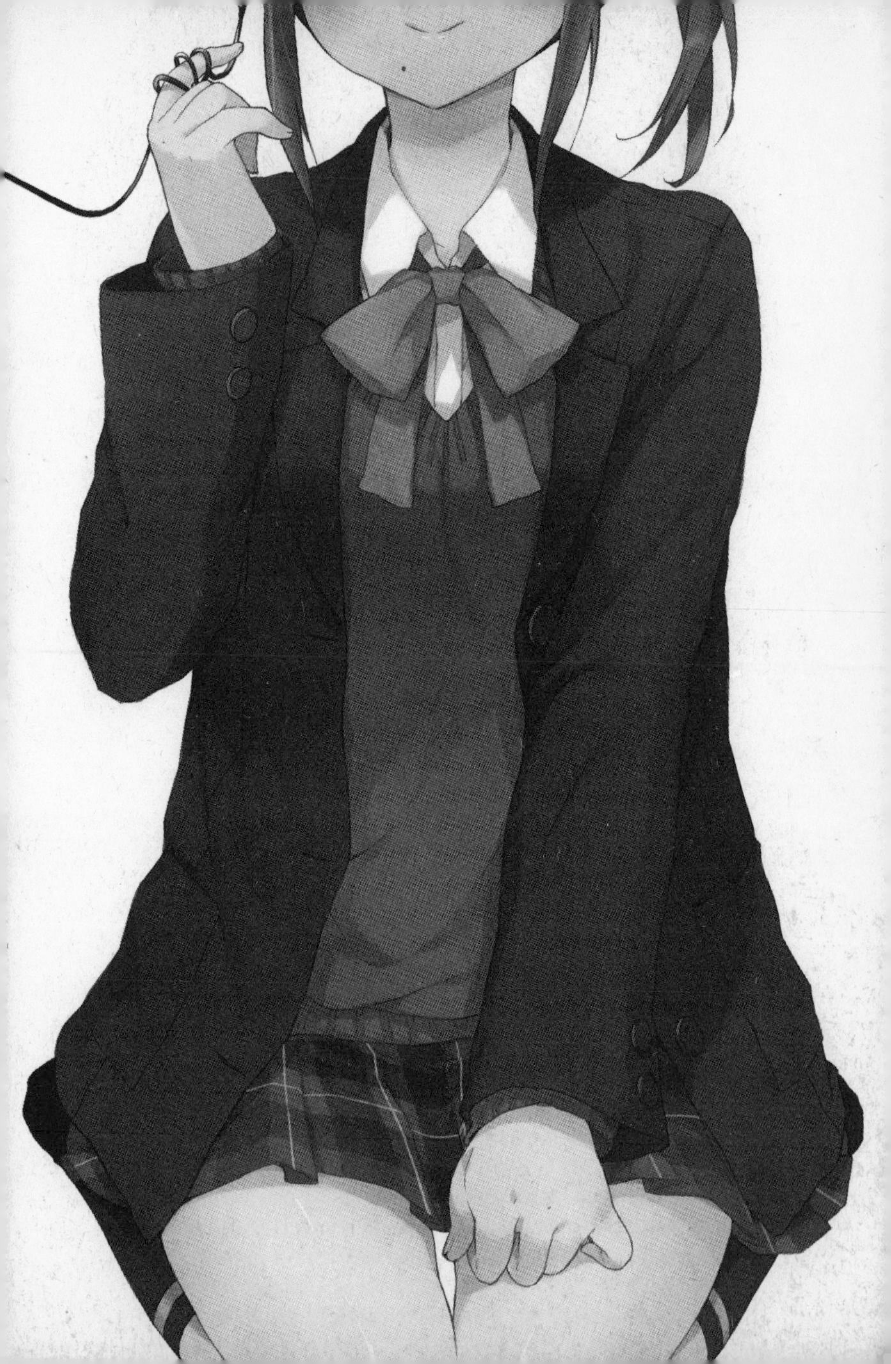

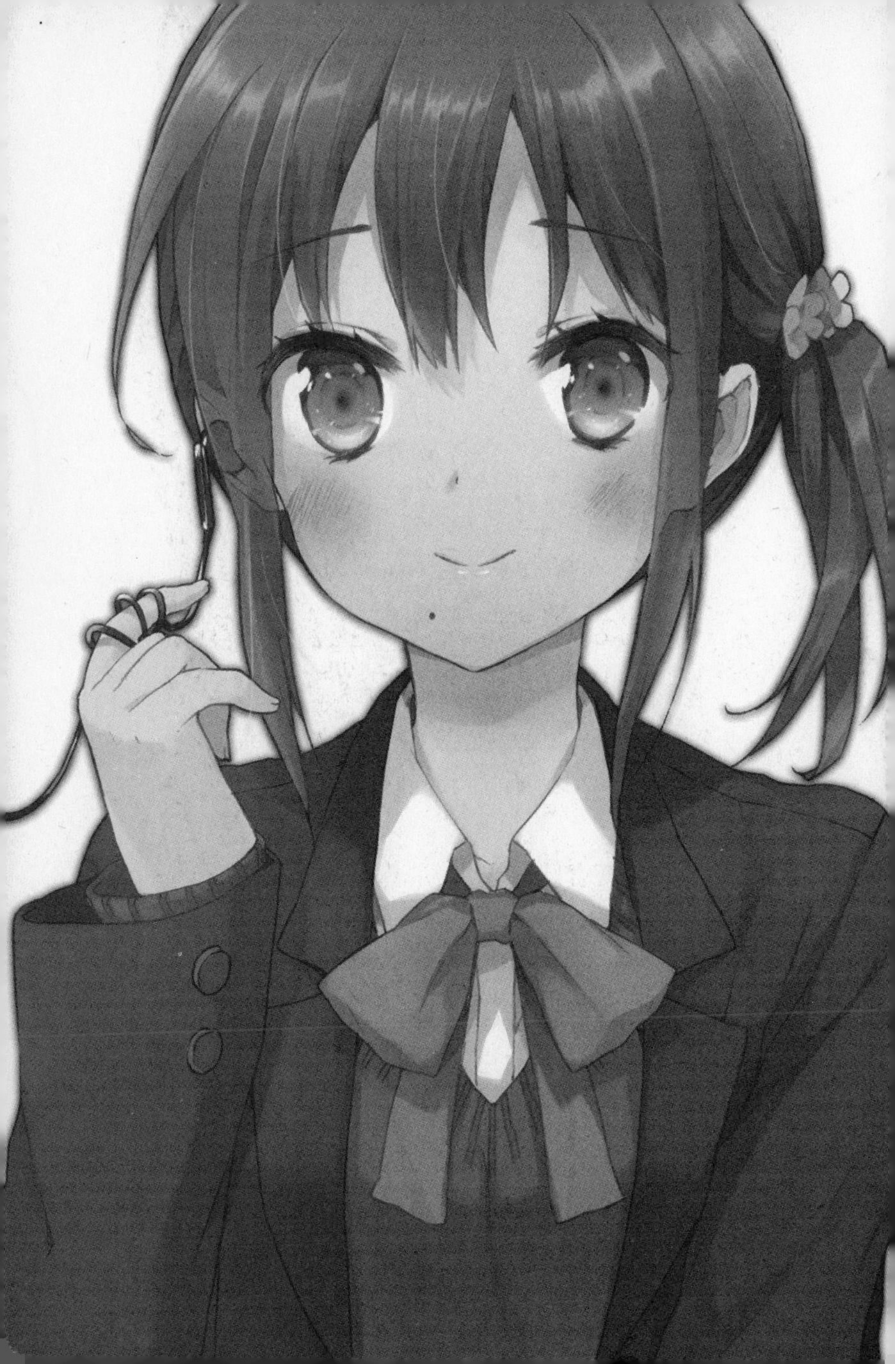

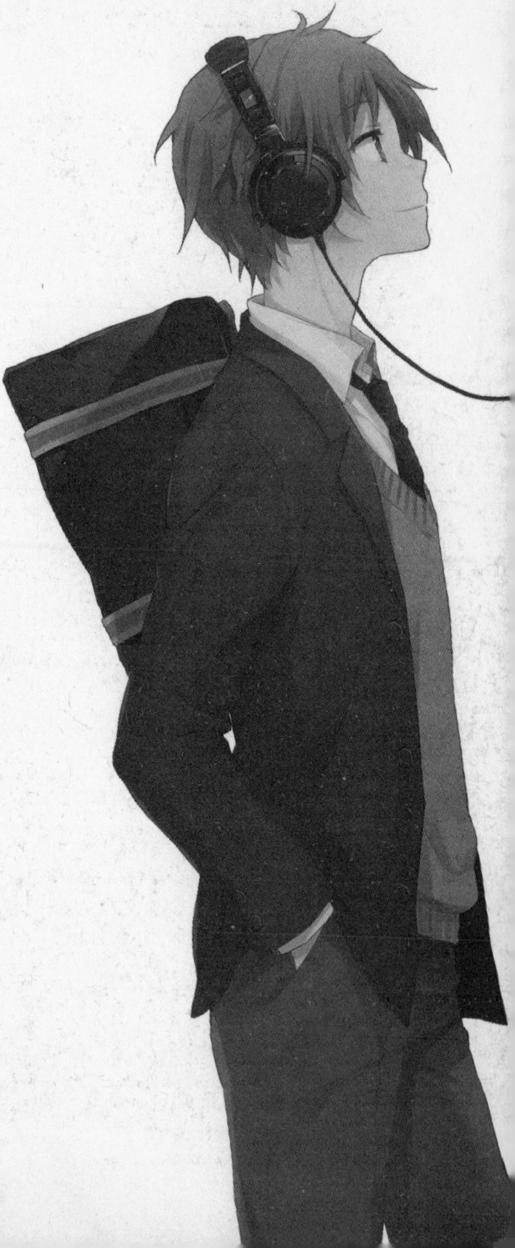

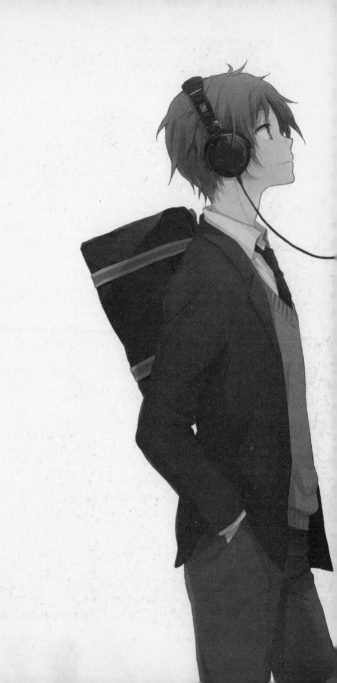

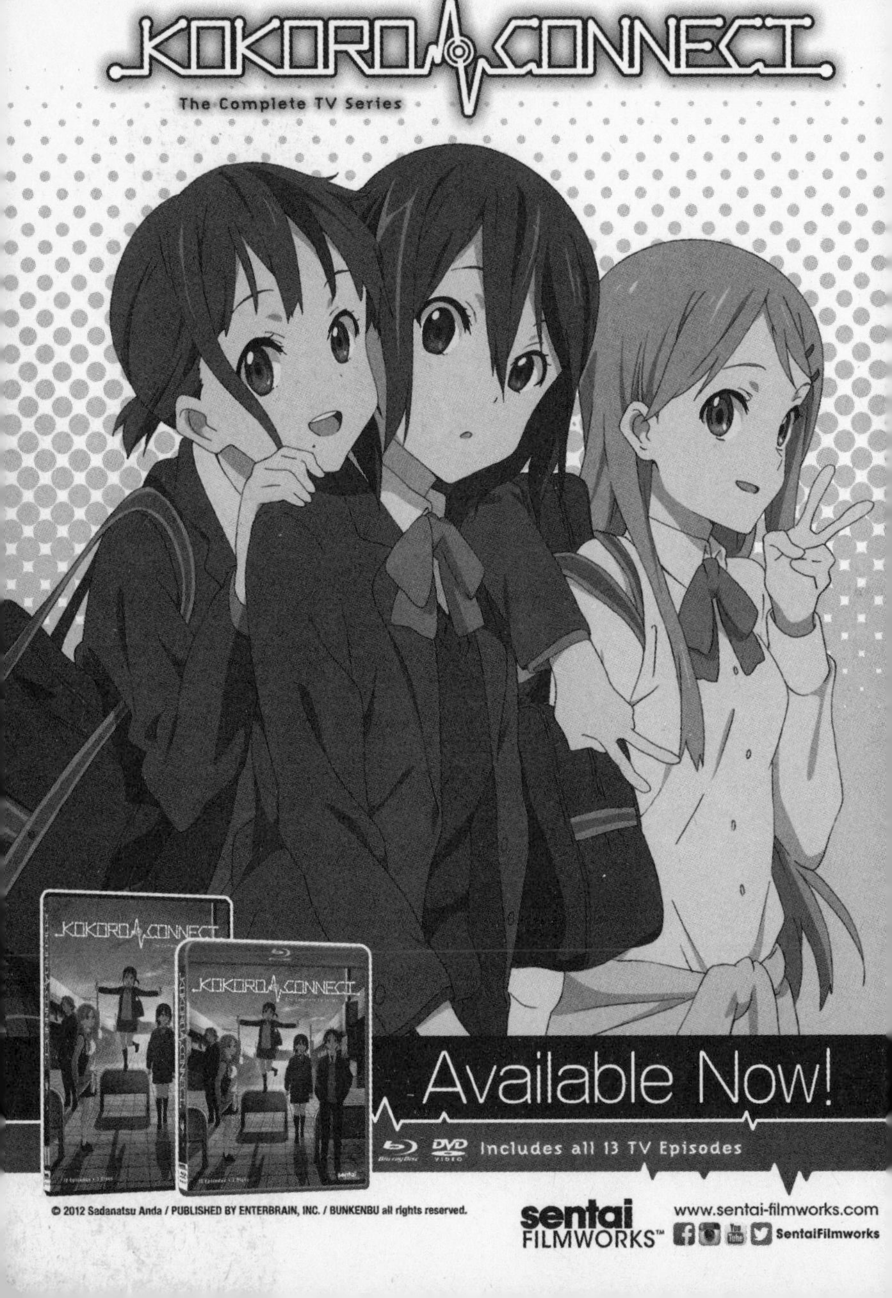
KOKORO CONNECT
The Complete TV Series
KOKORO CONNECT
KOKORO CONNECT
Available Now!
Includes all 13 TV Episodes
© 2012 Sadanatsu Anda / PUBLISHED BY ENTERBRAIN, INC. / BUNKENBU all rights reserved.
sentai FILMWORKS™
www.sentai-filmworks.com
SentaiFilmworks

KOKORO CONNECT

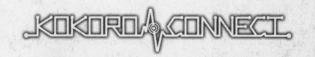